Incapacitating Biochemical Weapons

Incapacitating Biochemical Weapons

Promise or Peril?

EDITED BY ALAN M. PEARSON,
MARIE ISABELLE CHEVRIER,
AND MARK WHEELIS

LEXINGTON BOOKS

A division of
ROWMAN & LITTLEFIELD PUBLISHERS, INC.
Lanham • Boulder • New York • Toronto • Plymouth, UK

LEXINGTON BOOKS

A division of Rowman & Littlefield Publishers, Inc.
A wholly owned subsidiary of The Rowman & Littlefield Publishing Group, Inc.
4501 Forbes Boulevard, Suite 200
Lanham, MD 20706

Estover Road
Plymouth PL6 7PY
United Kingdom

Copyright © 2007 by Lexington Books

British Library Cataloguing in Publication Information Available

Library of Congress Cataloging-in-Publication Data

Incapacitating biochemical weapons : promise or peril? / edited by Alan Pearson, Marie
Chevrier, and Mark Wheelis.
    p. cm.
 ISBN-13: 978-0-7391-1438-4 (cloth : alk. paper)
 ISBN-10: 0-7391-1438-7 (cloth : alk. paper)
 ISBN-13: 978-0-7391-1439-1 (pbk. : alk. paper)
 ISBN-10: 0-7391-1439-5 (pbk. : alk. paper)
 1. Chemical arms control. 2. Disarmament. 3. Chemical warfare. I. Pearson, Alan. II.
Chevrier, Marie Isabelle. III. Wheelis, Mark.
 JZ5830.I53 2007
 358'.3882—dc22   2007028976

Printed in the United States of America

⊗™ The paper used in this publication meets the minimum requirements of American
National Standard for Information Sciences—Permanence of Paper for Printed Library
Materials, ANSI/NISO Z39.48–1992.

Contents

Abbreviations

5-HT	5-hydroxytryptamine (serotonin)
5-HTT	5-HT (serotonin) transporter
AIDS	Acquired Immune Deficiency Syndrome
ANLM	Airburst Non-Lethal Munition
ARCAD	Advanced Riot Control Agent Device
ARDEC	Army Research Development and Engineering Center
ATF	Bureau of Alcohol, Tobacco, and Firearms
BWC	Biological Weapons Convention
BZ	3-quinuclidinyl benzilate
cc	cubic centimeter
CCK	cholecystokinin
CCWC	Certain Conventional Weapons Convention
CFR	U.S. Code of Federal Regulations
CN	chloroacetophenone
CRF	corticotrophin-releasing factor
CS	o-chlorobenzylidene malononitrile
CWC	Chemical Weapons Convention
CWS	U.S. Army Chemical Warfare Service
DA	diphenylchlorarsine
DM	diphenylaminearsine
DNA	deoxyribonucleic acid
DoD	U.S. Department of Defense
ECBC	U.S. Army Edgewood Chemical Biological Center, Maryland; successor to ERDEC

ECHR	European Court of Human Rights
ED_{50}	effective dose, 50 percent; median effective dose
ENDC	Eighteen Nation Disarmament Committee
ERDEC	U.S. Army Edgewood Research, Development and Engineering Center, Maryland
ERK	extracellular signal-regulated protein kinase
FDA	U.S. Food and Drug Administration
GD-OTS	General Dynamics—Ordnance and Tactical Systems
HPA	hypothalamic-pituitary-adrenal
ICC	International Criminal Court
ICCPR	International Covenant on Civil and Political Rights
ICH	International Conference on Harmonization
ICJ	International Court of Justice
ICRC	International Committee of the Red Cross
IHL	international humanitarian law
IL-1β	interleukin 1β
IL-4	interleukin 4
IND	Investigational New Drug
JAG	Judge Advocate General
JNK	c-Jun N-terminal kinase
JNLWD	Joint Non-Lethal Weapons Directorate
LD50	lethal dose, 50 percent; median lethal dose
LOAC	Law of Armed Conflict
LSD	lysergic acid diethylamide
MAP	mitogen-activated protein kinase
MDMA	3, 4-methylenedioxymethamphetamine, (Ecstasy)
MKK	MAP kinase kinase
mRNA	messenger ribonucleic acid
NATO	North Atlantic Treaty Organization
NDA	New Drug Application
NK	neurokinin
NLMM	Non-Lethal Mortar Munition
NLW	non-lethal weapon
OC	oleoresin capsicum (pepper spray)
OICW	Objective Individual Combat Weapon
OLDS	Overhead Liquid Dispersion System
OPCW	Organization for the Prohibition of Chemical Weapons
PB	pyridostigmine bromide
PCP	phencyclidine
PhRMA	Pharmaceutical Research and Manufacturers of America
POW	prisoner of war

PTSD	PostTraumatic Stress Disorder
R&D	research and development
RAC-GWVI	Research Advisory Committee on Gulf War Veterans' Illnesses
RAP	Ring Airfoil Projectile
RCA	riot control agent
SAPK	stress-activated protein kinase
SBCCOM	U.S. Army Soldier Biological and Chemical Command
SBIR	Small Business Innovation Research
SIRUS	superfluous injury or unnecessary suffering
SOPs	Standard Operating Procedures
UK	United Kingdom
UN	United Nations
UNSCOM	United Nations Special Commission on Iraq
US	United States
VX	O-ethyl-S-(2-diisopropylaminoethyl) methyl phosphonothiolate, a nerve agent
WMD	weapons of mass destruction

Glossary

Agonist	a drug or other compound that binds to and activates a receptor to produce a response; an agonist often mimics the action of an endogenous biochemical.
Amygdala	a small oval structure in the temporal lobe of the brain that plays a role in the sense of smell, motivation, emotional behavior and emotionally laden memories.
Analgesia	the deadening or absence of the sense of pain without the loss of consciousness.
Anesthesia	the loss of the ability to feel pain, with or without the loss of consciousness, caused by administration of a drug or other medical intervention. General anesthesia induces a state of unconsciousness, whereas local anesthesia causes a loss of feeling in a part of the body without affecting consciousness.
Antagonist	a drug or other compound that binds to a receptor to block the action of an agonist or endogenous biochemical.
Biochemical	an organic compound produced by a chemical reaction in a living organism, or a biologically active synthetic analog or derivative of such a compound.

Biochemical (or chemical) incapacitant	a substance whose chemical action on specific biochemical processes and physiological systems, especially those affecting the higher regulatory activity of the central nervous system, produce a disabling condition (e.g., can cause incapacitation or disorientation, incoherence, hallucination, sedation, loss of consciousness). Also called "biotechnical agent," "calmative," "immobilizing agent."
Bioregulator	a naturally occurring organic compound, typically produced in small amounts, that regulates cellular processes in one or more organ systems and is essential for normal homeostatic function.
Calmative	synonym for biochemical incapacitant
Cholinergic	relating to compounds, cells or neurological systems that act on, employ or are affected by the neurotransmitter acetylcholine.
Cytokine	any of many small regulatory proteins released by cells which have a specific effect on the interactions between cells, on communications between cells or on the behavior of cells, particularly during an immune response. The cytokines include the interleukins, interferons, and cell signal molecules such as tumor necrosis factor.
Harassing agent	synonym for riot control agent
Hypothalamus-Pituitary-Adrenal (HPA) axis	the complex set of direct influences and feedback interactions between the hypothalamus in the brain, the pituitary gland (a small structure located just below the hypothalamus), and the adrenal gland (a small paired organ located at the top of each kidney); a major part of the neuroendocrine system that controls reactions to stress and regulates various body processes including digestion, the immune system, mood and sexuality, and energy usage.
Immobilizing agent	synonym for biochemical incapacitant
Incapacitant/Incapacitating agent	a chemical agent that "produces temporary physiological or mental effects, or both, which will render individuals incapable of concerted effort in the performance of their assigned duties"

(U.S. Army); in contemporary usage, the term refers to biochemical incapacitants, as opposed to riot control agents

Incapacitating biochemical (or chemical) agent
: see biochemical incapacitant

Incapacitating biochemical weapon
: a biochemical incapacitant in combination with a dissemination and delivery device.

Irritant
: synonym for riot control agent

Lacrimator/Lachrymatory agent
: synonym for riot control agent

Ligand
: any molecule that binds in a specific manner to another; in normal usage a soluble molecule, such as a hormone or neurotransmitter, that binds to a receptor.

Malodorant
: a foul smelling chemical typically used as a riot control agent or for area denial; generally causes tearing, gagging, nausea and/or vomiting

Neuroendocrine
: having to do with the interactions between the nervous system and the endocrine (hormonal) system.

Neurotransmitter
: a biochemical that is released by one nerve cell to transmit information to and thereby affect the activity of another nerve cell, muscle, or other tissue. Common neurotransmitters include acetylcholine, dopamine, gamma-aminobutyric acid (GABA), glutamate, noradrenalin (norepinephrine), and serotonin (5-HT), as well as various peptides.

Opioid/Opiate
: any of several narcotic drugs that have sedative or narcotic effects similar to opium or its derivatives and which are generally used to manage pain.

Organophosphate
: any of several organic compounds containing phosphorus, some of which are powerful inhibitors of acetylcholinesterase, which are used as insecticides and nerve gases.

Peptide
: a small molecule consisting of two or more amino acids linked in a defined order; peptides are smaller than proteins, which are also chains of amino acids.

Pharmacogenetics
: the study of genetic factors that influence an organism's reaction to a drug.

Proinflammatory   capable of promoting inflammation, the localized protective response of the body to irritation, injury, or infection.

Receptor   a structure on the surface of or inside a cell that selectively receives and binds a specific substance.

Respiratory depression   abnormally slow and shallow respiration, resulting in an increased level of carbon dioxide in the blood.

Riot control agent (RCA)   a locally acting chemical agent that rapidly produces sensory irritation of the eyes and upper respiratory tract which disappears within a short time (typically minutes) following termination of exposure. Examples include the tear gases CS and CR, the vomiting agent DM, and capsaicin (the principle component in oleoresin capsicum (OC) or pepper spray)

Safety margin
  (therapeutic index)   the ratio between the toxic dose and the therapeutic dose of a drug, or more generally, between the dose which produces a significant undesired effect and the dose which produces the desired effect; used as a measure of the relative safety of a drug for a particular treatment. The therapeutic index, which quantitatively measures the ratio of the dose producing the undesired effect in 50 percent of the population to the dose producing the desired effect in 50 percent of the population, is often used to approximate the safety margin.

Introduction[1]

Alan M. Pearson, Marie Isabelle Chevrier,
and Mark Wheelis

Revolutionary advances in the life sciences and biotechnology are generating new knowledge and new capabilities that promise tremendous benefits for health and society in the twenty-first century. These same advances are also making it possible to manipulate human consciousness, emotions, mental functions and behavior for coercion or warfare. Indeed, these advances and the changing nature of conflict and warfare in the twenty-first century are generating increasing interest in using incapacitating biochemical agents for military and law enforcement purposes.

The history of military interest in incapacitating biochemical weapons dates back more than fifty years. However, a recent event in Moscow first brought these weapons to contemporary public notice. On the evening of 23 October 2002 a group of male and female Chechen separatists raided the Dubrovka theater center during a performance of the play "Nord-Ost" and took more than 800 people hostage. The male hostage takers were heavily armed with assault rifles and pistols, and the women with pistols and high explosives. They demanded the withdrawal of Russian troops from Chechnya and threatened to kill the hostages if their demand was not met. A little over two days later, on the morning of October 26, Russian special forces troops disseminated an unknown biochemical agent through the theater's ventilation system, putting both hostages and the female hostage takers into a deep sleep (the male hostage takers left the main auditorium as the agent was disseminated, and prepared to battle Russian special forces in the hallways). Approximately thirty minutes later, the troops stormed the theater, killing all of the Chechen hostage takers, including the unconscious women, and ending the crisis. However, over 125 hostages died from the effects of the gas, and many more were severely injured. Several days later, the Russian Health Minister revealed that the gas contained a derivative of the potent narcotic fentanyl, a compound related to morphine, but did not reveal the specific identity of the agent(s) used.[2]

The Moscow incident was not met with significant public expressions of concern from other governments. Indeed, it may have generated even more interest on the part of governments in exploring the potential of incapacitating biochemical weapons.[3] Moreover, some may conclude that the development of effective and "non-lethal" incapacitating biochemical weapons for use by military and law enforcement forces is possible based on advances in science and technology and our rapidly increasing understanding of the human nervous system and of other physiological systems. The International Committee of the Red Cross has issued an urgent appeal for effective controls on technologies that could be used to manipulate the "life processes at the core of human existence."[4] But governments have largely been avoiding any real discussion of this highly contentious issue.

Defining Incapacitating Biochemicals

Any discussion of incapacitating biochemical weapons requires that "incapacitating biochemicals" first be defined. According to one widely used textbook, biochemistry is "the study of the molecular basis of life."[5] Another textbook says, even more simply, "biochemistry is the chemistry of life."[6] Accordingly, a biochemical is an organic molecule produced by a chemical reaction in a living organism. Synthetic versions or derivatives of such compounds are also considered to be biochemicals. A subset of biochemicals known as bioregulators, which are "naturally occurring organic compounds that regulate diverse cellular processes in multiple organ systems and are essential for normal homeostatic function,"[7] can cause severe adverse effects or death when introduced into the body in concentrations in excess of their normal trace amounts.[8] Toxins such as botulinum toxin and saxitoxin are produced by living organisms and hence are also biochemicals. In fact, many toxins owe their toxicity to their resemblance to endogenous bioregulators; the opiates, for instance, are structural analogs of bioregulators termed endorphins. An increasing number of biochemicals, including bioregulators, can be produced synthetically, i.e., by chemical reactions in the absence of living organisms.

Some biochemicals are not essential for fundamental life processes, yet through their chemical activity they can have a profound effect on such processes. For instance, the statin family of drugs can dramatically lower cholesterol levels by specifically inhibiting an enzyme essential for cholesterol biosynthesis. The statins were first discovered in certain strains of fungi,[9] but several synthetic statins have also been developed based on the fungal compounds, including atorvastatin (lipitor), which in 2004 was the largest selling drug in the world.[10] Like synthetic versions of naturally occurring biomolecules, synthetic compounds that are biologically active analogs of naturally occurring biomolecules are thus also considered biochemicals.

In the context of chemical and biological weapons, incapacitation is defined in military terms based on the desired behavioral consequence of the physiological action or effect of an agent rather than in scientific terms based on the action or effect itself. The meaning of the term "incapacitation" is thus context dependent and can be somewhat elastic, but importantly, *it must exclude death or permanent injury as an intended consequence.* According to U.S. Army Field Manual 3–11.9, "in a military context, incapacitation is understood to mean inability to perform one's military mission."[11] Two U.S. military authorities similarly note "when the word incapacitating is used, we should ask, 'incapacitating for what activity?' . . . Since missions vary, we could theoretically consider a particular agent to be incapacitating if it disrupts aspects of performance vital to a particular mission."[12] Incapacitation could mean reducing vision and otherwise harassing fighters with tear gas to impede their effectiveness; it could mean blunting cognition so as to impede effective concentration or cooperation among members of operational units; it could mean "knocking out" a target with an agent that induces anesthesia. These are all different endpoints pharmacologically. Regardless of the precise effect desired, incapacitation must be both predictable and significant from the user's point of view.

In turn, an "incapacitating agent" is a chemical agent that "produces temporary physiological or mental effects, or both, which will render individuals incapable of concerted effort in the performance of their assigned duties."[13] Incapacitating agents can be divided into two classes.[14] Class 1 agents generally act locally and have effects that disappear within minutes after exposure ceases. These include tear gases and are typically referred to as irritants, harassing agents or riot control agents (RCAs). Class 2 agents cause temporary incapacitation that lasts substantially longer than the time of exposure, up to hours or days, acting on and thereby altering specific biochemical processes and physiological systems, particularly those of the central nervous system.[15] These are the incapacitating biochemical agents. They have also been called incapacitating agents, incapacitants, immobilizing agents, calmatives, pharmacological agents, and biotechnical agents. They include neurotransmitters, other neuroregulators, and their synthetic analogs which are used as neuropharmacologic agents for anesthesia, sedation and other purposes. In the central nervous systems, these agents act as ligands for (that is, they bind to) specific receptor molecules located on the surface of nerve cells at the synapses (junctions) where one nerve cell transmits information to another. The distinction between these two classes is useful, but not always clear-cut; there are, for instance, incapacitating biochemical agents whose effects dissipate within minutes after exposure ceases.[16]

Incapacitating Biochemical Weapons: Science, Technology, and Policy

The Moscow theater siege illustrated both the potential and the limitations of incapacitating biochemical weapons. It also highlighted a number of scientific, operational, humanitarian, legal, and political issues surrounding the development and use of chemical and biochemical incapacitating agents for law enforcement and military purposes. This book originated in a symposium on incapacitating biochemical weapons, held in June 2005, that brought together more than sixty scientists, military experts, diplomats, policymakers, and representatives of international governmental organizations and civil society to examine these complex issues.[17] The chapters herein are based on presentations and papers delivered at or for this symposium.

Mark Wheelis provides a general overview and introduction to many of the issues surrounding incapacitating biochemical weapons in his chapter on nonconsensual manipulation of human physiology. Wheelis introduces a general theme running throughout this book: that incapacitating biochemical weapons will primarily be based on biochemical agents that affect the functioning of the nervous system. In this regard, he notes that the ability to manipulate neurophysiology, for either beneficial (therapeutic) or hostile purposes, will become increasingly specific as scientific understanding of the brain becomes more detailed. He also makes the important point that "whether there is substantial future development of [incapacitating biochemical] agents may be largely dependent on whether states embrace such weapons or eschew them." Thus, the types of weapons developed will reflect military and law enforcement interests, and Wheelis discusses potential military and law enforcement uses in some detail. He points out, however, that the utility of biochemical incapacitants for such uses will likely be diminished by a variety of technical and operational factors, including the ease with which prepared combatants could employ simple countermeasures and, ironically, the high level of lethality that can be expected (and was witnessed in Moscow) among those exposed.

Wheelis argues that once an incapacitating biochemical weapon system is developed and goes into production, it will likely become readily and widely available. Thus, he extends his discussion of use to include not only "traditional" modes of military and law enforcement action, but also use for political repression, interrogation and torture, use by poorly regulated private military corporations, and use by despots, terrorists, and criminals for their own purposes. Wheelis also describes two additional risks associated with military and law enforcement use of incapacitating biochemical weapons: the danger that they will significantly undermine both international arms control regimes and international humanitarian law, and their even broader consequences for long-standing ethical norms against the nonconsensual manipulation of human physiology. His conclusion is stark: "the capacity to manipulate human physiology to serve criminal or political purposes constitutes a serious threat to humankind. It is this context that makes [incapacitating biochemical] weapons, and the precedent they would establish, so worrisome. . . . [I]n choosing to develop [incapacitating biochemical] weapons, we . . . [may be] choosing a future in which human physiology becomes a target of soldiers, terrorists, criminals, and despots, while rejecting a future in which such manipulation is prohibited." The chapters that follow explore many of the points raised by Wheelis in greater detail.

The chapter by Alan Goldhammer provides additional contextual information. Incapacitating biochemical agents exert their effects by interacting with, and altering, the normal physiological functioning of one or more organ systems. They are thus very similar to pharmaceutical agents developed for therapeutic purposes; indeed, many potential incapacitating agents can be found among known pharmaceuticals. The Russian Federation has identified the agent used in the Dubrovka theater siege as a fentanyl derivative; it is thus either an anesthetic/analgesic already in medical or veterinary use, or is closely related to one. Consequently, understanding the process of drug development and testing is essential to understanding the context of development of incapacitating agents. While Goldhammer's chapter focuses on the United States, his description is broadly true of the pharmaceutical industry in most developed countries, from which nearly all new pharmaceuticals derive.

Goldhammer points out that the vigorous pharmaceutical industry in the United States rests in part on the investment of federal money into basic research, and on an intellectual property rights policy that allows recipients of federal money to patent the applications of their research. This patent policy was designed to encourage technology transfer from academic and research laboratories to the private sector, and it has been successful in doing so. In addition to the federal investment in basic research, large pharmaceutical companies maintain substantial research and development (R&D) departments, often exceeding $500 million annually. The development of a new pharmaceutical agent thus rests on a complex foundation of federal and private funding, and intellectual property law.

Despite this foundation on extensive basic research, Goldhammer observes that "drug development . . . remains a risky business." For every 5,000 candidate drugs in the R&D laboratory, only one proceeds to final licensure. The process takes twelve to fifteen years for development, followed by as much as a year of regulatory review, and costs an average of $800 million. Although R&D represents the largest single expense, on a per-compound basis clinical trials are the most expensive step in the process. Clinical trials are conducted in three successively larger and more expensive phases. Phase I trials are typically conducted on a small number of healthy volunteers and "are designed to evaluate drug safety and arrive at a clinically effective dosage." Phase II trials involve larger numbers of volunteers representative of the class of patient whom the drug is expected to benefit, and are designed to determine if there is significant evidence for efficacy and to gather additional evidence of drug safety. If Phase I and II trials provide evidence of safety and efficacy, the company may proceed to Phase III trials, which can involve thousands of subjects. Phase III trials are designed to gather additional evidence for safety and efficacy; because they involve significantly more subjects than earlier trials, they provide evidence with greater statistical significance. Nevertheless, rare adverse reactions may not be discovered even in Phase III trials, and so additional studies of drug safety during marketing are often required.

Goldhammer makes it clear that the benefits of advances in biology will be slow to be reflected in new therapeutic agents. The revolution in biology promises a greatly expanded pharmacopeia, with much higher specificity and many fewer side effects. But before any of the new generation of drugs can make it to the marketplace, they have to go through the arduous process that he describes. Thus the practical benefits of genomics and associated technologies will lag far behind the scientific advances. However, this will not necessarily be true of the use of pharmaceutical-like compounds as weapons. There are no established processes for weapon development and approval comparable to the highly formal process that regulates therapeutic drugs. Thus advances in the life sciences may provide opportunities for development of incapacitating biochemical weapons before they result in new drugs.

The chapter by Martin Furmanski provides an historical context for considering incapacitating biochemical weapons. Furmanski examines the history of military interest in incapacitants and riot control agents since the beginning of the twentieth century. Riot control agents were first developed for police use in Europe shortly before the World War I, stimulated by incidents in which police battles with barricaded criminal gangs led to police casualties. He documents military interest as well, despite a long-standing prohibition on munitions designed to deliver poisonous gases. When World War I broke out this interest increased, and there were sporadic uses of riot control agents in battle, mostly without effect. Like the earlier police interest, the hope was that these weapons could flush enemy troops from fortified positions to make them more vulnerable to lethal fires. The extensive use of other chemical weapons with permanent or lethal effects overshadowed the continued use of riot control agents throughout the war. After the war, use of riot control agents for controlling civilian unrest began, largely in the United States.

In contrast to World War I, World War II saw no use of chemical weapons of any kind on most fronts, although Japan made extensive use of riot control agents (as well as several more lethal agents) against Chinese troops and civilians. They were also not used to any significant extent in combat during the Korean War, although they were used in prison camps to control rioting POWs. In contrast, riot control agents were used extensively by the United States in Vietnam, with more than six million kilograms dispersed by 1969. Riot control agents were used primarily for military tactical purposes, such as terrain denial, enhancement of lethal fires, breaking contact after being ambushed, etc. Nevertheless the political argument justifying their development and deployment was that the agents would be used to avoid civilian casualties when combatants and civilians were intermixed. Such uses, however, were rare. There was also some use of riot control agents in the Iran-Iraq war in the 1980s, although the extent is unclear.

Furmanski documents military interest in incapacitating biochemical agents (although they were not then called that) beginning in the United States in 1949. By the early 1960s, the United States began stockpiling munitions. However, its agent of choice was never fully satisfactory. Among other problems, it had a slow onset, its effects were unpredictable, and the munitions were unstable. The weapons were never used; they were ultimately abandoned, and stockpiles destroyed in the late 1970s.

The chapter by Alan Pearson continues the story of military interest in incapacitating biochemical weapons to the present. Based on the extensive document archive of the Sunshine Project,[18] obtained by numerous Freedom of Information Act requests, Pearson documents the continued interest of the U.S. military in incapacitants. Although he focuses on the United States (because of the availability of documentation), his conclusions probably apply equally to a number of other countries. Certainly the Russian Federation has pursued such weapons, and has, from the evidence of their deployment in Moscow in 2002, produced and stockpiled them.

Pearson begins by addressing the central issue of incapacitants—the lethality that accompanies these ostensibly "non-lethal" weapons. As the Moscow theater siege showed, the use of incapacitating biochemical weapons may result in considerable lethality in addition to the desired incapacitation, and he discusses the reasons for this. The search for effective agents has been, in significant measure, a search for agents with high enough potency to be effective weapons, but with low enough lethality to warrant their classification as incapacitants.

The U.S. effort to identify effective incapacitating biochemicals was in full swing by the mid 1980s. A number of pharmaceutical compounds were studied in the Advanced Riot Control Agent Device (ARCAD) program, synthetic opioids attracting the most attention. The program tested a number of opioids, most in the fentanyl class, and noted the problems with respiratory depression that underlies much opioid lethality. However, there were claims that the program led to the discovery of agents with dramatically improved safety margins. These were probably mixtures of opioids with antagonists of opioid action. The program also began the development process for munitions to deliver agents once they had been identified and standardized.

The ARCAD program was cancelled in 1992, as the entry into force of the Chemical Weapons Convention (CWC) approached. However, exploratory work continued in the civilian sector, under contract to the National Institute of Justice. In 1997, renewed interest in the military led to additional civilian contracts funded by the Joint Non-Lethal Weapons Directorate (JNLWD), an interservice unit located in the Marine Corps. Perhaps most notable was a study that surveyed the medical and pharmaceutical literature and suggested ten categories of pharmaceutical agents that were considered to be potential incapacitating biochemical agents. Many of the identified candidates, however, present serious problems with lethality or efficacy, so it appears that the effort to identify a suitable agent remained mired at a preliminary stage. Efforts along these lines are documented through 2002; whether efforts have continued, and if so how serious or effective they have been, remains unclear.

Considerably more progress appears to have been made in developing munitions to deliver powders or liquids. Such munitions could deliver incapacitating biochemical agents and have sometimes been justified for their ability to do so. They could also deliver other agents, not so seriously constrained by treaty prohibitions, such as smoke. The prominent involvement of the JNLWD suggests that the capability to deliver incapacitating biochemical agents, should a suitable one ever be identified, was among the goals of the projects.

Following this review of U.S. efforts to develop incapacitating biochemical weapons, Pearson assesses what is known about efforts in other countries. The Dubrovka Theater siege provides evidence that the Russian Federation has developed a fentanyl compound as a weapon, has stockpiled it, and trained Special Forces troops in its use. He also notes that Israel has used fentanyl as an assassination weapon, and that there are some indications that China might be interested in these agents. Given the secrecy that commonly shrouds weapon development, other countries may also be pursuing incapacitating biochemical weapons. Pearson concludes that "[f]or all the effort that has been placed on the development of incapacitating biochemical weapons, there remains little evidence for success." However, he goes on to note that "whether incapacitating biochemical weapons are developed and used is likely to depend at least as much on the level of lethality and permanent harm that governments and the international community decide is 'acceptable,' as on advances in science and technology."

Col. George Fenton, a former director of the JNLWD, places incapacitating chemical weapons within the larger category of "less-lethal capabilities." He argues that, as conflict environments are becoming more complex, varied, urban-centric, and "inundated with non-combatants," such incapacitating capabilities are becoming increasingly important and even necessary for effective military and law enforcement operations and for minimizing casualties. Fenton writes that "[l]ess-lethal capabilities provide the commander in the field with additional options to address the situation at hand . . . particularly when the use of lethal force is not the desired option." This, he says, provides users with alternatives to having to choose between doing nothing or resorting to lethal force, thereby increasing their flexibility and responsiveness and decreasing the ability of adversaries to predict their actions.

Fenton enumerates several reasons why chemical incapacitants may be especially versatile and useful. They can be deployed using multiple means and can employ multiple media. They can influence the entire "human behavior target set," comprising the five senses plus motor ability and cognition, and thereby can physically and/or psychologically disrupt and impair the behavior of targets and their ability to complete tasks. They have minimal residual effects, and can be used to target multiple individuals at once. Finally, they have a wide range of applications including crowd and riot control, area denial, prisoner seizure or extraction, facility clearance, and armed combat operations.

According to Fenton, technological advances now enable the development and use of chemical incapacitants that would minimize unnecessary suffering. Moreover, he argues that chemical incapacitants, like other "less-lethal" weapons, satisfy and even support the principles of military necessity, distinction and proportionality that underlie the Law of Armed Conflict (international humanitarian law). For instance, they can increase the time and range of engagement, thereby enabling military and law enforcement personnel to better distinguish friend from foe, discern intent, determine threat level, and take the most appropriate and proportional action for the situation at hand. However, he says, the Chemical Weapons Convention bans the military use of chemical incapacitants. As a result, he says, "the generally accepted practice of *not developing certain chemically-based less-lethal capabilities* in order to comply with the letter of the CWC *may work against the principles underlying the Law of Armed Conflict*" (emphasis in original). Fenton argues that this practice should be re-examined.

In his chapter, Malcolm Dando assesses the scientific outlook for successful future development of incapacitating biochemical weapons. Dando argues that scientific advances in genomics, the neurosciences and our understanding of human behavior are revealing new ways to manipulate brain function, both for therapeutic purposes and for military and law enforcement applications. Dando examines specific examples of how new knowledge, and additional technological advances such as neuroimaging, might lead to new means of incapacitation in the future. He stresses that "incapacitation" means much more than simply putting people to sleep, noting that it could include disruption of the sense of balance or the generation of excessive fear. This view is consistent with Fenton's description of the immediate goal of military users of incapacitating chemicals: to influence the target's behavioral response, whether physiologically or psychologically, particularly including by producing a "sensory overload condition." Significantly, Dando observes that the ability to manipulate brain function results not from any single experiment or piece of knowledge but from the overall trajectory, or "research program," of some areas of civilian neuroscience. Dando says that there is such rapid progress in neuroscience today that those seeking incapacitating capabilities probably conclude that the scientific outlook for the development of new incapacitants is good, and will monitor civilian research programs for dual-use capabilities that may arise rather quickly. Efforts to prevent the development and use of incapacitating biochemical weapons will therefore, he argues, have to be undertaken by means outside of the science and technology alone.

While Fenton supports the development and ultimate use of chemical incapacitants, he notes that there remains much uncertainty about their human effects, their effectiveness, and the potential unintended consequences of their use. He asks "[w]hat other (side) effects have consequence to the human body?" and he argues strongly for further research, study and analysis. However, he notes, "understanding the science of the neuroendocrine and immune systems alone is sure to be overwhelming." Kathryn Nixdorff and Jack Melling address this issue in their chapter on the potential long-term consequences of exposure to incapacitating biochemicals. Through a series of selected examples, they illustrate some of the intricate interactions that exist between three complex physiological systems—the nervous system, the endocrine system and the immune system—and how their regulation "by biochemical substances produced within the systems themselves is highly interdependent." They also illustrate how the modulation or perturbation of one system with a biochemical agent can profoundly affect the others, with potentially detrimental and sometime long-term effects depending on the agent used and the physiological process(es) affected. They cite human and animal studies that show that "exposure to biochemical incapacitants may induce heterogeneous cognitive and physiological impairments and lead to long-term health effects."

The regulation of each one of these systems is already extremely complex. Nixdorff and Melling point out that their interaction with one another "raises this complexity to enormous proportions," and is just beginning to be understood. Thus, it is "extremely difficult to predict what the outcome will be if this balanced interaction is perturbed." Their chapter reminds us that the use of biochemical agents for hostile purposes (for which they may be neither as well tested nor as tightly controlled as therapeutic agents) can pose a particular threat to interacting physiological systems since they can disrupt the balanced operation of those systems, including in unpredictable ways. Nixdorff and Melling also make the important point that the ability to use biochemical incapacitants for military or law enforcement purposes is intimately tied to the ability to deliver the agents, and they briefly describe the intensive development of technologies for therapeutic drug delivery currently underway.

Following these chapters on the historical, technical and military aspects of incapacitating biochemical agents and weapons, subsequent authors describe the context of arms control treaties and international law as applied to their development and use.

In the first of these chapters, David Fidler addresses the legal interpretation of Article II.9 (d) of the CWC. According to this controversial clause, "law enforcement, including domestic riot control purposes" is not a purpose prohibited under the Convention. Thus, states that are parties to the Convention may possess toxic chemicals as long as the types and quantities of such chemicals are consistent with law enforcement purposes even though their use in warfare is prohibited. Applying the rules of treaty interpretation, Fidler considers the ordinary meaning of the words of the clause as well as state practice, in particular the siege of a Moscow theater using a toxic chemical. Fidler draws on international human rights and humanitarian law in his discussions and makes a number of finely crafted arguments.

Fidler rejects the argument that only chemicals that have the characteristics of riot control agents can be used for law enforcement, relying on several arguments including the interpretation that lethal chemicals can legitimately be used for capital punishment by States Parties to the CWC. Nevertheless, Fidler concludes that the use of incapacitating biochemicals when neither the dosage nor exposure can be controlled would be a violation of international human rights law except in extreme circumstances. This body of law, according to Fidler, "severely limits when law enforcement authorities could use incapacitating chemical or biochemicals against detained persons" but does not eliminate the possibility entirely.

Fidler goes on to argue that the obligation to apply relevant international law means that a state party may not use toxic chemicals to enforce domestic law extrajurisdictionally. Nor may a state use toxic chemicals to enforce international law. Nevertheless, Fidler argues that "the CWC permits the use of RCAs for law enforcement purposes undertaken by military forces during non-traditional military operations sanctioned by international law." The law enforcement clause, however, would not support the use of toxic chemicals, including riot control agents, against combat forces, even in nontraditional operations such as peacekeeping or counterinsurgency actions.

In the final section of his chapter, Fidler discusses the implications of his analysis. He disputes the notion that an interpretation of the CWC that allows a narrow use of incapacitating toxic chemicals would create a sizeable loophole for states to develop "large and diverse stockpiles of chemical and biochemical incapacitating agents . . . " Ultimately, he makes a case that such an interpretation "should not be considered a grave threat to the core object and purpose of either the CWC or the BWC."

Adolf von Wagner, the chairman of the CWC negotiations at their conclusion, makes a distinctly different argument. Relying on the negotiating history of the CWC Ambassador von Wagner sharply disagrees with certain aspects of Fidler's interpretation. Von Wagner bases his argument on the ordinary meaning of the terms of the Convention emphasizing that the meaning must be taken in context and must be consistent with the object and purpose of the treaty.

With regard to the Article II.9 (d), the law enforcement clause, von Wagner argues that riot control and law enforcement are not two separate categories of permitted use; rather, "law enforcement qualifies the conditions under which riot control measures shall be applied." Fidler and von Wagner agree that toxic chemicals may be used for capital punishment, but von Wagner states that "it was undisputed during negotiations and also in later academic discussions that the understanding related to the special case of capital punishment cannot serve as a tool for a wider interpretation of the term law enforcement . . . " Like Fidler, von Wagner uses state practice, specifically the decision not to allow German soldiers in Kosovo to use riot control agents against ethnic Albanians who were burning houses belonging to ethnic Serbs, to support his arguments. Von Wagner also relies on the 1925 Geneva Protocol to support a narrow interpretation of the purposes for which the use of toxic chemicals is permitted. He stresses that a common understanding of a narrow interpretation of the law enforcement clause is needed to bind all parties to the same obligations.

James Leonard, who led the U.S. delegation during negotiation of the Biological Weapons Convention (BWC), and Marie Chevrier discuss the Convention's relevance to incapacitating biochemical weapons. The BWC bans the development, production, stockpiling, acquisition, retention, and transfer of "[m]icrobial or other biological agents, or toxins . . . of types and in quantities that have no justification for prophylactic, protective, or other peaceful purposes." The central issue is whether incapacitating biochemical agents are "other biological agents, or toxins." Chevrier and Leonard argue that other biological agents can logically be inferred to include living agents that are not microbial (e.g., insect pests) and agents that are not living as the term is commonly understood (for example, prions, which are infectious but which replicate by a novel mechanism unlike any organism). They conclude that nonliving biochemical compounds are also included in the category of "other biological agents" and thus fall under the coverage of the BWC.

A similar argument could be made that incapacitating biological agents are also toxins in the normal meaning of the term: they are products of living organisms, and they are toxic at doses higher than the normally minute concentrations present in healthy living tissue. Thus natural bioregulators, neurotransmitters and the like, would be considered toxins (as well as other biological agents) under the BWC. Indeed, some have already been used as weapons; insulin, for instance, has been used for murder on several occasions.[19] Moreover many toxins produced by plants, arthropods, and vertebrates such as snakes, fish, and toads, are toxic because they mimic or antagonize the action of endogenous bioregulators. They do this by virtue of being structural analogs of the endogenous compounds. This makes it reasonable to think that synthetic analogs of endogenous bioregulators, such as the fentanyl opioids, should also be considered toxins. This interpretation is supported by action taken by the States Parties to the BWC at the Second Review Conference, which agreed that "toxins (both proteinaceous and non-proteinaceous) of a microbial, animal or vegetable nature *and their synthetically produced analogues* are covered" (emphasis added).[20]

Chevrier and Leonard go on to review the origins of the BWC, paying special attention to the 1968 UK Working Paper on Microbiological Warfare, the 1969 UK Biological Warfare Draft Convention, the 1969 report of the UN Secretary General on chemical and biological weapons and the effects of their use, and the unilateral renunciation of biological weapons by the United States in 1969 and of toxin weapons in 1970. They document that incapacitating as well as lethal agents were intended to be covered, and that at least in the United States, bioregulators were recognized as potential toxin agents. They point out that other countries, including Canada, Sweden, and the United Kingdom, have subsequently expressed the same view in background papers prepared for Review Conferences.

Based on their analysis of the wording and negotiating history of the BWC, Chevrier and Leonard conclude that "the development of biochemicals for deliberate use to impair the physical or mental functions of humans without their consent would be a violation of the Convention. Any attempt to reconcile the prohibitions of the BWC with an interpretation that would allow the development, production or use of such biochemical weapons would not be credible given the historical record."

Robin Coupland then considers the effects of incapacitating biochemical agents on health. He points out that the extensive human history with weapons that injure by physical force allows us to predict, with some confidence, the effects of a novel weapon that uses the same principles for its effect. But our lack of experience with weapons with other mechanisms of effect suggests that we may have difficulty understanding the consequences of their use. He raises a series of questions, the answers to which should be known with confidence before incapacitating biochemical agents could responsibly be deployed as weapons. He goes on to observe that the lethality of a weapon is dependent on the conditions of its use, and that there is little current experience to suggest that incapacitating biochemical agents would be significantly less lethal than other weapons. He points out that the lethality of sarin in the 1995 Tokyo subway attack was about 24 percent, whereas the lethality of the purportedly "non-lethal" fentanyl in the Dubrovka Theater siege was about 17 percent. Pointing out that "the only difference between a drug and a poison is the dose," he argues that under realistic field conditions of weapon use, controlling the dose to avoid lethality is not likely. He goes on to describe the opinion of the International Committee of the Red Cross (ICRC) that "non-lethal" weapons should be considered simply as weapons, and not placed in a different category based on their purported non-lethality. He also points out that two other categories of "non-lethal" weapon have been banned as weapons of war: blinding laser weapons and riot control agents.

Coupland says that if used as military weapons, incapacitating biochemical agents could jeopardize international humanitarian law (IHL) protections of soldiers. For instance, troops that are *hors de combat* are protected from further attack by IHL, but it might be difficult in the heat of battle to determine whether enemy troops are incapacitated. The result could be that these agents would increase, not decrease, the lethality of the modern battlefield by increasing the vulnerability of troops to lethal fires. Indeed, this was one of the effects of the use of riot control agents by the United States in Vietnam; although justified on humanitarian grounds, its use to force enemy soldiers from cover almost certainly increased the lethality of other weapons.

Finally, Coupland points out that Article 36 of the 1977 Additional Protocol I to the 1949 Geneva Conventions requires states to undertake a review of the legality of any new weapon or means of warfare. He calls for such consideration, encompassing not only tactical utility and potential benefits, but also effects on arms control agreements and IHL, before any movement to develop incapacitating biochemical weapons.

Francoise Hampson's chapter provides a primer on international law for the nonspecialist. She explains that the status of treaties varies with the legal tradition of the state that is party to the treaty. The role of customary international law, Hampson explains, faces a number of problems in the regulation of weapons, including the large amount of treaty law and the difficulty of establishing an international norm based on what states refrain from doing.

Following a brief discussion of the relevance of the CWC and the BWC to biochemical weapons, Hampson discusses international humanitarian law, also known as the law of armed conflict (LOAC), in considerable detail. IHL applies to intra-state conflicts as well as to armed conflict between or among states. It places restrictions on the weapons that parties to a conflict may employ: weapons that inflict superfluous injury or unnecessary suffering may not be used. Hampson next proceeds to a discussion of the relevance of human rights law. She concludes that all three disciplines have a role to play in determining the legal fate of incapacitating biochemical weapons, and that, ultimately, a new international treaty regime may be necessary to clarify international regulation of these weapons. In the meantime public engagement on each of the legal strategies currently available is needed.

William Aceves concentrates on the role of human rights law in restricting biochemical weapons. Recognizing that international humanitarian law and the treaties and other agreements that comprise the regimes controlling biological and chemical weapons are the most common legal frameworks of relevance to incapacitating biochemical weapons, Aceves nevertheless sees an important role for human rights law. Aceves discusses the origins of human rights law following the atrocities of World War II and its application in various contexts.

Because incapacitating biochemical weapons can cause death under some circumstances, the right to life norm is relevant—and it restricts the ways in which incapacitating biochemical weapons could be used. Aceves discusses this norm thoroughly and goes on to discuss the relevance of the prohibition in human rights law against cruel inhuman or degrading treatment. The second norm is absolute and thus plays a particularly strong role in restricting the use of incapacitating biochemical weapons. Aceves concludes with a discussion of the interplay between international humanitarian law and human rights law and makes a strong case for the inclusion of human rights law in the discussion of the regulation of biochemical weapons.

Peter Herby begins his chapter by restating that, despite the interest of armed forces in so-called non-lethal biochemical weapons, the use of any biological or chemical weapon in armed conflict would violate the BWC, the CWC and the 1925 Geneva Protocol. He argues for caution in considering whether their use in domestic law enforcement would be wise. Herby goes on to enumerate and discuss fundamental rules of international humanitarian law that would be undermined by any use of incapacitating biochemical weapons. Herby reminds readers of the "Marten's Clause," which is contained in international humanitarian law treaties; the clause allows weapons which are abhorrent to the public conscience to be prohibited on that basis alone. He also brings to light the sometimes subtle underlying messages that are reinforced by increasing attention to incorrectly described "non-lethal" weapons.

Herby proceeds with a discussion of how to strengthen the norms of international humanitarian law that are threatened by the interest in incapacitating biochemical weapons. Among his practical suggestions are to avoid using misleading terms such as "non-lethal" weapons, to call on all states to have a rigorous review of weapons under consideration for their compliance with international treaties including international humanitarian law treaties, to increase awareness of humanitarian law norms and their relevance, and to engage a wider audience, including scientists and funders, in a broader discussion of these issues. Herby concludes with a cautionary reminder from history that the use of lethal chemical weapons in many international conflicts was preceded by the use of incapacitating chemical weapons.

Concluding Remarks

This volume provides a comprehensive survey of the complex set of issues associated with the development and use of incapacitating biochemical weapons. The contributing authors have explored a wide range of topics from science to history to current military interest, arms control and international law. The issues that the authors raise have not been settled and decisions on whether to proceed with the development and use of incapacitating biochemical weapons are likely to continue to be marked by controversy and disagreement. Our own views are summarized in the concluding chapter of this book; but our principal intent in issuing this volume is that it will be read and discussed by scientists, diplomats, policymakers and the general public. A transparent dialogue between proponents and opponents of these weapons is likely to lead to a better decision-making process.

The symposium that served as the foundation of this volume would not have occurred without the key contributions of Dr. Barbara Rosenberg, long-time and tireless advocate of international biological and chemical weapons control efforts. The Geneva Forum, and in particular Mr. Patrick McCarthy, made all local arrangements in Geneva for the symposium. Our editor at Lexington Books, Mr. Joseph Parry, provided assistance throughout the publication process. Finally, we are grateful to the Carnegie Corporation of New York and an anonymous donor, whose financial support made both the symposium and this volume possible.

Notes

1. Parts of this chapter are reproduced with minor changes from Alan Pearson, "Incapacitating Biochemical Weapons: Science, Technology and Policy for the 21st Century," *Non-Proliferation Review* 13, no. 2 (July 2006): 151–88.

2. Paul M. Wax, Charles E. Becker, and Steven C. Curry, "Unexpected 'Gas' Casualties in Moscow: A Medical Toxicology Perspective," *Annals of Emergency Medicine* 41 (August 2003): 700–5.

3. Neil Davison and Nick Lewer, *Bradford Non-Lethal Weapons Research Project Research Report No. 5*, (Bradford: Centre for Conflict Resolution, University of Bradford, May 2004): 39 <http://www.bradford.ac.uk/acad/nlw/research_reports/docs/BNLWRPResearchReportNo5_May04.pdf> (15 July 2006).

4. International Committee of the Red Cross, "Appeal on Biotechnology, Weapons and Humanity," (25 September 2002), <http://www.icrc.org/web/eng/siteeng0.nsf/html/5EAMTT#a3> (8 February 2007).

5. Jeremy M. Berg, John L. Tymoczko, and Lubert Stryer, *Biochemistry, 6th Edition* (New York: W.H. Freeman, 2006): 3.

6. Donald Voet, *Biochemistry, 3rd Edition* (New York: Wiley, 2004), 13.

7. Elliot Kagan, "Bioregulators as Instruments of Terror," *Clinics in Laboratory Medicine* 21 (September 2001): 607–18.

8. United States Army Field Manual 3–11.9, *Potential Military Chemical/Biological Agents and Compounds*, (10 January 2005): I–7, <http://www.fas.org/irp/doddir/army/fm3-11-9.pdf> (10 July 2006).

9. Eva S. Istvan and Johann Deisenhofer, "Structural Mechanism for Statin Inhibition of HMG-CoA Reductase," *Science* 292 (11 May 2001): 1160–1164.

10. Bruce D. Roth, "The Discovery and Development of Atorvastatin, a Potent Novel Hypolipidemic Agent," *Progress in Medicinal Chemistry*, 40 (2002): 1–22. For sales data see IMS Health, "Leading Products by Global Sales, 2005," <http://www.imshealth.com/ims/portal/front/articleC/0,2777,6599_77478579_77479663,00.html> (1 July 2006).

11. Field Manual 3–11.9, I–6.

12. James S. Ketchum and Frederick R. Sidell, "Incapacitating Agents," in Frederick R. Sidell, Ernest T. Takafugi, and David R. Franz, eds., *Medical Aspects of Chemical and Biological Warfare*, TMM series, Part I (Washington, D.C.: TMM Publications, 1997): 288.

13. Field manual 3–11.9, I–6.

14. World Health Organization, *Public Health Response to Biological and Chemical Weapons: WHO Guidance* (Geneva: World Health Organization, 2004): 182.

15. U.S. Army Field Manual 8–285, Treatment of Chemical Agent Casualties and Conventional Military Chemical Injuries (22 December 1995), 3_1, <www.globalsecurity.org/wmd/library/policy/army/fm/8-285/index.html> (8 February 2007).

16. See information for Remifentanil at "Opioids" <http://www.anesthetist.com/anaes/drugs/opioids.htm> (1 July 2006).

17. The symposium was organized by the Scientists Working Group on Biological and Chemical Weapons of the Center for Arms Control and Non-Proliferation and was co-sponsored by the Geneva Forum, a collaboration of the United Nations Institute for Disarmament Research, the Quaker UN Office, and the Program for Strategic and International Security Studies of the Graduate Institute of International Studies.

18. See <http://sunshine-project.org> (25 February 2007).

19. Vincent Marks, "Murder by insulin," *Medico-Legal Journal* 67, no. 4 (1999): 147–163.

20. Final Declaration, Second Review Conference of the Parties to the Convention on the Prohibition of the Development, Production and Stockpiling of Bacteriological (Biological) and Toxin Weapons and on Their Destruction, BWC/CONF.II/13/II, 26 September 1986.

CHAPTER 1

Nonconsensual Manipulation of Human Physiology Using Biochemicals

Mark Wheelis

There is an ongoing revolution in biology that began in the mid 1970s with the development of recombinant DNA techniques and that has increased its momentum every year since. The revolution has been greatly accelerated in recent years by genomics, proteomics, and a host of related sub-disciplines and technologies. This revolution promises an unprecedented level of detailed knowledge of human physiology, extending to the functioning and interactions of the molecules that underlie health and disease.

This deep understanding of physiology and health will reveal, among other things, the nature, identity, and functioning of the molecules that mediate communication within the body. All physiological systems involve large numbers of cells. These cells communicate with each other via processes mediated largely by chemical compounds released by an originating cell that bind to specific receptor proteins on a recipient cell's surface. The enormous importance of cellular communication in human physiology is clear from the fact that over one quarter of the genes with tentatively identified functions in the human genome appear to encode proteins involved with this process.[1]

The binding of a signaling molecule to a receptor protein causes a change in the shape of the protein, which initiates a response inside the cell. As a class, these signaling molecules are termed bioregulators, but there are many specific terms for bioregulators in specific physiological systems, such as neurotransmitters for bioregulators in the nervous system, interleukins and cytokines in the immune system, and hormones for compounds that affect distant tissues. There are similar terminologies for the receptor proteins through which bioregulators exert their effect. Most importantly for the topic of this paper are the neuroreceptors, receptor proteins on the surface of cells in the nervous system whose stimulation either evokes the stimulated cell to initiate a nerve impulse or inhibits such firing.

Coupled with the emerging understanding of the chemistry of the brain are increasingly sophisticated methods of neuroimaging.[2] Noninvasive techniques can now identify in three dimensions the areas of the brain that are activated by various stimuli, by thoughts, or by intentions. Thus we are beginning to understand the spatial organization of neural circuits, at the same time that we are beginning to understand their chemistry. The ultimate result promises to be a very powerful synthesis that will further accelerate progress in understanding brain function. For the moment, we remain a long way from a complete understanding of the nervous system, much less its connections to the immune system and other systems. Nevertheless we may be close to a workable knowledge base for active and precise therapeutic intervention. A level of understanding that would allow informed and precise intervention in specific circuits appears imminent.

Manipulating the Brain

All brain functions are, so far as we know, the result of the activity of specific sets of neurons in the brain (often affected by other interactions, such as with the immune system). As such, they can in principle be manipulated by altering either the electrical activities of neurons or the chemistry of cell-to-cell communication. As we understand the chemistry of mental processes in increasing detail, we will be able to design pharmaceutical compounds (and combinations of compounds) whose interaction with neuroreceptors is increasingly specific. Over time, the ability to manipulate neurophysiology will thus become increasingly specific.

For example, the opioid fentanyl is a potent analgesic and anesthetic by virtue of its agonist action at a class of opioid receptors termed μ-receptors[3]. The natural bioregulator is a short peptide termed an endorphin. Fentanyl has a three dimensional shape and charge distribution that is similar to one part of the endorphin, so it can bind to some endorphin receptors. Unfortunately, several classes of neurons have μ-receptors, and fentanyl causes effects beyond its action on pain circuits and on awareness. The most serious of these effects are caused by its action on neurons in the pre-Boetzinger complex in the brainstem, where core physiological functions like respiration are controlled. Thus, fentanyl and other opioids cause respiratory depression, often lethal in cases of opioid overdose. However, recent animal studies demonstrate that simultaneous administration of a specific agonist of a different neurotransmitter, serotonin, can prevent respiratory depression without affecting analgesia.[4] Thus, by means of more precisely targeted agonists and antagonists of natural neurotransmitters, or by combinations of such compounds, more specific pharmaceuticals having higher potency and fewer (and milder) side effects can be expected.

In the more distant future, additional advances will likely come as a result of new abilities to affect specific regions of the brain separately from others, either by new technologies of drug delivery (biological or nanotechnological), or by stimulation of specific cells or groups of cells with electrodes or with electromagnetic fields. Therapeutic agents will also likely be tailored to individual or group genotypes, further reducing the occurrence and severity of side effects. Given the high cost of neurological disorders, and the large market for pharmaceuticals that treat such disorders, advances are expected to be rapid.[5]

The rate-limiting element in the development of new therapeutic agents is no longer the identification of new candidate agents, but rather the long, expensive process of development, testing, and approval.[6] But long before a new drug is approved, its mode of action is understood, and there is often significant information about its specificity and toxicity. Furthermore, many variants of the drug will have been synthesized and their properties studied. Thus our ability to manipulate the brain or other physiological systems will run significantly ahead of the approval of new therapeutic agents.

Of course, with the capability to interfere effectively for therapeutic reasons comes the capability to manipulate the nervous system for malign reasons.[7] A number of analysts have suggested that therein lies great potential for doing harm, most notably Matthew Meselson, Thomas Dudley Cabot Professor of the Natural Sciences at Harvard, who wrote prophetically that

> Every major technology—metallurgy, explosives, internal combustion, aviation, electronics, nuclear energy—has been intensively exploited, not only for peaceful purposes but also for hostile ones. Must this also happen with biotechnology, certain to be a dominant technology of the twenty-first century? . . . as our ability to modify fundamental life processes continues its rapid advance, we will . . . become able to manipulate . . . processes of cognition, development, reproduction, and inheritance . . . Therein could lie unprecedented opportunities for violence, coercion, repression, or subjugation . . . we appear to be approaching a crossroads—a time that will test whether biotechnology, like all major predecessor technologies, will come to be intensively exploited for hostile purposes, or whether our species will find the collective wisdom to take a different course.[8]

As Meselson observes, the ability to subvert neurobiology to do harm is only part of a broader capability to manipulate human physiology for hostile purposes; the reproductive and immune systems, for instance, may also provide targets that would serve malign political or military purposes. Here I will focus on the potential to misuse knowledge of the nervous system, because it is likely to be the first to be misused (indeed it already has been). However, many of the conclusions will apply generally to all hostile manipulations of human physiology.

Analogs of neurotransmitters could be developed as either lethal or incapacitating weapons. There appears to be relatively little interest in developing new lethal weapons based on these agents, in part because such weapons already exist—the nerve agents (both the G agents like sarin, soman, and tabun, and the V agents like VX, are analogs of the neurotransmitter acetylcholine, and are extremely potent). Further disincentives to development of additional such weapons are the prohibitions of the Chemical Weapons Convention (CWC), discussed below. Incapacitating agents are a different matter, and there has been considerable interest in them despite the CWC.[9] Such agents are here termed incapacitating biochemical agents. The term incapacitating biochemical weapon refers to the agent in combination with a delivery device.

It is worth noting that the long, expensive, and demanding approval process that a therapeutic agent must go through before approval does not apply to agents used for hostile purposes. There is no legally mandated process of safety and efficacy trials for weapons used for law enforcement purposes, nor any regulatory agency that must approve such weapons. New military weapons must be reviewed for consistency with international humanitarian law, but beyond that the requirements for testing and approval are entirely within the military, and are designed to serve military needs. Thus once the decision to develop incapacitating biochemical weapons is taken, implementation can be rapid compared with the process of approval of a new therapeutic agent.

Of course, the identification of an incapacitating biochemical agent is only the first step in developing a weapon. In some cases this step constitutes most of the weapon development—for instance, for use by Special Forces to subdue prisoners taken behind enemy lines, or for interrogation or torture, the agent loaded into a hypodermic syringe could constitute the fully developed weapon. In other cases, for instance to use at a distance against groups, considerable development would be necessary prior to fielding an agent/munition/propellant system that was sufficiently reliable, efficient, and safe. Such development efforts are most likely to be taken by states. Thus, whether there is substantial future development of incapacitating biochemical agents may be largely dependent on whether states embrace such weapons or eschew them. Once a weapon system is developed and goes into commercial production, it is likely to be rapidly imitated, to rapidly enter the international arms trade, and to become readily and widely available.

If states are, at least initially, the principal developers of incapacitating biochemical weapons, then the kinds of weapons developed will reflect the interests of military and law enforcement agencies. As discussed next, this suggests that the first incapacitating biochemical weapons to be developed will be ones that cause unconsciousness; indeed, it is clear that such a weapon has already been developed and used.

Use of Incapacitating Biochemical Weapons

USE FOR LAW ENFORCEMENT

There are many situations in which chemical incapacitating agents may be of interest to law enforcement agencies. The long history of police use of irritant agents, like tear gas and pepper spray, extends back to before World War I.[10] The reasons are clear. Much more than military forces, law enforcement agencies must necessarily avoid casualties, especially fatalities, and they normally operate within the civil society that they serve. There are few situations in which police have a clear right to kill, and most police interactions with both criminals and hostile civilians fall far short of this.

Particularly for hostage situations, the ability to rapidly and completely incapacitate without causing death or permanent disability could be of great utility. This is because it is unlikely in most situations that the hostage taker(s) could be incapacitated without simultaneously affecting the hostages; hence the need for safe incapacitants. The need for rapid acting agents is also clear, to prevent hostage takers from harming hostages in the interval between the moment when they realize they are being attacked with an incapacitating agent, and the time when the agent achieves its intended effect.

The Dubrovka theater siege in Moscow in 2002 exemplifies both of these features. Approximately 40 Chechen separatists took more than 800 theatergoers hostage, demanding that Russia withdraw its troops from Chechnya. The hostage takers were a mixed group of men and women. The men, including the leaders of the group, were armed with assault rifles, and the women were armed with handguns and had control of the detonators of numerous bombs, some worn on their bodies and some in packages that they placed next to them. The hostage takers threatened to blow up the theater and everyone in it unless their demands were met, and no one doubted their resolve to do so. To break the stand-off, Russian Special Forces pumped an anesthetic agent into the ventilation system of the theater to incapacitate the occupants. The agent is unknown, but is claimed to be an opioid of the fentanyl class. As the agent entered through the ventilation system, the male hostage takers exited into surrounding corridors to fight the Russians they expected to be storming the theater. However, Special Forces waited half an hour before they entered the building and engaged in a firefight that killed all the male Chechens. When Special Forces entered the theater itself, they found all the occupants unconscious. The female Chechens were executed while comatose, and the hostages were evacuated to nearby hospitals (with significant delay). Unfortunately, nearly 130 of the hostages died of overdose or of airway obstruction, and an unknown number died later of complications. An additional unknown number have suffered permanent disability.[11]

To some, the lessons are clear. The use of an incapacitating biochemical agent saved hundreds of lives, and proved its worth in such a situation. Equally, the large numbers of hostage deaths showed the urgent need for the development of a safer agent. However, the actuality may be quite different, and this event may be unique rather than a model for similar situations in the future. Clearly there was plenty of time for the women to detonate their bombs: some hostages made cell phone calls to family to say they were being gassed, and there was time for the male hostage takers to leave the room without being affected. Probably the principal element was the unexpected nature of the attack. With the leaders of the hostage takers out of the room, the women would probably have detonated their bombs when Russian forces entered. In the absence of such a defining event they waited, and were overcome by the anesthetic before they could think the situation through. If surprise was the critical element, future situations of the same kind might not turn out so well, and it may thus be difficult to replicate the success of this operation. It is worth noting that the hostage takers in the Beslan school hostage crisis in 2004, also Chechen separatists, were equipped with gas masks.

There are clear reasons for law enforcement to be interested in incapacitating biochemical weapons. Although future premeditated hostage situations can be expected to involve hostage takers prepared to deal with incapacitating biochemical agents, spontaneous hostage takers would not be expected to be so prepared, and these constitute most of the police experience. There are indications that this interest is being pursued; for example, the U.S. Department of Justice has commissioned several reports on possible uses of fentanyl agents.[12] However, it is unclear how far such interest has gone, whether there is continuing momentum, or what the status of law enforcement interest in other countries is. However, it seems implausible that interest is confined to the United States and Russia.

MILITARY USE

Most military use of incapacitating biochemical weapons is prohibited by the Geneva Protocol and by the CWC. Their development, production, and stockpiling is prohibited by the CWC and also by the Biological Weapons Convention (BWC).[13] There is thus in principle no opportunity for scrupulous nations to develop them for military use. However, if incapacitating biochemical weapons become too attractive to militaries of the world, this prohibition could crumble. Indeed, interest in developing this particular class of chemical weapon is probably the greatest threat to the chemical weapons ban, one of the great triumphs of modern arms control.[14]

Furthermore, many countries use military forces in police roles under certain circumstances. The forces used by Russia to resolve the Dubrovka theater and Beslan school hostage crises were military Special Forces, not civilian police. When militaries play such dual roles, they may legally develop an incapacitating biochemical weapon for law enforcement use, and then find the temptation to use it in military situations irresistible.[15]

We already see worrisome trends. As discussed above, Russia has already used an incapacitating biochemical weapon at the Dubrovka theater in 2002, and Special Forces appear to have been prepared to use it again during the Beslan school hostage crisis in 2004, but events preempted them. More recently, another use of the weapon was reported in Nalchik in 2005, again to resolve a hostage crisis.[16] While these are arguably law enforcement actions (not prohibited by either the Geneva Protocol or CWC), it is nevertheless worrisome that the Russian military has developed, produced, stockpiled, and used a chemical agent as a weapon against opponents in the context of an ongoing civil war. That such use has not elicited a protest, or even a request for consultation, from any State Party to the CWC is equally worrisome.

Other nations may also have developed incapacitating biochemicals as military weapons. In 2002, Rear Admiral (ret.) Stephen Baker claimed that U.S. Special Forces were equipped with "knock-out gases," and he speculated that they would be used in Iraq. Although the Pentagon issued an immediate denial that the U.S. had plans to use such agents in Iraq, it conspicuously did not deny that its special forces were so equipped.[17] A knowledgeable source within the U.S. Special Forces has confirmed Admiral Baker's allegation. It is also corroborated by a "former high-level Defense Department official," who is quoted as saying "We can do things on the ground, too, but it's difficult and very dangerous—put bad stuff in ventilator shafts and put them to sleep."[18] If, as all of this suggests, U.S. Special Forces are so equipped, this would appear to be a violation of the CWC.

The allegation that U.S. Special Forces are already equipped with incapacitating biochemical weapons gains plausibility in the context of long-standing U.S. military interest in such weapons.[19] However, it does not appear that any agents have been standardized for use other than by Special Forces. For overt military weapons, the CWC constraints appear to have been largely respected thus far. Nevertheless, multiple munitions specifically designed to deliver chemical agents have been developed or are under development. These include mortar

rounds, rifle-propelled grenades, 155 mm artillery shells, and airburst munitions. If the United States were to decide to add incapacitating biochemical
agents to its arsenal, it could have a fully mature weapon system soon after an
agent was standardized.

More recently, Czech scientists have reported on their work to develop incapacitating biochemical agents as weapons for law enforcement.[20] France has
also been noted to probably have an interest in incapacitating biochemical
weapons,[21] and Israel (which is not a party to either the CWC or the BWC) has
used fentanyl in assassination attempts.[22] It is likely that other countries are also
quietly developing such weapons.

It thus appears that two of the major military powers in the world have already adopted incapacitating biochemical weapons for certain limited military
activities, and that others are actively developing them. Even if these activities do
not lead to tactical or strategic munitions stockpiles, they could easily expand
significantly. In addition to their utility in quasi-law enforcement situations, incapacitating biochemical weapons could be attractive to militaries for their ability to aid in the covert taking of prisoners in uncooperative countries or behind
enemy lines, and in their transport to friendly territory. They could be useful
when transporting POWs, or in controlling aggressively hostile POWs. They
might also be useful in military interrogations (see below). If such weapons become an acceptable part of military arsenals, then an expanded role, including
combat uses, would be likely.

Of course, when we think of military use of incapacitating biochemical
weapons, we normally think of their use by our own forces. But once developed, we can expect that most militaries of the world would soon be armed
with such weapons, as would insurgent forces and terrorists. In considering the
wisdom of developing such weapons, we thus need to consider not just how
we might use them, but also how they might be used against us. One of the
abilities that incapacitating biochemical weapons will clearly enhance is the
ability to take prisoners, by allowing targets to be incapacitated rather than
killed, and by allowing them to be pacified during their captivity and transport. Regular military troops, either of nations or under UN command, are
particularly vulnerable to being taken prisoner and mistreated, since the ability to take hostages will likely have asymmetric value in conflicts between states
and insurgent or terrorist forces. Moreover, the legacy of Abu Ghraib,
Baghram, Guantanamo Bay, the "torture memo," and the refusal to apply the
protections of the Geneva Conventions to detainees in the U.S. "war" on terrorism will likely linger for a long time, and American forces in particular will
be at great risk. Significant numbers of military prisoners in terrorist or insurgent hands could have serious political and military ramifications, which it
would be foolish not to anticipate.

Another concern is the rise in importance of private military corporations—private companies under contract to the military that provide armed personnel for security, prison services, and other tasks. Such companies can field large, heavily armed forces under contract to, but operationally independent of, government. Because they do not come under the regular military chain of command their use of incapacitating biochemical weapons could be more difficult to control and could be more likely to result in abuses than the same weapons in military hands.

USE FOR INTERROGATION OR TORTURE

There is a long history of coercive interrogation, as military and police forces often feel they have security concerns that override humanitarian law and constitutional protections. For example, the United States, a country that has been one of the world leaders in support of individual rights, has recently been in the news for interrogation practices that are considered by most people to constitute torture. Clearly some segments of the U.S. government feel that the need to prevent another terrorist attack like the al-Qaeda attacks in 2001 takes precedence over the normal rights and protections afforded to detainees. In this kind of situation, any pharmaceutical agent that offers the potential for reliable information extraction might be quite attractive. Indeed, released detainees have claimed that they were forcibly medicated, and detainees' medical records were illegally provided to interrogators.[23] What purpose these practices served is unclear, but they may have been designed to aid interrogation. This would be consistent with past efforts of the U.S. Central Intelligence Agency to develop chemical aids to interrogation.[24]

In the future, chemical agents that make captives more compliant, trusting and eager to please their captors will likely be available, and could greatly enhance interrogation. Other agents will likely allow captors to cause acute depression, psychosis, pain, panic, and other states, and to relieve the effects at will. This kind of chemical torture would almost certainly be far more effective than traditional physical torture in breaking the will of captives. It would be naive to think that such agents will not be used if the nonconsensual manipulation of human physiology becomes acceptable.

Indeed, there is a long history of the use of chemicals for torture. Most egregiously, the Soviet Union used imprisonment in state psychiatric hospitals as a punishment for political dissent, and in that context injected various chemicals for torture.[25] As the dissident psychiatrist Dr. Anatoly Koryagin wrote secretly to his western psychiatric colleagues

> I appeal to you, my colleagues, not for a moment to forget those who
> have stood up for the rights and freedoms which people need, and

now are condemned to spend years in the nightmarish (for a healthy person) world of psychiatric wards, exhausting themselves in a debilitating struggle to preserve their psyches, a struggle against torture[r]s armed with drugs.[26]

There is no reason to believe that this history of abuse of medicine will not be repeated, as the capabilities for pharmacological torture become refined by orders of magnitudes over what was available to the Soviet Union. And it will not only be despotic states that might be tempted to use incapacitating biochemical agents in this way; any state that sees itself under siege will be tempted to rationalize torture by appeal to overriding national security concerns.

USE BY DESPOTS

Dictatorial regimes, in which individuals have few protections against abuse by the state, are more likely than democracies to use incapacitating biochemical agents in unethical or illegal ways. All of the above abuses would likely be more prevalent and brutal in dictatorships, and there would be additional uses of incapacitating biochemical agents to despots for improving their ability to suppress dissent. In addition to the uses for torture and interrogation, the ability to control crowds by incapacitation rather than dispersal (with traditional riot control agents) would be a powerful tool for repression, as it would allow the leaders of popular dissenting movements to be more readily captured.

USE BY CRIMINALS

"Knock-out drops" slipped into a drink to make a "Mickey Finn" have featured in detective fiction throughout the twentieth century. The active ingredient in a Mickey Finn is widely reputed to be chloral hydrate (ethyl chloride), one of several halogenated alkane anesthetics. Although chloral hydrate is a gas at room temperature, it is readily soluble in water and might well have been used for incapacitation. Whether it was in fact used by criminals for this purpose is unclear. But the potential attraction of such use to criminals is strongly suggested by the fictional scenarios.

Recent experience has confirmed criminal interest in such drugs. Apparently widespread use of several categories of drug to facilitate rape seems to be a major law enforcement problem. The central nervous system depressant gamma-hydroxybutyric acid (GHB), an analog of the natural neurotransmitter gamma-aminobutyric acid (GABA), and the sedative rohypnol (trade name for fluni-trazepam, a benzodiazepine class sedative) have both been widely used to facilitate "date rape." These drugs cause stupor and unconsciousness. More importantly, they commonly induce amnesia of events during the period of intoxication, concealing as well as facilitating rape. They are rapidly cleared from the body, eliminating forensic evidence of intoxication unless assayed very soon after the crime. Actual prevalence of such use is very difficult to quantify, but it is recognized as a significant social problem in many western countries.[27]

Other potential criminal uses of such drugs include incapacitating victims to facilitate robbery, burglary, or kidnap; incapacitating security guards to gain access; keeping victims of kidnap or hostage-taking docile; facilitating jailbreaks; etc. Pepper spray has been used with increasing frequency for some of these purposes.[28] It is reasonable to presume that if new incapacitating biochemical weapons for law enforcement are developed, they will rapidly find their way into criminal hands and be used for criminal purposes.

USE BY TERRORISTS

Terrorists might also find incapacitating biochemical agents useful—to facilitate hostage-taking, to incapacitate security guards, to keep hostages docile, etc. They might also find the ability to use biochemical agents to extract information during interrogation to be of value in planning attacks on secure targets, such as nuclear power plants, or facilities storing decommissioned nuclear warheads or nerve agents. Biochemical agents released into airplane cabins could allow small numbers of terrorists to control large numbers of potential adversaries, preventing passenger revolt and penetrating cockpit doors. Since chemical weapons have the potential to complement firearms and other traditional weapons, other applications could undoubtedly be imagined, tailored to particular terrorist plans. It is worth remembering that al Qaeda has repeatedly demonstrated imaginative planning of complex operations; if biochemical weapons could give them capabilities they do not now have, we can expect them to be interested.

Benefits and Risks of Incapacitating Biochemical Weapons

Like any other weapon, incapacitating biochemical weapons would have advantages and disadvantages. On the positive side, they could have the potential to save lives in certain situations. Examples include law enforcement situations in which hostages are being held, and perhaps military situations in which combatants and noncombatants are intermixed. The former would be legal under existing arms control regimes, but the latter would require substantial change to, or substantially changed interpretations of, both the CWC and the BWC. Whether this could be done without destroying the treaty regimes is unclear.

However, the utility of incapacitating biochemical agents for these purposes is likely to be significantly diminished due to several complicating factors. First, there are at present no incapacitating biochemical agents that could be legitimately considered "non-lethal," even if by that term we only mean that lethality is less than some arbitrary low number, like 0.5 percent of the targeted population (a definition used by the U.S. Joint Non-Lethal Weapons Directorate). All currently licensed pharmaceuticals that can rapidly induce unconsciousness have narrow safety margins,[29] and most unlicensed relatives are likely to have equal or narrower safety margins. Second, even if a compound that was completely safe pharmacologically could be found, any time people are rendered rapidly unconscious, a significant number will collapse in ways that obstruct their airway, or will aspirate vomit and choke. Because of these two complications, military and law enforcement use of incapacitating biochemical agents that cause unconsciousness can be expected to almost always be accompanied by fatalities, and their use on innocent bystanders or hostages has to be evaluated accordingly.

Added to this is a third complication: existing incapacitating biochemical candidate agents have readily available countermeasures. Simple masking will prevent their action, and antidotes are available for the most promising candidates, the opioids. Thus criminals or terrorists with forethought, and all modern military forces, will be easily able to defend against them.

It is worth noting here that there is scant reason to believe the humanitarian argument advanced by most advocates of incapacitating biochemical weapons that they are desirable because they replace lethal force. This argument might certainly be true in limited law enforcement situations, but history suggests that it would not be the norm for military use. In previous situations where "non-lethal" weapons have been used in combat, they have augmented, not replaced, lethal force. This was true repeatedly in Vietnam, where the United States used 10,000 tons of the tear gas CS, much of it to drive enemy troops from cover in order to make them more vulnerable to other fires, and virtually none of it for humanitarian purposes.[30] This also appears to be happening to a limited extent in Iraq, where there are reports of "non-lethal" acoustic weapons being used to drive snipers from cover so that they can be more effectively killed.[31]

In addition to the immediate risks associated with military and law enforcement use of incapacitating biochemical weapons, the pursuit of such weapons also poses broader risks to humanity. These risks fall into three major categories: the abuse potential they bring; their consequences for international arms control regimes and for international humanitarian law; and their consequences for long-standing ethical norms.

The potentials for abuse have been sketched out previously. In short, even if incapacitating biochemical weapons are developed for legitimate ends, like almost all other weapons they will also be diverted to illegitimate ones. Criminals, terrorists, and despots will all find uses for these weapons. And as with many other weapons, they may find incapacitating biochemical weapons more suited to their ends than legitimate users find them to theirs. This is in part because illegitimate users will not be constrained to the same extent that legitimate users are to use incapacitating biochemical weapons humanely, or to behave humanely after their use. Thus, policy decisions involved in deciding whether to pursue incapacitating biochemical weapons, and for what purposes, must include careful consideration of the potential risks of these weapons in the wrong hands.

The implications of the pursuit of incapacitating biochemical weapons for international norms and laws are unquestionably serious. The CWC establishes a categorical prohibition on the hostile use of toxic chemicals except for law enforcement, or for uses in which the toxicity is incidental. The BWC establishes a similar categorical prohibition on the hostile use of biological agents or toxins (which category includes incapacitating biochemical agents),[32] without an explicit exception for law enforcement. Thus the use of incapacitating biochemical weapons for any purpose would conflict with the BWC, and for any use other than law enforcement would conflict with the CWC. The categorical nature of these bans is one of their great virtues, and is consistent with the purposes of the Conventions as stated in their preambles:

> Determined for the sake of all mankind, to exclude completely the possibility of bacteriological (biological) agents and toxins being used for weapons [BWC]
>
> Determined for the sake of all mankind, to exclude completely the possibility of the use of chemical weapons [CWC]

A partial ban that allows some chemical agents and toxins to be used for hostile purposes while banning others is inconsistent with these high principles, is fraught with ambiguity, and interferes with the detection of noncompliance. Indeed, the development of incapacitating biochemical weapons has been identified as one of the major threats to the ban on chemical and biological weapons generally, and there is concern that they could lead to the entire regime crumbling. As these bans constitute one of the great achievements of twentieth century arms control, this is a possibility that should not be taken lightly, no matter how improbable advocates of incapacitating biochemical weapons might consider it.

There are also serious implications for international humanitarian law: most importantly, the provisions of the Geneva Conventions that prohibit the deliberate targeting of civilians by military forces, and the prohibition on harming enemy combatants who are *hors de combat*.[33] Since one of the principal uses anticipated by advocates of the military use of incapacitating biochemical weapons is to target groups of people that include both civilians and combatants, there is a clear intent to prepare to violate the ban on targeting civilians. And there is very real concern that incapacitated enemy troops would be vulnerable to lethal force, as it may be very difficult to determine in the field how incapacitated they are, or how long the incapacitation may last. It is worth noting that in the Moscow theater siege, Russian Special Forces executed all the comatose Chechens, presumably for exactly these reasons.

Very serious ethical issues are also raised by incapacitating biochemical weapon development. There is currently a clear ethical norm that the manipulation of human physiology without the consent of the manipulated is wrong, except in certain very limited medical situations. Few would contest that it is both wrong and criminal to get someone drunk, or to give them LSD or other drugs, without their knowledge and consent. Administration of licensed prescription drugs is restricted to physicians, and they are constrained by the ethics of their profession to do so only for the benefit of the patient, and only with informed consent. While there are some exceptions, primarily for instances when patients are unable to give informed consent and represent a danger to themselves or to others, such situations are very limited, very tightly regulated, and require stringent oversight. To allow weaponry to move into the arena of physiological manipulation would set a precedent that might well serve us poorly in the future, as the ability to manipulate human physiology for specific, nontherapeutic purposes becomes increasingly powerful.

Conclusion

I am not arguing here that there should be no development of incapacitating biochemical weapons. I do suggest that if such development is to proceed, it should be done with great deference to existing arms control and humanitarian law, and with full consideration of the social, political and ethical implications of incapacitating biochemical weapons. I have suggested elsewhere that such a program should be open and transparent; should be administered, funded, and conducted by nonmilitary agencies such as departments of justice; should be justified solely on the basis of law enforcement needs; and should involve the development only of munitions and delivery devices that are characteristically used by police forces.[34] All current programs of incapacitating biochemical development fail to satisfy these criteria, and are thus provocative, destabilizing, unwise, and arguably illegal.

In the long term, the capacity to manipulate human physiology to serve criminal or political purposes constitutes a serious threat to humankind. It is this context that makes incapacitating biochemical weapons, and the precedent they would establish, so worrisome. Rather than developing incapacitating biochemical weapons, we might serve humanity and our posterity better by working to ban the nonconsensual manipulation of human physiology except for very tightly constrained medical situations where the benefit of the individual requires it, and where that individual is unable to give informed consent. I have elsewhere suggested that an international convention with that purpose might be usefully added to the corpus of international humanitarian law.

While it may seem melodramatic to put the issue in such terms, it may nevertheless be accurate to say that in choosing to develop incapacitating biochemical weapons, we are choosing a future in which human physiology becomes a target of soldiers, terrorists, criminals, and despots, while rejecting a future in which such manipulation is prohibited. Given a choice, which future would we choose for our children?

Notes

1. J. C. Venter, M. D. Adams, E. W. Myers, P. W. Li, and others, "The Sequence of the Human Genome," *Science* 291 (2001): 1304–51.

2. J. D. Haynes and G. Rees, "Decoding Mental States from Brain Activity in Humans," *Nature Reviews: Neuroscience* 7 (2006): 523–34.

3. An agonist is a compound that mimics the effects of a naturally occurring neurotransmitter. A compound that prevents the natural effects is called an antagonist.

4. T. Manzke, U. Guenther, E. G. Ponimaskin, M. Haller, M. Dutschmann, S. Schwarzacher, and D.W. Richter, "5-HT$_{4(a)}$ Receptors avert Opioid-Induced Breathing Depression Without Loss of Analgesia," *Science* 301 (2003): 226–29. See also H. Eilers and M. A. Schumacher, "Opioid-Induced Respiratory Depression: Are 5-HT$_{4(a)}$ Receptor Agonists the Cure?" *Molecular Interventions* 4, no. 4 (2004): 197–98.

5. The chapter by Malcolm Dando discusses in greater detail the emerging capability to specifically alter brain function, affecting mood, emotion, cognition, perception, alertness, memory, or any other function rooted in the brain.

6. See the chapter by Alan Goldhammer.

7. M. Wheelis and M. R. Dando, "Neurobiology: A Case Study of the Imminent Militarization of Biology," *International Review of the Red Cross* 87 (2005): 553–68.

8. M. Meselson, "Averting the Hostile Exploitation of Biotechnology," *Chemical and Biological Weapons Conventions Bulletin* 48 (2000): 16–19.

9. See the chapters by George Fenton and Alan M. Pearson.

10. See the chapter by Martin Furmanski.

11. J. Hart, F. Kuhlau, and J. Simon, "Chemical and Biological Weapon Developments and Arms Control," in *SIPRI Yearbook 2003: Armaments, Disarmament and International Security* (Oxford: Oxford University Press, 2003): 646–82; Dan Reed, Director, "Terror in Moscow," HBO documentary film, 2003.

12. See the chapter by Alan Pearson.

13. See the chapters by David Fidler, and by Marie Isabelle Chevrier and James F. Leonard.

14. Editorial, "'Non-Lethal' Weapons, the CWC and the BWC," *Chemical and Biological Weapons Conventions Bulletin* 61 (September 2003).

15. See the chapter by David Fidler for a discussion of the limits that the CWC places on the use of incapacitating biochemical weapons by militaries operating in law enforcement modes.

16. A. Osborn, "Troops Crush Chechen 'Bandits' as Putin Promises No Mercy," *The Independent,* 17 October 2005.

17. G. Lean and S. Carrell, "U.S. Prepares to Use Toxic Gases in Iraq," *The Independent,* 2 March 2003; See also: V. Clarke, *The Independent,* 9 March 2003.

18. S. Hersh, "The Iran Plans," *The New Yorker,* 17 April 2006, col. 32, p. 30–37.

19. See the chapter by Alan M. Pearson.

20. L. Hess, J. Schreiberova, and J. Fusek, "Pharmacological Non-Lethal Weapons," in Fraunhofer-Institut für Chemische Technologie, ed., *Non-Lethal Options Enhancing Security and Stability: 3rd European Symposium on Non-Lethal Weapons, May 10–12, 2005* (Ettlingen, Germany: Fraunhofer-Institut für Chemische Technologie, 2005).

21. Sunshine Project, "A Survey of Biological and Biochemical Weapons Related Research Activities in France," *Country Study* 2 (November 2004), <http://www.sunshine-project.org> (25 February 2007).

22. A. Cowell, "The Daring Attack that Blew Up in Israel's Face," *New York Times,* 15 October 1997; See also: L. Beyer, "A Hit Gone Wrong: Israel Tries to Whack a Hamas Leader but Winds up the Loser," *Time,* 13 October 1997; See also: L Beyer, "Don't Try this at Home—or in Amman," *Time,* 27 October 1997.

23. J. Meek, "People the Law Forgot," *The Guardian,* 3 December 2003; P. Sleven and J. Stephens, "Detainees' Medical Files Shared: Guantanamo Interrogators' Access Criticized," *Washington Post,* sec. A01, 10 June 2004.

24. M. R. Dando and M. Furmanski, "Midspectrum Incapacitant Programs" in M. Wheelis, L. Rozsa, and M. R. Dando, eds., *Deadly Cultures: Biological Weapons Since 1945* (Cambridge, MA: Harvard University Press, 2006): 236–51.

25. T .C. Smith and T. A. Oleszczuk, *No Asylum: State Psychiatric Repression in the Former U.S.S.R.* (New York: New York University Press, 1996): 39–42.

26. Amnesty International, "Political Abuse of Psychiatry in the USSR." Report EUR 46/01/83, March 1983.

27. Office of National Drug Control Policy, Fact Sheet on Club Drugs, <http://www.whitehousedrugpolicy.gov/drugfact/club/index.html> (25 February 2007).

28. Sunshine Project, "A Survey of Biological and Biochemical Weapons," <http://www.sunshine-project.org> (25 February 2007)

29. The safety margin is the ratio of the dose that will cause the desired effect (incapacitation in this case) in half of the exposed population, to the dose that causes death or serious harm in half.

30. See the chapter by Martin Furmanski.

31. B. Bender, "U.S. Testing Non-Lethal Weapons Arsenal for use in Iraq," *Boston Globe*, 5 August 2005.

32. See the chapter by Marie Isabelle Chevrier and James F. Leonard.

33. See the chapter by Robin Coupland.

34. Mark Wheelis, "'Non-Lethal' Chemical Weapons: A Faustian Bargain," *Issues in Science and Technology* (Spring 2003): 74–78.

CHAPTER 2

Drug Development in the Twenty First Century and the Role of New Biotechnologies

Alan Goldhammer

Introduction

According to a survey conducted by the Pharmaceutical Research and Manufacturers of America (PhRMA), the United States pharmaceutical industry will spend over $38 billion during 2004 in the search for new cures.[1] Unlike the development and marketing of many consumer products, bringing a new pharmaceutical to the patients who need it is not an overnight process. Rather, it takes years, not months, and costs in the neighborhood of $800 million. Not every drug that is synthesized in the laboratories of a pharmaceutical company makes it through development. In fact, the overwhelming majority are dropped by the company because of toxicity or lack of efficacy. For those that do receive approval from the U.S. Food and Drug Administration (FDA), only a few realize full market potential. The estimate is that only three out of ten marketed drugs produce revenues that match or exceed average research and development costs.[2]

The remainder of this chapter will focus on drug development decisions, the regulatory requirements administered by the FDA, and the role of biotechnology. While the emphasis is on U.S. regulatory requirements, considerable efforts have been made over the past decade to harmonize regulatory requirements in the three major pharmaceutical-producing regions of the world: the United States, Japan, and the European Union. This effort, the International Conference on Harmonization or ICH, has brought together regulators and industries from these regions. A great number of consensus documents have come out of the deliberations that outline various testing and analysis regimes for preclinical, clinical, and product development and quality. Further information on ICH activities and all the guidance documents can be found at the organization's website.[3]

The costs of drug development have been evaluated by the Tufts University Center for the Study of Drug Development and are outlined in Table 2.1.[4] Several factors contribute to the high cost including the out of pocket drug discovery and preclinical costs, the costs of human clinical trials, clinical success and attrition rates, the development time and the cost of capital.[5] Each of these factors will be dealt with in subsequent sections of this chapter.

The pharmaceutical industry is heterogeneous in terms of the size and research focus of companies. Over the past fifteen years, a significant consolidation has taken place among the large multi-national pharmaceutical companies. These companies are characterized by research and development budgets (R&D) that exceed $500 million with large divisions capable of sustaining the research enterprise throughout the drug development process. Although large in size, these companies may focus their research efforts on selective therapeutic areas.

The significant basic research investment by the National Institutes of Health in the United States during the period from 1955 through the present resulted in numerous advances in the basic biological sciences. The Bayh-Dole (Public Law 96-517) and the Stevenson-Wydler (Public Law 96-480) Acts, both passed in 1980, clarified the assignment of patents derived from federally-funded research conducted either at government research laboratories or university laboratories receiving federal funding. The purpose of these two laws was to encourage the transfer of technology to the private sector so that it could be appropriately commercialized.

Clarification of intellectual property rights coupled with dramatic scientific advances in the biological sciences resulted in the creation of numerous companies seeking to develop new therapeutics. Some of these companies were founded by university scientists who had a particular invention or compound that was thought to be clinically important. Two key inventions referred to as biotechnology, recombinant DNA technology (the ability to move disparate genetic information between organisms) and monoclonal antibody technology (the ability to express large amounts of a specific antibody in animal cell culture) were key to attracting venture capital necessary to the establishment of these companies.

Table 2.1. Increases in the costs of developing a new pharmaceutical

Year	Cost ($million, adjusted to year 2000)
1975	$138
1987	$318
2000	$802

There is no firm number of how many companies were founded during the past thirty years. Not all of them were true biotechnology companies. A number were focused on small molecule drug development using innovative new screening technologies. Despite initial capitalization, a number of companies were forced to retrench or cease operations because of a lack of ongoing capital or possession of a technology that turned out not to be clinically useful. Others merged to create synergistic larger enterprises (Amgen's acquisition of Immunex). Still others licensed technology to more established pharmaceutical companies in return for royalty payments. Finally, there has been limited outright acquisition of companies by the major pharmaceutical companies (for example, Centocor's acquisition by Johnson & Johnson).

Regardless of the size of the company and whether it is a start up or an established multinational pharmaceutical company, the drug development process is the same. Fundamental research must be translated into clinical evidence. Significant investments into research and development must go into the necessary clinical research to support licensure of the drug by regulatory authorities.

Drug Development—Typical Research and Development Factors

Prior to initiation of a clinical program, the costs of product manufacture must be considered. If the candidate drug is a small molecule, large scale synthesis must be feasible. Prospective compounds with too many chiral centers cannot be cost effectively synthesized in quantities necessary for large scale clinical use. In such cases a biological mode of production is necessary. The vast majority of antibiotics whose structures are chemically complex are produced through fermentation processes involving select microorganisms. Production processes for biotechnology products such as recombinant proteins or monoclonal antibodies are now well established and can be readily scaled up. However, their cost of manufacture is still higher than that for small molecules. These protein products are administered via injection or infusion and must be manufactured under sterile conditions.

At the outset of a development project the candidate compound must demonstrate in vitro activity against a particular receptor or target. Potential safety concerns can be inferred from knowledge of the compound's interactions or interference with any metabolic pathways. The efficacy and any potential toxicities of the compound must be assessed in animal models. Except in the rare case of treating certain life threatening diseases, the compound should be non-mutagenic. It is important to note that human proteins and monoclonal antibodies may not be active in animal models and such evaluation is not useful.

Except for most biotechnology products, oral administration is preferred. Formulation and bioavailability via this route must be evaluated. Only after there is a significant amount of preclinical data indicating that the compound offers promise and the gross toxicities are known is it moved into human clinical trials.

Compounds that move into clinical trials must have favorable manufacturing profiles. The costs of starting materials and any owed royalties generally must be less than 15–25 percent. There must be an industrial infrastructure for production, or capital investment to achieve it, for the pharmaceutical class.

Multinational pharmaceutical companies operate in world markets. Consideration of products for development is for peak year worldwide sales of greater than $500 million over the lifespan of the product (defined by the patent exclusivity which may vary from market to market). Optimal pricing of the pharmaceutical is contingent on whether it is the first in a new class of therapies or if it offers a marked therapeutic benefit relative to existing therapies.

The other major consideration in pricing is the complexity of the clinical development program. Increasingly regulatory agencies are requiring more safety data, both preclinical and clinical. Additional animal testing and increased patient enrollment in clinical trials both drive up costs.

Despite intense efforts to make drug development more predictable, it remains an inherently risky business. Figure 2.1 shows the attrition rates during the drug development process. For every 5,000 compounds that are synthesized

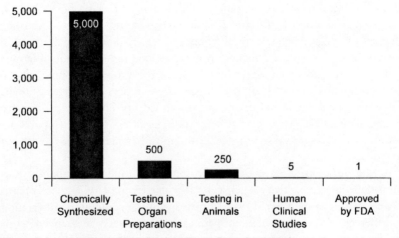

Figure 2.1. Attrition Rate During Drug Development
Source: Pharmaceutical Research and Manufacturers of America

in the laboratory only one makes it all the way through development to approval by the regulatory agency. There has been a recent trend of decreased productivity throughout the development process that has worried some experts.[6]

Human Clinical Trials

Of all the factors critical to drug development, human clinical trials that evaluate safety and efficacy are pivotal. It is this cumulative stage that is the most costly, on a per-compound basis (research and development consume more total expenditure, but that is averaged over thousands of compounds). Failures that occur late in the process are a major setback regardless of the size of the company. For the small venture-capital funded company that has no products on the market failure may doom the company. For the established company, failure represents lost capital that might have been deployed to another project.

Figure 2.2 is a schematic showing the various phases of drug development and the average time frame for each. The company driven process takes twelve to fifteen years to complete. Regulatory review and approval takes another six to twelve months. In addition, there may be further regulatory requirements once the product reaches the market.

The early part of the process is the basic research that was covered in the previous section. In general, the various required animal preclinical safety tests take up to two years to complete. A sound understanding of the metabolism, organ

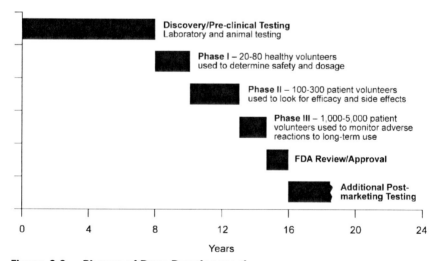

Figure 2.2.   Phases of Drug Development
Source: Pharmaceutical Research and Manufacturers of America

dispersal, and gross toxicity of the drug is needed prior to administering an experimental drug to humans. At this stage information from all these tests is submitted to the FDA in the form of an Investigational New Drug application or IND. FDA reviews the data and unless the Agency puts the trial on hold for safety reasons, it can proceed.

Most importantly, pharmaceutical research involving human subjects is conducted in accordance with the highest ethical standards. The principles derive from the Declaration of Helsinki that outlines how research involving human subjects should be conducted.[7] It is the ultimate goal of pharmaceutical companies to develop new cures or treatments for a wide variety of disabling diseases that afflict human kind, while conducting studies that accord with those ethical standards.

The regulatory requirements of the FDA require that any clinical investigation subject to an FDA-approved IND must be reviewed by an Institutional Review Board and the clinical investigator must have the informed consent of the subject. This regulation is codified at 21 CFR Part 50 (all of the FDA regulations for this and other drug regulatory issues related to the development and production of pharmaceuticals are available over the internet)[8] and is similar to the "common rule" for informed consent that the U.S. Department of Health and Human Services applies to other types of research involving human subjects. Several years ago, the FDA did codify an exception from informed consent for emergency research (21 CFR Part 50.54). This was particularly needed for the study of drugs to treat life threatening conditions where the available treatments were unproven or unsatisfactory and it was not possible to get the informed consent from the subject or the subject's legally authorized representative, i.e., where the subject arrives for medical treatment unconscious.

Phase I trials are designed to evaluate drug safety and arrive at a clinically effective dosage. This trial is usually conducted on a small number of healthy volunteers. After the pharmacokinetics (drug absorption, distribution, metabolism and elimination), pharmacodynamics (drug actions or effects) and toxicity have been evaluated, an exploratory trial to explore the effectiveness of the drug is started. Increased numbers of patients are enrolled in this Phase II trial. Although infrequent, some drugs for serious or life threatening diseases have been approved on the basis of solid Phase II clinical data (e.g., cancer and AIDS). In such cases, further studies are carried out once the drug is approved for marketing to confirm these clinical observations.

Information from the Phase I and II clinical trials is used by the company to plan the pivotal Phase III clinical trial that will serve as the basis of the company's submission to the FDA for marketing. It is common for the company to meet with the regulators to assure that this trial is well designed, that the clinical endpoints are robust, and that enough patients will be enrolled in the trial so that statistically meaningful results are observed. It is routine for such trials to involve several thousand patients. Vaccine clinical trials involve many more patients in order to gain a maximal understanding of all the safety issues associated with the vaccine. Since vaccines are given to healthy children and adults, dangerous side effects, even if rare, are not tolerated. It is routine for these Phase III trials to be conducted at multiple clinical research sites.

The total number of patients involved in a clinical trial for a new pharmaceutical may range from 750 at the low end to several thousand. A clinical development program for any new pharmaceutical is established only after discussion with the FDA to agree on clinical end points. Thus, it is difficult to conceive of how investigator bias can be introduced at any one of the points in clinical development. Furthermore, it is critical to trial sponsors that only data of the highest quality be collected and submitted to the FDA. Questionable data or interpretation thereof will result in review delays and potentially non-approval of the product.

Clinical trial design is another factor that contributes to the length of the trial and the number of patients enrolled. There has been much discussion about the use of placebo controlled clinical trials and the discussions will likely continue.[9] The long-standing consensus of medical research and ethical opinion is that placebo controlled studies are not only critical to the understanding of the efficacy and safety of most treatments, but do not of themselves compromise unacceptably the ethical treatment or clinical well being of the study participants. Placebo controlled studies, and not other designs, allow an active drug's therapeutic gain and safety profile to be measured and evaluated in the most objective fashion.

Certainly, there are some examples of potential drug candidates where it would be unethical to carry out a clinical trial against placebo. Antibiotics for the treatment of infectious disease and clot-busting agents for the treatment of myocardial infarction are two excellent examples. There are existing treatments in each category and clinical end points are well defined. Other medical conditions such as depression or schizophrenia are less amenable to such an approach. Diagnosis and treatment are, in many cases, quite subjective. In such cases, carrying out a clinical trial against a placebo presents the best opportunity to acquire high quality data that can be used to support licensure.

It also must be pointed out that clinical research carried out using an active control, e.g., using a second medication that also treats the underlying condition, is fraught with difficulties. In many cases the drug sponsor may be testing the drug that was developed by another manufacturer and will not have access to the underlying scientific data, or assumptions used in the conduct of that earlier trial. This may lead to problems in comparing the clinical data. Additionally, active control trials may be more costly and time consuming compared to a placebo-controlled trial. The number of patients required to show statistical superiority to the control is estimated to be three times that required to show simple non-inferiority.

Current Federal Regulations on Good Clinical Practices (21 CFR Parts 50, 54, 56, 312, 314) and the ICH Guideline on Good Clinical Practices (ICH E6) provide a standard for designing, conducting, recording, and reporting research studies that involve the participation of human subjects. In addition, evaluation of the conduct of a clinical study and the quality of the data produced are also addressed in these guidelines. These references also provide direction and guidance regarding measures to remove any potential for bias in a study.

Sponsors' responsibilities include: ensuring that they and investigators comply with the laws and guidelines, monitoring payments to investigators and subjects, and delivering high quality data to marketing authorities to support licensing. Investigators are educated about the regulatory compliance process via the contract language, which identifies important safety issues, investigator meetings and training, site initiation monitoring visits, and clinical field monitors. Sponsors implement and maintain independent quality assurance groups and quality control systems with written Standard Operating Procedures (SOPs) to ensure that trials are conducted and data are generated, documented (recorded), and reported in compliance with the protocol, the Good Clinical Practices and applicable regulatory requirements.

As part of implementing quality assurance oversight, sponsors periodically perform audits which are independent of and separate from routine monitoring or quality control functions. These audits evaluate trial conduct and compliance with the protocol, SOPs, Good Clinical Practices (administrative, regulatory, source data verification) and the applicable regulatory requirements.

A uniform cost for each aspect of clinical development is difficult to come by. However, surveys of PhRMA member companies provide a general breakdown of research and development expenses (See Table 2.2). While the discovery/preclinical expenditures look large, these are spread out over thousands of compounds and are relatively modest on a per molecule basis. However, for Phase III the costs are significant as fewer compounds out of those screened make it through clinical development to this point. Companies are reluctant to carry development programs through Phase III unless there is a reasonable expectation of approval.

Because the costs of development escalate as the drug moves through development, there is increasing pressure to make continuation decisions early in the process where the sunk costs are low. This presents a conundrum for pharmaceutical companies as they may not have enough information on either the inherent safety or efficacy of the drug to make an informed decision. Complicating the decision-making even further is that the company probably does not have

Table 2.2.   Research & Development costs by activity for the U.S. Pharmaceutical Industry in 2002

Activity	Cost ($ millions)	Percent Share
Discovery/Preclinical	10,983.3	31.9
Phase I	2,333.6	6.8
Phase II	3,809.6	11.1
Phase III	8,038.1	23.3
Approval	4,145.4	12.0
Phase IV	3,698.1	10.7
Uncharacterized	1,445.2	4.2
Total	34,456.2	100

full information on the progress of competitors with similar investigational drugs.

Drug safety is continually studied throughout the development process and extensive efficacy data is acquired. Throughout this entire process patient safety is of paramount importance.[10] In the case of placebo-controlled clinical trials impartial Data Safety Monitoring Boards are routinely employed to provide real time review of results and are empowered to stop trials if safety concerns arise or if it appears the product is efficacious and should be provided to all patients in the trial.

FDA Review and Postmarket Requirements

After this development phase, which usually lasts about seven years, the analyzed data is submitted in a New Drug Application (or NDA) to the FDA. The Prescription Drug User Fee Act (Public Law 102-571) passed in 1992 provides additional resources to the FDA in the form of user fees paid by the pharmaceutical industry. This program has been reauthorized by the U.S. Congress twice, in 1997 and 2002. An outline of the broad impact of this legislation on drug development and review can be found on the FDA site.[11]

In return for the additional resources, the Agency commits to reviewing NDAs in a timely manner. FDA has six months to act on a priority application (for those drugs treating life threatening medical conditions) and ten months for a standard application. An action is defined as a complete review of all the data submitted in the license application. FDA may have substantive questions about certain aspects of the application. These are detailed in a letter back to the sponsor of the NDA and the application may enter a second review cycle. A perspective on the average review times for NDAs is presented in Table 2.3.

Table 2.3. Approval times for Priority and Standard New Drug Applications and Biologics License Applications

Calendar Year	Priority			Standard		
	# Approved	Median FDA Review Time (months)	Median Total Review Time (months)	# Approved	Median FDA Review Time (months)	Median Total Review Time (months)
1993	19	16.3	20.5	51	20.8	26.9
1994	16	13.9	14.0	45	16.8	21.0
1995	16	7.9	7.9	67	16.2	18.7
1996	29	7.8	7.9	67	16.2	18.7
1997	20	6.3	6.4	101	14.7	15.0
1998	25	6.2	6.4	65	12.0	12.0
1999	28	6.1	6.1	55	12.0	13.8
2000	20	6.0	6.0	78	12.0	12.0
2001	10	6.0	6.0	56	12.0	14.0
2002	11	13.8	19.1	67	12.7	15.3
2003	14	7.7	7.7	58	11.0	15.4
2004*	29	6.0	6.0	90	11.9	12.0

Source: U.S. Food and Drug Administration. http://www.fda.gov/cder/rdmt/NDAapps93-04.htm (15 August 2005).

The FDA approval decision is based on a thorough evaluation of the benefits of the drug versus the risks the drug presents to the patient. The benefit is the expected positive clinical outcome. The risk is the probability of harm times the severity of harm (e.g., the side effects observed during clinical development). No drug is free of risk, though in many cases side effects from the medicine may be minor and well tolerated by patients. Patients suffering from life threatening diseases such as cancer and human immunodeficiency virus (HIV) infection are willing to accept more risk from treatments in return for successful therapy. Such factors figure into the FDA approval decision.

For many drugs FDA requires certain studies to be performed once the drug is on the market. Clinical trials to confirm an efficacy endpoint are common for most cancer drugs as they may have been approved based on a surrogate marker (a measurable quantity, such as the level of a serum protein that is known to be correlated with specific clinical outcomes, such as Prostate-Specific Antigen and prostate cancer). In other cases a specific drug safety trial may be required to further amplify the safety profile of the drug.

Not all of the safety issues can be determined during the development phase of the drug. Rare adverse drug reactions are often not seen as the patient population is not large enough. In order to reliably detect a 1 in 10,000 rare event, 30,000 patients would be needed in the clinical trial. Such a large trial would take considerable time and resources to conduct, delaying introduction of the drug to the wider population. To address this, companies maintain large dedicated divisions that study safety issues when the drug is marketed. Serious and life threatening adverse drug reactions must be reported to the FDA within fifteen days. During the first three years the product is on the market companies file quarterly reports outlining all new safety issues that have come to the company's attention. Thereafter annual reports are filed for as long as the company markets the drug.

Finally, the dynamics of drug development make it extraordinarily difficult to research every possible clinical indication for the new drug candidate. The cost and time are too overwhelming. Companies select the clinical indication that appears most amenable to treatment and pursue other indications post-approval. One of the best examples of this approach is alpha-interferon, approved seventeen years ago for hairy cell leukemia, a relatively rare disease. Continued research led to other approvals, among them treatments for genital herpes, Kaposi's sarcoma, and Hepatitis. There are numerous other examples in the oncology arena where an initial direction of research leads to a product with multiple uses.

Clinical Trial Design Issues and Bioterrorism Agents

Heightened public awareness of terror attacks using pathogenic microorganisms and/or toxins has led to increased federal support for programs in the biodefense arena.[12]

One of the principal difficulties in developing new treatments and/or vaccines to such agents is that the normal clinical trial process cannot be followed. Many of the putative biothreat agents are not endemic in the United States. Thus, there is a major question about how the necessary efficacy data to support licensure can be acquired. It is likely that animal testing will be the necessary surrogate. FDA has changed its regulations to allow for the approval of drugs where human clinical trials may not be possible (21 CFR Part 314.600). Whether such evidence will allow for the widespread use of a drug or vaccine in the absence of a confirmed threat is uncertain. One further approach would be to administer such drugs/vaccines under an IND and require informed consent of the patient.

Role of Biotechnology in the Twenty-First Century Drug Development

Although modern biotechnology is just over thirty years old, it is expected to play an increasing role in drug development in the years to come. The initial uses of biotechnology were in the large scale production of human proteins for therapeutic use. Human insulin, approved in 1982, revealed the potential of recombinant DNA technology. According to the Biotechnology Industry Organization over 200 biotechnology drugs have been approved through 2004.[13] Some of the products on this list are small molecules and special formulations, so the true number of biotechnology products is less than the reported total. Nevertheless, the large scale production of cell growth factors, anti-clotting agents, immune system modulators, angiogenesis inhibitors and hormones has been profound. Eight biotechnology products are listed among the top fifty drugs by sales, with each over $1 billion per year.[14]

It may be that biotechnology's biggest role will be in providing new approaches to traditional drug development. The sequencing of the human and a number of pathogenic microorganism genomes will provide new target opportunities for research scientists. Pharmacogenetics is already helping to identify pathways of drug toxicity that should lead to better predictive models resulting in drugs with improved safety parameters.

One excellent example of such an approach is the study of liver toxicities of drugs. The liver is responsible for metabolizing foreign substances including drugs. While liver function is robust in most individuals, a subset of the population suffers from liver injury when given certain medicines. If not promptly detected progression to acute failure may result leading to death or requiring transplantation. Drug-induced liver injury is a major reason for regulatory actions concerning drugs, including failure to approve, withdrawal from the market, restrictions on use, and warnings to physicians.

In order to address this matter, the Pharmaceutical Research and Manufacturers of America, the FDA, and the American Association for the Study of Liver Diseases convened a workshop in 2001 to explore this issue in detail. The outcome of the conference led to an ongoing collaboration between the three groups. Meetings have been held annually to discuss how liver toxicity can better be predicted, detected, and managed.[15]

Detoxification of drugs by the liver routinely involves a series of oxidations of the molecule. Not all patients suffer drug induced liver injury, indicating some type of genetic linkage. Because well over 99 percent of the sequence of the human genome is shared, it makes sense to focus genetic studies on the 0.1 percent that is heterogeneous. The majority of these differences result from a single nucleotide substitution. Such substitutions are commonly called single nucleotide polymorphisms and can be readily detected. One of the common mutations linked to drug induced liver injury is to a gene coding for the cytochrome P450 protein.

A broader perspective on the use of pharmacogenetics was presented by Roses at the 2005 steering committee meeting.[16] This technology can be used both prospectively and retrospectively to look at both safety and efficacy. It is the prospective use of the tool that is of most importance to the pharmaceutical industry, particularly as it can assist in making decisions on whether to carry a drug on in development. It is important to note that pharmacogenetics will not increase costs of drug development but will provide new safe and effective drugs for more people. It will provide the opportunity to find effective drugs for definable [and perhaps overlapping] segments of the patient population and reduce attrition in the late pipeline, significantly translating to safer and more effective therapies.

Similarly, specific gene sequences can help identify sub-group responders to therapies. Ultimately the identification of specific genetic components could lead to "personalized medicine" where the therapeutic benefit to a specific patient can be identified and the risk of the medication appropriately managed. However, the regulatory pathway to approval may be complex as clinical trials will have to be structured in a way to identify responders to the drug under study. There will be ethical issues related to patient privacy that will have to be managed when the drug is approved. However, these are not insurmountable and can be addressed using secure data management systems.

Research Costs Must be Controlled

Much has been written on the "blockbuster syndrome," where pharmaceutical research and development is increasingly targeted on chronic diseases that afflict large numbers of patients.[17]As was shown in Table 2.1, the current costs of development exceed $800 million for a new drug. This has directed much of the research effort towards drugs whose peak year sales were expected to exceed $1 billion. This has the effect of targeting research into some very narrow therapeutic areas, principally chronic conditions, at the expense of research into acute conditions such as bacterial infections. Drugs to treat such conditions are given for short periods of time relative to diabetes and cardiovascular drugs that in most cases are administered to the patient over his/her lifetime.

A move towards personalized medicine will similarly result in smaller patient populations to be treated. Thus, the overall expectation may be smaller markets for future drugs. If the sales income drops, there will be pressure to control costs on the development side to maintain company profitability. Companies may seek to narrow research portfolios.

The Pharmaceutical Industry and Incapacitating Biochemical Weapon Development

The arduous and expensive pathway of new drug development makes it unlikely that this mechanism would be used by any country seeking an incapacitant capability for law enforcement or military purposes. There is no equivalent of the systematic testing of safety and efficacy, through three successive clinical phases, in the requirements for developing a new weapon, nor are there restrictive licensing requirements. It is much more likely that promising new biochemical agents will be identified in the scientific research literature, and developed as a weapon by the interested party.

Of course, drugs already developed, and on the market (or about to be marketed), constitute a pool of possible biochemical weapon agents. However, the legal uses of licensed human, veterinary, and investigational drugs are severely constrained by national law, and their use as a weapon could raise significant legal issues.

However, new technologies being applied to early stages of drug discovery, such as combinatorial methods of synthesis and high throughput screening techniques, greatly expand the number of potential compounds of interest as an incapacitant or chemical weapons agent. Much of this discovery research will not result in new pharmaceutical compounds and is not likely to be published or patented. Thus, potential diversion of such compounds towards development of a chemical weapon must be deemed unlikely unless there is collaboration (whether overt or covert) between the technology company and an interested party.

Notes

1. PhRMA, "Pharmaceutical Industry Profile, 2005; From Laboratory to Patient: Pathways to Innovation," Pharmaceutical Research and Manufacturers of America, 1100 Fifteenth Street, NW, Washington, D.C., 2005, <http://www.phrma.org> (1 March 2007).

2. H. Grabowski and J. Vernon, "Returns to R&D on New Drug Introductions in the 1980s," *Journal of Health Economics* 13 (1994): 383–406.

3. Food and Drug Administration Regulations on Pharmaceuticals can be accessed from the internet at: <http://www.accessdata.fda.gov/scripts/cdrh/cfdocs/cfcfr/cfrsearch.cfm> (1 March 2007).

4. J. A. DiMasi, R.W. Hansen, and H.G. Grabowski, "The Price of Innovation, New Estimates of Drug Development Costs," *Journal of Health Economics* 22 (2003): 151–85.

5. Tufts Center for the Study of Drug Development, "BACKGROUNDER: A Methodology for Counting Costs for Pharmaceutical R&D," <http://csdd.tufts.edu/InfoServices/Publications.asp> (2 August 2005).

6. J. Mervis, "Productivity Counts—But the Definition is the Key," *Science* 309 (2005): 726–27.

7. World Medical Association, "Declaration of Helsinki—Ethical Principles for Medical Research Involving Human Subjects," *Journal of the American Medical Association* 284 (2000): 3043–45.

8. See note 3.

9. R. Temple and S. Ellenberg, "Placebo-Controlled Trials and Active-Control Trials in the Evaluation of New Treatments. Part 1: Ethical and Scientific Issues," *Annals of Internal Medicine* 133 (2000): 455–63; R. Temple and S. Ellenberg, "Placebo-Controlled Trials and Active-Control Trials in the Evaluation of New Treatments. Part 2: Practical Issues and Specific Cases," *Annals of Internal Medicine* 133 (2000): 464–70.

10. M. J. Schmidt, "Human Safety in Clinical Research." *Applied Clinical Trials* 10 (2001): 40–50.

11. Food and Drug Administration Regulations on Pharmaceuticals and Fees can be accessed from the internet at <http://www.fda.gov/oc/pdufa/default.htm> (1 March 2007). In addition, this website contains all the program performance objectives, yearly progress and financial reports.

12. For a summary of projects supported by the U.S. National Institutes for Allergy and Infectious Diseases, see <http://www2.niaid.nih.gov/biodefense/> (1 March 2007).

13. BIO, "Approved Biotechnology Drugs," (2005), <http://www.bio.org/speeches/pubs/er/approveddrugs.asp#I> (15 August 2005).

14. "The Top 500 Prescription Drugs," *Med Ad News* May Issue (2005), <http://www.pharmalive.com/magazines/medad/?date=05 percent2F2005> (1 March 2007).

15. All the proceedings from the initial workshop and ongoing meetings of the steering committee are archived at <http://www.fda.gov/cder/livertox/default.htm>

16. A. D. Roses, "Pipeline Pharmacogenetics: Efficacy and Safety Applications," Presentation to FDA/CDER-AASLD-PhRMA Hepatotoxicity Steering Committee in 2005. This can be found at <http://www.fda.gov/cder/livertox/presentations2005.htm> (1 June 2005).

17. R. F. Service, "Surviving the Blockbuster Syndrome," *Science* 303 (2004): 1796–99.

CHAPTER 3

Historical Military Interest in Low-lethality Biochemical Agents

AVOIDING AND AUGMENTING LETHAL FORCE

Martin Furmanski

In these early years of the twenty-first century, we are witnessing the reemergence of military interest in developing biologically active agents whose primary purpose is not to kill, but to temporarily manipulate target personnel's physiology or behavior, potentially with little or no lasting effects. The obvious examples of this renewed interest are the Moscow theater event of 2002, and the reported subsequent Russian use of "knockout gas" grenades in a hostage situation in October 2005.[1] The U.S. military has supported investigation and possible development of novel non-lethal biochemical interventions such as calmatives and malodorants.[2] An article in a military periodical by civilian authors from the People's Republic of China advocates the development of sophisticated biochemical weapons.[3]

In the twentieth century a number of national military establishments showed interest in developing and using a variety of chemical and pharmaceutical agents where the expected effects were of low lethality. Previous authors have summarized the historical features of these programs.[4] This study will present the history of the military interest in these agents, particularly stressing the dichotomy between uses that augment lethal force and those that seek to avoid it.

This study will use the history of irritant chemical agents (also known as riot-control agents [RCAs]) to provide the context for low-lethality chemical agents that have achieved widespread acceptance in civilian police applications for their utility at reducing the need for lethal force but that have in the past also been used in military combat applications to augment lethal force. It will also examine the U.S. program to develop incapacitating biochemical agents, concentrating on the program that weaponized and stockpiled the psychochemical incapacitant BZ (3-quinuclidinyl benzilate).

Irritant Chemical Agents

This paper will use the term Irritant Chemical Agents (ICA) to refer to a class of chemical agents that which can produce rapidly in humans sensory irritation or disabling physical effects which disappear within a short time following termination of exposure. Irritant chemical agent is used in preference to the commonly used term riot control agent (RCA) because it more accurately describes the agents, rather than naming them for a specific application. It was the official designation of these agents before 1965 in U.S. chemical weapon documents. Moreover, a wide variety of chemical agents have been used as irritant chemical agents in a variety of military and civilian applications, while only three, the agents CN (1-Chloroacetophenone), CS (o-Chlorobenzylidene malononitrile) and DM (Adamsite, diphenylaminearsine), have actually been used to control rioting crowds. Moreover, the agents considered appropriate for riot control purposes have changed over time. The vomiting agent DM was used as a standard U.S. military agent for riot control from 1932 to 1965, but was considered unsuitable for such purposes after 1965.

EARLY DEVELOPMENT OF IRRITANT CHEMICAL AGENTS

Both civilian and military organizations developed a variety of irritant chemical agents, then termed lachrymators or tear gases, in the years immediately preceding WWI in a parallel fashion. Both sought to develop a gaseous or aerosol weapon capable of forcing an adversary to vacate a fortified shelter, and thus avoid casualties suffered storming such defensive positions.

Chemists of the police department in Paris developed irritant chemical agents and delivery munitions in response to a series of violent sieges against barricaded heavily armed criminal gangs that had required use of high explosives and had resulted in multiple police fatalities in 1912. In 1913 and 1914 these "asphyxiating revolvers" were used against armed and barricaded deranged single individuals on at least two occasions.[5] However, use of tear gases against civil disorders in France did not begin until 1948.[6]

All European belligerents prior to WWI recognized a prohibition against poison gas warfare: the 1899 and 1907 Hague agreements had banned "poisonous weapons" and shells "whose sole purpose was delivery of poisonous gases." Nevertheless, before the war some military officers in France, Germany and

Britain saw potential utility in gas weapons that could penetrate fortifications, and these advocates sought to circumvent the treaty restrictions by developing nontoxic irritant gases. All these countries had apparently tested some agents, but at the beginning of the war only the French army held a small supply of tear gas grenades and small-caliber tear gas shells they had obtained from the civilian police.[7]

MILITARY USE OF IRRITANT CHEMICAL AGENTS IN COMBAT 1914–1918

When WWI broke out, the military tear gas programs were accelerated, gathering some influential scientific advocates, such as Sir William Ramsay of the Royal Society and Lord Dundonald in Britain, and Fritz Haber and Hermann Nernst in Germany. Britain decided that first use of irritant gas munitions violated the spirit if not the text of the Hague agreements and declined to introduce them into combat. In contrast, France and Germany used irritant gas munitions in small engagements in early 1915, but without dramatic effect because they were employed in low doses and under unfavorable weather conditions. Although the pragmatic field commanders initially showed little enthusiasm for these apparently ineffective new "tear gas" munitions, the advocates of gas warfare pressed further development and deployment, relying upon professional prestige and personal contacts. France ordered new supplies of tear gas munitions and protective goggles for a spring offensive, and in Germany advocates convinced the government to breach the Hague agreements and to initiate toxic gas warfare.

The German April 1915 chlorine cloud attack at Ypres succeeded in breaking the Allied line but the Germans were unprepared to exploit the advantage. After this demonstration of military effectiveness in battle, the pragmatic military commanders on all sides embraced gas warfare.

Even after toxic chemical agents were introduced, the existing irritant chemical agents continued to be used in considerable amounts throughout the war. In August 1915, before gas masks were issued, the Germans mounted several large artillery attacks delivering tear gases as the primary chemical agent against the French and British, resulting in at least one episode reportedly resulting in the capture of 2,400 temporarily blinded French soldiers.[8] After the development of effective gas masks, the role of primary chemical agent for offense was given to more toxic agents. The irritant tear gases continued to be used extensively however, because a small number of irritant chemical agent containing shells could produce a harassing effect, forcing enemy forces to mask, reducing combat efficiency and interfering with eating and sleeping.[9]

Two new irritant chemical agent agents, chloropicrin (PS) and the vomiting agent diphenylchlorarsine (DA), were developed and introduced into combat and used in large amounts after the introduction of lethal chemical agents and the issuing of gas masks. Although these agents were potentially lethal at high doses, they were used predominantly at low concentrations because they could penetrate the existing gas masks. At low doses they produced violent sneezing or vomiting, and they could force demasking and hence expose an enemy to more lethal gases delivered in the same attack. Although they caused few deaths from direct toxicity, they were used extensively. British procurement of chloropicrin and other irritating agents for shell filling (9,912 tons) exceeded their procurement of the highly toxic classic "war gases" Phosgene and Mustard (8,141 tons). In the much larger German chemical warfare program, chloropicrin, DA and other irritant agents accounted for 22 percent of all German gas shell fills.[10]

IRRITANT CHEMICAL AGENTS USED IN COMBAT 1919–1925

In the wake of the wholesale use of chemical agents in WWI, the legal status of such use was ambiguous. British troops intervening in the Russian Civil War in 1919–1920 reportedly used "toxic smoke pots" containing the irritant chemical agent DA against Red Army elements, but apparently without success. These munitions had been prepared for use in WWI, but had not been used in combat by the British, and this use was to some extent a field trial for an irritant chemical agent new to the British arsenal.

Spanish forces initially used chloropicrin, an irritant chemical agent, with phosgene in initial chemical attacks against native rebels in Morocco in 1923–1924, but rapidly adopted the more toxic mustard as a chemical weapon of choice.[11]

NEW IRRITANT CHEMICAL AGENTS ARE DEVELOPED POST-WWI

Developing new irritant chemical agents was an important part of the immediate post-war U.S. chemical program. At the end of the war, irritant chemical agents, both irritant "tear gases" and vomiting agents, were considered valuable military munitions in a chemical arsenal that included many highly toxic agents. They were considered important both for their potential battlefield uses and as simulants for toxic agents in training exercises. The U.S. Army Chemical Warfare Service (CWS) continued research and development on them, adopting improved post-war variant agents CN and DM by 1922, and building production plants for these agents at Edgewood Arsenal. These were to remain standard U.S. irritant chemical agents in the U.S. chemical arsenal until the mid-1960s.[12]

U.S. CHEMICAL WEAPONS ADVOCATES PRESS CIVILIAN USE OF IRRITANT CHEMICAL AGENTS

In the immediate post-WWI period there were extensive episodes of civil unrest in the United States: on 29 occasions between 1919 and 1921 federal troops or National Guard units had to be called to restore order in violent strikes or civil riots. These troops and demobilized soldiers now returned to police duties sought tear gases for riot control. Although the CWS was enthusiastic and willing to provide irritant chemical agents to civilian police departments, the Army Staff,[13] like the general public,[14] was hostile to any sort of chemical warfare and refused permission for the CWS to provide irritant chemical agents to civilian police forces, National Guard units, or for irritant chemical agents to be used by federal troops in actions to restore civil order.[15] In 1922 the Chemical Warfare Service was ordered to discontinue all offensive programs and cease production of toxic agents and to concentrate on defensive developments and training only. The restrictions on CWS activities had the effect of focusing its attention on irritant chemical agents. Because irritant chemical agents were used as simulants for more toxic chemical agents in defensive training programs, production of irritant chemical agents and limited stockpiling of irritant chemical agent agents and munitions continued.

Collaboration between the CWS and the civilian chemical industry arose, supporting civilian use of irritant chemical agents for law-enforcement purposes. This effort was motivated by a general belief among chemical weapons advocates that both toxic and nontoxic chemical agents were humane, effective weapons and that use of irritant chemical agents in civilian law enforcement would demonstrate that general principle to the public.[16] The CWS developed a tear gas hand grenade specifically designed for civilian crowd control. This ideological motive was bolstered by commercial self-interest: several commercial companies were formed by demobilized or retired chemical officers for the manufacture and marketing of irritant chemical agent munitions to police departments.

Although Army Staff restrictions prevented the CWS from directly supplying irritant chemical agents to civilian police or National Guard units, the CWS developed a "back door" program to support civilian use of irritant chemical agents. Based on the existing program of research cooperation with chemical companies supplying the CWS, the CWS diverted finished tear gas munitions and bulk tear gas agent to the private companies promoting civilian tear gases, allowing large-scale demonstrations of tear gas to police departments in 1921–1922.[17] A substantial market for police tear gas was established, and irritant chemical agents became common in U.S. police arsenals by the mid 1920s.

Irritant chemical agents had not been used for civilian riot control before this promotional campaign. The 1920 U.S. Army publication addressing riot control[18] surveys both U.S. and European experience in the control of civil disorders, makes no mention of the use of chemical agents, despite discussing such drastic interventions as the use of machine guns and artillery against civil insurrections and riots.

Beginning in 1921, reports of instances of the use of tear gas by police against barricaded individuals began to appear.[19] The first reported use of tear gas against a rioting crowd appears in 1922.[20] Tear gas was also promoted for static defense installations in bank vaults, and in prisons for riot control.[21] These uses received favorable publicity.[22] The civilian police use of tear gas preceded such use by military forces in civil disorder, and was an important factor in "normalizing" non-lethal gases, at least to the U.S. public. Tear gas was used by National Guard units in riot situations beginning in 1926,[23] and by federal troops after 1932.

The U.S. chemical companies attempted to market tear gases to police and governments worldwide,[24] but in Europe tear gases were seldom adopted by civilian police organizations, or if adopted, were seldom used to control civil disturbances until after World War II. Despite widespread and recurrent civil unrest in many countries in the 1920s and 1930s, police preparations to use tear gas are seldom mentioned, and then usually in situations where it was not ultimately used. Only in Sweden,[25] Ireland[26] and Austria[27] do single reports of police use of tear gas for riot control on domestic populations appear before WWII. France maintained a capability to employ irritant chemical agents against barricaded criminals,[28] but no use against civil disorders is recorded until 1948.[29]

U.S. IRRITANT CHEMICAL AGENT POLICY 1925–1932

Chemical weapons advocates in the United States succeeded in blocking U.S. ratification of the 1925 Geneva Protocol, in part by advocating that non-lethal tear gases would provide a military advantage in the U.S. military interventions against "primitive" foes, such as those encountered in the recurrent military interventions in Latin America.[30] Although U.S. military manuals[31] consistently stated that the United States was party to no treaty that prohibited the use of chemical weapons, U.S. public opinion still overwhelmingly condemned gas warfare, and few U.S. military officers outside of the Chemical Warfare Service looked upon chemical warfare favorably. The 1922 restrictions limiting CWS activities to defense remained in force until 1934–1936. The U.S. military made no effort to differentiate irritant chemical agents from more toxic chemical agents, or to use either in combat. For instance, U.S. troops fighting an insurgency in Nicaragua in the 1920s and 1930s did not use tear gases.

MILITARY IRRITANT CHEMICAL AGENT USE IN CIVIL DISORDERS 1932

The program begun in the early 1920s to market tear gas to civilian police forces in the United States was very successful: tear gas (CN) became a standard police weapon in the United States in the later 1920s and 1930s. The pragmatic benefits of tear gas, reducing injuries and fatalities to both police and crowds/criminals were recognized, and use of tear gas was accepted.

The most prominent use of irritant chemical agents by the regular U.S. military in this period was the dispersal of the "Bonus Army" from squatter's encampments in Washington, D.C. in 1932. In the depths of the Depression, several thousand veterans and their families had marched to Washington, D.C. to demand early payment of a veteran's bonus that had been previously authorized by Congress. Gen. Douglas MacArthur was ordered to evict the "Bonus Army" from public land. With Dwight Eisenhower and George Patton commanding units, the military proceeded to evict the squatters with a vigorous use of tear and vomiting agents. Reports circulated that two small children had died, apparently from the effects of the gas, but this story was disputed by the U.S. Attorney General,[32] and no clear resolution of the cause of death is clear from contemporary accounts. The use of tear gas on the Bonus Army and the popular conviction that it had caused the children's deaths drew widespread public disapproval as a political act, but did not discredit military or police use of irritant chemical agents in domestic riot control. George Patton had commanded the cavalry unit that cleared the squatter's camp and he praised irritant chemical agents as being "essential" in such operations, pointing out that his troops had cleared the camp without firing a shot.[33]

U.S. CHEMICAL WEAPONS POLICY 1933–1948

In the mid 1930s, there was a resurgence of popular concern, particularly in Europe, that chemical weapons would become important in any foreseeable European war, a concern underlined by the rise of fascism in Italy, Germany, and Japan, and emphasized by reports of use of chemical weapons by Italy in Ethiopia in 1935 and Japan in China in 1937. In 1934 the Secretary of War authorized the CWS to make "all necessary preparations for the use of chemical warfare from the outbreak of war." This increased activity included some additional development of irritant chemical agents, specifically the development of a combined CN-DM irritant grenade for riot control, standardized in 1941.[34]

The United States maintained a policy of no first use of chemical agents during WWII, a position forcefully articulated by President Roosevelt on several occasions. Although both irritant chemical agents and toxic agents were positioned for possible retaliation in combat theaters, none were authorized for use in combat.

IRRITANT CHEMICAL AGENTS AND VIOLATIONS OF THE 1925 GENEVA PROTOCOL IN THE 1930s AND 1940s

In a series of disarmament discussions in the early 1930s, the major adherents to the 1925 Geneva Accords made it clear that they considered irritant chemical agents as well as more toxic agents to be forbidden in warfare by that document.[35] In these discussions the United States, not an adherent to the 1925 Geneva Protocol, presented an inconstant position regarding irritant chemical agents in warfare, on some occasions suggesting they should not necessarily be considered prohibited weapons in war in the context of a draft disarmament agreement then under discussion,[36] and on other occasions acquiescing to the European consensus that they were prohibited.[37]

In 1935 Italy used tear gases to disperse formations of Ethiopian soldiers who had no protection from gas attack, and this use of irritant chemical agents foreshadowed the later introduction of mustard gas into the conflict.[38]

In 1936 a report appeared of tear gas use in the Spanish Civil War,[39] but this remained unconfirmed. Neither irritant chemical agents nor toxic agents played a significant role in the fighting, though both sides might have been supplied with these agents by their Soviet and Fascist sponsors.[40]

After 1937, the Japanese found that irritant chemical agents were highly effective against Chinese troops, who did not have gas masks, and the Japanese used irritant chemical agents in hundreds of engagements.[41] The Japanese also used irritant chemical agents to drive the civilian population from hiding places, often resulting in atrocities.[42] For these types of engagements, irritant chemical agents were much more useful than the more toxic agents phosgene, mustard and lewisite which produced effects only after hours or days. Irritant chemical agents produced an immediate effect, and gas masks allowed Japanese troops to attack into areas gassed with irritant chemical agents without delay. Moreover, mustard and lewisite were persistent agents, presenting a hazard to advancing Japanese troops. Japanese gas masks provided poor protection against hydrogen cyanide, the only rapidly acting lethal agent in the Japanese chemical arsenal.[43] The Japanese infantry was routinely supplied with gas masks and irritant chemical agents of the tear gas type (CN) and the vomiting gas type (DA).[44]

Only after the United States demonstrated in April 1942 that U.S. carrier based aircraft could attack the Japanese home islands, and after President Roosevelt in June 1942 warned Japan that continued chemical attacks against China would result in U.S. chemical warfare retaliation against Japan,[45] did the Japanese irritant chemical agent and toxic chemical attacks against China abate.

Except for the Japanese use of irritant chemical agents and toxic agents against China, no belligerent in WWII used either irritant chemical agents or toxic chemical warfare agents.[46]

IRRITANT CHEMICAL AGENTS IN THE KOREAN WAR 1950–1953

U.S. field commanders sought authorization to use chemical agents in combat in the Korean War, but even requests limited to the use of irritant chemical agents to clear enemy fortifications were refused.[47]

During the Korean War the United States faced well-organized, violent riots and defiance of orders in U.S. controlled POW camps. These confrontations between armed guards and POWs initially resulted in multiple fatalities, particularly among the disarmed POWs. In response to protests by the International Committee of the Red Cross (ICRC) against the use of unnecessary lethal force and adverse worldwide publicity engendered by communist propaganda reports, the U.S. army adopted a "tear gas first" policy to deal with POW disorders. This policy gave considerable experience to the U.S. military on the use of irritant chemical agents, particularly against large numbers of motivated and disciplined (if disarmed) soldiers. Guards soon found that CN alone was often insufficient to subdue a determined, disciplined and well-trained opponent. DM was frequently added for additional effect. The tear gas first policy was not popular with line officers, and on occasion the United States reverted to initial use of lethal force.[48] This experience was to motivate a search for a more powerful irritant chemical agent, a search that later was to lead to the change from CN to CS as the standard irritant chemical agent in the U.S. military arsenal.

Further militarization of irritant chemical agents was attempted with the development of heavy weapon irritant chemical agent devices. Modified flamethrowers, including a large, tank-mounted one, were developed that could deliver streams of bulk liquid irritant chemical agent agents. These were used against rioting POWs in the Korean POW camps, but it was found that direct contact with the sprayed liquid caused second-degree (blistering) chemical burns resembling mustard gas lesions.[49] Further development included a dedicated armored personnel carrier with a similar spray device mounted and other irritant chemical agent munitions and dispersal equipment inside, meant for controlling anti-American demonstrations in foreign countries.[50] The project was dropped when it was realized such use might well allow allegations of U.S. "gas warfare" against civilians and cause a propaganda disaster.[51]

MILITARY USE OF IRRITANT CHEMICAL AGENTS IN CIVIL DISORDERS AND THE INTRODUCTION OF CS GAS, 1956–1960

British military forces used irritant chemical agents to deal with civil disorders in Cyprus beginning in 1956, but found that the standard CN agent was inadequate against determined rioters. The United Kingdom sought a more effective irritant chemical agent, and after screening many candidate compounds introduced CS as an irritant chemical agent in Cyprus in 1958. CS was more rapid in action, more severe in effect, and less toxic. While CN was a true "tear gas" affecting the eyes almost exclusively, CS was a general mucosal irritant, and affected the upper and lower airways as well as the eyes, and was capable of causing skin blistering and nausea in heavy exposures. While tight fitting goggles (or even tightly closing the eyes) could protect against CN effects, a full gas mask was necessary to protect against CS. However, CS had a higher margin of safety than CN in lethality tests in animals, and caused less permanent eye damage after heavy exposure. The United States, seeking a more effective irritant chemical agent since its Korean War POW experience, adopted CS as a standard irritant chemical agent in 1959, but also maintained stocks of CN and DM until the mid 1960s.

CN remained the standard "tear gas" for domestic police forces in the United States until the antiwar and civil rights riots of the late 1960s.

FUNDAMENTAL CHANGE IN U.S. CHEMICAL AND BIOLOGICAL WEAPONS POLICY 1956

An interim U.S. chemical warfare policy adopted in October 1950 had continued the retaliation only policy of WWII, but provided for reevaluation when modern chemical weapons became available.[52] Once nerve gas agents and munitions were standardized and stockpiled,[53] U.S. chemical and biological weapons policy changed. In 1956 the National Security Council adopted a policy on chemical weapons to allow their use whenever militarily advantageous, at direction of President. Neither Congress nor the public was informed, and this policy change remained classified until 1990.[54]

IRRITANT CHEMICAL AGENTS IN THE VIETNAM WAR ERA 1960–1975

A result of the 1956 change of national policy was increasing interest in low-lethality chemical agents. The U.S. military adopted CS in June 1959, and by early 1960 stated: "Specifically, the Army wishes to obtain immediately the freedom to use CS, a powerful tear gas, against indigenous populations or unfriendly military forces in any area of the world when the accomplishment of a mission assigned to a U.S. commander justifies such use."[55] During 1960 Army proposals circulated to either obtain advanced Presidential delegation of authority to military commanders to use irritant chemical agents, or to remove non-lethal chemical weapon agents from the National Security Council policy requiring Presidential authorization. Ultimately the Joint Chiefs of Staff requested neither an advanced Presidential authorization nor any formal change of policy, instead informing the Secretary of Defense in June 1960 that "the riot control agents, such as CN, CS and DM, are considered to fall outside the meaning of the term chemical warfare as used in the national policy."[56] U.S. Army Field Manuals were modified in 1961 to state: "There are no restrictions on the initial employment of irritant chemical agents, smoke agents, and flame, subject to policy guidance of the theater commander."[57]

South Vietnam received irritant chemical agents from the United States beginning in 1962, and used them against civilian demonstrations.[58] South Vietnamese forces had also used irritant chemical agents against the Viet Cong tunnel complex at Cu Chi in 1963, but they proved ineffective because of efficient partitioning of tunnel segments.[59] This military irritant chemical agent use, though reported in the press,[60] caused little controversy. U.S. and South Vietnamese responses to Communist charges of "chemical warfare" made at the time addressed the initiation of defoliation operations rather than irritant chemical agent use.[61] The legal status of South Vietnamese use of irritant chemical agents in 1963 was uncertain. South Vietnam was not a party to the 1925 Geneva Protocol and in 1963 did not recognize Viet Cong as belligerents and had not declared a formal state of war existed.[62]

U.S. advisors had been active with the South Vietnamese army since the early 1960s, but by late 1963 South Vietnamese forces were losing battles and the Saigon regime was in danger of losing the war.[63] In early 1964 the U.S. advisors in Vietnam began considering the possibility that South Vietnamese forces might effectively use low-lethality chemical weapons in the antiguerilla campaign. Initial proposals suggested the use of the established irritant chemical agents of CS, CN and DM, and the newly standardized psychochemical incapacitant BZ. Approval to introduce the standardized irritant chemical agents into combat was granted in September of 1964.[64]

The first use of irritant chemical agents (including agents CS, CN and DM) in combat was on 23 and 24 Dec 1964 by U.S. Special Forces (with a token South Vietnamese Ranger component) in attempts to rescue U.S. Special Forces advisors who had become POWs. Irritant chemical agents were intended to suppress ground fire and avoid the risk of making the POWs casualties. The irritant chemical agents proved ineffective and no POWs were located. These raids were secret and remained unpublicized. The third use, in February 1965, was a pre-emptive delivery of irritant chemical agents by South Vietnamese troops to a vil-lage in the Phu Lac peninsula where a mixing of civilians and combatants had been anticipated during a search and destroy mission. The expected admixture of civilians and combatants did not develop, however, and once again the irritant chemical agents were ineffective tactically.[65]

The use of irritant chemical agents in Vietnam became public in March 1965, when a photojournalist noted troops carrying gas masks, and a U.S. spokesman in Vietnam admitted tear and vomiting agents had been used in combat by South Vietnamese forces in cooperation with U.S. forces.[66] U.S. of-ficials characterized the gases as non-lethal and similar to those commercially available for police uses. They expressed surprise that such use of irritant chem-ical agents would draw comment, saying area commanders, rather than the Pres-ident, had authorized their use.[67] Severe criticism of the use of gas in warfare was raised in the British Parliament,[68] and by the British Foreign Secretary who de-cried its use in a speech to the National Press Club[69] and to President Johnson.[70] The communist press soon mounted a propaganda campaign with significant in-ternational success.[71] Secretary of State Dean Rusk defended the use of non-lethal gas in a press conference, but stated, erroneously, that the Phu Lac inci-dent had actually involved admixed or captive civilians and that this had prompted the use of irritant chemical agents to avoid the use of artillery or aer-ial bombs. Speaking to the "essential policy aspects" of the problem, he stated, "We do not expect that gas will be used in ordinary military operations."[72] Fol-lowing this controversy Secretary of Defense McNamara ordered General West-moreland, the U.S. military theater commander in Vietnam, to withhold further approval of irritant chemical agent use in combat.[73]

In September 1965, LtCol LN Utter, without authorization, used irritant chemical agents to clear a cave where enemy combatants had retreated with civil-ian hostages.[74] The irritant chemical agent attack allowed capture of twenty-two combatants and liberation of almost 400 civilians without fatality. An investiga-tion showed Utter was unaware of the prohibition of using irritant chemical agents, and he was cleared of wrongdoing. Utter's success in employing irritant chemical agents to avoid civilian casualties was used by General Westmoreland as a justification to request reinstatement of his authority to authorize irritant chemical agent use in combat.[75] At the time a veteran investigative reporter con-sidered the Utter incident to have been a ploy calculated to gage and shape U.S. public opinion in favor of wider use of irritant chemical agents in combat in Vietnam,[76] and a later evaluation concludes the event was skillfully handled to allow reinstatement of authority to use irritant chemical agents in combat.[77] Au-thority to authorize use of irritant chemical agents in combat was gradually returned to General Westmoreland in the fall of 1965.[78] He was given full authority to authorize irritant chemical agent use on 3 November 1965, and on 15 November 1965 authorized his subordinate commanders to use CS in tunnels or caves, or when civilians were intermingled with combatants. On 23 December 1965 Westmoreland modified these instructions to permit unrestricted use of CS and CN at the discretion of the senior commander concerned. Use of DM was never authorized.[79]

General Westmoreland's September 1965 requests to lift the irritant chemical agent ban stressed not only the potential of saving civilian lives, but also the military advantage and decreased friendly casualties irritant chemical agents offered to U.S. and South Vietnamese troops in clearing caves and tunnels.[80] Once authority was returned to Westmoreland, he authorized subordinate commanders to use irritant chemical agents in combat without restriction.[81]

Use of irritant chemical agents in Vietnam became routine, grew to massive levels, and special preparations of CS were developed for persistent military effects.[82] The U.S. military used irritant chemical agents to complement or increase the lethality of conventional munitions and in circumstances that did not serve to protect civilians. Early well publicized examples were the blind aerial dropping of massive amounts of irritant chemical agents in target areas immediately prior to carpet-bombing with conventional munitions, in order to force persons out of bomb shelters into the open.[83] Irritant chemical agents were used to attempt clearance of caves, bunkers and tunnel systems, forcing occupying combatants into conventional zones of fire. Irritant chemical agents were used defensively to break off ambushes, or protect fixed bases from infiltration. Irritant chemical agents were used to suppress ground fire during rescues of downed U.S. pilots. Extensive use of irritant chemical agents to drive enemy troops from cover occurred in urban fighting against regular enemy troops in Hue and Saigon during the Tet offensive.

Massive amounts of persistent irritant chemical agent preparations were used in attempts to deny enemy reoccupation of underground facilities and to attempt to interdict enemy transportation routes by aerial contamination. The amount of irritant chemical agents used rose dramatically, totaling 13.7 million pounds (6.2 million kgs) by September 1969.[84] A sharp protest came from concerned U.S. scientists[85] and a renewed international propaganda campaign was mounted by the communist world.

U.S. Army reports in 1969[86] and 1974[87] failed to conclude that use of irritant chemical agents had saved civilian lives. The 1974 report found that most of the anticipated humanitarian benefits of irritant chemical agents had not been realized. In considering mixed civilian/combatant situations, it found no demonstrable benefit, concluding: "[i]t was thought that CS could be used to prevent civilian casualties in these situations; however, this has not been the case. Reports

of the use of CS against noncombatants or to save civilians were not available."
It found irritant chemical agents had not become accepted as a method of choice
for clearing tunnels or neutralizing bunkers, and that there was no objective evidence that the massive use of persistent irritant chemical agents on enemy supply routes had impaired enemy logistics. It found the major usefulness of irritant
chemical agents was as an adjunct to conventional weapons in conventional
combat situations, where irritant chemical agents provided a reduction in
friendly casualties.

The U.S. faced increasing condemnation of its irritant chemical agent policy at home and abroad, and in 1966 faced a UN resolution calling for all states
to abide by the 1925 Geneva Protocol banning chemical and biological warfare.
In contrast to its response in 1952, the United States supported the resolution
and voted in favor,[88] but contended, contrary to the general international consensus, that use of irritant chemical agents in war was not prohibited by the
1925 Geneva Protocol, because they were non-lethal agents. The United States
further argued that since civilian police used tear gas on their own citizens in
suppressing civil disorders, CS was not a "banned" weapon and it did not cause
needless suffering.

During the period of U.S. military involvement, Communist forces used irritant chemical agents sporadically, most notably in attacks against fixed fire base positions.[89] However, after withdrawal of U.S. ground troops, Communist forces began using substantially increased amounts of irritant chemical agents. This was
particularly apparent during the large scale conventional attacks to take or hold
strategic areas in the "Easter Offensive" ("Nguyen Hue Offensive") of 1972,[90] and
in later attacks against South Vietnamese troops.[91]

THE INTRODUCTION OF CS GAS INTO CIVILIAN USAGE

The U.S. contention that use of CS gas in Vietnam had precedence in civilian
police use was by analogy to other irritant chemical agents only, since in 1966
civilian police forces worldwide uniformly used the older, milder CN gas.
CS gas was introduced to control civilian disorders in the United States only
after it had been widely used in combat in Vietnam, and not, as some important con-temporary summaries state, in the "late 1950s."[92] The Army Chemical Corps produced guidelines for civilian use of CS gas in October 1967.[93] A
Presidential Advisory Commission on Civil Disorders specifically endorsed
"massive" civilian use of CS gas instead of CN gas in March 1968,[94] and the
U.S. Army began training civilian police and National Guard in the use of CS
gas for riot control in March 1968, recognizing the police were familiar only
with CN.[95]

A standard text of riot control for police departments published in 1969 documents the late introduction of CS into civilian police usage. This text characterized CS as a military chemical agent, and stated, "until recently civil law enforcement had not expressed any active interest in replacing the older, and time-proven CN agent with the more potent CS tear and nauseating agent. CS has not yet been used by civil law enforcement on any large scale . . ."[96]

The first reported major use of CS gas against civilians in the United States occurred during the May 1969 student disorders in Berkeley, California, where it was released over a crowd confined in the central quadrangle area from a National Guard helicopter using a military dispersing apparatus.[97] CS agent overcame both persons in the quadrangle and large numbers of peaceful non-participants working in adjacent buildings, such as the Research Library.[98]

When President Nixon unilaterally disavowed biological weapons and first use of lethal incapacitating chemical weapons in 1969, White House spokesmen specifically reserved the right to continue to use irritant chemical agents and herbicides in combat. International opinion remained critical of this U.S. contention, and a UN committee, by a vote of 58 to 3 (with 35 abstentions) found that the United States violated the 1925 Geneva Protocol with its irritant chemical agent use in Vietnam,[99] a vote the United States denied constituted an international consensus.[100] A subsequent UN General Assembly vote similarly found the United States in violation, this time by an 80 to 3 vote, with 36 abstentions, prompting an editorial in *The New York Times* to urge U.S. renunciation of irritant chemical agent use in war.[101] The U.S. military strongly resisted any encroachment on their freedom to use irritant chemical agents as an unrestricted military weapon in combat.[102]

BRITISH DECLARE CS GAS DOES NOT VIOLATE THE 1925 GENEVA ACCORDS 1970

The UK had long articulated that irritant chemical agents, as well as the classic chemical weapons agents, were prohibited in warfare by the terms of the 1925 Geneva Protocol,[103] and had protested vigorously the U.S. introduction of irritant chemical agents into the Vietnam War in 1965. However, in February 1970 Britain reversed this long-standing position, stating that because CS gas was "not significantly harmful to man in other than wholly exceptional circumstances" that its use in war did not violate the 1925 Geneva Protocol.[104] In addition to diplomatic pressure from the United States, it is likely British domestic political concerns contributed to this reversal of policy.

British military forces had used large amounts of CS in controlling civil disorder in the Bogside area of Northern Ireland in August of 1969, and many civilians not participating in the disorders reported being incapacitated by CS while sheltering in their dwellings. The Bogside CS use had been highly controversial. British civil police had not been issued any tear gases before 1965, and their use was restricted to use on deranged individuals. Use in civil disorders had been prohibited.[105] The British military had previously used irritant chemical agents only in overseas possessions such as Palestine,[106] Egypt[107] and India,[108] and CS gas only in Cyprus and British Guiana.[109] A British governmental commission established to investigate the safety of CS concluded that "margin of safety is . . . large" and stated that "despite the extreme discomfort that follows inhaling this, it is only under quite exceptional circumstances that exposure doses . . . could be received that might cause serious injury or death."[110] This policy on CS apparently remained in force until the British accession to the CWC in the 1990s.

THE U.S. RESTRICTS IRRITANT CHEMICAL AGENT USE AND RATIFIES THE 1925 GENEVA ACCORDS

The U.S. position on irritant chemical agents complicated efforts to gain the Senate ratification of the 1925 Geneva Protocols. The U.S. military wanted to retain the option of using irritant chemical agents in combat without restriction, but large numbers of Senators were unwilling to support this reservation to the international consensus. The U.S. Senate ratified the 1925 Geneva Protocol in 1975, after a compromise was reached with the U.S. military in which it agreed that it would not use irritant chemical agents in an unrestricted way in regular combat, but still reserved the right to use irritant chemical agents in combat in certain more limited specified military circumstances, delineated in Executive Order 11850 of 8 April 1975.[111] These exceptions include military irritant chemical agent use to control civilian or POW riots, use of irritant chemical agents in situations where civilians are used as screens, use of irritant chemical agents in rescue operations in remote isolated areas, or use in rear echelon areas outside the zone of immediate combat to protect convoys from civil disturbances, terrorists, and paramilitary organizations.

IRRITANT CHEMICAL AGENTS AND THE "YELLOW RAIN" ALLEGATIONS

In the 1980s the U.S. government alleged Communist forces had made chemical attacks in Southeast Asia and Afghanistan. U.S. investigators concluded both irritant chemical agent and lethal chemical attacks had occurred, but because the

United States held that irritant chemical agents were not forbidden in combat, and because deaths were reported, the U.S. allegations stressed that potentially lethal mycotoxins had also been used.[112] The mycotoxin allegations have been largely discredited,[113] though the U.S. military[114] and some scholars[115] continue to maintain that lethal chemical attacks of some sort did occur. Symptoms of mycotoxin or irritant chemical agent exposure can be quite similar: eye and skin irritation, blistering, nausea and diarrhea. High doses of the irritant chemical agent CN have been fatal. Recently declassified documents confirm that both CS and CN were identified in specimens collected from an attack site.[116]

Use of irritant chemical agents in combat by Vietnamese forces in Southeast Asia can be seen as a continuation of the unrestricted irritant chemical agent use in combat originally initiated by the United States in that theater in 1965.

THE FALKLANDS (MALVINAS) WAR 1982

Argentina had endorsed the international consensus that the 1925 Geneva Protocol outlawed irritant chemical agents in war.[117] However, the 1970 British announcement that it did not consider CS gas to be prohibited under this treaty removed any restraint on other nations from initiating use of CS against Britain.

In its invasion of the Falkland (Malvinas) Islands in 1982 Argentine Special Forces were ordered to use irritant chemical agents against the small British garrison of Royal Marines to minimize British casualties with the aim of avoiding propaganda complications following the seizure of the islands.[118] Irritant chemical agents were fired against British Army barracks, but the barracks were vacant, and apparently this use of irritant chemical agents went unnoticed by the British and unreported until publication of Argentine memoirs of the fighting. This use of irritant chemical agents in open combat to reduce casualties between two professional military forces is, perhaps, unique.

Despite the 1970 announcement that the UK government did not consider use of CS gas to violate the 1925 Geneva protocol, the British military did not apparently integrate irritant chemical agents into its military doctrine, and did not utilize them in their recapture of the Falkland Islands.

IRRITANT CHEMICAL AGENTS IN THE IRAN-IRAQ WAR

Irritant chemical agents played an important role in the introduction of chemical warfare into the Iran-Iraq war.[119] U.S. intelligence identified that Iraq first employed irritant chemical agents in July 1982 against Iranian human wave attacks "quite effectively," a successful experience that arguably accelerated their pursuit of more toxic chemical and biological agents. The first lethal chemical weapon attacks by Iraq followed in October 1982.[120]

Although Iraq declared to the UN Special Commission (UNSCOM) that 50 percent of its chemical munitions had been filled with irritant chemical agents,[121] UNSCOM could not independently determine a precise assessment of Iraqi irritant chemical agent production and use.[122] It did identify that at least 20,000 CS filled munitions were destroyed during the 1991 Gulf War.

The extent of irritant chemical agent use by Iraq is not always apparent in intelligence summaries of U.S. origin, because U.S. policy makes a sharp distinction between use of irritant chemical agents and toxic chemical weapons, and do not include instances of tear gas use in combat as instances of [lethal] chemical attack.[123] Similarly, summaries by non-governmental U.S. organizations sometimes make a distinction that suggests military munitions containing irritant chemical agents do not constitute a violation of chemical weapons prohibitions, such as "The [UNSCOM] inspectors found that Iraq actually possessed 46,000 battlefield munitions filled with chemical agents, although many of these contained tear gas."[124]

IRRITANT CHEMICAL AGENT USE IN THE 1990s–2000s

The United States authorized use of irritant chemical agents in the 1991 Gulf War under EO 11850, but no use of irritant chemical agents was reported. The United States did, however, use irritant chemical agents in UN peacekeeping missions in the Balkans against unarmed civilian crowds on several occasions.

The United States ratified the Chemical Weapons Convention (CWC) in 1997. The CWC does not allow for reservations by adherent states, and the U.S. Senate, while maintaining it had the right to make such reservations, chose to make no such formal reservations. However, in its ratification resolution the U.S. Senate placed "conditions" on the treaty,[125] some of which relate to the status of irritant chemical agents. These conditions specifically reserve the right for U.S. troops on peacekeeping missions to use irritant chemical agents in civil disorders to avoid casualties in noncombatants, subject to approval by the UN or host nation. The conditions also state that EO 11850 remains in force. Current U.S. military doctrine maintains that the United States retains the option of using irritant chemical agents under the conditions of EO 11850, subject to presidential authorization.[126] President Bush authorized use of irritant chemical agents in the 2003 Iraq War under EO 11085, prompting a British response that UK troops would not transport or participate in military actions where irritant chemical agents were used.[127] As of October 2005, the United States has not used irritant chemical agents in Iraq during the 2003–2005 invasion and occupation.

Incapacitating Biochemical Agents

Incapacitating biochemical agents are a class of low lethality chemical agents distinct from classical irritant chemical agents because they produced incapacitation for extended periods (hours, days or weeks) following exposure. Unlike irritant chemical agents suitable for riot control purposes, possession of incapacitating biochemicals is prohibited by the CWC.

PSYCHOCHEMICAL AGENTS SOUGHT BY UNITED STATES 1945–1975

During the Cold War the United States and other nations developed incapacitating biochemical agents. Although the Soviet Union, Yugoslavia, and quite likely other nations developed incapacitating biochemical munitions, sufficient information is available only from the U.S. program to allow a discussion of the development of interest in these weapons.

The origins of the U.S. military's incapacitating biochemical program were in a 1949 paper by a Chemical Service officer who proposed that psychoactive chemicals used in military engagements might allow victory without the horrific destruction seen in WWII and foreseen in atomic warfare.

The military interest in incapacitating biochemicals was largely motivated by the desire to obtain irritant chemical agents to be used in conjunction with the newly deployed lethal nerve agents. Chemical warfare doctrine in the 1950s and 1960s sought to offer a flexible spectrum of agents, ranging from highly lethal to incapacitating, so that chemical weapons might be used in a variety of strategic and tactical situations, particularly in dealing with the overwhelming Soviet superiority in conventional weapons in Europe. A non-lethal incapacitant chemical warfare agent was desired to allow effective but non-lethal chemical weapons attacks against NATO territory overrun by Soviet forces, or against Warsaw pact forces that might easily shift alliance away from the Soviets. Irritant chemical agents were also desired because they might increase combat effectiveness and reduce casualties and in limited wars and in fighting insurgencies.[128]

The requirements for the new chemical psychochemical incapacitant were summarized in 1955:[129]

1. onset of action less than one hour
2. no permanent effect a desirable but not essential characteristic
3. as potent as nerve gases as a munition fill
4. low toxicity in handling and stable in storage
5. capable of dissemination from aircraft in all weather conditions

A variety of candidate agents, including anesthetic agents, sedatives, opiates, and muscle paralyzing agents were evaluated in human and animal studies. The U.S. military began a public relations campaign to gather support for such research into "humane" chemical weapons in the late 1950s,[130] including Congressional hearings and a memorable film showing a cat, under the influence of a psychochemical, being terrified by a mouse. Although military testimony before Congress stated a variety of different candidate agents with different effects would be useful in military action and possessed wide margins of safety,[131] in fact only psychochemical agents approached a satisfactory margin of safety and were potent and robust enough to be delivered in munitions. Over 2,000 active duty U.S. soldiers were exposed to psychoactive agents in a program of testing operated by the U.S. Chemical Corps.[132]

In mid 1961 a psychochemical agent designated BZ (3-quinuclidinyl benzilate) was selected to provide a military chemical incapacitant capability. Approximately 130,000 pounds (60,000 kgs) of BZ was manufactured under contract, and two munitions were type-standardized as standard B in early 1962. Production of munitions was begun in early 1963 and completed in early 1964.[133] BZ containing weapons entered the U.S. arsenal in 1964.

In 1964 the U.S. military had proposed initiating use of BZ along with CS in the Vietnamese conflict.[134] However unlike irritant chemical agents, incapacitating biochemicals retained their "chemical weapon" status and still required Presidential authorization. The military chose to pursue employment of only irritant chemical agents. When the United States endorsed the aims of the 1925 Geneva Protocol in a 1966 UN vote, it reserved the right to use irritant chemical agents in combat but did not mention incapacitating biochemicals. However, during 1967 and 1968 internal U.S. documents show that the U.S. Defense Department continued to reserve a Presidential option of initiating incapacitating biochemical use.[135]

LIMITATIONS OF BZ AS AN INCAPACITATING BIOCHEMICAL

Although BZ was standardized, it had important shortcomings and was never fully accepted by the pragmatic field organizations. Its standardization as a level B munition acknowledged it was not fully suitable, and U.S. Army publications issued in 1966 and 1971 on its employment cautioned that it had "critical limitations."[136]

Physiologically, BZ had important drawbacks as a military incapacitating biochemical. It had a relatively slow onset of action: at a dose that eventually incapacitated 50 percent of subjects for twenty-four hours, initial effects would require an hour to appear, and eight hours to reach full effect. The onset, severity, and duration of its action varied greatly depending on the dose received. At target dose levels some subjects, though impaired if tested as individuals, appeared to operate satisfactorily if placed in a unit where less severely affected members could give guidance and maintain order. Those who were completely incapacitated displayed greatly variable behavior over time: an initial period of inert apathy and docility would progress to fearfulness, panic and paranoia, complicating "mop up" procedures and the handling of POWs. The apathy and irrationality that it caused could be an important defect: inert civilians would be unable to evaluate and flee threats, and later might panic and flee from cover, exposing themselves to fields of fire. Enemy soldiers might panic rather than surrender in a hopeless tactical situation, fighting to the death, or commanders or units controlling nuclear or lethal chemical weapons might fire them without proper authorization, causing unintended escalation.

The physiological characterization of BZ as a benign agent was also questionable. The U.S. military suitability tests indicated it was benign, but these tests were made on military personnel who had no physical health problems and who were specially screened for psychological health. Doses given to human subjects were kept low and physical conditions kept benign in the interest of the safety of the subjects. Such highly selected subjects and benign conditions produce minimum severe complications. It indeed appears the army studies on psychochemicals underestimated severe complications compared to less controlled doses of psychoactive agents on unselected populations in more stressful situations. For instance, the army evaluated phencyclidine (PCP) in its psychochemical program, and experienced few significant adverse reactions.[137] The army experience with PCP is markedly different from the civilian experience with PCP effects in recreational drug users, where severe acute reactions are common, persistent psychological sequelae well described, and where acute deaths have been reported.[138] Concern was expressed also because BZ impaired thermoregulation, and its margin of safety might have been quite small in hot, humid tropical conditions.[139] When the British evaluated BZ, they apparently found it more hazardous than the Americans had, and in 1965 rejected it as a candidate chemical incapacitant.[140]

Operationally, BZ weapons had major drawbacks. BZ munitions used a pyrotechnic mixture that delivered the agent as a visible smoke, making clandestine delivery impossible. The standard chemical-biological-radiological defensive act of masking (or fleeing) when confronted by an unknown smoke munition would protect an enemy from its effects.

Overriding technical problems with the instability of the pyrotechnic component of the BZ munitions were encountered. Multiple fires and explosions occurred during manufacture of the original munitions,[141] and accelerated storage testing revealed a critical instability in the pyrotechnic mixture that had been used in all stockpiled munitions. In 1966 this instability caused a ban on this agent-pyrotechnic mixture, necessitating a radical redesign of the development program for third-generation BZ munitions.[142] As of 1968 no satisfactory BZ/ pyrotechnic mixture had been identified. Concerns of agent/pyrotechnic instability apparently caused cancellation of the production of second-generation munitions developed using the unstable mixture, and apparently also restricted release of the existing BZ munitions from storage at Pine Bluff Arsenal. Full data on storage and shipping of BZ munitions did not appear in the 1967 field chemical munitions publication, though such data on level B munitions containing other agents such as nerve gas and irritant chemical agents did.[143] Unlike lethal chemical weapons and irritant chemical agent munitions, BZ munitions were never shipped to forward depots. Special handling because of pyrotechnic instability was implemented during demilitarization operations of the existing BZ munitions.[144]

INCAPACITATING BIOCHEMICAL FIRST USE DISAVOWED BY THE UNITED STATES, 1969

Despite the substantial amounts of BZ that had been manufactured, stored as bulk agent or loaded in munitions in the early 1960s, it was never fully accepted as a useful chemical munition, and in the reevaluation of chemical and biological weapons ordered by President Nixon in 1969, it was determined that BZ was "unlikely to be employed due to its wide range of variability of effects, long onset time, and inefficiency of existing munitions." Perhaps recognizing the embargoed status of the existing BZ munitions, the review concluded that "The United States currently does not have an effective operational incapacitating chemical capability."[145]

When President Nixon unilaterally disavowed use of biological weapons in November 1969, he also announced a no first use policy for both lethal and incapacitating chemical weapons (though not irritant chemical agents and herbicides).

BZ AND INCAPACITATING BIOCHEMICAL PROGRAM UNILATERALLY TERMINATED BY THE UNITED STATES, 1970–1990s

Although U.S. laboratory investigation into other incapacitating psychochemical agents continued until 1975,[146] no other incapacitating biochemical agent was standardized. The termination of human experimentation played a role in limiting new psychochemical investigations.[147] The United States apparently abandoned its incapacitating biochemical program and declared BZ obsolete in 1976[148] and began planning destruction of the BZ stockpiles the same year.[149] Discussion of psychochemical incapacitants was dropped from chemical warfare training manuals in the 1977 and 1983 editions.[150] The destruction of BZ stocks occurred from 1988 to 1990. This unilateral destruction began before any bilateral agreements for chemical weapons reduction with the Soviet Union and well before the CWC was negotiated.

Conclusions

Historically, military organizations have sought low-lethality chemical arms for a variety of applications. They have been sought to provide an alternative to lethal force in circumstances where lethal force is undesirable or unacceptable, such as in the control of riots by unarmed civilians or prisoners of war. Riot-control irritant chemical agents proved effective in these applications, and have become established as legitimate.

These same irritant chemical agents have been used in circumstances where they provide a military advantage in the application of lethal force, as in forcing an unprotected enemy to vacate a concealed or fortified position and thereby exposing him to lethal force. Although irritant chemical agents have proven effective in these applications, the international consensus against the use of any chemical agent in military combat has neutralized this pragmatic military finding. The United States, which controversially claims the option to use irritant chemical agents in some combat situations, has thus far refrained from such use.

The development of effective non-irritant low-lethality biochemical agents has proven technically difficult, as the U.S. military incapacitant program and the unintended deaths and disabilities caused by the Moscow theater event have demonstrated. While new incapacitating biochemical agents may be developed and tried, it is likely that their ultimate acceptance will depend both upon their native margin of safety and the method of their employment. It is hoped that the historical experience of riot-control irritant chemical agents will serve as a model, and the ultimate measure will be whether a novel agent reduces the need for lethal force.

Notes

1. N. P. Walsh, "Russian Troops Root out Militants after Days of Fighting Leave 100 Dead," *The Guardian*, 15 October 2005.

2. National Research Council of the National Academies, *An Assessment of Non-Lethal Weapons Science and Technology* (Washington, D.C.: National Academies Press, 2003): 26–28, 63–64, 80–82, 106–7, 159–60.

3. Ji-wei Guo and Yang Xue-sen, "Ultramicro, Non-Lethal, and Reversible: Looking ahead to Military Biotechnology," *Military Review* (July–August 2005): 75–78.

4. J. P .Perry Robinson with the Stockholm International Peace Research Institute, *The Problem of Chemical and Biological Warfare: The Rise of CB Weapons, vol. 1* (New York: Humanities Press, 1971); H. F. Haber, *The Poisonous Cloud: Chemical Warfare in the First World War* (Oxford: Clarendon Press, 1986).

5. "Asphyxiating Revolvers: A New Police Weapon," *The Scotsman*, 15 March 1913, 6; "Heat Wave Incident in Paris," *The Scotsman*, 2 July 1914, 7. This sequence of events has been obscure to previous historians of chemical weapons in this period. Early accounts had erroneously attributed first use of tear gases in France to the 1912 "Motor Bandit" sieges, and later historians could not confirm this use. See Robinson *SIPRI* vol. I, 126, and note 6, pages 126 and 128; H. F. Haber, *The Poisonous Cloud: Chemical Warfare in the First World War* (Oxford: Clarendon Press, 1986).

6. O. Fillieule and F. Jobard, "The Policing of Protest in France: Toward a Model of Protest Policing" in D. Della Porta and H. Reiter, eds., *Policing Protest: The Control of Mass Demonstrations in Western Democracies* (Minneapolis: University of Minnesota Press, 1998): 83.

7. Haber, *The Poisonous Cloud*, 1986: 18–28.

8. J. B. S. Haldane, *Callinicus: A Defense of Chemical Warfare* (New York: Dutton, 1925): 19–20.

9. A. H. Waitt, *Gas Warfare* (New York: Duel, Sloan & Pierce, 1942): 58–66.

10. Haber, *The Poisonous Cloud*, 261.

11. S. Balfour, *Deadly Embrace: Morocco and the Road to the Spanish Civil War* (Oxford: Oxford University Press, 2002): 133–39.

12. L. P. Brophy, W. D. Miles, and R. C. Cochrane, "The Chemical Warfare Service: From Laboratory to Field," *The United States Army in World War II: The Technical Services.* (Washington, D.C.: Department of the Army, 1959): 70–74.

13. "Letter from John J. Pershing to Senator W. E. Borah, Chairman Foreign Relations Committee, December 10, 1926," *Congressional Record* (Senate) 69th Congress 2nd Session, vol. LXVIII–part 1, 10 December 1926, 226.

14. "Gas as a Humane Weapon: Protests from Sufferers against Rear Admiral Sims's Theory," *The New York Times,* 30 July 1922, 95.

15. D. P. Jones, "From Military to Civilian Technology: The Introduction of Tear Gas for Civil Riot Control," *Technology and Culture* 19, no. 2 (April 1978): 151–68.

16. "Non-Toxic Gases: Argument for their Humane Use as Weapons of War," *New York Times,* 25 June 1922, col. E4.

17. "250 Policemen Weep in Face of Riot Gas," *The New York Times*, 23 July 1921, 14; "Tear Gas and Masks Asked for by Police," *The New York Times*, 1 February 1922, 4; E. Russel, *War and Nature: Fighting Humans and Insects with chemicals from World War I to Silent Spring.* (Cambridge: Cambridge University Press, 2001): 62.

18. H. A. Bellows, *A Treatise on Riot Duty for the National Guard*, (Washington, D.C.: U.S. Government Printing Office, 1920).

19. "To Use Tear Gas on Fugitives in Cave," *The New York Times,* 16 December 1921, 27; "Police Use Tear Gas to Dislodge Maniac," *The New York Times,* 27 July 1922, 3.

20. "Tear Gas Holds Back Mob," *The New York Times,* 15 June 1922, 9.

21. "Tear Gas Stops Riot," *The New York Times,* 30 August 1922, 1.

22. L.G. Edwardson, "Noxious Tear-Gas Bomb Mightier in Peace than in War," *The World Magazine,* 27 July 1924, 4–5.

23. "Bombs Rout Crowd at Negro's Trial: Delaware Troops Hurl Tear Gas as an Angry Throng Storms Court at Georgetown," *The New York Times,* 9 February 1926, 3.

24. "Missionary Shown as Gas Salesman," *The New York Times,* 21 September 1934, 9.

25. "Swedish Troops Kill Five in Strike Riot," *The New York Times,* 15 May 1931, 3.

26. "O'Duffy Injured by Mob in Ireland," *The New York Times,* 7 October 1933, 18.

27. "Styrian Peasants Rebel," *The New York Times,* 3 January 1933, 14.

28. "Daudet and Reds Pardoned in France," *The New York Times,* 31 December 1929, 6.

29. O. Fillieule and F. Jobard, "The Policing of Protest in France": 83.

30. "Excerpt from Senate Debate on the Geneva Protocol" (Congressional Record, 9 December 1926: 150) reproduced in *Chemical-Biological Warfare: U.S. Policies and International Effects,* Committee on Foreign Affairs, House of Representatives, 16 May 1970 (Washington, D.C.: U.S. Government Printing Office, 1970): 40–41.

31. U.S. War Department, *Rules of Land Warfare Basic Field Manual FM 27–10* (Washington, D.C.: U.S. Government Printing Office, 1940).

32. "Text of Mitchell's Report on the Records of Members of the BEF," *The New York Times,* 12 September 1932, 8.

33. G. S. Patton, "Federal Troops in Domestic Disturbances," The Patton Society Research Library, (November 1932), <http://www.pattonhq.com/textfiles/federal/html> (24 April 2005).

34. Brophy, "The Chemical Warfare Service," 71–72.

35. "Statements of Japan, Spain, USSR, France, China, Italy, Canada, Turkey, British Empire," *Documents of the Preparatory Commission for the Disarmament Conference, Series X* (Geneva: League of Nations Publications, 15 January 1931): 313–14.

36. "Proposal by United States Delegation," *Documents of the Preparatory Commission for the Disarmament Conference, Series X* (Geneva: League of Nations Publications, 15 January 1931): 312.

37. Robinson, *The Problem of Chemical and Biological Warfare;* Haber, *The Poisonous Cloud,* 53, footnote 34.

38. Robinson, *The Problem of Chemical and Biological Warfare;* Haber, *The Poisonous Cloud,* 142–46.

39. "The Battle for Toledo: Use of Tear Gas Shells," *The Scotsman,* 28 September 1936; Robinson, *The Problem of Chemical and Biological Warfare;* Haber, *The Poisonous Cloud,* 146–47.

40. "Gas as a Weapon" in *Chemical Warfare Bulletin* 24, no. 1 (January 1938): 23–28. (Reprinted from *Army Ordnance.*)

41. Robinson, *The Problem of Chemical and Biological Warfare;* Haber, *The Poisonous Cloud,* 147–52.

42. S. H. Harris, *Factories of Death: Japanese Biological Warfare, 1932–1945, and the American Cover-up* Revised Edition (New York: Routeledge, 2002): 331.

43. U.S. War Department, *Handbook on Japanese Military Forces* TM-E 30-480 (Washington, D.C.: U.S. Government Printing Office, 1944): 256.

44. U.S. War Department, *Handbook on Japanese Military Forces*, 266–68.

45. "U.S. Warns Japan," *The New York Times*, 6 June 1942, 1 and 2.

46. F. J. Brown, *Chemical Warfare: A Study in Restraints* (Princeton, NJ: Princeton University Press, 1968): 259.

47. C. C. Crane, *American Airpower Strategy in Korea 1950–1953* (Lawrence, KS: University Press of Kansas, 2000): 67–68; J. H. Rothschild, "Germs and Gas: The Weapons Nobody Dares Talk About." *Harper's Magazine* 218, no. 1309, June 1959, 30.

48. Military History Office, *The Handling of Prisoners of War during the Korean War*, June 1960. NARA RG 338 Entry A1 224 Box 1950.

49. Military History Office, *The Handling of Prisoners of War during the Korean War*, June 1960. NARA RG 338 Entry A1 224 Box 1950.

50. "Memo: Training of Armored Non-Toxic Gas Squads for Control of Civil Disturbances, November 19, 1954," NARA RG 175 Entry 1B Box 219, 1–6.

51. "Memo: Employed [sic] of CNB Filled Flame Throwers in Control of Civil Disturbances, December 20, 1954," NARA RG 175 Entry 1B Box 219.

52. "Chemical Warfare Policy: A Report to the National Security Council by the Secretary of Defense Feb 1, 1950," NSC62. Record number 54852, Chemical and Biological Warfare Collection, Box 2, National Security Archive, George Washington University, Washington, D.C.

53. "Chemical (Toxic) and Biological Warfare Readiness: Joint Strategic Plans Committee JSPC 954/29, August 13, 1953," Record #54828, Chemical and Biological Warfare Collection, Box 2, National Security Archive, George Washington University, Washington, D.C.

54. U.S. Department of State, "National Security Document NSC5062/1 11 March 1956," in *Foreign Relations of the United States, 1955–1957. Volume XIX: National Security Policy* (Washington, D.C.: U.S. Government Printing Office, 1990): 206–8.

55. JCS 1837/112, 563.

56. JCS 1837/116, 593.

57. *Chemical, Biological and Radiological (CBR) Operations* FM 3-5 Department of the Army, September 1961, 5.

58. D. Halberstam, "Buddhists in Saigon Clash with Police," *The New York Times*, 16 June 1963, 1; P. Grose, "Regime's Foes Riot in Streets of Saigon," *The New York Times*, 23 November 1964, 1; "Khanh Says Use is New," *The New York Times*, 23 March 1965, 2.

59. T. Mangold and J. Penycate, *The Tunnels of Cu Chi* (New York: Berkeley Books, 198): 88–89.

60. "Reds' Tunnel Network Is Found Near Saigon," *The New York Times*, 5 July 1963, 2.

61. "Washington Rebuts Poison Gas Charge," *The New York Times*, 11 March 1963, 4; "Germ-War charge is denied by Saigon," *The New York Times*, 21 March 1963, 4.

62. J. F. Gebhardt, "The Road to Abu Ghraib: U.S. Army Detainee Doctrine and Experience," *Global War on Terrorism Occasional Paper* 6 (Fort Leavenworth, KS: Combat Studies Institute Press, 2005): 41–42.

63. D. Halberstam, "Tactics of Enemy and Political Pressures on Army Pose Major Problems," *The New York Times*, 27 October 1963, 167.

64. Headquarters, United States Military Assistance Command, Vietnam [hereafter HQ U.S.M.A.V.], *Command History 1964*, 95, 133.

65. G. J. Veith, "The 'Real' Tailwind: The first POW raids and the tear gas controversy of 1965" (presented at the 3rd Triennial Vietnam Symposium, Vietnam Center, Texas Tech University, Lubbock, TX), <http://www.aiipowmia.com/sea/veithgas.html> (21 October 2005).

66. M. Frankel, "U.S. Reveals use of Non-Lethal Gas against Vietcong," *The New York Times,* 23 March 1965, 1–2.

67. Raymond, "Decision on Gas not President's, White House Says: Area Commanders Control Weapon, Reedy Asserts—Chemical Called Mild," *The New York Times,* 24 March 1965, 1, 7.

68. C. H. Farnsworth, "War-Gas Debate Stirs Commons: Wilson Parries Criticism; Many Nations Aroused," *The New York Times,* 24 March 1965, 6.

69. J. Raymond, "Decision on Gas not President's," 1, 7.

70. "Memorandum of Conversation in Washington on March 23, 1965 at 11:45A.M, document 240," NARA RG 59, conference files, Lott 66 D 347, CF2482, <http://www.state.gov/r/pa/ho/frus/johnsonlb/xii/2279.htm> (20 October 2005).

71. "Asian Reds Make Gas a Top Issue: Propaganda Drive Believed Effective Though Belated," *The New York Times,* 25 March 1965, 14.

72. J. W. Finney, "Rusk Defends use of Non-Lethal Gas in War in Vietnam," *The New York Times,* 25 March 1965, 1,13; "Excerpts from Transcript of Rusk News Parley on Use of Gas in Vietnam," *The New York Times,* 25 March 1965, 13.

73. "U.S. Chief Seeks a Ruling on Gas: Westmoreland Seeking Right to Use Tear Gas; U.S. Chief in Vietnam said to Believe it Would be More Humane at Times than Weapons of Lethal Force," *The New York Times,* 23 September 1965, 1–2; G. J. Veith, "The 'Real' Tailwind."

74. R. W. Apple, "Marine Officer Uses Tear Gas in Vietnam, Setting Off Inquiry," *The New York Times,* 8 September 1965, 1, 3.

75. Veith, "The 'Real' Tailwind."

76. S. Hersh, *Chemical and Biological Warfare* (New York: Bobbs-Merrill Co., 1968): 173–77.

77. Veith, "The 'Real' Tailwind."

78. "GIs in Vietnam Can Use Tear Gas; Westmoreland Empowered to Employ It When It Would Save Lives," *The New York Times,* 6 October 1965, p.1; G. J. Veith, "The 'Real' Tailwind."

79. HQ U.S.M.A.V., *Command History 1965*, 443–44, 447.

80. Veith, "The 'Real' Tailwind."

81. P. L. Howard, "U.S. Explains New Tactic," *The New York Times,* 22 February 1966, 2; *Chemical-Biological Warfare: U.S. Policies and International Effects,* Report of the Subcommittee on National Security Policy and Scientific Developments of the Committee on Foreign Affairs, House of Representatives, 16 May 1970. (Washington, D.C.: U.S. Government Printing Office, 1970): 4–10; "Employment of Riot Control Agents, Flame, Smoke, Antiplant Agents, and Personnel Detectors in Counterguerilla Operations," Department of the Army Training Circular TC 3-16, April 1969.

82. R. Blumenthal, "U.S. Now Used Tear Gas as Routine War Weapon," *The New York Times,* 6 December 1969, 13.

83. "Copters Spread Tear Gas," *The New York Times,* 3 January 1966, 8; N. Sheehan, "Tear Gas Dropped Before B-52 Raid," *The New York Times,* 22 February 1966, 1–2.

84. Smith, "U.S. Command in Saigon, 11.

85. "22 Scientists Bid Johnson Bar Chemical Weapons in Vietnam," *The New York Times,* 20 September 1966, 1, 3.

86. Smith, "U.S. Command in Saigon 11; P. L. Howard, *Operational Aspects of Agent CS (Technical Report) DTC-FR-S700M* (Fort Douglas, UT: Deseret Test Center, April 1973): 1–12, 107–19.

87. *Operational Aspects of Agent CS,* 116.

88. "Bar on Poison Gas Backed 101-0 in U.N.," *The New York Times,* 24 November 1966, 12.

89. HQ U.S.M.A.V., *Command History 1966* (March 1966): 820; "Siege & Fall of Lang Vei Special Forces Camp," (February 1968), <www.members.tripod.com/~vet4/specialforces.html> (9 November 2005); "Attack on Ngok Tavak information," (10 May 1968), <http://www.flyarmy.org/panel/battle/68051001.htm> (9 November 2005); J. Prados, "The NVA's Operation Dien Bien Phu: The 1969 Siege of Ben Het." *The VVA Veteran* (August-September, 2003).

90. HQ USM.A.V., *Command History 1972–1973,* A-51.

91. W. E. LeGro, *Vietnam: Cease Fire to Capitulation* (U.S. Army Center of Military History: CMH Publication, (90–29), 1985: html version not paginated. See: Chapter 11, "Hill 1062," and chapter 12, "Nui Mo Tau, Nui Bong and Hill 350." <http://libraryautomation.com/nymas/Vietnamfulltext2.html> (4 September 2007).

92. F. Sidel, "Riot Control Agents" in R. Zajtchuck, ed., *Textbook of Military Medicine* (Washington, D.C.: Bordon Institute, 1997), ch. 12, 310.

93. Characteristics of Riot Control Agent CS (EASP 600-1) Edgewood Arsenal, October 1967, referenced in Applegate, *Riot Control Material and Techniques* (Harrisburg, PA: Stackpole Books, 1969): 165.

94. Report of the National Advisory Commission on Civil Disorders, March 1968, referenced in R. Applegate, *Riot Control Material and Techniques,* 165.

95. "Army Helps Police Learn About Riots," *The New York Times,* 22 March 1968, 49.

96. Applegate, *Riot Control Material and Techniques,* 132-134, 165-168.

97. "Copter Breaks up Berkeley Crowd," *The New York Times,* 21 May 1969, 1.

98. (M. Furmanksi, pers. experience, 20 May 1969).

99. "U.N. Rebuffs US on Tear-Gas Use," *The New York Times,* 11 December 1969.

100. T. Szulc, "U.S. Criticizes Vote in U.N. on Meaning of Chemical Warfare Ban," *The New York Times,* 12 December 1969, 18.

101. Editorial, "Banning Tear Gas," *The New York Times,* sec. E14, 21 December 1969.

102. "Pentagon Defends Use of Tear Gases," *New York Times,* 23 March 1971, 3.

103. "Statement of British Empire," *Documents of the Preparatory Commission for the Disarmament Conference, Series X* (Geneva: League of Nations Publications, 15 January 1931), 313–14.

104. A. Lewis, "Britain Asserts CS Gas Is Not Banned," *The New York Times,* 3 February 1970, 3.

105. "On This Day: May 20, 1965: British police to be issued with tear gas." *BBC News,* available online at: <http://news.bbc.co.uk/onthisday/hi/dates/stories/may/20/newsid_2510000/2510539.stm> (28 February 2007)

106. "Tear Gas," Statement in Commons, *The Scotsman,* 30 May 1936, 14; "Search for Arms," *The Scotsman,* 24 June 1936, 15.

107. *The Scotsman,* 15 November 1938, 1.

108. "Troops and Police Fire on Calcutta Mobs," *The Scotsman,* 29 October 1946, 5.

109. "Riot Gasses Used 124 Times in Last 5 years," *The New York Times,* 2 April 1965, 5.

110. H. Himsworth, *Report of the Enquiry into the Medical and Toxilogical Aspects of CS (Orthochlorobenzylidene Malononitrile): Part II, Enquiry Into Toxicological Aspects of CS and its Use for Civil Purposes,* H.M.S.O. 1971, 46,48, <http://www.bopcris.ac.uk/bopall/ref13616.html> (5 June 2005).

111. G. Ford, *Executive Order 11850—Renunciation of Certain Uses in War of Chemical Herbicides and Riot Control Agents,* April 8, 1975. 40 FR 16187 CGR, 1971–1975 Comp., 980, <http://www.archives.gov/federal-register/codification/executive-order/11850.html> (25 February 2007).

112. A. M. Haig, *Chemical Warfare in Southeast Asia and Afghanistan,* Special Report no. 98, U.S. Department of State, 22 March 1982, 7–8, 11, 16.

113. J. P. P. Robinson, Jeanne Guillemin, and Matthew Meselson, "Yellow Rain in Southeast Asia: The Story Collapses" in Susan Wright, ed., *Preventing a Biological Arms Race* (Cambridge, MA: MIT Press, 1990), 220–38.

114. "Multiservice Tactics, Techniques, and Procedures for Nuclear, Biological and Chemical Defense Operations," *U.S. Army, Marine Corps, Navy & Air Force Field Manual FM 3–11 (FM3-100),* March 2003.

115. R. L. Katz, *Yellow Rain Revisited: Lessons Learned for the Investigation of Chemical and Biological Weapons Allegations.* PhD dissertation, Princeton University Woodrow Wilson School of Public and International Affairs, May 2005.

116. Katz, *Yellow Rain Revisited,* 128.

117. Robinson, Guillemin, and Meselson "Yellow Rain in Southeast Asia," 167–68.

118. M. Middlebrook, *The Argentine Fight for the Falklands* (South Yorkshire, England: Pen and Sword Books, 2003).

119. J. Ali, "Chemical Weapons and the Iran-Iraq War: A Case Study in Noncompliance," *The Nonproliferation Review* (Spring 2001): 47–48.

120. "Department of State, Office of the Assistant Secretary for Near Eastern and South Asian Affairs Action Memorandum from Jonathan T. Howe to Lawrence S. Eagleburger: Iraqi Use of Chemical Weapons", including cable entitled "Background on Iraqi Use of Chemical Weapons, November 21, 1983," Document 25 in National Security Archive Electronic Briefing Book No 82: *Shaking Hands with Saddam Hussein: The U.S. Tilts toward Iraq,* 1980–1984,<http://www.gwu.edu/~nsaarchiv/NSAEBB/NSAEBB82/index.htm> (29 April 2005).

121. Matthew S. Meselson and J. P. P. Robinson, "'Non-Lethal' Weapons and Implementation of the Chemical and Biological Weapons Conventions" in *The BWC Intercessional Process towards the Sixth Review Conference and Beyond,* 20th Pugwash Workshop Study Group on Implementation of the CBW Conventions 8–9 November 2003, Geneva, Switzerland, 3 <http://www.pugwash.org/reports/cbw/cbw20/cbw20-meselson-robinson.htm> (30 April 2005).

122. United Nations, *U.N.S.C.O.M. Report S/1995/284,* 10 April 1995, para. 35. <http://www.fas.org/news/un/iraq/s/s1995-0284.htm> (28 February 2007).

123. For instance, the U.S. intelligence reports that identified the initial CS attacks have extensive disclaimers that these do not constitute chemical weapons attacks according to U.S. policy. These CS attacks do not appear in chronologies of Iraqi chemical weapons attacks produced from U.S. governmental sources; Central Intelligence Agency, *Iraq's Weapons of Mass Destruction Programs: Chemical Warfare Programs, October 2002,* Table: Documented Iraqi Use of Chemical Weapons, 8.

124. Henry L. Stimson Center, "U.N. Inspectors to Continue Hunt for Iraq's Biological and Chemical Weapons," *The CBW Chronicle* 2, no. 4 (May 1998), <http://www.stimson.org/chw/?sn=cb2002011327> (30 April 2005).

125. A. Gordon, "Implications of the US Resolution of Ratification," *The CBW Conventions Bulletin* 38 (December 1997): 1–6.

126. R. Maguire. *Morality, Law and War.* U.S.M.C. Power Point Presentation August 29, 2002, frames 12 and 13, <http://www.tecom.usmc.mil/cce/references/pme/Law%20of%20War%20-%20McGuire,%2029%20Aug%2002.PPT> (28 February 2007).

127. N. Wade and E. Schmit, "Bush Approves Use of Tear Gas in Battlefield: Weapons Experts Fear Violation of Law," *The New York Times,* 2 April 2003.

128. J. H. Rothschild, "Germs and Gas: The Weapons Nobody Dares Talk About," *Harper's Magazine* 218, no. 1309, June 1959, 34.

129. U.S. Army Chemical Corps, "Summary of Major Events and Problems, FY56" (Army Chemical Center, MD: U.S. Army Chemical Historical Center, November 1956), 128–30 [hereafter CmlC Hist FY56].

130. Rothschild, "Germs and Gas."

131. J. A. Hebbeler, Brig Gen., "Chemical and Biological Warfare: Briefing at the Request of Congressman Richard McCarthy," National Security Archive Record 55210, 4 March 1969, 3.

132. D. A. McFarling, "LSD Follow-Up Study Report," U.S. Army Medical Department (Washington, D.C.: U.S. Government Printing Office, October 1980); *Possible Long Term Health Effects of Short-Term Exposure to Chemical Agents, vol. 1: Anticholinesterases and Anticholinergics* (Washington, D.C.: National Academy Press, 1982): vii–xi.

133. Chemical Systems Laboratory, "Proposal for Demilitarization of Incapacitating Agent BZ and Munitions," U.S. Army Armament Research and Development Command. (Aberdeen Proving Ground, MD: February 1978), 6, 18–20.

134. HQ U.S.M.A.V., *Command History 1964,* 95, 133.

135. "Letter, Secretary of Defense to Secretary of State, November 17, 1966," cited in "Interdepartmental Political-Military Group in response to NSSM 59," in *U.S. Policy on Chemical and Biological Warfare and Agents: Report to the National Security Council*, National Security Archive Briefing Book no. 58, (10 November 1969), document 6a, 6b, page 10; "N. B. Katzenback Memorandum for Mr. Walt W. Rostow, The White House. Subject: Policy on Chemical and Biological Weapons, February 20, 1967," NSA record 54869.

136. Department of the Army, *Chemical and Biological Weapons Employment: Field Manual FM3-10* (U.S. Government Printing Office, Washington, D.C., March 1966), 24; *Department of the Army, Chemical Weapons Employment: Field Manual FM3-10* (U.S. Government Printing Office, Washington, D.C., March 1966), Change 1, and 26 February 1971, 24.

137. "Volunteer Screening, Selection and Classification" in *Possible Long Term Health Effects of Short-Term Exposure to Chemical Agents. vol 2: Cholinesterase Reactivators, Psychochemicals, and Irritants and Vesicants*, vol. 1 (Washington, D.C.: National Academy Press, 1982): 48–53.

138. National Institute on Drug Abuse, *NIDA Info Facts: PCP (Phencyclidine)*, <http://www.nida.nih.gov/Infofacts/PCP.html> (28 February 2007).

139. *Possible Long Term Health Effects of Short-Term Exposure to Chemical Agents. vol 1: Anticholinesterases and Anticholinergics* (Washington, D.C.: National Academy Press, 1982): 60–61.

140. J. P. P. Robinson, "Disabling Chemical Weapons: A Documentary Chronology of Events, 1945–2003," *Harvard Sussex Program*, 52, footnote 207. (Hereafter Robinson Chronology).

141. Chemical Systems Laboratory, "Proposal for Demilitarization of Incapacitating Agent BZ and Munitions," 17–19.

142. *BLU-30/B (Nonhazardous) Bomblet*, Honeywell Inc. Hopkins, MN Ordnance Div. July 1968, NTIS publication AD501759, 83.

143. Department of the Army, *Chemical Corps Reference Handbook: Field Manual FM3-8* (Washington, D.C.: U.S. Government Printing Office, January 1967).

144. Chemical Systems Laboratory, "Proposal for Demilitarization of Incapacitating Agents BZ and Munitions," 17–18, 30.

145. Interdepartmental Political-Military Group, "U.S. Policy on Chemical and Biological Warfare and Agents: Report to the National Security Council (in response to NSSM 59)" in R.A. Wampler, ed., "National Security Archive Briefing Book No. 58: Volume III" in *Biowar: The Nixon Administration's Decision to End the U.S. biological Warfare Programs* (10 November 1969), doc. 6a and 6b, p.11, 31–32; HAK talking points in R.A. Wampler, ed., "National Security Archive Briefing Book No. 58: Volume III" doc. 11, 7.

146. Allen M. Hornblum, *Acres of Skin: Human Experiments at Holmsburg Prison* (New York: Routledge, 1998), 127–30.

147. U.S. Chemical Corps Obligations Report FY 1977 cited in Robinson Chronology entry 761000, 73.

148. Robinson Chronology entry 760200, 73, footnote 269.

149. Chemical Systems Laboratory, "Proposal for Demilitarization of Incapacitating Agent BZ and Munitions," 4, 6.

150. Department of the Army, *Field Manual FM 21-40: NBC (Nuclear, Biological and Chemical) Defense* (Washington, D.C.: HQ Department Army, 14 October 1977): 1–13, 1–18; U.S. Army Ordnance and Chemical Center and School, *Introduction to Chemical and Radiological Operations and Biological Defense*, Interschool Subcourse 220 (Washington, D.C.: U.S. Government Printing Office, 1983): 39–46.

CHAPTER 4

Late and Post–Cold War
Research and Development
of Incapacitating
Biochemical Weapons

Alan Pearson

In the previous chapter, Martin Furmanski explored the history of military interest in incapacitating biochemical weapons from World War I to the early
1970s. By the late 1980s, military and law enforcement agencies in the United
States were expressing renewed interest in biochemical incapacitants and had begun research and development activities that could lead to new incapacitating
biochemical weapons. However, such activities, which have continued into the
twenty-first century, have not been limited to the United States. Relatively little
is known about these activities as they have generally been kept out of the public eye.

    This chapter will review what is publicly known about recent military
and law enforcement research and development efforts directed toward incapacitating biochemical weapons. Any biochemical weapons system will comprise at least two components—the payload, in this case the biochemical
compound(s) used to render an effect on the target, and the delivery system.
This chapter will consider these components in turn. As more is publicly
known about U.S. efforts than about those of any other nation,* this chapter
will focus on the United States. Efforts in other nations will be addressed as
possible.

---

*This is due in no small part to the substantial efforts by the Sunshine Project to obtain documents
from the U.S. government under the Freedom of Information Act (FOIA). This chapter could not have
been written without access to documents that the Sunshine Project has provided through its efforts.

Payloads

According to Furmanski, the United States continued to pursue incapacitating biochemicals for several years after President Nixon announced a no first-use policy for chemical weapons in 1969. At the time, according to the Interdepartmental Political-Military Working Group, the one standardized incapacitating agent, BZ, was "unlikely to be employed due to its wide range of variability of effects, long onset time, and inefficiency of existing munitions." In 1968, R. B. Fisher, the chair of the Chemical Defence Advisory Board in the UK, pointed out a fourth complication: "any chemical agent, a small dose of which is capable of profound disturbance of bodily or mental function, is certain to be able to cause death in large dose . . . and no attack with a chemical warfare agent is likely to be designed with the primary objective of avoiding overhitting."[1]

Fisher is referring to what could be termed the "dose-response problem," at once a problem of science, technology, application, morality and politics. The "safety margin," or "therapeutic index," of a drug is the ratio of the drug dose that causes severe or adverse effects or lethality in 50 percent of a target population (LD_{50}) to the drug dose that causes the desired effect in 50 percent of that population (ED_{50}) (see figure 4.1). For BZ this ratio has been estimated to be approximately 40,[2] considered inadequate by most if not all observers today.

Ultimately, however, it is the ability of a prospective weapon to meet military and political requirements, within existing political and operational constraints, which determines whether the weapon is developed, fielded and used.[3] Thus, the relevant ratio to consider in assessing any proposed incapacitating biochemical weapon agent is not the therapeutic index but rather, the ratio of the dose which results in the "maximum acceptable" level of mortality and serious long-term morbidity to that which achieves the minimum required operational impact. That ratio is *determined by moral, military and political considerations*. In the early days of the U.S. Cold War chemical weapons program, advocates within the U.S. Army Chemical Corps promoted the use of mustard gas as an incapacitating agent because it had "only" a 2 percent lethality rate among U.S. troops in World War I.[4] Today, U.S. military requirements appear to be at least 99 percent incapacitation, including no more than 0.5 percent mortality and no more than 1.0 percent combined mortality and serious long-term morbidity.[5]

As Klotz et al have shown, an agent that could fulfill such requirements would need to have an exceptionally large safety margin.[6] Even if a lethality rate of up to 5 percent were accepted,[7] a very large safety margin would be required. Moreover, the reported safety margin of a potential incapacitating agent can be very misleading, for at least three reasons. First, safety margins can only be determined in animal models. Yet, different animal models can yield significantly different results and extensive experience has shown that "animal data cannot be

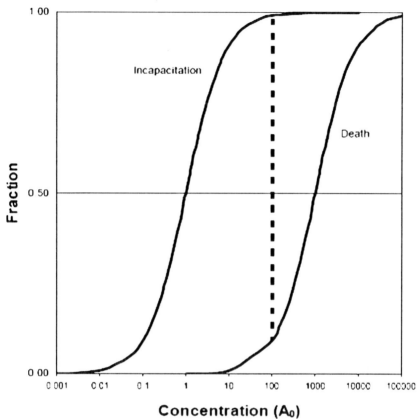

Figure 4.1.   Relationship Between Dose, Incapacitation and Lethality.
Source: Klotz, Furmanksi and Wheelis, "Beware the Siren's Song," 2003

extrapolated directly to human beings," most especially at the upper limits of exposure.[8] Second, the characteristics (slope, location, threshold effects) and predictive value of dose-response curves depend on the effect being measured and on the range of doses being tested. Yet, "no drug produces a single effect, and, depending on the effect being measured, the therapeutic index for a drug will vary."[9] Definitions of desired effects can be quite subjective and may not be operationally relevant, while dose ranges tested can be quite narrow due to safety concerns, thus failing to provide important information about the tails of the curves. For instance, BZ was tested to only twice the ED_{50} due to safety concerns.[10]

Third, dose-response curves determined under idealized and controlled settings don't reflect real operational contexts. In military studies, human-effects testing typically use healthy young adults who are exposed to defined doses for a defined length of time in noncombat settings where they can be carefully monitored for adverse effects. Such tests fail to take into consideration the uncontrollable variability that would occur in the field, both in exposure (uneven concentration and exposure time) and within the target population (age, size, gender, health status, and individual susceptibility). In the real world, pharmacologic therapy must be individualized, as "therapists of every type have long recognized and acknowledged that individual patients show wide variability in response to the same drug or treatment method . . . the concentration or dose of drug required to produce a therapeutic effect in most of the population will usually overlap the concentration required to produce toxicity in some of the population."[11] As a 1997 report from Lawrence Livermore National Laboratory noted, "typically, in a clinical setting, the lethal dose of an anesthetic is only two to four times the therapeutic dose."[12] For this reason, pharmaceutical agents must be tailored to individuals and delivered under controlled circumstances within a narrow range of doses. Yet, unavoidable differences in exposure time and agent distribution after an agent is disseminated in the field make the uniform delivery of precisely controlled doses of incapacitating agents nearly impossible. This only encourages users to deliver more agent than needed to incapacitate most individuals in order to compensate for those individuals who inevitably would not receive enough.[13] This problem is complicated even more by the need for rapid incapacitation in most scenarios, as this requires the delivery of higher doses than would normally be used for nonmilitary purposes. It is thus no surprise to hear one developer of incapacitating biochemical agents say that "it's a very complex situation—it is hard enough to use them in the operating room without compounding the problem with larger groups."[14]

Wheelis and Dando maintain that early efforts to develop effective incapacitating biochemical weapons failed primarily because scientific understanding of neurobiology and neuroreceptors was insufficient for enabling the development of agents with adequate specificity to safely (i.e., non-lethally) elicit a narrow range of rapid and predictable responses.[15] However, as one recent report noted, advances in science and technology have continually revealed new possibilities:

> Since the mid 1960s . . . the premier status of the U.S. pharmaceutical industry . . . combined with the exponential developments in the fields of pharmacology, neuroscience, anesthesia, and biotechnology fields . . . has brought forth a diverse array of compounds that produce sedation and/or a calm state as either a primary or secondary effect.[16]

The fervor in neuropharmaceutical drug discovery and development is illustrated by the fact that one class of such drugs alone, the antidepressants, are the fourth largest class of pharmaceuticals sold worldwide today—at nearly $20 billion in sales in 2005.[17] As Dando points out in chapter 6, the increasing knowledge about the brain, and in particular about the structure, distribution, function and integration of receptor sub-types within complex neurological circuits and systems, suggests that it might be possible to find more specific drugs for treating neurological and other mental disorders.

By the mid 1980s the U.S. Army had a significant program underway to apply these advances to the development of effective incapacitating weapons. At first under the Incapacitating Chemicals Program, and later under the Advanced Riot Control Agent Device (ARCAD) program, the Army Edgewood Research, Development and Engineering Center in Maryland (ERDEC) conducted research and development activities on a range of "chemical systems for anti-material and antipersonnel NLWs [non-lethal weapons], such as *calmatives*, lacrimators [tear gases], and malodorants" (emphasis added).[18,19] The ARCAD program explored at least two different classes of incapacitating biochemical agents, alpha-2 adrenergic receptor agonists (compounds that bind to and activate a receptor) and synthetic opioids.

The canonical alpha-2 adrenergic receptor agonist clonidine has been prescribed since the 1960s for its antihypertensive effects. It also has neurological effects and is prescribed at lower doses for the treatment of attention deficit hyperactivity disorder and Tourette's Syndrome. At high doses clonidine can cause "immobilization by profound sedation." However, it can also cause hypotension and bradycardia, potentially leading to cardiac arrest, and upon sudden withdrawal "rebound" hypertension can result. Moreover, clonidine and other alpha-2 adrenergic receptor agonists have long-lasting effects and, even at high doses, slow onset times. By the mid-1980s more selective compounds were being discovered, in particular the sedative dexmedetomidine, first developed as a veterinary sedative-analgesic and now also used as an anesthetic for sedation of intensive care patients. The ARCAD program explored relationships between the structure and the activity of the alpha-2 adrenergic receptor agonists and attempted to design and synthesize new agonists that overcame some of the problems that rendered clonidine a poor choice for an incapacitating agent.[20] It is likely that dexmedetomidine was among the compounds studied, and the program reportedly identified "a naphthalene analog of medetomidine [that] is also a very potent and selective 2-adrenergic stimulant."[21]

Greater interest and effort was apparently placed on the synthetic opioids, especially the fentanyl family of opioids, which act on the same set of receptors as morphine and related compounds found in opium. The fentanyls are among the strongest analgesics (pain relievers) known, and among the fastest acting neurochemical agents. Fentanyl, for example is 100 times more potent than morphine and also acts more rapidly (onset time of 1–2 minutes versus 15–30 minutes) and with shorter duration (1 hour versus 3–5 hours). In addition to providing relief from pain, opioids can cause sedation and, at high doses, un-consciousness. These are unwanted side effects when opioids are used for anal-gesia, but are the intended effect when they are used during anesthesia. Indeed, the fentanyl class opioids have been widely used for both analgesic and anesthe-sia since the discovery of fentanyl in 1960.[22]

Opioid compounds, including fentanyl and probably etorphine (a potent analog of the minor opium constituent thebaine), were investigated by U.S. mil-itary researchers as potential biochemical incapacitants during the early Cold War program. However, they were found to be unsatisfactory as their lethal doses were only ten to twenty fold greater than their incapacitating dose as defined militarily.[23] Indeed, in addition to causing sedation and unconsciousness, the opioids can cause hypotension, bradycardia (reduced heart rate), muscle rigidity, and most seriously, severe and life threatening respiratory depression. However, a series of compounds related to fentanyl were discovered during the 1970s that were both more potent and said to have a much higher safety margin. One such compound, sufentanil, is five to ten times more potent than fentanyl and is the most potent opioid currently in routine clinical use. A second compound, the veterinary drug carfentanil, is perhaps the most potent analgesic currently known with roughly 10,000 times the potency of morphine. Like fentanyl, both of these opioids are fast acting and have a relatively short duration of effect.[24]

According to a research proposal submitted by ERDEC in April 1994, the newer fentanyls had "shown promise in previous studies" and were "excellent candidates for situations where a quick knock-down agent is needed." The pro-posal noted, however, "they also have drawbacks. Earlier materials showed high safety ratios in rodents, but much lower ratios in primates because of respiratory depression. Previous studies at Edgewood under the . . . ARCAD program led to materials with dramatically improved safety ratios."[25]

Several points can be made about this work. First, U.S. Army research on the fentanyl compounds, including both carfentanil and sufentanil, began at least as early as 1985, and continued into the early 1990s.[26] Second, the work apparently included studies that demonstrated effective aerosol delivery of these opioids in nonhuman primates.[27] Third, the early results clearly illustrate the point made above—that safety margins determined in animal models of analge-sia can be highly misleading indicators of agent "safety" in applications where militarily-relevant incapacitation is the goal. The original developer of these agents, Janssen, had reported safety margins based on studies of analgesia in rats of 277 for fentanyl, 25,000 for sufentanil, and 10,000 for carfentanil.[28] How-ever, opioid doses used for anesthesia, perhaps more relevant to military require-ments, are typically ten times or more the doses used for analgesia.[29] Indeed, the therapeutic index for sufentanil is reported to be twenty-five fold lower for anesthesia in dogs, 800 fold lower in ferrets, and not much more than one in humans.[30] Carfentanil can cause severe respiratory depression and death in non-human primates at doses ranging from 2–14 micrograms/kg, only 7–50 times the median effective dose for analgesia in rats.[31] In this sense, opioids such as sufentanil and carfentanil may be even more toxic than the nerve agent VX, which has a median lethal dose of approximately 15 micrograms/kg.[32]

To solve this problem the ARCAD program took two approaches. First, it tried mixing a fentanyl-type agonist with an antagonist that blocks the respiratory depression. It was this work that led to the "materials with dramatically improved safety ratios,"[33] although the actual success of this approach was later questioned (see below). Second, it continued to search for potential new incapacitating agents, including synthetic opioids that exhibit, in a single compound, "both agonist and antagonist properties toward the opioid receptor."[34] This approach was apparently not successful. However, other searches for new agents resulted in the identification of a class of compounds referred to as the "azabicyclononanes."[35] In preliminary studies these were found to be very potent and "to probably have much better safety ratios" than the fentanyls in rodents and ferrets, but also have slower onset times.

The ARCAD program pursued the development of both payloads and delivery systems (see more below). According to one source, the ARCAD was in advanced development but had not yet progressed to demonstration and validation when it was cancelled in early 1992. Importantly, the program was cancelled not because the problem of developing a highly potent, deliverable and "safe" agent was seen as intractable, but "because of multilateral treaty [i.e., Chemical Weapons Convention] language restricting the use of riot control agents to internal law enforcement only."[36] Despite cancellation of the ARCAD program, military work on potential biochemical payloads continued through at least 1993, when the Army conducted research and development activities on an unidentified chloropyridylazabicycloheptane reported to have "analgesic properties equivalent to the opioids" but thought to operate via a different mechanism, and also synthesized and characterized "novel" sedatives and "a series of new analgesics/anesthetics."[37]

A low level of military research and development (R&D) activity may have continued beyond 1993 as well. In late 1992 or early 1993 the U.S. Army issued a Small Business Innovation Research (SBIR) Program solicitation for proposals that would "suggest, acquire, evaluate and develop chemical immobilizing materials." The request noted that "most recent less-than-lethal programs at U.S. Army ERDEC focused on the fentanyls as candidate compounds," but that for many applications "they have safety ratios that are too low and durations of action that are too long. . . . Thus, candidate chemical immobilizers with improved safety ratios and shorter duration of action are needed."[38] Similarly, ERDEC submitted three proposals in 1994 for research and development of incapacitating biochemical agents, including "calmative agents" related to the serotonin receptor antagonist ketanserin (probably including an agent known as R51703), alpha-2 adrenergic receptor agonists as sedative "chemical immobilizers," previously identified synthetic opioids and azabicyclononanes, and extensive studies (including inhalational exposure) of a series of compounds based on remifentanil, a very fast and ultra-short acting synthetic opioid discovered in the early 1990s.[39] A fourth proposal was submitted for an "advanced concept technology demonstration" of chemical immobilizers designed to "select, acquire and demonstrate the effectiveness and safety of a chemical immobilizer(s) on test animals" including rodents and primates, "with an emphasis on inhalation" and with "limited prototype hardware tests."[40] It is unknown whether these proposals, which requested a total of $3 million for FY1995–FY1997, were funded.

Exploratory research on incapacitating biochemical weapons did continue past 1993 in the civilian sector. Following on earlier studies it had funded at ERDEC starting in 1987, the National Institute of Justice, part of the U.S. Department of Justice, funded work at the Lawrence Livermore National Laboratory to explore the feasibility of "utilizing anesthetic compounds in combination with antidotes to enhance the dose safety of chemical incapacitants" for both civilian law enforcement and "special military operations, and low intensity conflict."[41] The earlier work had focused on the ultra-short acting opioid alfentanil as a candidate incapacitating agent based on the results of animal studies involving delivery via intramuscular injection and inhalation, and had begun development of a dart delivery system. However, the prototype delivery system failed tests and alfentanil was found to be unsatisfactory due to a very low safety margin (of only four "in a hospital setting,") in striking contrast to the reported safety margin of over 1,000 in rats.[42] The new study focused particular attention on sufentanil and another highly potent opioid, lofentanil, and recommended a weapon design that integrated "a timed-release combination of naloxone (an opioid receptor antagonist that would act as a time-delayed antidote) with an ultrafast-acting fentanyl based anesthetic formulation" in a skin-penetrating solvent such as dimethylsulfoxide for rapid transdermal delivery, all delivered by a felt-pad projectile. Work on this or a similar system continued at least until 2002; the funder is unknown.[43] At the same time, the National Institute of Justice funded studies of combining oleoresin capsicum (OC, or pepper spray) with calmative agents.[44] None of this work was far removed from the military, as the Department of Justice and the Department of Defense signed a memorandum of understanding to collaborate on the development of "dual-use technologies for law enforcement agencies and military operations other than war."[45]

The U.S. military renewed its pursuit of incapacitating biochemical weapons in 1997, when the Joint Non-Lethal Weapons Directorate (JNLWD) was established to manage a new Joint Non-Lethal Weapons Program and to provide a central focal point within the Department of Defense for coordinating and integrating "non-lethal" weapons technologies and systems, including research and development activities.[46] Two political and legal factors helped enable this pursuit. First was the U.S. Senate's consent to ratification of the Chemical Weapons Convention (CWC) in April 1997. The Senate included a condition requiring the President to certify that "the United States is not restricted by the Convention in its use of riot control agents, including the use against combatants who are parties to a conflict," in certain military operations, and prohibiting the President from altering or eliminating Executive Order 11850 (8 April 1975). The executive order permitted the use of riot control agents (RCAs) "in defensive military modes to save lives," including use "in situations in which civilians are used to mask or screen attacks and civilian casualties can be reduced or avoided."[47]

Second was the November 1997 release of a "Preliminary Legal Review of Proposed Chemical-Based Nonlethal Weapons," prepared in response to a request from JNLWD, by the Office of the US Navy Judge Advocate General (JAG). The review suggested two legal routes through which incapacitating biochemical weapons might be found to be consistent with the international legal obligations of the United States. In one approach, "convulsives and calmative agents may . . . be RCAs," which, the review says, "are only constrained by the 'method of warfare' restriction" in the CWC and may be used in accordance with EO11850 (according to Article I.5 of the CWC, riot control agents may not be used as a "method of warfare;" see also chapters by Fidler and von Wagner). Alternatively, if calmatives and gastrointestinal convulsives are found to "rely on their toxic properties to have a physiological effect on humans . . . [and] are not considered RCAs, in order to avoid being classified as a prohibited chemical weapon, they would have to be used for the article II(9)(d) 'purpose not prohibited,' the law enforcement purpose . . . the limits of this 'purposes not pro-hibited' are not clear and will be determined be the practice of states."[48] In effect, according to a commentary published in the *Naval War College Review*, "calmatives and gastrointestinal convulsives, if classified as riot control agents, can be acceptable." If not so classified, the "use of chemical-based antipersonnel NLWs . . . in operations other than war" would still be allowable.[49]

The extent of recent U.S. military efforts to develop incapacitating biochemical weapons remains unclear. Several documents shed light on JNLWD's pursuit of this specific capability through 2002, and on its continued pursuit of technologies that could be directly applied to the development of such weapons in the future. Most relate to systems being developed primarily to deliver liquids and powders, including in aerosol form, for counter-personnel applications. The only known agent being tested with these systems at present is the tear gas CS, but each could carry a variety of potential chemical payloads including, in the words of one Army project manager, "markers, taggants, incapacitants, malodorants [and] OC/RCA."[50] Indeed, for each system a use in delivering incapacitating biochemical agents has been envisioned. Whether any decision has been made to actually integrate development of a delivery system with development of a biochemical payload is unknown.

If "incapacitants" in this usage are clearly neither malodorants nor riot control agents,[51] they seem to be what U.S. government officials and advisors now often call "immobilizers" or "calmatives," as in the U.S. Navy JAG opinion discussed above. According to a 2000 presentation by the Director of JNLWD, they belong to the "biotechnical" category of "non-lethal" technologies.[52] Calmatives were also identified as one of twelve key technologies for further development by the participants in a Joint Mission Area Analysis Conference sponsored by JNLWD in October 2000.[53] These "calmatives" were little more than the same types of incapacitating biochemical agents that have already been discussed. A reference book published by the U.S. Air Force Institute for National Security Studies defines calmatives as "biotechnical agents which are sedatives or sleep-inducing drugs; includes alfentanil, fentanyls, ketamine, and BZ."[54] Indeed, a committee of the U.S. National Research Council (part of the National Academies of Science) also included fentanyls as an example of the agents it terms calmatives in a 2003 report, and testimony by an official at the U.S. Department of Justice in 2002 uses the terms "calmative" and "anesthetic" synonymously.[55]

One indication of renewed U.S. military efforts to develop incapacitating biochemical weapon payloads was a comment in the National Research Council report that calmatives were "under study by ECBC [Edgewood Chemical Biological Center, the successor to ERDEC] after [a] lull in R&D for 10 years."[56] Indeed, such study was underway by 1999, according to the 1999 JNLWP annual report,[57] and not just at ECBC. In 2000, for example, the JNLDW—funded at the University of New Hampshire Non-lethal Technology Innovation Center—awarded a grant for a study entitled "NLW and the blood-brain barrier."[58]

Earlier, in October 1999, the U.S. Department of Defense (DoD) Chemical and Biological Defense program issued an SBIR solicitation on behalf of JNLWD for research and development projects that would "demonstrate the feasibility of a safe, reliable chemical immobilizing agent(s) for non-lethal (NL) applications in appropriate military missions and law enforcement situations."[59] Envisioned military uses included peacekeeping missions, crowd control, embassy protection, rescue missions, and counter-terrorism. The solicitation noted that previously developed or proposed agents had been "deficient in one or more technical aspects," including low safety margins and poor reliability in terms of onset time and duration of effects. It went on to note, however, that "recent pharmaceutical developments suggest that new approaches to safer Chemical immobilizers with improved performance characteristics may be available."

SBIR solicitations typically describe three phases of work: phase I start-up and feasibility studies (six months), phase II research and development (up to two years), and phase III technology maturation (funded by private sector or other non-SBIR federal sources). The phase I goals of the 1999 solicitation were as follows: to assess the route of entry of potential immobilizing agents; to conduct an analysis of promising new agents or agent combinations, including "recent breakthroughs in the pharmacological classes such as anesthetics/analgesics, tranquilizers, hypnotics and neuromuscular blockers"; to select the most promising agents and review existing data to identify knowledge gaps relevant to their proposed use; to conduct toxicological tests in order to fill these data gaps; to establish the "mode of immobilization," effective dose, onset time, duration of effects, and safety ratio "in the most appropriate animal species;" and to correlate these results with existing data from other studies, especially those conducted in humans and nonhuman primates, in order to "establish feasibility of use for nonlethal applications."[60]

In early 2001, a phase I contract under this SBIR was awarded to Optimetrics, Inc., whose lead researcher had previously worked on biochemical incapacitants at ERDEC. According to the abstract submitted by Optimetrics, phase I studies would consist of a "Front End Analysis" that would: review existing data on "three new agent combinations with potential for meeting user objectives; define scenarios of use and operational parameters; and conduct toxicological animal tests, and correlate the results with those from previous studies."[61] The fourth 1994 ERDEC research proposal discussed above had also proposed a front end analysis of chemical immobilizers in order to "select candidates with the highest probability of success versus the most likely scenarios of use." Similar to the SBIR solicitation, the 1994 proposal described chemical immobilizers as "chemical compounds that produce incapacitation through immobilization, disorientation, or unconsciousness . . . [potentially including] anesthetics, analgesics, sedatives and hypnotics."[62] The relationship, if any, between the three agent combinations identified in 2000 and the various agents and agent combinations discussed in the 1994 ERDEC proposals is not known.

If the phase I studies were successful, funding would be sought for phase II studies. According to the SBIR solicitation, the goals of phase II would be to establish "desired performance/operational characteristics versus potential scenarios of use," with input solicited from a range of potential military and law enforcement users; to determine the implications of the CWC for the proposed use scenarios; to select "optimum" scenarios; to conduct nonhuman primate and clinical tests "to establish safety and performance characteristics"; and to design and demonstrate "an appropriate delivery technique" such as an aerosol generator for inhalational delivery or a dart for intra-muscular injection. Optimetrics proposed in addition to conduct human volunteer studies to test various routes of entry (inhalation and intramuscular). Although phase I studies were completed, the U.S. military has not commented on their results or whether phase II studies were initiated.[63]

In FY2001 JNLWD also launched its own two-year "Front End Analysis for Non-Lethal Chemicals" in collaboration with ECBC and the U.S. Army's Soldier Biological Chemical Command (SBCCOM, now called RDECOM). The project involved "workshops and analyses culminating in a database of all potential riot control agents, calmatives, etc. with an emphasis on technology advances in the past ten years" in order to "identify feasible non-lethal chemical materials for further testing which have minimal side effects for immobilizing adversaries."[64] Military user workshops would identify the range of desired operational effects during potential applications including crowd control, area denial and clearing facilities. Advances in the pharmaceutical industry would receive particular attention, and a list of promising candidates would be provided to the Judge Advocate General's office for preliminary legal review. As described, the project appears to be both broader (considering more than three specific agent combinations) and shallower (limited to expert elicitation combined with literature analysis) than the Optimetrics effort.

The JNLWD staff expected the front end analysis to be completed by June 2002. Again, any results generated by this effort are not publicly known. However, a three-person study completed in October 2000 by the Applied Research Laboratory at Pennsylvania State University, a leading contractor for JNLWD that is run by a former JNLWD Director, may give some indication of the results that could be expected.[65] The study team, which included two anesthesiologists, conducted a comprehensive review and analysis of the medical research literature and several commercial sources of pharmaceutical information in order to identify pharmaceutical agents that can "produce sedation and/or a calm state as either a primary or secondary effect." The team also provided recommendations for further research and development. The researchers generated a database containing over 7,800 relevant references and, based on their review of this database, identified ten classes of pharmaceutical agents and thirty-two representative agents or agent combinations as having a "high potential" for use in incapacitating biochemical weapons (Table 4.1).

In fact, in contrast to the "high potential" cited by the researchers, many of the agents identified are of questionable value. It is hard to imagine fluoxetine and valium as significant incapacitating agents, while the problems associated

Table 4.1.   Potential Incapacitating Biochemical Agents Identified by the Pennsylvania State University Study

Drug Class	Selected Compounds	Effect[a]
Benzodiazepines	diazepine (valium), midazolam (Versed)	sedation, hypnosis, anxiolysis
Alpha-2 adrenergic receptor antagonists	clonidine dexmedetomidine	sedation, anxiolysis
Dopamine D3 receptor agonists	pramipexole, CI-1007, PD 128097	antipsychotic
Selective Serotonin Reuptake Inhibitors	fluoxetine (Prozac), sertraline (Zoloft), paroxetine	anti-depressant
5-HT1a receptor agonists	buspirone, lesopitron, alnespirone, MCK-242	anxiolysis
Opioid receptor agonists	morphine, carfentanil	sedation, hypnosis
Neurolept anesthetics	propofol, innover (droperidol/fentanyl)	hypnosis
Corticotropin-Releasing Factor receptor antagonists	CP 154,526	anxiolysis
Cholecystokinin B receptor antagonists	CCK-4, CI-988	anxiolysis

[a] hypnosis, in the context of anesthesia, means the induction of sleep; anxiolysis means the reduction of anxiety, mild sedation.

with carfentanil and similar agents have been well documented above. Propofol and Versed are similarly dangerous agents when used outside of the controlled setting of the operation room.[66] Moreover, as the National Research Council's Naval Studies Board concluded in 2003 upon reviewing the results of the ARCAD program and its attempts to find agonist/antagonist combinations that would increase the safety of incapacitating biochemical weapons, "the principal effect was still unconsciousness, which is unacceptable under most interpretations of the CWC."[67] And as a former lead researcher for the U.S. military concluded in 2002, no one has yet "solved the safety-effectiveness problem."[68]

More important than the particular agents identified by the Pennsylvania State researchers may be the fact that they cast a wide net in their search for potential biochemical incapacitants. They noted that "new compounds are in 'the drug development pipeline' that will have an improved ease of delivery, specific control of duration of effect, specific sites of action and other properties that may prove advantageous," and concluded that "new classes of pharmaceutical agents and new compounds are poised to meet the unique requirements of the non-lethal warfare arena."[69] And they made two critical conclusions regarding the process for identifying and developing biochemical incapacitants: (1) that results obtained from clinical research are "vitally needed in [the] assessment of calmative pharmaceutical agents" because preclinical research (animal studies) is not adequate for confirming effective doses and routes of administration or for determining the incidence of unwanted side effects; and (2) that the pharmaceutical and biotechnology industries often surpass academia in conducting basic and applied pharmacology research, and thus that partnerships with the pharmaceutical industry should be developed in order "to better incorporate their knowledge and expertise."[70]

Delivery Systems

THE ADVANCED RIOT CONTROL AGENT DEVICE (ARCAD)[71]

The ARCAD was "a hand held grenade, or device, that can also be shoulder fired from a weapon currently being used or developed" that would deliver a "potent riot control compound . . . [that] will be effective primarily through the respiratory tract." The types of "potent riot control compounds" being considered have been discussed above. According to the acquisition plan approved in May 1991, the ARCAD was to transition to the demonstration and validation phase of development by the end of 1991, with proof of principle tests scheduled for FY1993. The FY1992–FY1993 budget for this phase of development was $10.2 million, exploratory development during FY1991–92 having already cost $4.4 million. However, as noted earlier, the ARCAD program was apparently cancelled in 1992.

THE 81 MM NON-LETHAL MORTAR MUNITION (NLMM)[72]

In May 1997, JNLWD issued a call for proposals for, among other things, "non-lethal delivery systems that provide capabilities for longer ranges and larger payloads." The Army Research Laboratory subsequently submitted a proposal for the development of an 81 mm mortar munition capable of delivering payloads to ranges of 400 meters or more and consisting of two parts, a delivery vehicle and a payload unit.[73] Although it is not publicly known if this project was funded, the proposal described what would be some key elements of the NLMM effort, particularly the focus on an 81 mm caliber munition that could be launched from an existing mortar system and delivered with reduced kinetic energy relative to existing munitions.

Thus, when JNLWD sought industry proposals for long range "non-lethal" delivery systems through its Technology Investment Program in 1998, the requirements included that the delivery system be based on an existing weapons platform, that it be capable of delivering a variety of potential payloads including liquids, powders, solids and "aerosols" at ranges of greater than 200 m and with a coverage area of >25 m², and that no portion of the system could impact the target area with a kinetic energy of greater than 58 foot-pounds.[74] Over time, the range requirement increased, first to 1500 m and later to 2500 m.

In May 1999, and again during FY2001, JNLWD awarded contracts to two companies for initial exploration of various concepts for an 81 mm mortar munition that could meet these requirements. JNLWD simultaneously supported similar in-house activities at the Army Research Development and Engineering Center (ARDEC), which was subsequently asked to manage the overall program in September 2000. The most challenging problem facing the NLMM project, aside from the nature of the payload itself (which remained unspecified), was meeting the requirement for a maximum terminal kinetic energy of <58 foot-pounds. A variety of technical solutions were proposed, including lightweight (composite) delivery vehicles with one or more parachutes, various drag technologies, and combustible or frangible cartridge casings. It was surmised that "the best technical approach will be some mix" of technologies.[75] A forward ejection parachute system based on the M853A1 illumination round and jointly developed by ARDEC in collaboration with one of the contractors ultimately passed proof of principle tests in November 2002 and February 2003.

Also in 1999, JNLWD awarded a contract to PRiMEX Aerospace Company (now General Dynamics—Ordnance and Tactical Systems (GD-OTS), for a proof-of-concept demonstration of a payload dissemination unit called the Overhead Liquid Dispersion System (or OLDS, originally called the Overhead Chemical Agent Dispersion System). According to the final report submitted by PRiMEX, the OLDS was "conceived as a method to rapidly distribute non-lethal crowd control liquids . . . from distances of greater than 350 feet. . . . The dispersed liquid could be any one of a range of materials including malodorants, tear gas agents, marking agents, pepper sprays, etc."[76] The key component of the OLDS was the dispersion system that consisted of a container housing a liquid agent and a dispersion gas generator. The system was designed such that, upon pressurization caused by release of an inert gas by the gas generator, the container would fragment uniformly to ensure even dispersion of the liquid agent. The pressurization rate was optimized to disperse the liquid over a large area in sufficiently sized droplets. In tests carried out in March 2000, the payload unit "demonstrated rapidly dispersing nearly 90 in³ [1475 cc] of liquid payload over a 40 foot diameter area at distances of more than 350 feet from where it was launched, while minimizing any hazards associated with debris size and shape."[77] U.S. Army program managers considered these tests to be successful. The system could be optimized to deliver different sized droplets (from 0.5 inches to vapor) depending on the physical properties of the agent and the desired application. The final report noted that "determining the non-lethal substance or substances to pursue for use in the OLDS is critical for dispersion system optimization."[78]

In September 2001, JNLWD awarded a follow-on contract to GD-OTS to adapt the OLDS for use in delivery vehicles that were simultaneously undergoing concept development. In a March 2003 presentation, the program manager for the NLMM project described the ARDEC delivery vehicle as incorporating a single ejectable payload canister and then went on to discuss the "overhead dispersion concept," with specific reference to the GD-OTS work just described. The manager noted that "successful live-fire demos" were conducted in November 2002 and February 2003 "using a frangible case configuration," and a simulated CS payload. The manager also noted that GD-OTS was continuing its liquid payload dispersal studies, and that ECBC had begun a malodorant payload study.[79]

Significant changes were made in the 81 mm NLMM, re-named the Non-Lethal Mortar Carrier Projectile, between 2003 and 2005. Whether the OLDS was still being considered for inclusion in this munition is not publicly known, but would have required further design changes to the system. The NLMM as presented in 2005 appears to include four payload units, each of which is capable of holding approximately 35 cc of agent. It seems likely that work on the NLMM continues, although it is unclear if or when the first critical go/no-go decision point in the U.S. weapons development process (called "Milestone A") required for advancement of the program was reached. Authority and funding for continued development of the system would have transferred from JNLWD to the Army soon after a positive Milestone-A decision was reached. In this regard, FY2005 was the last year of documented JNLWD funding for the NLMM. By this time, JNLWD had spent approximately $5.5 million on the NLMM program since FY2000,[80] and the Army was expected to spend at least $42 million more on the program through FY2009.[81] While the FY2006 and FY2007 Army budget documents suggest that the program is continuing, they do not provide enough information to make a more definitive assessment of its status.[82]

In addition to the 81mm NLMM, work was initiated in 2003 on a 120 mm mortar cartridge design based on the XM984 munition currently in development for use in the Future Combat System Non Line-of-Sight (NLOS) Mortar.[83] The XM984 can deliver up to fifty-four submunitions at distances of up to 12 km.[84]

ARTILLERY

Sometime before or during 2004 work was also initiated on a 155 mm munition called the "XM1063 Non-Lethal Personnel Suppression Projectile." This projectile, based on the M864 artillery projectile currently in use, is also being designed for the Non Line-of-Sight Cannon. It will have a range of at least 20 km, and perhaps as much as 28 km.[85] "Preliminary advanced concept non-lethal payload designs" were developed and tested in FY2004 at Yuma Proving Grounds.[86] Contracts totaling at least $640,000 were awarded in October 2004 and February 2005 to GD-OTS for an extensive list of activities in support of ongoing design and test efforts, including payload design refinements and effectiveness assessments (including agent concentration, area coverage, and agent effectiveness testing at ECBC). Other activities include completing prototype design and fabrication, conducting component and subsystem tests, developing and testing the liquid payload dissemination system (presumably similar to the OLDS), conducting a non-lethal "personnel suppression payload delivery full up demonstration using the final projectile design with impact energy mitigated submunitions at 20 km," and compiling data "for legal and compliance review." No additional information is publicly available on either the 120 mm or the 155 mm systems or their payloads.

SMALL ARMS

The Airburst Non-Lethal Munition (ANLM)[87]

In the mid 1990s, the U.S. Army began development of the XM29 Objective Individual Combat Weapon (OICW), a dual component 5.56 mm assault rifle/20 mm grenade launcher designed to provide "greater than five times the lethality at twice the range" of the M16 assault rifle and the M203 grenade launcher. The grenade launcher component would use airburst munitions that could be set to explode at a defined location in space relative to the target. In 2004 the Army decided to split the system, now years behind schedule and facing major engineering problems, into two separate weapons—the XM8 assault rifle and the XM25 grenade launcher—and to increase the caliber of the airburst munition to 25 mm.[88] Work on the XM8 was halted in October 2005, while work on the XM25 continues with the final development phase set to begin in FY2006 and initial production and fielding in FY2009.[89]

In March 2000, JNLWD initiated development of a 20 mm "Airburst Non-Lethal Munition" (ANLM) for the XM29 in order to "exploit [the] ability of the OICW to airburst munitions at a precise location in space to emplace or employ NL [non-lethal] concepts."[90] ANLM design requirements included the ability to deliver liquids, powders, "aerosols," and objects at a range of 5 m to 1000 m, and the ability to scale the design to other size rounds. Primary interest focused on the delivery of powder, liquid and aerosol payloads, potentially including "taggants, incapacitants, malodorants, [and] OC/RCA [pepper spray/riot control agent]."[91] The preliminary focus was on CS because "there is significant data available on CS dissemination, it is typically easy to weaponize." However, according to one program manager "there may be many other RCAs . . . once the development program begins . . . other payloads and dissemination methods can be more thoroughly investigated."[92] All publicly known dissemination tests have been performed using CS in either powder or small pyrotechnic pellet form.

According to an independent technology assessment report issued in 2002, the ANLM's main challenge is its small size. In fact, to be successful the ANLM must overcome three coupled challenges: preventing serious injury or lethality due either to inadequate minimization of the projectile's terminal kinetic energy or to the air-burst itself; overcoming payload volume limitations which might limit the practical effectiveness of the munition; and achieving effective payload dissemination. According to the report, "the key component of this non-lethal delivery is the fusing mechanism used to initiate the bursting charge. If it fails, the projectile could be lethal."[93] However, this critical component occupied over 60 percent of the total payload volume, yielding a theoretical maximum of 4.5 grams of CS dissemination per munition.[94] The program managers therefore generally assumed that several munitions would have to be fired at any given target to achieve effective results, but the independent report concluded that for some payloads "too many rounds might be needed to achieve an effect."[95] Thus, the review panel recommended that a front end analysis be conducted to identify other payloads, stating that "there may be better and more concentrated agents" that are "well suited" for the ANLM, and that "new agents are continually emerging."[96] As noted earlier, JNLWD was in fact doing just that. In the final analysis, the review panel concluded that an effective payload dissemination mechanism had not yet been achieved, and that "understanding . . . payload dissemination is the munition's highest risk area, especially for chemical agent payloads."[97] According to one program manager, "very little is known about the dissemination of small size munitions such as the [20] mm OICW configuration. In our opinion, the difficulty of scaling down in size was [a] larger problem than anticipated."[98]

These challenges were recognized early on by program managers, who stated that the "preliminary focus is on [the] CS effect and overcoming the KE [kinetic energy] of [the] projectile near [the] target."[99] Several technical solutions were being explored as of 2002, including proximity fuzes and MEMS (micro-electro-mechanical systems)—based fuzes, the latter of which could increase the payload volume available for agent to approximately 12 cc. Modeling and simulation studies and payload (CS) effectiveness studies, including the effects of burst height, dosage, dissemination method, and weather, and the determination of a "suitable concentration/dosage metric" were continuing in collaboration with SBCCOM/ECBC.[100] In addition, an initial scalability analysis for a 40 mm munition for the

M203 (theoretical maximum of 26.5 grams of CS) and the automatic Mk19 (theoretical maximum of 16.1 grams of CS) grenade launchers was completed in May 2001.

Little additional information on the ANLM is available past 2002. With the decision in 2004 to shelve the XM29 and pursue the XM25 grenade launcher independently, the caliber size of the ANLM was increased to 25 mm. A 2005 presentation by the Acquisition Division Chief of JNLWD suggested that efforts on both 25 mm and 40 mm ANLM rounds containing chemical agent payloads were continuing. Like the XM29 and XM25 programs, the ANLM program has moved more slowly than planned. Initial goals to reach Milestone A by the first quarter of FY2002 and Milestone B by the first quarter of FY2004 were pushed back a year or more by the middle of 2002. The FY2007 budget request for JNLWD includes $1.94 million for continued development of the 25 mm round, and since JNLWD typically does not fund projects beyond Milestone B[101], this suggests that the target dates have further slipped. Of note, over $5.6 million had already been spent or budgeted from FY2002 to FY2006.[102]

"Smart" Bullets/Rocket Assisted Safe Projectile

JNLWD awarded two Small Business Innovation Research contracts to Agentai Inc. in 2002 for work to develop "smart" bullets and a Rocket Assisted Safe Projectile that would be "non-lethal over their entire range, from muzzle to max range" [11 m for the bullets, 500 m for the projectile fired from an M203]. In addition to delivering blunt trauma as their primary role, the projectiles would also be "designed to deliver secondary payloads . . . includ[ing] chemical agents that can further incapacitate or maintain the incapacitation of the targeted individual."[103] Work on the payloads themselves was not included in the contract, and the outcome of this high-risk effort is unknown. The somewhat fanciful language describing the technology was matched by language describing the outcome: "Once . . . this new technology is widely presented, demonstrated and accepted by police forces, security personnel and security forces, a vast ammunition market will open up. This provides for great commercial opportunity, which can later extend to the entire ammunition world market."[104] Regardless of the viability of the specific technology being pursued by Agentai, such proliferation of incapacitating biochemical weapons is among the greatest concerns of those who seek to prevent their development.

The Bullet Trap Rifle Grenade Cargo Projectile

In February 2003 the U.S. Army received United States Patent number 6523478 for a "rifle-launched non-lethal cargo dispenser," described as "a projectile adapted for launching from the end of a rifle muzzle for safely and effectively de-livering a payload."[105] Among the payloads claimed in the patent were electronic devices, unmanned aerial vehicles, flash-bang munitions, sting balls, concussion grenades and explosive devices. Most relevant to this discussion were payloads "consisting of an aerosol composition . . . further selected from the group con-sisting of smoke, crowd control agents, biological agents, chemical agents, ob-scurants, marking agents, dyes and inks, chaffs and flakes."[106] The U.S. Army re-cently secured a correction that eliminated chemical and biological agents from the list of potential payloads after news of the patent sparked concerns that the development of the projectile violated the Biological and Chemical Weapons Conventions.[107]

Although the patent was changed, it is clear that the projectile was designed to disseminate agents as aerosols, and was envisioned as potentially carrying a wide variety of agent payloads. According to the patent, "the mechanism gener-ally comprises a frangible casing defining a filler space containing particles of a powder, a liquid or an aerosolizable . . . as the fill space is pressurized [by an ex-panding propellant], the contents . . . are deagglomerated and fluidized until the frangible casing ruptures and releases the contents in the form of an aerosol cloud."[108]

The rifle launched projectile was collaboratively developed by Engineering Technologies Inc. and ECBC as the "bullet trap rifle grenade cargo projectile." According to a 2002 presentation, it has a maximum range of over 500 ft and is capable of delivering up to 230 grams of payload agent. The projectile is one of several "methods of use" envisioned for the "propellant based aerosol generating device" developed by Engineering Technologies Inc and ECBC and patented in 2000. Other delivery mechanisms in development as of 2002 included 38 mm and 40 mm cartridges holding at least 60 cc of agent, 18 and 54 chamber dis-penser units, and a 12-shot vehicle mounted cartridge launcher capable of deliv-ering cartridges holding 121 cc of agent to a distance of 25 m to 300 m.[109]

The Ring Airfoil Projectile and Launcher

The National Institute of Justice has funded efforts by Vanek Prototype to de-velop and improve a multi-shot launcher and associated ring airfoil projectiles for delivering pepper spray under its Civilian Less Lethal Program. Ring Airfoil Projectiles (RAPs) were first developed by the U.S. Army in the early 1970s as high explosive fragmentation projectiles. Their unique shape, described as "like an airplane wing curled into a ring," generates high lift and low drag, and by spinning them at launch, relatively flat trajectories with extended range are achievable. RAPs with bodies made of a rubber-like material containing cavities for holding "chemical-incapacitation agents" (in this case, CS) that would be dispersed upon impact were also designed, but never used.[110] Little additional research on RAPs was conducted for approximately twenty years until, in 1997, the National Institute of Justice showed renewed interest in the concept. Most recently, in 2004 the National Institute of Justice funded Vanek Prototype to develop a multi-round RAP launcher (previous launchers were all single shot) and to "continue development of RAP as agent carrier [by] initiat[ing] work on blister pack strip as a means of loading and maintaining a chemical agent in the RAP until impact (sic)."[111] Earlier, Vanek had noted that the RAP could deliver payloads including "incapacitants, irritants, malodorants, and marking agents."[112] Vanek Prototype recently received United States Patent for its "multi-shot ring airfoil projectile launcher."[113] In addition to the RAP, the National Institute of Justice is developing a pepper spray projectile and dispenser with a 100 foot launch range able to disperse pepper spray, and presumably other chemicals, in a room within one second.[114]

OTHER DELIVERY SYSTEMS

Dart and paintball type systems were discussed above in the context of work funded by the National Institute of Justice. Although dart-based delivery appears to have been rejected, paintball type systems were apparently still in development as of 2002.[115] Finally, from 1999 until at least 2002, JNLWD funded work at the University of New Hampshire to develop microencapsulants that would offer "significantly improved ways of delivering chemical agents." The microcapsules could be delivered by most of the delivery vehicles discussed above. Indeed, the University of New Hampshire partnered with one of the companies working on the 81 mm NLMM for this project.[116] The microcapsules would decompose after contact with skin and water to release the chemical agent inside. They would be compatible with a wide range of agents, including tear gas, malodorants, markers, and anesthetics.

Research and Development of Incapacitating Biochemical Agents in Other Nations

As recent events in Russia illustrate, the United States has not been alone in its pursuit of incapacitating biochemical weapons. Indeed, these events imply that Russia has not only developed such weapons, but that it has also stockpiled them and trained troops in their use. On the evening of 23 October 2002 a group of Chechen rebels raided the Dubrovka theater center in Moscow during a performance of the play Nord-Ost and took approximately 800 people hostage. The hostage takers were well armed and the women were wearing high explosives. They demanded a withdrawal of Russian troops from Chechnya and threatened to kill the hostages if their demand was not met. A little over two days later, on the morning of October 26, Russian military Special Forces disseminated an unknown biochemical agent through the ventilation system, apparently putting both hostages and the Chechen women into a deep sleep. Approximately thirty minutes later, the troops stormed the theater, killing all of the Chechen hostage takers (including the apparently unconscious women) and ending the crisis. However, approximately 125 hostages died from the effects of the gas, and many more were severely injured. Several days later, the Russian Health Minister revealed that the gas contained a derivative of the potent narcotic fentanyl, a compound related to morphine.[117] Carfentanil and sufentanil have been the subject of most speculation, and it is possible that whatever opioid was used was also mixed with another agent. Russian Special Forces again used a "knockout gas" in October 2005 against Chechen rebels holding two women hostage in a shop in the city of Nalchik.[118]

Interestingly, a paper presented by several Russian researchers at the third European Symposium on Non-Lethal Weapons in 2005 reported the results of their efforts to model "the scenario of calmative application in a building with deterred hostages," in order to identify ways to reduce or eliminate fatalities.[119] The researchers noted the well known "factors of uncertainty," namely, individual variation in vulnerability to the effects of a gas, "non-homogeneous spatial distribution of gas in the building," and "scattering of waiting time since gas attack to medical aid," and focused their efforts on modeling the effects of the latter two factors. As baseline criteria for "acceptable interval of impact," the researchers set as a minimum dose that which effectively incapacitates 95–97 percent of individuals exposed, and as a maximum, that which causes severe injury or death in 3–5 percent of individuals exposed. Even so, they found that, because of variations in spatial distribution of the agent and exposure time, "the 'desired operating envelope' simply disappears. If the level of 95 percent efficiency is absolutely required to neutralize terrorists and to prevent mass destruction, there is no chance to eliminate hard consequences and fatalities. Calculations show that the majority of the hostages can get serious poisoning and part of them— fatality. This is the cost of releasing if no other solutions [are] left."[120] The researchers thus concluded that either the safety margin of the biochemical weapon must be expanded or the influence of variations must be reduced. One possible approach suggested by the researchers, which they noted was "under discussion," was "to apply gaseous calmative agent and antidote together in the same composition or consequently after some delay."[121] This approach is reminiscent of that taken by U.S. military researchers, with little apparent success, in the late 1980s and early 1990s. Another possible approach was to develop optimal strategies for rendering medical aid to affected individuals, such as prioritizing those individuals who appear most affected rather than treating all individuals equally.[122] This approach also has its supporters, who claim that the Russian use of incapacitating biochemicals should in fact be seen as a success, the high death toll being due solely to poor planning and execution.[123] It should be noted, however, that in light of the inability to separate a weapon from the context of its use, such an interpretation is of questionable validity. Whatever the ultimate outcome, the researchers noted that "the full solution [to this difficult problem] . . . demands the big intensive work of many scientific teams within several years."[124]

In early 2004 one expert close to the U.S. incapacitating biochemical weapon program remarked that "it would not be surprising if a number of countries were conducting more detailed and renewed research as a result" of the Moscow theater siege.[125] The Czech military has been conducting research on incapacitants since the year 2000, including studies in rabbits, nonhuman primates and human volunteers to examine the effects of different mixtures of various drugs in order to determine which combinations and doses result in "reversible immobilization."[126] The drugs being studied include ketamine (a dissociative anesthetic), medetomidine and dexmedetomidine (alpha 2 adrenergic receptor agonists), midazolam (a benzodiazepine), and fentanyl (an opioid), as well as remifentanil, alfentanil and etorphine (all opioids, tested only in rabbits). The agents were delivered via intramuscular injection—all were found to have relatively long (>1 minute) onset times via this delivery route. Animal studies further investigated nasal and inhalation administration, oral administration, and transdermal administration. None of the drugs and techniques studied could yet be said to be "successful." For instance, the researchers noted that "[i]f using dexmedetomidine for primate immobilization, close monitoring of heart rate during immobilization is absolutely essential."[127] Such monitoring would not, of course, be possible for most applications of incapacitating biochemical weapons.

NATO has similarly listed "chemical technologies [that] could act on the central nervous system by calmatives, dissociative agents, [and] equilibrium agents," and "by convulsives" as two of its seventeen antipersonnel "non-lethal" "technologies of interest."[128] Israeli special forces are known to have attempted at least one assassination using fentanyl sprayed into the ear of the target, suggesting that Israel has also investigated and developed biochemical weapons.[129] And there are indications that China may be interested as well—an article written by two Chinese analysts that appeared in the U.S. Army journal *Military Review* in July 2005 argued that the "times call for new kinds of weapons, and modern biotechnology can contribute such weapons." "War through the command of biotechnology," they said, will ultimately "lead to success through ultramicro, nonlethal, and reversible effects. . . . Modern biotechnology offers an enormous potential military advantage."[130]

Conclusion

For all of the efforts have been placed on the development of incapacitating biochemical weapons, there remains little evidence for success. There is no publicly available evidence that the United States has developed and fielded incapacitating biochemical weapons for either military or police use, other than scattered reports that U.S. Special Forces are equipped with "knock-out" agents.[131] The experiences of the United States and Russia suggest that the challenges to developing incapacitating biochemical weapons remain substantial. As noted earlier, one former lead researcher for the U.S. military said in 2002 that, to his knowledge, no one had yet "solved the safety-effectiveness problem."

Nonetheless, at least several nations continue to pursue incapacitating biochemical weapons. In 2004, an anesthesiologist close to the U.S. incapacitants program spoke of "recent and current research in this area," which he said is focusing on improving delivery mechanisms and developing "more potent, faster acting, safer compounds."[132] Little information is publicly available about U.S. activities since early 2003, when the Front End Analysis was briefly posted on the JNLWD website. No U.S. government documents concerning delivery systems have made references to immobilizers, calmatives, or incapacitants other than malodorants, tear gas and pepper spray since 2002. This may reflect a decision to discontinue or put a hold on such work, or it may simply mean that the work is continuing under conditions of increased secrecy. A third possibility also exists—that the U.S. military has already identified a short list of biochemical incapacitants it considers adequate and has placed payload development on hold pending further improvement of delivery and dissemination devices. Indeed, as we have seen, delivery and dissemination itself is one of the most challenging problems facing the development of incapacitating biochemical weapons. At some point, however, a precise payload must be identified in order to complete development of a dispersion system. Indeed, the design process for the NLMM has apparently been impeded due to a lack of information about the precise payload it will be carrying.[133]

In contrast to the United States, almost no information is available concerning efforts by other nations to develop incapacitating biochemical weapons. Yet, as discussed above, such efforts are certainly occurring, perhaps spurred on by the hope that advances in science and technology will allow the significant current challenges to be overcome. As the U.S. anesthesiologist noted, "remarkable progress has been made in the techniques to deliver immobilizing agents and in the development of safer, faster-acting potent compounds of extremely short duration in the last decade." Much of this work, he wrote, "is either privileged or currently not available to the public [i.e., classified or proprietary] and therefore unpublished."[134]

In the end, whether incapacitating biochemical weapons are developed and used is likely to depend at least as much on the level of lethality and permanent harm that governments and the international community decide is "acceptable," as on advances in science and technology. All that is really needed is for a biochemical incapacitant to be viewed as being "good enough." Advances in science and technology may indeed ultimately be sufficient to enable the development of weapons that are, or more to the point that *appear* to be, "good enough." And what will be considered "good enough" will very likely differ from one time and place to another. Thus, when one proponent poses the question "human immobilization: is the experience in Moscow just the beginning?"[135] the answer may well be "yes."

Notes

1. M. Dando and M. Furmanski, "Midspectrum Incapacitant Programs," in Mark Wheelis, Lajos Rozsa, and Malcolm Dando, eds., *Deadly Cultures: Biological Weapons Since 1945* (Cambridge, MA: Harvard University Press, 2006): 243, 250.

2. J. S. Ketchum and F. R. Sidell, "Incapacitating Agents," in Frederick R. Sidell, Ernest T. Takafugi, and David R. Franz, eds., *Medical Aspects of Chemical and Biological Warfare*, (Washington, D.C.: Borden Institute, 1997). Also in Part I of B.G. Russ Zajtchuk and Col. Ronald F. Bellamy, ed., *Textbook of Military Medicine* (Washington, D.C.: TMM Publications, Borden Institute, 1997): 295.

3. J. P. Zanders, "Assessing the Risk of Chemical and Biological Weapons Proliferation to Terrorists," *Nonproliferation Review* 6 (Fall 1999): 23–25.

4. M. Furmanski, "Military Interest in Low-Lethality Biochemical Agents: The Historical Interaction of Advocates, Experts, Pragmatists, and Politicians" (background paper at Symposium on Incapacitating Biochemical Weapons: Scientific, Military, Legal and Policy Perspectives and Prospects, delivered in Geneva, Switzerland on 11 June 2005): 19, <http://www.armscontrolcenter.org/cbw/symposium/papers/pdf/20050601_symposium_military_interest.pdf> (1 July 2006).

5. J. M. Kenny, "Human Effects Advisory Panel Program" (power point presentation at the Non-Lethal Defense IV Conference, sponsored by the National Defense Industrial Association, March 20–22, 2000), slide 23, <http://www.dtic.mil/ndia/nld4/kenny.pdf> (15 July 2006).

6. L. Klotz, M. Furmanski, and M. Wheelis, "Beware the Siren's Song: Why 'Non-Lethal' Incapacitating Chemical Agents are Lethal," Scientists Working Group and Biological and Chemical Weapons (March 2003), <http://www.armscontrolcenter.org/cbw/wg/wg/wg_2003_sirensong_nonlethal_chemical_agents.pdf>, (8 March 2007).

7. V. L. Klochikhin, A. A. Lushnikov, and V. A. Zagaynov, "Principles of Modeling of the Scenario of Calmative Application in a Building with Deterred Hostages" (paper presented to the Third European Symposium on Non-Lethal Weapons, Stadthalle, Germany, 10–12 May 2005).

8. P. M. Wax, C. E. Becker, and S. C. Curry, "Unexpected 'Gas' Casualties in Moscow: A Medical Toxicology Perspective," *Annals of Emergency Medicine* 41 (August 2003): 700–5.

9. A. S. Nies, "Principles of Therapeutics," in Joel G. Hardman and Lee E. Limbard eds., *Goodman and Gilman's The Pharmacological Basis of Therapeutics,* 10th edition (Dallas, TX: McGraw-Hill, 2001): 51.

10. See, for example, Ketchum and Sidell, "Incapacitating Agents," 296. Actually, some information on upper exposure limits can be gained from clinical data on surgical patients, as higher doses than would normally be tested in healthy individuals are often used in hospital settings. This is possible because the doses can be tightly controlled, the patients are constantly monitored and often ventilated, rapid intervention can be administered in the case of adverse effects and a host of other measures are taken to ensure patient safety. Toxicological data based on overdose cases can also provide some indication of upper exposure limits. As noted in the text, these sources of data indicate that potential biochemical incapacitants have low safety margins in humans. The author is indebted to Martin Furmanski for these observations. On the use of anesthesia in clinical settings, see, for example, D. A. E. Shephard, "The Changing Pattern of Anesthesia, 1954–2004: A Review Based on the Content of the *Canadian Journal of Anesthesia* in its First Half-Century," *Canadian Journal of Anesthesia* 52 (March 2005): 238–48.

11. Nies, "Principles of Therapeutics," 48.

12. B. D. Anderson and P. M. Grant, "Dose Safety Margin Enhancement for Chemical Incapacitation and Less-Than-Lethal Targeting," NIJ Final Report (Lawrence Livermore National Laboratory, January 1997).

13. Klochikhin, Lushnikov, and Zagaynov, "Principles of Modeling." The authors arrive at the following important conclusion on the basis of their study: "If the level of 95 percent efficiency is absolutely required to neutralize terrorists and to prevent mass destruction, there is no chance to eliminate hard consequences and fatalities. Calculations show that the majority of hostages can get serious poisoning and part of them—fatality. This is the cost of releasing if no other solutions left," 3; Klotz, Furmanski, and Wheelis, "Siren's Song," 4.

14. G. Gugliotta, "U.S. Finds Hurdles in Search for Non-Lethal Gas," *Washington Post*, 1 November 2002, A30, quoting C. Parker Ferguson.

15. M. Wheelis and M. Dando, "Neurobiology: A Case Study of the Imminent Militarization of Biology," *International Review of the Red Cross* 87 (September 2005): 561; M.R. Dando, "The Danger to the Chemical Weapons Convention from Incapacitating

Chemicals," *First CWC Review Conference Paper* no. 4 (Bradford, UK: Department of Peace Studies, University of Bradford, March 2003): 11.

16. J. M. Lakoski, W. B. Murray, and J. M. Kenny, "The Advantages and Limitations of Calmatives for Use as a Non-Lethal Technique," Applied Research Laboratory, College of Medicine of The Pennsylvania State University, 2000.

17. For sales data see IMS Health, "Leading Therapy Classes by Global Pharmaceutical Sales, 2005," <http://www.imshealth.com/ims/portal/front/articleC/0,2777,6599_77478579_77479683,00.html> (18 July 2006).

18. Committee for an Assessment of Non-Lethal Weapons Science and Technology, Naval Studies Board, National Research Council, *An Assessment of Non-Lethal Weapons Science and Technology*, (Washington, D.C.: National Academies Press, 2003), 27, 63–64; Edgewood Research, Development & Engineering Center (hereafter ERDEC), "Antipersonnel Chemical Immobilizers: Synthetic Opioids" (research proposal, 17 April 1994), <http://www.sunshine-project.org/incapacitants/jnlwdpdf/edgeopiate.pdf> (1 July 2006); J. P. P. Robinson, "Disabling Chemical Weapons: A Documentary Chronology of Events, 1945–2003" (unpublished working paper, Harvard Sussex Program, University of Sussex, November 1, 2003, hereafter Robinson Chronology). The author is indebted to J. P. Perry Robinson for sharing his Documentary Chronology, which provides by far the most complete account of publicly available information on attempts to develop and use incapacitants between 1945 and 2003.

19. One report suggests that this effort may have extended as far back as the 1970s. See D. Ruppe, "United States: U.S. Military Studying Non-Lethal Chemicals," *Global Security Newswire*, 1 November 2002, <http://www.nti.org/d_newswire/issues/newswires/2002_11_4.html#7> (18 July 2006).

20. ERDEC, "Antipersonnel Chemical Immobilizers: Sedatives" (research proposal, 27 April 1994), <http://www.sunshine-project.org/incapacitants/jnlwdpdf/edgesedate.pdf> (19 July 2006).

21. News Chronology, *Chemical Weapons Convention Bulletin* 26, Harvard Sussex Program on CBW Armament and Arms Limitations, December 1994, (entry for 15–18 November 1994): 29.

22. P. L. Bailey, J. Wilbrink, P. Zwanikken, N. L. Pace, and others, "Anesthetic Induction with Fentanyl," *Anesthesia and Analgesia* 64 (January 1985): 48–53.

23. Ketchum and Sidell, "Incapacitating Agents," 293; C. McLeish, "The Governance of Dual-Use Technologies in Chemical Warfare" (M.Sc. dissertation, University of Sussex, 1997): 55–65; Dando and Furmanski, "Midspectrum Incapacitant Programs;" Robinson Chronology.

24. L. E. Mather, "Clinical Pharmacokinetics of Fentanyl and its Newer Derivatives," *Clinical Pharmacokinetics*, 8 (September-October 1983): 422–46; W. F. Van Bever, C. J. Niemegeers, K. H. Schellekens, and P. A. Janssen, "N-4-Substituted 1-(2-Arylethyl)-4-Piperidinyl-N-Phenylpropanamides, A Novel Series of Extremely Potent Analgesics with Unusually High Safety Margin," *Arzneimittel-Forshung* 26 (no. 8, 1976): 1548–51.

25. ERDEC, "Synthetic Opioids."

26. R. G. Thompson, D. Menking, and J. J. Valdes, "Opiate Receptor Binding Properties of Carfentanil," Technical Report A736781, Chemical Research Development and

Engineering Center, Aberdeed Proving Ground, MD (November 1987), <http://www
.stormingmedia.us/73/7367/A736781.html> (June 2006); ERDEC, "Demonstration
of Chemical Immobilizers" (research proposal, 27 April 1994), <http://www.sunshine-
project.org/incapacitants/jnlwdpdf/edgedemon.pdf> (14 July 2006).

27. T. Stanley, "Human Immobilization: Is the Experience in Moscow Just the Beginning?" *European Journal of Anesthesiology* 20 (June 2003): 427–28.

28. Van Bever, Niemegeers, Schellekens, and Janssen, "Novel Series"; C. J.
Niemegeers, K. H. Schellekens, W. F. Van Bever, and P. A. Janssen, "Sufentanil: A Very
Potent and Extremely Safe Intravenous Morphine-Like Compound in Mice, Rats, and
Dogs," *Arzneimittel-Forschung* 26, (no. 8, 1976): 1551–56.

29. "Opioids," <http://www.anesthetist.com/anaes/drugs/opioids.htm> (accessed 1
July 2006); Taylor Pharmaceuticals, "Sufenta (Sufentanil Citrate) Injection," package insert, at <http://www.akorn.com/documents/catalog/package_inserts/1/098/050-01.pdf>
(14 July 2006).

30. J. de Castro, A. Van de Water, L. Wouters, R. Xhonneux, and others, "Comparative Study of Cardiovascular, Neurological and Metabolic Side Effects of 8 Narcotics in
Dogs," *Act Anesthesiologica Belgica* 30 (March 1979): 55–69; Klotz, Furmanski, and
Wheelis, "Siren's Song," 7; U.S. Patent Number 5834477, "Opiate Analgesic Formulation with Improved Safety," assigned to Secretary of the Army, U.S.A., 10 November
1998, <http://www.patentstorm.us/patents/5834477-fulltext.html> (11 July 2005); and
"Opioids," <http://www.anesthetist.com/anaes/drugs/opioids.htm>, (8 March 2007).
Extensive clinical experience demonstrates that the fentanyls can have significant adverse
effects in a substantial portion of patients when used at doses required for anesthesia, and
even at doses required for analgesia. They are considered safe in hospital settings because
dosages can be individualized and for the reasons discussed in note 10. One authoritative
source has this to say: "SUFENTA (sufentanil citrate) SHOULD BE ADMINISTERED
ONLY BY PERSONS SPECIFICALLY TRAINED IN THE USE OF INTRA-
VENOUS AND EPIDURAL ANESTHETICS AND MANAGEMENT OF THE
RESPIRATORY EFFECTS OF POTENT OPIOIDS. AN OPIOID ANTAGONIST,
RESUSCITATIVE AND INTUBATION EQUIPMENT AND OXYGEN SHOULD
BE READILY AVAILABLE," (emphasis in original), Taylor Pharmaceuticals, "Sufenta."

31. K. S. Kearns, B. Swenson, and E. C. Ramsay, "Dosage Trials with Transmucosal Carfentanil Citrate in Non-Human Primates," *Zoo Biology* 18 (24 January 2000): 397–402.

32. D. R. Franz, "Defense Against Toxin Weapons," in Frederick R. Sidell, Ernest T.
Takafugi, and David R. Franz, eds., *Medical Aspects of Chemical and Biological Warfare* in
Part I of B. G. Zajtchuk and Col. Ronald F. Bellamy, eds., *Textbook of Military Medicine*
(Washington, D.C.: TMM Publications, Borden Institute, 1997): 607.

33. ERDEC, "Opioids."

34. Robinson chronology, entry for 13 November 1990.

35. ERDEC, "Opioids."

36. ERDEC, "Demonstration of Chemical Immobilizers."

37. Robinson chronology, entry for 6 January 1994.

38. New Chronology, *Chemical Weapons Convention Bulletin* 22, Harvard Sussex Program on CBW Armament and Arms Limitations, December 1993, (entry for 12 August
1993): 11.

39. ERDEC, "Synthetic Opioids"; ERDEC, "Sedatives"; ERDEC, "Anti-Personnel Calmative Agents" (research proposal submitted 27 April 1994).

40. ERDEC, "Demonstration of Chemical Immobilizers."

41. Anderson and Grant, "Dose Safety Margin"; Robinson chronology, entry for 3 March 1989.

42. L. Pilant, "Less-than-Lethal Weapons: New Solutions for Law Enforcement," *Science and Technology* (Publication of the International Association of Chiefs of Police, December 1993): 3; Mather, "Clinical Pharmacokinetics."

43. Naval Studies Board, *Non-Lethal Weapons*, 124.

44. A. T. DePersia and J. Cecconi, "Less–than–Lethal Program" (PowerPoint presentation to Non-Lethal Technology and Academic Research Symposium III, University of New Hampshire, November 2003), slide 14, <http://www.sunshine-project.org/incapacitants/jnlwdpdf/NIJcalm.pdf> (20 July 2006).

45. J. Lancaster, "Pentagon, Justice Dept. Set Plans for Sharing Non-Lethal Technology," *Washington Post*, March 23, 1994, A3; U.S. Department of Justice, National Institute of Justice, *NIJ Research Plan 1995-1996* (Washington, D.C.: Department of Justice, 1995), 20. Cooperation is ongoing, including with the Department of Homeland Security. See T. DePersia, "Homeland Security Advanced Research Projects Agency" (PowerPoint presentation dated 25 January 2004) <http://www.hsarpabaa.com/main/HBCU/9_DePersia.pdf> (17 July 2006).

46. Department of Defense Directive 3000.3, 9 July 1996, <http://www.dtic.mil/whs/directives/corres/pdf/d30003_070996/d30003p.pdf> (20 July 2006); M.-A. Coppernoll, "The Non-Lethal Weapons Debate," *Naval War College Review* 52 (Spring 1999), <http://www.nwc.navy.mil/press/review/1999/spring/art5-sp9.htm> (13 July 2006); http://www.jnlwp.com/history.asp> (7 June 2006).

47. United States Senate, *S. Exec. Res. 75 To Advise and Consent to the Chemical Weapons Convention, Subject to Certain Conditions*, 17 April 1997, <http://frwebgate.access.gpo.gov/cgi-bin/getdoc.cgi?dbname=105_cong_bills&docid=f:sr75is.txt.pdf> (20 July 2006); Executive Office of the President, *Executive Order 11850—Renunciation of Certain Uses in War of Chemical Herbicides and Riot Control Agents* (Washington, D.C., 8 April 1975) appears at 40 FR 16187, 3 CFR, 1971–1975 Comp., 980, <http://www.armscontrolcenter.org/archives/001943.php> (13 July 2006).

48. Department of the Navy, Office of the Judge Advocate General, International & Operational Law Division, *Preliminary Legal Review of Proposed Chemical-Based Non-Lethal Weapons* (30 November 1997), <http://www.sunshine-project.org/incapacitants/jnlwdpdf/jagchemi.pdf> (14 July 2006).

49. Coppernoll, "Non-Lethal Weapons Debate."

50. C. A. Sanchez, "Non-Lethal Airburst Munition(s) for Objective Individual Combat Weapon" (powerpoint presentation at 2001 National Defense Industry Association Joint Services Small Arms Symposium, 15 August 2001), <http://www.sunshine-project.org/incapacitants/jnlwdpdf/sanchez.pdf> (14 July 2006).

51. A conclusion reinforced by U.S. Army Field Manual 3–11.9, which classifies "incapacitating agents" (including the fentanyls) as "chemical warfare agents," distinct from "RCAs" which it classifies as "military chemical compounds," see United States Army, Field Manual 3-11.9, *Potential Military Chemical/Biological Agents and*

Compounds, (10 January 2005): 1–5, <http://www.fas.org/irp/doddir/army/fm3-11-9.pdf> (10 July 2006).

52. Col. G. Fenton, "The U.S. Department of Defense Joint Non-Lethal Weapons Program, March 2000 Overview" (power point presentation at the Non-Lethal Defense IV Conference, sponsored by the National Defense Industrial Association, 20–22 March 2000), <http://www.dtic.mil/ndia/nld4/fenton.pdf>, slide 10 (14 July 2006).

53. Naval Studies Board, *Non-Lethal Weapons*, 24.

54. Robert Bunker, ed., *Non-Lethal Weapons: Terms and References*, INSS Occasional Paper 15 (Colorado: United States Air Force Academy, USAF Institute for National Security Affairs, December 1996), 10, <http://www.usafa.af.mil/df/inss/OCP/ocp15.pdf> (14 July 2006).

55. Naval Studies Board, *Non-Lethal Weapons*, 27, 124; S.V. Hart, "Less-Than-Lethal Weapons" (statement before the Subcommittee on Aviation, Committee on Transportation and Infrastructure, U.S. House of Representatives, 2 May 2002), <http://www.house.gov/transportation/aviation/05-02-02/hart.html> (20 July 2006).

56. Naval Studies Board, *Non-Lethal Weapons*, 125.

57. Cited in the Sunshine Project, "Non-Lethal Weapons Research in the US: Calmatives and Malodorants," *Backgrounder Series* no. 8 (July 2001), <http://www.sunshine-project.org/publications/bk/bk8en.html>.

58. G. Shwaery, "Non-Lethal Technology Innovation Center (NTIC)" (PowerPoint presentation to 2002 Non-Lethal Defense V Symposium: Non-Lethal Weapons: Now, More Than Ever, National Defense Industrial Association, 26–28 March 2002), <http://www.dtic.mil/ndia/2002nonlethdef/Shwaery.pdf> (25 July 2006).

59. United States Army, "Chemical Immobilizing Agents for Non-Lethal Applications, Topic CBD 00-108," Small Business Innovation Research Solicitation CBD 00.1, <http://www.acq.osd.mil/osbp/sbir/solicitations/sbir001/cbd001.htm> (18 January 2006).

60. United States Army, "Chemical Immobilizing Agents."

61. Optimetrics, Inc., "Chemical Immobilizing Agents for Non-Lethal Applications," SBIR phase I award from the CBD 00.1 Solicitation, <http://www.nttc.edu/resources/funding/awards/dod/2000sbir/001cbd.asp> (18 January 2006).

62. ERDEC, "Demonstration of Chemical Immobilizers."

63. Ruppe, "U.S. Military Studying Non-Lethal Chemicals."

64. Joint Non-Lethal Weapons Directorate, "Front End Analysis for Non-Lethal Chemicals," appeared for a short time on JNLWD website in early 2003, <http://www.sunshine-project.org/incapacitants/jnlwdpdf/feachemical.pdf> (20 July 2006); J. Cline and Maj. A J. Aragon, Jr. "Non-Lethal Technologies for the Objective Force" (PowerPoint presentation to the National Defense Industries Association Firepower Conference, Parsippany, NY, 18–20 June 2001), slide 18, <http://www.dtic.mil/ndia/2001armaments/cline.pdf> (20 July 2006); LTC R. Copeland, "Joint Non-Lethal Weapons Program," (PowerPoint presentation to National Defense Industries Association Mines Conference, June 2002), slide 18, <http://www.dtic.mil/ndia/2002mines/copeland.pdf> (1 July 2006); U.S. Joint Non-Lethal Weapons Directorate, *Joint Non-Lethal Weapons Directorate Newsletter*, 2nd Quarter, 2001 as cited in T. Feakin, *Bradford Non-Lethal Weapons Research Project, Research Report 3* (Bradford: Department of Peace

Studies, University of Bradford, August 2001), <http://www.brad.ac.uk/acad/nlw/research_reports/researchreport3.php> (14 July 2006).

65. Lakoski, Murray and Kenny, *Advantages and Limitations.*

66. Roche Pharmaceuticals, "Versed (Midzolam HCl) Injection," package insert at <http://www.fda.gov/ohrms/dockets/dailys/01/Mar01/032101/cp00001_exhibit_02.pdf> (24 July 2006); Bedford Laboratories, "Propofol Injectable Emulsion 1 percent," package insert at <http://66.70.89.95/information/propofol.pdf> (24 July 2006).

67. Naval Studies Board, *Assessment of Non-Lethal Weapons*, 27. This may reflect a difference in goals, as the committee noted that "prior research had been aimed at understanding margins of safety between loss of consciousness and death, whereas in crowd and riot control situations, the goal is to ensure a wide margin of safety between quieting and unconsciousness," 107.

68. Ruppe, "New Research."

69. Lakoski, Murray and Kenney, *Advantages and Limitations*, 6.

70. Lakoski, Murray and Kenney, *Advantages and Limitations*, 9 and 48.

71. Robinson chronology, entries for January 28 and January (unspecified day), 1992.

72. In addition to sources specifically cited, information in this section is compiled from Cline and Aragon, "Non-Lethal Technologies"; D. H. Lyon, R. F. Johnson, and J. Domanico, "Design and Development of an 81 mm Non-Lethal Mortar Cartridge" (PowerPoint presentation to Non-Lethal Defense IV Symposium, National Defense Industrial Association, 20–22 March 2000), <http://www.sunshine-project.org/incapacitants/jnlwdpdf/udlpmort.pdf> (25 July 2006); U.S. Army TACOM-ARDEC, "Fabrication of Composite Mortar Components and Investigation of Mortar Cartridge Kinetic Energy Mitigation Techniques for the 81 mm Non-Lethal Mortar Cartridge" (Purchase Order/Contract Number DAAE30-01-M-1289, 6 June 2001), <http://www.sunshineproject.org/incapacitants/jnlwdpdf/udlp81mm.zip> (25 July 2006); U.S. Army TACOM-ARDEC, "81mm Frangible Case Cartridge," Contract Number DAAE30-01-C-1077, 28 June 2001, <http://www.sunshine-project.org/incapacitants/jnlwdpdf/m281mm.zip> (25 July 2006); U.S. Army TACOM-ARDEC, "Liquid Payload Dispensing Concept Studies Techniques for the 81mm Non-Lethal Mortar Cartridge," Contract Number DAAE30-01-M-1444, 18 September 2001, <http://www.sunshine-project.org/incapacitants/jnlwdpdf/gd81mm.zip> (25 July 2006); M. Evangelisti, "Delivery of Non-Lethal Mortar Payloads by Mortar Systems: Joint RDT&E Pre-Milestone A Program" (PowerPoint presentation to 2002 International Infantry & Joint Services Small Arms Systems Symposium, Exhibition & Firing Demonstration, National Defense Industries Association, 13–16 May 2002), <http://www.dtic.mil/ndia/2002infantry/evangelisti.pdf> (25 July 2006); S. Han, A. Ponikowski, and R. Trohanowsky, "The 81mm Non Lethal Mortar Carrier Projectile (MoCaP)" (PowerPoint presentation to the 40th Annual Armament Systems: Guns—Ammunition-Rockets-Missiles Conference & Exhibition, National Defense Industries Association, 25–28 April 2005), <http://www.dtic.mil/ndia/2005garm/thursday/han.pdf> (25 July 2006).

73. U.S. Army Research Laboratory, "Non-Lethal Delivery System for Non-Lethal Mortar Payload, FY98/FY99," Non-Lethal Technology Investment Funding Proposal, 1997, <http://www.sunshine-project.org/incapacitants/jnlwdpdf/arlmortar.pdf> (25 July 2006).

98   ALAN PEARSON

74. For comparison, a typical 81mm munition, the M853A1 illumination round, weighs 9 pounds and is delivered at a terminal velocity of >300 feet/second, corresponding to a kinetic energy of >2700 foot-pounds.

75. M. Evangelisti, "Joint RDT&E Pre-Milestone 0 & Concept Exploration Program: 81mm Non-Lethal Mortar" (presentation to Joint Non-Lethal Weapons Program 1QFY01 Director's Review, 20 November 2000), <http://www.sunshine-project.org/incapacitants/jnlwdpdf/jnlwdmort.pdf> (25 July 2006).

76. Primex Aerospace Company, "Overhead Liquid Dispersion System (OLDS) Non-Lethal Demonstration Program," Final Report for Contract DAAE30-99-C-1072, 19 April 2000, <http://www.sunshine-project.org/incapacitants/jnlwdpdf/primexolds.pdf> (25 July 2006).

77. Primex, "OLDS."

78. Primex, "OLDS."

79. R. Hegarty, "Joint Non-Lethal Weapons Program: Non-Lethal Mortar Cartridge (NLMC)" (PowerPoint presentation to 2003 Picatinny Chapter/PEO Mortars Conference, Morristown, NJ, 1–3 October 2003), <http://www.sunshine-project.org/incapacitants/jnlwdpdf/usamort03.pdf> (25 July 2006).

80. Evangelisti, "81mm Non-Lethal Mortar"; United States Department of the Navy, "Fiscal Year (FY) 2006/FY2007 Budget Estimates Submission, Justification of Estimates, Research, Development, Test and Evaluation, Navy Appropriation, Volume II, Budget Activity 4," (Washington, D.C.: Department of the Navy, February 2005), Program Element Number 0603851M, <http://www.finance.hq.navy.mil/fmb/06pres/rdten/RDTEN_BA_4_book.pdf> (24 July 2006); see data for same Program Element in budget documents for FY2003, FY2004 and FY2005, <http://www.dod.mil/comptroller/defbudget/fy2007/index.html> (24 July 2006).

81. Hegarty, "Non-Lethal Mortar Cartridge."

82. United States Department of the Army, "Supporting Data FY 2007 President's Budget, Research, Development, Test and Evaluation Army Appropriation, Budget Activities 1, 2, and 3, Volume I," (Washington, D.C.: Department of the Army, February 2006), see entry for Program Element 0603004A, Project 232, <http://www.asafm.army.mil/budget/fybm/FY07/rforms/vol1.pdf> (25 July 2006).

83. Hegarty, "Non-Lethal Mortar Cartridge."

84. Globalsecurity.org, "M984 120 mm Extended Range DPICM Mortar Cartridge," <http://www.globalsecurity.org/military/systems/munitions/m984.htm> (25 July 2006).

85. U.S. Army, Picatinny Center, "Non-Lethal Artillery Structural Firing (FY04) Purchase Order Contract in Support of the FY04 155mm Non-Lethal Artillery Projectile Program," Contract Number W15QKN-04-M-0328, 14 September 2004, <http://www.sunshine-project.org/incapacitants/jnlwdpdf/XM1063.pdf> (25 July 2006); Globalsecurity.org, "M864 Base Burn DPICM," <http://www.globalsecurity.org/military/systems/munitions/m864.htm> (25 July 2006).

86. U.S. Army, Picatinny Center, "155mm XM1063 Non-Lethal Artillery Engineering Support Contract," Contract Number W15QKN-05-C-1225, 24 February 2005, <http://www.fbodaily.com/archive/2005/02-February/26-Feb-2005/FBO-00758148.htm> (25 July 2006).

87. Sanchez, "Non-Lethal Airburst Munition(s)"; Fenton, "Joint Non-Lethal Weapons Program"; Cline and Aragon, "Non-Lethal Technologies"; C. A. Sanchez, "OICW Non-Lethal Munition" (PowerPoint presentation to the 2002 International Infantry & Joint Services Small Arms Symposium, National Defense Industrial Association, Atlantic City, NJ, 13–16 May 2002), <http://www.dtic.mil/ndia/2002infantry/sanchez.pdf> (23 July 2006); K. J. Swenson, "Joint Non-Lethal Weapons Program: Brief to the Joint Services Small Arms Symposium" (PowerPoint presentation to International Infantry & Joint Services Small Arms Systems Annual Symposium, Exhibition and Firing Demonstration, National Defense Industrial Association, Atlantic City, NJ, 16–19 May 2005), <http://www.dtic.mil/ndia/2005smallarms/tuesday/swenson.pdf> (23 July 2006); "Independent Technology Assessment Report of Findings: The Objective Individual Combat Weapon Non-Lethal Munition," Applied Research Laboratory, College of Medicine of The Pennsylvania State University, 10 October 2002, 10 and 15, <http://www.sunshine-project.org/incapacitants/jnlwdpdf/oicwairburst.pdf> (1 July 2006).

88. Globalsecurity.org, "XM29 Integrated Airburst Weapon," <http://www.globalsecurity.org/military/systems/ground/m29-oicw.htm> (23 July 2006).

89. United States Army, Armament Research Development and Engineering Center, "OICW Increment II Airburst Weapon System—SDD & LRIP Phases," Solicitation Number W15QKN-05-X-0446, 8 June 2005.

90. Sanchez, "Non-Lethal Airburst Munition(s)," slide 2.

91. Sanchez, "Non-Lethal Airburst Munition(s)," slide 2.

92. "Independent Technology Assessment," Applied Research Laboratory, 39.

93. "Independent Technology Assessment," Applied Research Laboratory, 14.

94. Sanchez, "Non-Lethal Airburst Munition(s)," slide 8.

95. "Independent Technology Assessment," Applied Research Laboratory, 28.

96. "Independent Technology Assessment," Applied Research Laboratory, 38.

97. "Independent Technology Assessment," Applied Research Laboratory, 21.

98. "Independent Technology Assessment," Applied Research Laboratory, 35.

99. Sanchez, "Non-Lethal Airburst Munition(s)," slide 12.

100. Sanchez, "Non-Lethal Airburst Munition(s)," slide 12.

101. Col. G. Fenton (ret.), personal communication, 3 March 2006. This is also apparent from U.S. Navy budget documents, which demonstrate that JNLWD funds activities up to, but not beyond, the advanced technology development stage, which is pre-Milestone B.

102. United States Department of the Navy, "Fiscal Year (FY) 2007 Budget Estimates Submission, Justification of Estimates, Research, Development, Test and Evaluation, Navy Appropriation, Volume II, Budget Activity 4," (Washington, D.C.: Department of the Navy, February 2006), Program Element Number 0603851M, <http://www.finance.hq.navy.mil/fmb/07pres/rdten/RDTEN_BA_4_book.pdf> (24 July 2006); See data for same Program Element in budget documents for FY2004, FY2005 and FY2006, <http://www.dod.mil/comptroller/defbudget/fy2007/index.html> (24 July 2006).

103. Agentai, Inc. "Smart Non-Lethal Bullets," Topic # Navy 02-122; and Agentai, Inc. "Rocket Assisted Safe Projectile," Topic # Navy 02-119, Navy Small Business Innovation Research Awards, 2002, available at <http://www.sunshine-project.org/publications/pr/pr080903support.html> (4 January 2006).

104. Agentai, Inc. "Smart Non-Lethal Bullets"; Agentai, Inc. "Rocket Assisted Safe Projectile."

105. United States Patent 6523478, "Rifle-Launched Non-Lethal Cargo Dispenser," assigned to United States Army, 25 February 2003, <http://patft.uspto.gov/netacgi/nph-Parser?patentnumber=6523478> (24 July 2006).

106. United States Patent 6523478

107. D. Ruppe, "U.S. Army Grenade Patent Changed," *Global Security Newswire*, 31 January 2006, <http://www.nti.org/d_newswire/issues/2006_1_31.html#76D99711> (24 July 2006).

108. United States Patent 6523478.

109. D. Hartman, E. Maldonado, and N. Gonzalez, "Application of Propellant Dissemination Technologies for Non-Lethal Aerosols" (PowerPoint presentation to 2002 Mines, Demolition and Non-Lethal Conference & Exhibition, National Defense Industrial Association, 3–5 June 2002), <http://www.dtic.mil/ndia/2002mines/hartman.pdf> (24 July 2006).

110. Vanek Prototype Co., "Proposal for a Multi-Shot Launcher with Advanced Less-than-Lethal Ring Airfoil Projectile." Research proposal submitted to National Institute of Justice, 23 March 2002, <http://www.sunshine-project.org/incapacitants/jnlwdpdf/dojrap.pdf> (24 July 2006).

111. National Institute of Justice, "Rapid Development of an LTL System Based on a Multishot RAP Launcher and Advanced Segmented Projectiles." Continuation award to Vanek Prototype Co., Project Number 2004-IJ-CX-KO54, May 2004, <http://www.sunshine-project.org/incapacitants/jnlwdpdf/vanekrapdoj.pdf> (24 July 2006).

112. Vanek, "Proposal for a Multi-Shot Launcher."

113. United States Patent 7007424, "Multi-Shot Ring Airfoil Projectile Launcher," March 7, 2006, <http://patft.uspto.gov/netacgi/nph-Parser?patentnumber=7007424> (24 July 2006).

114. DePersia and Cecconi, "Less-Than-Lethal Program."

115. Naval Studies Board, *Non-Lethal Weapons*, 124.

116. Y. G. Durant, "White Paper: Delivery of Chemicals by Microcapsules." Proposal submitted in response to BAA-98-R-0016, (Advanced Polymer Laboratory, University of New Hampshire, 1998), <http://www.sunshine-project.org/incapacitants/jnlwdpdf/unhmicrocap.pdf> (24 July 2006); Y. Durant, M. Thiam, C. Petcu, N. Vashista, and others, "Encapsulation Technology for NLWs," (PowerPoint presentation to Non-lethal Technology and Academic Research II Symposium, University of New Hampshire, 17 November 2000), <http://www.unh.edu/apl/communications/NTAR percent202.pdf> (24 July 2006).

117. Wax, Becker, and Curry, "Unexpected 'Gas' Casualties."

118. D. Holley "Russian Forces Crush Rebels After Two Days of Fighting," *Los Angeles Times*, 15 October 2005, A3.

119. Klochikhin, Lushnikov, and Zagaynov, "Principles of Modeling."

120. Klochikhin, Lushnikov, and Zagaynov, "Principles of Modeling," 3.

121. Klochikhin, Lushnikov, and Zagaynov, "Principles of Modeling," 3.

122. Klochikhin, Lushnikov, and Zagaynov, "Principles of Modeling," 13-14.

123. N. Davison and N. Lewer, *Bradford Non-Lethal Weapons Research Project Research Report No. 8,* (Bradford: Centre for Conflict Resolution, University of Bradford, March 2006), 52, <http://www.brad.ac.uk/acad/nlw/research_reports/docs/BNLWRP ResearchReportNo8_Mar06.pdf> (15 July 2006).

124. Klochikhin, Lushnikov, and Zagaynov, "Principles of Modeling," 4.

125. T. Stanley, quoted in N. Davison and N. Lewer, *Bradford Non-Lethal Weapons Research Project Research Report No. 5,* (Bradford: Centre for Conflict Resolution, University of Bradford, May 2004): 39, <http://www.bradford.ac.uk/acad/nlw/research_ reports/docs/BNLWRPResearchReportNo5_May04.pdf> (25 July 2006).

126. L. Hess, J. Schreiberova, and J. Fusek, "Pharmacological Non-Lethal Weapons." Paper presented to the 3rd European Symposium on Non-Lethal Weapons, Stadthalle, Germany, 10–12 May 2005; Davison and Lewer, *Bradford Report No. 8,* 50; reporting on Czech Army Project MO 03021100007.

127. Hess, Schreiberova, and Fusek, "Pharmacological Non-Lethal Weapons," 6–7.

128. NATO Research and Technology Organization, *Non-Lethal Weapons and Future Peace Enforcement Operations,* RTO-TR-SAS-040, (December 2004), 3–10, <http://www .rta.nato.int/Main.asp?topic=sas.htm#> (15 July 2006).

129. News Chronology, *CBW Conventions Bulletin,* 38 (Harvard Sussex Program on CBW Armament and Arms Limitations, December 1997), entry for 25 September 1997, 29.

130. Guo Ji-wei and Xue-sen Yang, "Ultramicro, Nonlethal, and Reversible: Looking Ahead to Military Biotechnology," *Military Review* (July-August 2005): 75–78, <http:// usacac.army.mil/CAC/milreview/download/English/JulAug05/yang.pdf>. Like much of the work by non-lethal weapons enthusiasts and technology boosters, this article, which talks about a wide range of biotechnology-enabled weapons, is more science fiction than science fact. But it reveals a clear interest in the future of biotechnology for military purposes. It also includes such statements as "such devastating, non-lethal effects will require us to pacify the enemy through postwar reconstruction efforts and hatred control," 76; and "[w]e can control the degree of injuries and damage produced and even provide an antidote or a cure . . . Providing such an anodyne to our enemies would represent real 'mercy,'" 77.

131. M. Wheelis, "'Non-Lethal' Chemical Weapons: A Faustian Bargain" *Issues in Science and Technology* (Spring 2003), <http://www.issues.org/19.3/wheelis.htm> (14 July 2006), citing statement by retired Rear Admiral Stephen Baker that U.S. special forces were equipped with "knockout gases." Also see S. M. Hersh, "The Iran Plans," *New Yorker* (17 April 2006), quoting a former U.S. defense official as saying in regards to military action against Iran, "we don't have to knock down *all* of their air defenses. Our stealth bombers and standoff missiles really work, and we can blow fixed things up. We can do things on the ground, too, but it's difficult and very dangerous to put bad stuff in ventilator shafts and put them to sleep."

132. T. Stanley, quoted in Davison and Lewer, Bradford Report No. 5, 39.

133. Sunshine Project, "The MCRU Calmatives Study and JNLWD: A Summary of (Public) Facts," 19 September 2002, <http://www.sunshine-project.org/incapacitants/ mcrucalmfacts.html> (25 July 2006).

134. Stanley, "Human Immobilization."

135. Stanley, "Human Immobilization."

CHAPTER 5

Current and Prospective Military and Law Enforcement Use of Chemical Agents for Incapacitation

George P. Fenton

Making the Case:
Chemical Agents for Incapacitation

THE ADVENT OF AND NEED FOR LESS-LETHAL CAPABILITIES

When wanton death and destruction were the intended consequences of armed combat, certain uses of chemicals and chemically-based substances in open conflict were justifiably bounded during the twentieth century to limit needless human suffering—beginning with the Washington Treaty of 1922 following World War I and culminating with the Chemical Weapons Convention (CWC). Ironically, during the same century, technological advances created new potential capabilities, in which the use or application of chemicals in hostilities would actually result in limiting needless human suffering. This paradox presents a challenge in that the generally accepted practice of *not developing certain chemically-based less-lethal capabilities* in order to comply with the letter of the CWC *may work against the principles underlying the Law of Armed Conflict*. Rigid interpretation of policies and treaties of the last century may, in fact, be counterproductive or self-defeating.

The urgent need for less-lethal capabilities became evident at the turn of the century as paradigms of warfighting evolved beyond those, such as

---

Disclaimer: The views presented in this paper are my own, and are not to be interpreted to represent the views or position of the United States Government, the United States Marine Corps, the Joint Non-Lethal Weapons Directorate, American Systems Corporation, or those individuals who took the time to offer their thoughts and counsel to me.

large-scale movement and force-on-force combat, which characterized the traditional state-versus-state warfighting of the past. The current global migration of people to the urban city and its consequent demographic implications has forced a paradigm shift in military operations. Combat operations are now becoming more urban-centric and are typically, albeit unofficially, described by the moniker "The Three Block War. "The term "Three Block War" typifies the uncertainty and complexity of modern war. The "first block" relates to humanitarian relief operations, with soldiers aiding and assisting in the distribution of material goods. The adjacent "second block" relates to peacekeeping operations, with soldiers separating warring factions with an aim to keep the peace and disarm troublemakers. Finally, the "third block" relates to actual combat operations, with soldiers returning fire against an adversary determined to kill. In this urban setting, each of the three blocks is inundated with noncombatants—women, children, elderly, and the feeble and infirm. As witnessed in the cities subjected to war during the past fifteen years in several countries and geographic regions (such as Somalia, the Balkans, Haiti, East Timor, Rwanda, and Iraq to name a few) innocent people remain in the crossfire and in harm's way. Furthermore, the once well-defined interpretations of the conventions that apply to war now have become less certain as the lines amongst the fighters themselves—the insurgent, the revolutionary, the terrorist, the para-militiaman, the conventional state soldier, and the gang member, the thug, the trafficker, the criminal and the law-enforcer— have become blurred.

While the use of less-lethal capabilities is not new to warfare or law enforcement, the impetus for the United States to formally institutionalize the pursuit of such capabilities is generally believed to be found in the United States' involvement in the Somali civil war of the early 1990s.[1,2] Then-Lieutenant General Anthony Zinni,[3] United States Marine Corps, introduced less-lethal capabilities into the 1995 U.S. Concept of Operations for the withdrawal of forces from Somali soil. General Zinni later, in his testimony before the U.S. Congress, underscored the importance of such capabilities as a military need. In 1996,[4] the U.S. Congress mandated that the Department of Defense formally establish a less-lethal weapons program. The following year, the Commandant of the Marine Corps was named Executive Agent for the U.S. Department of Defense Joint Non-Lethal Weapons Program, and accordingly, the Joint Non-Lethal Weapons Directorate was established at Quantico, Virginia.

Less-lethal capabilities provide the commander in the field with additional options to address the situation at hand. This is true for both the law enforcement officer and the military officer, particularly when the use of lethal force is not the desired option. The less-lethal capability is an *additional* arrow in the quiver . . . it provides the on-scene commander with another option that fits neatly between the bullhorn and the bullet. Less-lethal capabilities provide an alternative to "Hobson's Choice," which can be described as "do nothing, or use what is at hand," i.e., resort to lethal force. The numerous susceptible frailties of the human body can be easily exploited through the use of chemically-based substances, which thus provide the on-scene commander with multiple options to disable a subject without having to unavoidably kill him/her. Chemically-based substances have become an important complement to the current tool kit of options.

THE CHEMICAL WEAPONS CONVENTION AND INCAPACITATION

The Chemical Weapons Convention contains a number of definitions and specific language on prohibited and non-prohibited activities. For example, CWC Article I, paragraph 1 states in part:[5]

Each State Party to this Convention undertakes *never under any circumstances*:

(a) To develop, produce, otherwise acquire, stockpile or retain chemical weapons, or transfer, directly or indirectly, chemical weapons to anyone;
(b) *To use chemical weapons*;

Article II, paragraph 1 includes, in part, the following relevant definition:

"*Chemical Weapons*" *means* the following, together or separately:

(a) *Toxic chemicals and their precursors*, except where intended for purposes not prohibited under this Convention, as long as the types and quantities are consistent with such purposes;

Additionally, Article II, paragraph 2 contains the following important definition:

"*Toxic Chemical*" *means*:
Any chemical that through its chemical action on life processes *can cause death, temporary incapacitation or permanent harm* to humans or animals.

In Article II, paragraph 9, the CWC further explains relevant purposes that are not prohibited:

Purposes Not Prohibited Under this Convention:

(c) *Military purposes* not connected with the use of chemical weapons and *not dependent on the use of the toxic properties of chemicals as a method of warfare*;
(d) *Law enforcement including domestic riot control purposes.*

The CWC does provide a specific definition for the term "Riot Control Agent" in Article II, paragraph 7:

> *"Riot Control Agent" means:*
> Any chemical not listed in a Schedule, which can produce rapidly in humans *sensory irritation or disabling physical effects* which disappear within a short time following termination of exposure.

However, the CWC does not offer any definition or specificity for the term "temporary incapacitation." This is important because of its reference to those purposes not prohibited under the convention—specifically the terms "method of warfare" and "law enforcement including riot control agents" specified in Article II, paragraph 9.

In the context of the CWC, is incapacitation within the bounds of law enforcement? And if chemical weapons are not used as a *method* of war, (meaning at the operational, strategic or strategic-national levels of war) but rather as a *means* for policing/peacekeeping actions at the tactical level during stability operations following the cessation of combat operations, is their use in keeping with the spirit of the Convention?

Regardless of interpretation, a definition for "incapacitation" needs to be agreed upon. For example, the Merriam-Webster on-line dictionary offers the following definition for incapacitation:

> Main Entry: in·ca·pac·i·tate
> Function: *transitive verb*
> 1: to make legally incapable or ineligible
> 2: to deprive of capacity or natural power:—in·ca·pac·i·ta·tion *Noun*

Within the U.S. Department of Defense (DoD), no formal definition exists for the term "incapacitation." However, a formal definition for "incapacitating agent" may be found in DoD Joint Publication 1-02, *Dictionary of Military and Associated Terms* (5 September 2003): "an agent that produces temporary physiological or mental effects, or both, which will render individuals incapable of concerted effort in the performance of their assigned duties." Interesting, in addition, are two unofficial working definitions of the term "incapacitation" as used by military personnel.[6] The first is provided in relation to lethality; the second is from a less-lethal perspective:

> Incapacitation: (Lethal Perspective) The inability to perform physical or mental tasks required to be effective in a particular role. Probability of Incapacitation (Pi) is the measure of a soldier's inability to perform activities critical to his tactical situation. Pi encompasses a system-level approach that addresses weapon delivery accuracy, munitions effectiveness against the target, and variations between targets.
>
> Incapacitation: (Less-lethal Perspective) Weapon munitions' effects that result in either rendering a person physically incapable (real or perceived) or mentally disinclined to resist or pose a threat to friendly forces.

The significant words in each reference—deprive of capability, [create conditions to ensure an] inability to perform, and render incapable—are suggestive of non-fatal engagement. In the context of less-lethal weapons in which one key underlying principle is reversibility of effect,[7] to inflict some form of incapacitation *without the intention to kill* is certainly in keeping with the spirit of the CWC.

THE BEHAVIOR TARGET SET

The most deadly thing on the battlefield is one well-aimed round.[8] But if the soldier or law enforcer aims to incapacitate rather than to kill, then just exactly what is the intent of his use of force? Those less-informed might suggest the aim is to get "some kind of less-lethal effect" on the target. However, the correct response is to influence a subject's motivational behavior. It is the *subject's behavior response* that is of importance to the soldier or law enforcer. Specifically, the aim is to influence the motivational behavior of the targeted subject so as to render him/her incapable of intended task performance. Figure 5.1[9] shows the key elements of a notional less-lethal engagement. The culminating element is Behavior Response. Within this element, sensory overload or some other less-lethal effect is the means to the end.

The objective of sensory overload is to influence the target subject's ability to maintain situational awareness and his ability to act, thereby denying the subject the opportunity to carry out his intended task. In other words, the objective is to defuse the offensive nature of the subject and place the subject in a defensive mindset. The aim is to subdue the subject through incapacitation. This strategy is based on the fact that in day-to-day activity, a subject has a normal,

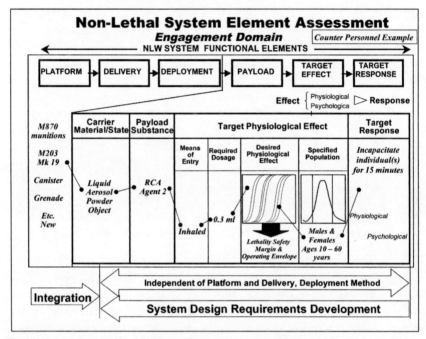

Figure 5.1.   Less-lethal System Element Assessment
Source: American Systems, amended by U.S. Dept. of Defense Joint Non-Lethal Weapons Program.

comfortable "sensing zone" composed of human sensing factors. The five senses (*sight, hearing, taste, smell*, and *touch/feel*), *motor ability* and *cognition* together comprise the human factor behavior set. When any one of these human factors is disrupted in such a way that it no longer functions within its comfortable sensing or acting zone, the subject is forced to react and/or respond to the external disrupting influence. When multiple senses are affected, the subject can be forced into a sensory overload condition wherein he is no longer able to carry out his intended action.

Chemical agents show promise when mapped to the behavior target set. The attractiveness of these less-lethal capabilities is their wide range of applications, minimal residual effects, and ability to target multiple individuals at once.[10] Law enforcement and military personnel are ever more frequently involved in circumstances where there exists a need for an effective yet less-lethal means by which to manage crowds, deny an area, seize or extract prisoners, resolve barricade situations, clear facilities, and break up civil disturbances. Currently available capabilities are typically limited to blunt impact (kinetic energy) items such as rubber ball grenades, bean bag rounds, batons, or rubber bullets; human electro-muscular incapacitation devices (Taser® M26 and X26); and chemically-based riot control agent (RCA) products. Each of these capability types is effective to a degree, but none can be considered a one hundred percent solution.

There are a multitude of riot control agent products used by military and law enforcement organizations around the world. While each product ultimately has the same purpose—to temporarily incapacitate the targeted subject(s)—the means of dissemination vary. The "best" riot control agent to use will typically depend upon the intended goals and environmental elements of the situation at hand. Other types of chemically-based substances include calmatives, malodorants, anti-traction substances, and foams. The intended effects of the latter two are not dependent on the toxic properties of the chemical;[11] therefore their use is not prohibited by the CWC and they will not be considered further here.

Within the DoD Joint Non-Lethal Weapons Program, three core areas are identified for application of less-lethal capabilities: Counter-Personnel, Counter-Materiel, and Counter-Capability. When examining chemical agents as they pertain to Counter-Personnel capabilities, three key attributes are also noted—the Human Behavior Target Area, the Transitory Effect and the Target Response. Table 5.1 addresses various relationships.

For riot control agents, four of the five senses comprise the human behavior target (sight, smell, taste, and touch). The transitory effect, typically of short duration in terms of time,[12] causes sensory irritation.[13] To the law enforcer and military soldier, the most critical attribute is the *intended* consequence—the Target Response. Disrupted behavior and inability to complete a task are the main, anticipated reasons for using riot control agents.

The use of calmatives, while they provoke a change in the state of mind, have *the same intended consequence* as riot control agents—disrupted behavior

Table 5.1.   Less-lethal Capability Attributes

Chemical	Counter-Personnel Human Target Area	Transitory Effect Target Effects	Target Response Intended Response
RCAs	Olfactory Vision Skin Breathing	Wheezing, coughing Gagging, tearing Blurred vision Drowsiness	Task disruption Behavior disruption Distraction Departure
Calmatives	Cognition	Drowsiness Incoherence Sleepiness	Task disruption Behavior disruption Distraction
Malodorants	Olfactory	Non-tolerance Wheezing, coughing Gagging, tearing	Task disruption Behavior disruption Distraction Departure

and inability to complete the intended task. And while they may not cause sensory irritation, they do disable physically *as well as* psychologically.

However, the fear or reluctance to use calmatives is anchored in the *unintended consequence* of their use. What other (side) effects have consequence to the human body? Scientific research, study, and analysis must lead to the examination of consequence and potential application.

Malodorants are emerging substances of interest. A recent summer episode in New York City heightens awareness for the potential application for such a capability. Next to a garbage bin on a corner street in Upper East Side Manhattan, a big garbage bag was the source of a rather pungent smell that caused local havoc:

> "Office-bound residents stumbled and picked up their pace, workers
> covered their noses, police officers used masks. The smell was so bad
> you could practically see it . . . [T]he smell was unbearable."[14]

The stench was horrific; people vacated nearby premises and avoided the area. The source of the smell was dead fish. As suggested by this "fish story," malodorants, while not necessarily producing any sensory irritation or disabling effects, produce heightened sensory activity/awareness[15] via an offensive rancid odor and clearly have potential to influence the motivational behavior of personnel.

THE NEED FOR AND BENEFITS OF INCAPACITATING CHEMICAL AGENTS

When an engagement demands law enforcement or military action but does not necessitate the use of lethal force, the aim is to influence the motivational behavior of an adversary in order to create the conditions to resolve the crisis at hand. In a tactical situation, a range of responses may be possible, but the preferred response must balance a number of factors and many variables may play into the action. Knowing key essential elements of information, which will vary from scenario to scenario, will enable an enforcer to make a better-informed decision regarding the specific course of action to be undertaken. The intention of the adversary may be the most important variable. Other key variables include the size of the group being encountered, the current and anticipated activities of the adversary(s), their location(s), with whom they are affiliated (or whether they are independently-acting individuals), the time, and the equipment they may have.

Other equally important elements will include information about the physical and cultural environment, infrastructure, avenues of approach into and out of the area, communications, access to food and water, etc. As these elements of information are gathered and analyzed to best prepare a course of action, the law enforcement/military unit looks to maintain an edge by respecting time-proven axioms:

- *Be Flexible*—The professional abilities of a well-trained unit, which will have honed standard operating procedures (SOPs), will also have the ability to remain flexible, allowing freedom of action and the ability to make audible changes to an established plan. The unit is not tied to a lock-stepped sequential set of tasks that must be followed. For example, having the ability to employ any one or more means from a tool kit of multiple capabilities facilitates tailoring the right capability for the problem at hand.
- *Do Not Be Predictable*—No unit engaged with an adversary should ever be predictable. Again, the more options available to an on-scene commander, the stronger his odds that he won't be predictable in his actions.
- *Maintain and Employ Redundant Capabilities*—Capabilities at hand need to be complementary and redundant. The enforcing unit must guard against counter-capabilities by having depth and breadth in its own kit to be able to prosecute the action without allowing defeat of its mission.

An attractive aspect of chemically-based substances is found in the multitude of deployment means and employment mediums. Representative deployment means include aircraft, unmanned aerial vehicles (UAVs), "paint balls," canisters, man-packs, sprayers, direct and indirect fire, hand-held dispensers and others. Employment mediums include aerosols, liquids, powders, foams, capsules and pellets, and paints. Because of their versatility in employment schemes as well as their influence on the full set of human behavior target areas, chemically-based substances enable an enforcing unit to hold true to established practices to ensure mission success. Again, the more options the enforcing unit has at its disposal, the more flexible, less predictable, and more responsive it can be in conducting its mission.

The characteristics and effects of less-lethal capabilities, and specifically of the chemically-based substances outlined above, allow for directive actions rather than reactive responses. For example, they may enable military and law enforcement personnel to:

- Discern hostile intent *before* the [re]-action to shoot to kill
- Neutralize the subject *before* any escalation of force
- Avoid reaching the lethal engagement threshold

The real benefit is that the soldier or law enforcer is better able to distinguish between friend (noncombatant) and foe. Creating a delay or a deterrent to a

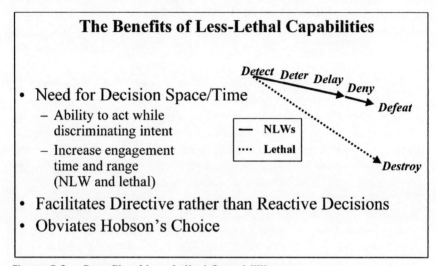

Figure 5.2.   Benefits of Less-Lethal Capabilities
Source: Butch Foley and John Nelson, American Systems, with modification

potentially hostile action through the use of less-lethal capabilities provides additional time for the user to better decide on the level of threat presented and determine the most appropriate action to take. See figure 5.2.[16]

MILITARY AND LAW ENFORCEMENT USE OF CHEMICAL AGENTS FOR INCAPACITATION

Counter-personnel less-lethal capabilities enabled through chemically-based substances include, but are not limited to:

- Target discrimination (i.e., being able to distinguish possible targets from non-threatening personnel)
- Target isolation/separation
- Event isolation
- Denied area/access
- Facility clearing
- Crowd control
- Target incapacitation

These needed counter-personnel capabilities fall within both law enforcement and military mission sets. Chemically-based substances, through their diverse set of properties, enable the enforcer to effectively engage in a multitude of situations, many of which may happen simultaneously during the same incident.

LEVERAGING THE PRINCIPLES OF THE LAW OF ARMED CONFLICT

The Law of Armed Conflict (LOAC) serves as a basis of the Geneva Convention, and by extension of the Chemical Weapons Convention, to which the signatory states adhere. Three important LOAC principles govern armed conflict—military necessity, distinction, and proportionality. Military necessity requires combat forces to engage in only those acts necessary to accomplish a legitimate military objective. Distinction means discriminating between lawful combatant targets and noncombatant targets, e.g., civilians, prisoners of war, etc. Proportionality refers to the application of force, and prohibits excessive use of force to accomplish the military objective. Moreover, an extension of the principle proportionality is the need to minimize unnecessary human suffering.

Table 5.2 provides a framework for examining chemically-based substances in terms of the principles of the Law of Armed Conflict.

Table 5.2.   Chemically Based Substances (CBS) and their Relationships to the Law of Armed Conflict (LOAC)

LOAC Principle	Concepts for CBS Less-Lethal Use	Implications Without CBS Less-Lethal Use
Military Necessity	*Mission Set* Target discrimination Target isolation/separation Event isolation Denied area/access Facility clearing Crowd control Target incapacitation	*Other Options* Lethal force Less-capable less-lethal methods that raise risk to the using unit
Distinction/ Discrimination	*Discern Intention* Isolate combatant Separate noncombatants	Potential for no discrimination and more fatalities
Proportionality	*Apply the right tool* Onset time Magnitude & duration	Lethal consequence Escalation because a less capable less-lethal was used
Minimize Unnecessary Suffering	*Manage Consequence* Type of effect/response Degree of spread and recovery	Overwhelming force with a probability of kill likely

- *Military Necessity.* The mission set falls within the force continuum of military operations. These mission tasks are undertaken in armed combat, peacekeeping and stability operations. Some degree of force will be likely. The use of chemically-based substances can help mitigate or defuse the crisis/incident(s). Alternative means include the use of lethal force, or some other less-lethal but potentially less capable tool.
- *Distinction and Discrimination.* The central theme of distinction is to be able to engage only lawful military combatants. Such force-on-force engagement is indicative of the world wars of the twentieth century and ages past when conflicting states armies drew battle against one another in pursuit of state political aims. Today's conflict is that of the three-block war construct described earlier. The need to distinguish between the combatants and the noncombatants takes form in the desire to discriminate between the oft-mixed intermingled individuals or groups, with the intention to separate one group from another, or the belligerent from the harmless civilian. Chemically-based substances can serve this cause.
- *Proportionality.* Proportionality prohibits excessive of use of force to accomplish the military objective. Lethal force is not the preferred option for the mission set described; less-lethal force to include chemically-based substances provides a reasonable alternative that lessen the chances for unintended fatal consequence or permanent injury. Features such as onset time, magnitude and duration, when properly managed, help mitigate the unintended consequences.
- *Minimized Unnecessary Suffering.* Lethal suffering is absolute! Capabilities that lessen the chance for fatality merit favorable support and are in keeping with the spirit of the Geneva Convention. Use of chemically-based substances, those that have a low probability for—or do not result in—permanent injury, facilitate consequence management and lessen unnecessary suffering.

Chemically-based substances appear to satisfy the principles of the Law of Armed Conflict and yet the CWC bans the military use of them.

GOALS FOR AND VALUE OF THE USE OF CHEMICALLY-BASED SUBSTANCES

The goals for less-lethal capabilities that include chemically-based substances, are ideal and perhaps altruistic, and can be mapped to the LOAC principles. The goals include:

- *Informed, Nonreactive Decision Making.* Through the use of less-lethal capabilities, the intent is to create conditions in which the soldier (or law enforcer) may be able to discern the intent of the adversary, and thus make an informed decision regarding his own actions as opposed to reacting to the circumstances at hand. To this end, the soldier is able to make a conscious decision whether to shoot to kill or not shoot, enabling adherence to the principles of military necessity and proportionality.
- *Repeatable, Universal Bio-Effect with Reversibility.* Given the nature of human sensory disruption, the ideal less-lethal capability is one that has the same safe universal bio-effect on *every* human target regardless of gender, age, weight, physique, health, and any other physiological characteristics. The universal bio-effect must be reversible without having any consequence for permanent injury. These goals also enable adherence to the principles of military necessity and proportionality.
- *Eliminate Casualties.* Through the use of less-lethal capabilities, the aim is to reduce if not eliminate friendly and non-hostile casualties, in keeping with the principles of discrimination and minimizing unnecessary suffering.
- *Environmentally Friendly.* The less-lethal capability should not be harmful to the environment by any form of contamination or lingering effects, also in keeping with the principles of discrimination and minimizing unnecessary suffering.

The value of less-lethal chemically-based substances is apparent when the goals are mapped to the LOAC principles. Once again, chemically-based substances appear to satisfy the principle of the Law of Armed Conflict.

Three Scenarios

David Koplow, Professor of Law at the Georgetown University Law Center Washington, D.C., recently published a manuscript entitled, *Tangled Up in Khaki and Blue: Lethal and Non-Lethal Weapons in Recent Confrontations.*[17] Koplow provides a detailed, documented account of three confrontations in the form of mini-case studies, each examined through a lens focused either on the use or non-use of less-lethal capabilities. In each case, Koplow provokes debate on the use of such capabilities, including chemically-based substances. The first study is a law enforcement operation that examines the Branch Davidians fiasco in Waco, Texas in 1993, in which CS gas was used; the second study is the 2002 Dubrovka theater affair having both law enforcement and military undertones, in which a narcotic calmative agent related to fentanyl was used; and the third study is of the British military in

Basra Iraq 2003, in which no chemically-based substances were used. The case studies merit review because they help put in perspective the application of chemically-based substances for less-lethal purposes. In each case violence erupted, people died, and the use/non-use of chemically-based substances has been debated. There are certainly lessons to be learned in all cases.

THE BRANCH DAVIDIANS—WACO, TEXAS, U.S.A. 1993

The Branch Davidians affair centered on a radical religious cult-like group that lived in a commune sanctuary in a series of ramshackle buildings on a seventy-seven acre compound. The compound was home to over 100 men, women, and children. The Davidians were suspected to have a firearms arsenal comprising over $200,000 worth of weapons, explosives, munitions, and equipment including illegally possessed automatic weapons. Moreover, David Koresh, the leader of the group, was suspected of engaging in frequent child sexual abuse. The alleged illegal possession of automatic weapons and David Koresh's alleged child abuse behavior led to a yearlong investigation, and ultimately warrants for his arrest and a search of the compound. The end result was a fifty-one day standoff between the federal Bureau of Alcohol, Tobacco, and Firearms (ATF) and the Branch Davidians. Offensive action was taken on the fifty-second day with over 300 law enforcement officials from ATF, the Federal Bureau of Investigation, the Texas Rangers, the Waco police, the McLennan County Sheriff office as well as members of the Texas National Guard converging on the compound. The original plan of action called for the gradual introduction of dispensed CS gas into selected buildings over a period of time in order to incrementally contaminate the compound to flush out the Davidians. The plan failed. An exchange of gunfire ensued, buildings burned, and seventy-five adults and children perished. Not clear, and perhaps never to be known, was the role CS gas played in the clash. Intended to serve as a flushing tool with the aim to clear the buildings of occupants, the use of gas may have been just another contributing factor that hardened the will of resistance of the main belligerents. Another thought—the CS canisters may have started a fire.[18] In the post-incident examination when the tactics, techniques, procedures and equipment used in the assault are scrutinized, other less-lethal capabilities are debated as to their relative worth and potential for success of the mission.

In this case, could a more effective, faster-acting riot control agent have been employed? Could a less aggressive substance like a malodorant have been used instead to yield the desired outcome? Could a universal sleeping agent have been introduced under the cover of night? Could some other form of chemically-based substance been introduced into either the food or water supply that could over-

whelm any of the senses in the human factor behavior set? Could any of these op-
tions have been done safely, and in a manner consistent with the goals of using
less-lethal capabilities? An expanded toolkit of capabilities could certainly bear on
the outcome of the crisis.

THE DUBROVKA THEATER—MOSCOW, RUSSIA 2002

The Dubrovka theater incident was not a protracted affair. This incident had the markings of terror, in which nearly 800 hostages were taken, the facility was barricaded, and the belligerents were bent on a suicide mission. Moscow authorities reluctantly concluded that a peaceful resolution was not forthcoming. Early in the morning around 5:15 a.m., Russian Special Forces executed their hastily-drawn plan, beginning by pumping a quantity of a chemical narcotic gas (thought to be a fentanyl derivative) through the Dubrovka Theater's ventilation system. Apparently, a few of the terrorists recognized what was happening but were unable to decisively act; [19] fifteen to thirty minutes of chemical effect rendered nearly everyone inside the theater immobile with the exception of some terrorists positioned in the hallways adjacent to the theater. By 6:00 a.m. the Russian elite *Spetsnaz* forces launched their assault. By the end of the attack, all terrorists engaged or found were shot dead. The troops began defusing the terrorist's explosives, escorting/pulling hostages out of the building, and engaging medical personnel on scene and across the city. Some 450 emergency teams were on standby, and local transportation was commandeered to serve as medical transport. However, the Russian authorities had not advised the medics to be prepared for the chemical casualties as well as gunshot and explosion wounds and, in the chaos of the moment, emergency triage sputtered. In the end, the death toll for the assault included all 50 terrorists (killed by firearms) and 129 hostages (all but two killed by the narcotic gas). None of the assaulting troops was hurt in the fighting, but the effects of the gas injured nine. Almost all of the surviving hostages were hospitalized after the rescue due to the gas; many required treatment for an extended period and may have incurred permanent injuries. Proponents of the raid have argued that it represented mission success. Certainly, when compared to what could have been the loss of all hostage lives, the fact is that over 600 hostages lives' were saved, albeit leaving some with disabling permanent injury.

Could proper training, tactics, techniques, and procedures have reduced the
number of noncombatant casualties? Can additional research regarding the proper-
ties of narcotic gases and their influences on the human anatomy and physiology
prove promising for future crises of this type? Can such research lessen the probability
of long-term effects?

THE BRITISH IN BASRA—BASRA, IRAQ 2003

The military plan for the 2003 combined multinational Operation Iraqi Freedom called for British forces to take Basra. An immediate objective of the battle strategy was to pounce on Basra; the Americans would quickly dispatch any organized resistance in the area, then advance north toward Baghdad, leaving the British the tasks of neutralizing any lingering pockets of resistance in the south and occupying Basra. The coalition's initial concept of operations called for the British to advance to, but not quite into, Basra; there the forces would pause, anticipating a surrender of the city, perhaps to be spurred by a spontaneous, indigenous Shia uprising against their long-time repressors. At all costs, the invaders wanted to avoid the specter of a prolonged urban fight. House-to-house fighting against the Fedayeen would be both costly in terms of British soldiers' lives, and devastating to the process of building support from the Iraqis. The residents would surely despise any army that succeeded in liberating them only at the cost of destroying their homes, businesses, and their city as well as killing innocent civilians.

The run-up to Basra succeeded, but the first consequence of battle was a humanitarian crisis. The city's electricity supply failed, resulting in power loss to water treatment facilities. Sixty percent of the population was without electricity and without safe drinking water. The result was that the Fedayeen still controlled the city; but more importantly, they controlled the local populace. The defenders adopted a variety of tactics of asymmetric warfare, employing guerrilla, terrorist, and patently illegal maneuvers. For example, they co-located military and civilian sites, dressed and fought as civilians, and coerced family members into suicide missions. There were fake surrenders, amounting to perfidy under the Law of Armed Conflict. The Fedayeen used human shields, grabbing children as personal cover in order to keep the British troops from returning fire. The defending Fedayeen savagely repressed any dissent inside Basra, peremptorily executing resisters and those suspected of collaborating with the invaders.

Most distressing to the British was the apparent absence of any large-scale popular uprising; the plan had overlooked or missed one key factor—the paralyzing fear Saddam's minions had imposed on Basra. For two weeks a stalemate persisted, with the British perched just outside the city. Steadfastly refusing to be drawn into the city, the British did undertake occasional probing raids well into the city. The perception was an illustration of Westerners getting bogged down in the Middle East, and they were being blamed for the slow pace of humanitarian relief and the failure to dislodge the Fedayeen. Seventeen days later, the British did attack into the heart of the city with the intention to stay. The local population reacted with enthusiasm, but also violently took matters into their own hands against individual antagonists—lynch mobs, revenge beatings, and vigilante killings ensued.

Within a few short days of fighting, Basra was relatively secure. Yet a rampage of widespread looting occurred within government buildings—universities, utilities, hospitals were all stripped bare. The British suddenly found themselves called upon to play a variety of incompatible roles—conventional warfighter, guerilla fighter, humanitarian relief worker, and policeman. The UK forces temporized on the last of those responsibilities, declining to turn their attention to "governance" tasks so long as active combat was still being waged. As fighting dwindled, it became apparent that the city of Basra had indeed been spared the worst ravages of urban warfare. But there was loss of life, loss of property, and loss of infrastructure. In the aftermath, humanitarian aid did come online, but only very gradually.

Could less-lethal capabilities have played a successful role, particularly in the policing actions necessary to quell civil disobedience? Could riot control gas have enabled the soldiers to keep looters away from critical areas? Could malodorants have been used to temporarily contaminate or make foul critical infrastructure in order to keep them from being ransacked?

Each of the three case studies poses perplexing questions for the use of chemically-based substances for less-lethal purposes. Yet, the scenarios should put in perspective why law enforcement and military authorities see value in employing them. For those who get "mud on their boots" and risk their lives on the forward edge of hostility, the additional capabilities enabled by chemically-based substances increase chances for mission success while lessening the chances for loss of their own and others' lives.

In Closing

Varied human factors—age, gender, weight, size, and other anatomical and physiological factors—influence the characterization of human effects of chemically-based substances. The state-of the-*human effectiveness*- art for less-lethal capabilities has only begun to be defined and understood. Only within the past decade has there been a concerted effort to do more to understand human effects characterization, and develop the construct to weigh the merits of emerging technologies as capabilities for less-lethal force, as witnessed within the U.S. DoD Joint Non-Lethal Weapons Program. The business as it pertains to chemically-based substances is no different. Aside from simply understanding potential physically disabling effects, understanding the science of the neuroendocrine and immune systems alone is sure to be overwhelming. Yet, the payoff to safeguard life through well-researched initiatives shows promise if we are to believe that the utility of chemically-based substances can make a difference for our military and our law enforcement personnel. To this end, the generally accepted practice of not developing chemically-based less-lethal capabilities in order to comply with the letter of the CWC should be reexamined.

Acknowledgements: I would like to acknowledge Professor David Koplow, John Nelson, Alicia Conrad, Joseph Rutigliano, and John "Butch" Foley, who each provided valuable insight in the preparation of this paper.

Notes

1. In one case, U.S. military personnel became engaged in an extended firefight where hostile personnel used local residents as "human shields." One consequence of the event was that a large number of noncombatants may have been unintentionally killed by U.S. gunfire as troops defended themselves. Less-lethal capabilities such as "tear gas" were not used in this case, but could have lessened the number of casualties if they had been employed.

2. Other nations too had already institutionalized their interest, or were actively doing so about this time. For example the British had a less-lethal project office within the Ministry of Defense to develop capabilities for use in domestic affairs, i.e., Northern Ireland. In the 1990s, NATO formally promulgated guidance for the use of less-lethal weapons.

3. In the summer of 2000, Anthony Zinni retired from the United States Marine Corps as a four-star general. General Zinni's final active duty tour was Commander in Chief, United States Central Command.

4. Department of Defense Directive 3000.3, 9 July 1996, <http://www.dtic.mil/whs/directives/corres/pdf/d30003_070996/d30003p.pdf> (20 July 2006)

5. In this and subsequent quotes from the Chemical Weapons Convention, text is italicized for emphasis.

6. See the Joint Service Small Arms Program's Joint Capabilities & Integration Development System analysis, January 2006.

7. U.S. Joint Non-Lethal Weapons Program, *Master Plan*, October 1998, 6.

8. Anonymous source.

9. Figure 5.1, taken from the public domain, was created in support of the U.S. DoD JNLW program.

10. The text of this paragraph, in part, is paraphrased from research conducted by Alicia Conrad.

11. Antitraction substances may be found in the form of liquid sprays and graphite powders. Foams may be found in the form of liquid foam or sticky foam.

12. Duration in this case is defined in terms of minutes and may be hours, but normally not days. However, the key attribute is the reversibility of the effect(s). Over time, effects dissipate without any lingering permanent effect.

13. Not reflected in this chart but of considerable importance is onset time. RCAs typically have a near-instantaneous effect.

14. A. Allam, "What Could Stink So Much," *The New York Times*, 10 June 2005.

15. The author acknowledges that appropriate research needs to substantiate the cause and effect relationships of malodorants.

16. Fig. 5.2, taken from the public domain, was created for the U.S. DoD JNLW program. The author, while serving as the Director of the DoD JNLWD, co-created this diagram in collaboration with John "Butch" Foley of American Systems Corporation.

17. David A. Koplow, "Tangled Up in Khaki and Blue: Lethal and Non-Lethal Weapons in Recent Confrontations," *Georgetown Journal of International Law* 36, no. 3 (Spring 2005): 703–808. The author's presentation of each of the three case studies is paraphrased from a 2005 version of Dr. Koplow's manuscript. Any error, misinformation, or mistake is the sole responsibility of the author, with no malice intended toward Professor Koplow.

18. The research reveals that three near-simultaneous fires broke out at once. The suspicion is that those fires were deliberately set by cult members.

19. Failure to have an immediate action drill in place can lead to indecision to act; if this was the case, enough time may have lapsed for the narcotic gas to take effect before the terrorists could set off their explosives.

CHAPTER 6

Scientific Outlook for the Development of Incapacitants

Malcolm R. Dando

> It was a very elegant set of presentations on the search for agents to modulate memory. . . .Very elegant work on neurobiology . . . was presented and a series of aged rats were paraded with newly augmented memory functions. . . . And some very elegant structural chemistry was placed onto the board in which various chemicals displayed varied effects in augmented memory. And then with the most casual wave of the hand the individual said, "Of course, modification of the methyl group at C-7 completely eliminates memory. Next slide, please." This is the level of naivete that . . . exists in the community . . .
>
> —George Poste speaking at the National Academies meeting on "Scientific Openness and National Security" 9 January, 2003, Washington, D.C.

Introduction

Given the history of state-level offensive biological and chemical weapons programs during the last century[1] it is natural for those concerned to prevent the use of such weapons in this century to focus first on how to best stop the outbreak of more such state-level programs. Given the simplification and spread of modern chemical and biological technology, it is also understandable for there to be growing concerns about sub-state (terrorist) development and use of such weapons.

What is perhaps surprising is that the 2001 anthrax letter attacks in the United States initiated an additional concern about experiments carried out in civil organizations that might unwittingly provide help to terrorists seeking new forms of chemical and biological weapons. The first experiment that raised such concerns was the inadvertent creation of a lethal mousepox virus by insertion of a single mouse gene encoding the immune system regulator IL-4 into the mousepox genome. This work, published in the *Journal of Virology* in 2001,[2] raised the concern that a deadly human virus might be created in the same way—say by adding the IL-4 gene to the smallpox genome.

Similar concerns were raised the following year when researchers demonstrated that it was possible to artificially synthesize infectious polio virus from lengths of appropriate DNA purchased from commercial companies.[3] Polio is a simple virus, and this experiment had long been considered a possibility, but the fact that it had been done raised the question of whether other, more complex and deadly human viruses like Ebola might be made in the same way by those with hostile intentions.

A third experiment had been carried out in the late 1990s, but what was done also came to be questioned in the developing climate of concern. Researchers had been attempting to discover tissue from victims of the 1918 Spanish Influenza epidemic and to recover parts of the RNA genome of the virus in order to sequence them.[4] They reasoned that as the virus had killed some 20 million people, and unusually for influenza had been particularly lethal for young adults, it was worth trying to discover as much as possible about it. Sequencing of the 1918 Spanish Influenza genome segments was followed by attempts to discover which of these had been responsible for the extreme lethality of the virus[5] and then to the sequencing and recreation of the whole genome.[6,7]

As more attention was given to the subject, however, some observers began to argue that the focus on single experiments risked misunderstanding the nature of the problem. Rather, they argued, it was necessary to look at where a series of related experiments was leading—in what might be termed a "research program."[8] Thus the mousepox recombinant virus was made even more lethal by other researchers who made a more effective insertion of the IL-4 gene, and other pox viruses, including cowpox that can infect humans, were subjected to the same manipulation. Similarly, technical improvements had led to much faster and more efficient creation of viral genomes.[9,10]

Professor Matthew Meselson of Harvard University has indicated where a continuing series of such research programs are likely to lead:[11]

> During the century ahead, as our ability to modify fundamental life processes continues its rapid advance, we will be able not only to de-

vise additional ways to destroy life, but also be able to manipulate it including the processes of cognition, development and inheritance.

And he added:

A world in which these capabilities are widely employed for hostile purposes would be a world in which the very nature of conflict had radically changed. Therein could lie unprecedented opportunities for violence, coercion, repression or subjugation . . .

As Meselson correctly pointed out, all previous scientific and technological revolutions have been extensively exploited for hostile purposes and thus we face the grim possibility that the same will happen to modern biology. There are clear dangers in many fields such as immunology[12] and agriculture.[13] The intention here is to focus on the dangers that may arise from the clear military interest in new chemical incapacitating agents and the ongoing advances in neuroscience.

Incapacitating Biochemical Weapons

An incapacitating (bio)chemical weapon may be defined as an agent that "produces a disabling condition that persists for hours to days after exposure."[14] Specifically the term now means agents that are "highly potent . . . [and] able to produce their effects by altering the higher regulatory activity of the CNS [central nervous system]." Clearly therefore we are not discussing the well known domestic riot control agents such as the tear gas CS as they do not have such effects.

As the revolution in biology has proceeded over the last few decades the distinction between chemical and biological weapons has become less and less useful. It appears better to consider a chemical and biological threat spectrum that ranges from classical chemical agents, through mid-spectrum agents such as toxins and bioregulators, to traditional and genetically modified biological agents (see figure 6.1).

While we classify bioregulators together with toxins as mid-spectrum agents an important difference needs to be kept in mind. Toxins have been subject to the forces of natural selection in very direct predator/prey relationships over evolutionary time. The chances that greatly improved functions can be achieved by chemical manipulation are therefore likely to be limited. Toxins are tightly honed in for the receptor molecule they affect. Bioregulators, on the other hand, while certainly impacted by evolutionary forces, have not been subject to such direct predator/prey relationships. As has been known for decades, very great changes

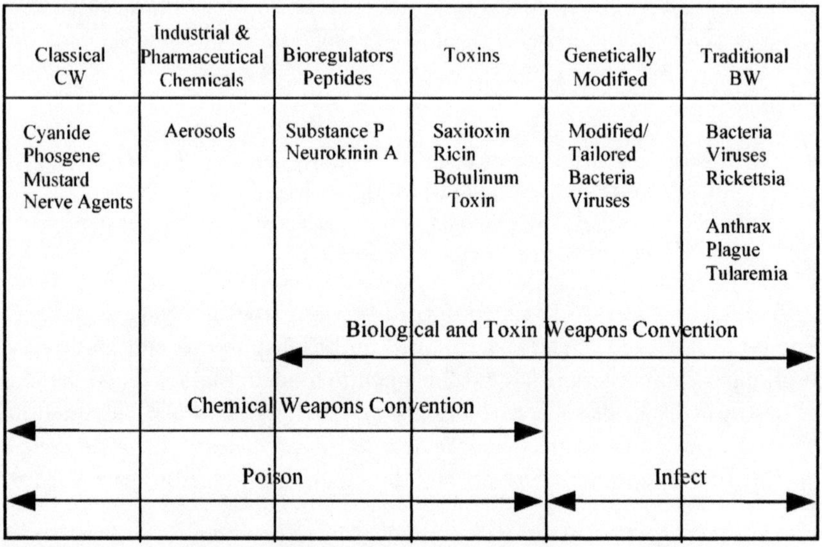

Classical CW	Industrial & Pharmaceutical Chemicals	Bioregulators Peptides	Toxins	Genetically Modified	Traditional BW
Cyanide Phosgene Mustard Nerve Agents	Aerosols	Substance P Neurokinin A	Saxitoxin Ricin Botulinum Toxin	Modified/ Tailored Bacteria Viruses	Bacteria Viruses Rickettsia Anthrax Plague Tularemia

Biological and Toxin Weapons Convention ◄───────►

Chemical Weapons Convention ◄───────►

Poison ◄───────►   Infect ◄───────►

Figure 6.1.   The Biochemical Threat Spectrum

can be made in the strength, or even the characteristics, of their functions by chemical changes in their structures.

During the Cold War, considerable efforts were made by both sides to develop incapacitating agents that disrupted normal bioregulatory functions in the nervous system, the endocrine system, and the immune system.[15] These efforts were largely fruitless due to the limited understanding of these systems available to researchers at the time (see the chapter by Furmanksi in this volume). However, the revolution in biology is now opening up new possibilities for the development of bioregulatory agents as was clearly recognized in a recent report from the U.S. National Academies.[16]

Moreover, the use of bioregulatory agents as weapons is not science fiction. On 23 October 2002 some fifty Chechens took over 800 people hostage in a Moscow theater. Three days later Russian forces stormed the building after pumping large quantities of a "gas" (chemical agent) into the structure. The intention was to incapacitate the hostage takers with the chemical agent so that they could not interfere with the operation—for example by detonating bombs. All of the hostage takers were killed in the assault and over 120 of the hostages died, but a large number were saved. The "gas" used was reported to be a derivative of fentanyl, an opiate chemical related to morphine, perhaps mixed with other agents.[17]

The operation, however, also demonstrated the well-known problems of using such agents. Fentanyl is an anesthetic that will certainly put people to sleep, but in higher concentrations it will stop people breathing. It was first synthesized in Belgium in the 1950s. It has an analgesic potency about eighty times greater than morphine. Fentanyl is one of a number of related compounds widely used in medicine, but there are also analogs used as illegal "designer" drugs. The concentration of fentanyl in any particular part of the building was difficult to control, the effects of any given concentration of it on any particular individual would not have been known in advance, and, crucially, the separation of the lethal and incapacitating effects of the drug are not sufficiently large to eliminate the chance that some of the hostages were going to die or suffer neurological problems after the event.

Nevertheless, it is probable that some military forces have seen the saving of so many people from a group of determined terrorists as a success and may be keen to see if an improved agent could be developed so that such an operation would be more successful in the future. Such notions are not fanciful either as there is clear evidence of military interest in new incapacitating agents. In the United States, where there is more chance of recovering official documentation through the Freedom of Information Act, this recent and continuing interest has been documented in some detail.[18] Moreover, an organization known to have a close relationship to the military in the United States has published a survey of routes of incapacitation thought to be possible at the present time.[19] It was reported, for instance that "[t]he researchers identified several drug classes (e.g., . . . alpha$_2$-adrenoreceptor agonists) and individual drugs (. . . dexmedetomidine) found appropriate for immediate consideration as non-lethal [agents]."

Such findings are hardly surprising as a U.S. Army Chemical and Biological Defense Command Edgewood Research, Development and Engineering Center annual research conference in the early 1990s had a paper that stated that:[20]

> Centrally acting alpha$_2$-adrenergic compounds show antihypertensive actions with sedative properties. More selective alpha$_2$-adrenergic compounds with potent sedative activity have been considered to be ideal next generation anesthetic agents which can be developed and used in the Less-Than-Lethal [non-lethal] Technology program . . .

Similar interest is also evident in European groups presenting at recent meetings on so-called non-lethal weapons.[21]

This paper will begin by taking up the possibilities at the level of the 1990s as the genomics revolution began to allow a better understanding of the complexity of the nervous system at the molecular level. The new knowledge generated by the genomics revolution gives hope that more specific drugs might be found for benign purposes (reducing the difficult side effects that still led many people to stop taking modern drugs for mental health problems). It also suggests that more specific and useable incapacitating agents might be discovered.[22]

The main intention in this paper, however, is to look further forward and to give some examples to indicate what some might consider possible means of incapacitation in the future. Incapacitation is understood here to be a much wider concept than just putting people to sleep. It could, for example, range from disruption of the sense of balance through to the generation of excessive fear. Historically we know that military forces sought many such forms of incapacitation. Additionally, of course, chemical agents were sought by other agencies for different purposes.[23]

Understanding the Human Nervous System

Our understanding that human behavior is a product of the nervous system's operations is very recent and really dates only as far back as the seventeenth century. Detailed understanding of the structure and function of the nervous system is even more recent than that. Only at the end of the nineteenth century, through the work of the great Spanish neuroscientist Cajal, did it become clear that the nervous system was made up of billions of individual nerve cells (neurons). Today we divide these neurons into three major functional groups: those of the autonomic nervous system (involved in functions like control of blood pressure); those of the peripheral nervous system (controlling functions of our skeletal muscles); and those of the central nervous system in the brain and spinal cord.

We now know that information is conveyed within individual neurons by electrical means. Gradually, after Loewi had shown in the 1920s that a chemical was released by neurons to control the heart, it became clear that most information transfer between neurons is by chemical means. When an electrical nerve impulse reaches the end of the long extension (axon) of the neuron it causes the release of a chemical, called a neurotransmitter, into the junction (synapse) between that cell and the next one in the information chain. The effect of this release will depend on the specific neurotransmitter released by the pre-synaptic cell, the nature of the receptors on the postsynaptic cell that recognize the neurotransmitter, and the state of that cell. In general, neurotransmitters are thought to exert either excitatory or inhibitory effects on the possibility of a nerve impulse being initiated in the postsynaptic cell, but the mechanisms can be complex. After its release, the neurotransmitter is cleared from the synapse by other mechanisms, such as reuptake into the presynaptic cell, so that its effect is relatively precise.

Conceptually then there are many ways in which chemical agents or drugs can affect the operations of the central nervous system. A chemical agent might have the same effect as a natural transmitter, or it might lock on to the receptor protein of the postsynaptic cell so that the natural transmitter cannot function at all, or it might prevent the reuptake or enzymatic destruction of the neuro- transmitter in the synaptic region and therefore enhance its natural effects. Just before the Second World War lethal nerve agents were discovered that disrupted acetylcholine neurotransmission, and just after the war a series of chance discov- eries led to the first really useful modern drugs for dealing with mental illnesses. Since that time there has been every reason to try to understand the circuits in the brain that have developed over evolutionary time to control aspects of be- havior and the functions of the neurotransmitter/receptor systems within such circuits. Clearly, the more we understand such systems the more we will be able to reduce the suffering of the many people who have mental illnesses.[24] The re- verse side of the coin is that this knowledge may also increase the possibilities for malign manipulation.

Again it is important not to see such considerations as farfetched. In May 2002, for example, the London *Economist* had a front page headlined "The Fu- ture of Mind Control" and a lead article[25] which contrasted the concerns being voiced over the potential misuse of genetics with the apparent unconcern over the advancing understanding of the nervous system. It argued "If you want to predict and control a person's behavior, the brain is the place to start," and a linked detailed article stated that:[26]

> pharmaceutical companies are only just beginning to mine the spec- trum of psychological ailments that flesh is heir to. Drugs to combat shyness, forgetfulness, sleepiness and stress are now in or close to clin- ical trials, not to mention better versions of drugs that have already swept society . . .

Such concerns, expressed in a general journal widely read by many profes- sionals, have an increasingly solid foundation in the scientific literature. For ex- ample, the journal *Nature* in June 2005 carried a paper[27] titled "Oxytocin in- creases trust in humans." The paper reported on a study of human behavior in a game designed to test levels of trust. Crucially, the game was played under two different conditions. In one people were not given a dose of oxytocin by in- tranasal administration before they played, but in the other condition the oxy- tocin was given. The results were clear-cut. According to the paper "We found that intranasal administration of oxytocin causes a substantial increase in trust- ing behavior." Oxytocin is a neuropeptide (a transmitter chemical found in the brain) which has been extensively studied for several decades and is known to be involved in the regulation of complex behaviors such as reproduction, attach- ment and social recognition in mammals.[28]

A follow-up neuroimaging study to this paper on oxytocin and trust demon- strated that the administration of oxytocin has a specific effect on the amygdala.

The amygdala is the hub of the mammalian neurocircuitry regulating fear and social cognition, and it is where oxytocin receptors have been found to be densely located.[29] The researchers found that "compared with placebo, oxytocin potently reduced the activation of the amygdala and reduced coupling of the amygdala to the brainstem regions implicated in autonomic and behavioral manifestations of fear." Given the increasing knowledge of the structure and function of amygdala receptors provided by the genomics revolution, it is highly probable that the molecular mechanisms underlying the action of oxytocin on the amygdala will be elucidated rapidly.[30]

While the researchers in this field are obviously motivated by a desire to help people suffering from social dysfunctions such as social phobia and autism, they are not unaware of the potential for misuse of their work. The authors of the original paper showing how oxytocin administration impacts on trusting noted that "Of course, this finding could be misused to induce trusting behaviors that selfish actors subsequently exploit."

In short, we have here an example of aerosol delivery of an agent that has a specific effect on a known brain circuit in humans that contains particular neuroreceptors affected by the agent. Moreover, administration of the agent produces a significant effect on social function and this effect could be misused by those with malign intent. It is the contention here that as the genomics and associated revolutions proceeds we shall see many more such examples in a variety of different "research programs." This point will be illustrated below by reference to some of the programs that, if successful in their benign intent, would unfortunately also facilitate other—and perhaps more dangerous—forms of misuse.

In 1999 at a special meeting of the National Academies of Sciences in Washington and the Society of Neuroscience,[31] noted that "The past decade has delivered more advances than all previous years of neuroscience research combined." What lay behind such a remarkable claim? In basic terms, the genomics revolution in biology affected neuroscience as it affected everything else in biology. The body's signaling chemicals, such as bioregulators, affect specific receptors on the cell membrane (or sometimes the cell interior). The first neurotransmitters to be discovered were simple small molecules like acetylcholine, noradrenalin and serotonin (or 5-hydroxytryptamine (5-HT)). During the 1990s, it became increasingly clear that there were a large number of previously unsuspected peptide (short strings of amino-acids) neurotransmitters. At the same time, a large number of genes encoding neurotransmitter receptors were identified and because these receptors fall into a relatively small number of general categories, a vast amount of knowledge was collected very quickly. As the editors of one standard catalogue of receptors noted,[32] in 1990 the listing was thirty pages long and had structural information on a quarter of the receptors. By contrast, in 1999 they pointed out that "In this tenth edition, 106 pages are required to accommodate current information on approximately fifty receptor and ion channel[33] classes, for which structural information is presented for over 99 percent." This large increase in structural information has led to a similarly large increase in our understanding of what that information demonstrates about the complexity of the neurotransmitter systems and the possibilities for manipulation.

The genomics revolution is crucial because:[34]

> the genome sequence information will allow us to make a short-list of proteins with a high probability of becoming drug targets. In the neuroscience area, G protein-coupled receptors (GPCRs)[35] and ion channels are obvious candidates because most existing drugs for neurologic and psychiatric diseases act on these classes of target . . .

And of course these advances have been monitored by the military. As one review noted:[36]

> Advances in discovery of novel bioregulators, especially bioregulators for incapacitation, understanding of their mode of operation and synthetic routes for manufacture have been very rapid in recent times . . .

The review continued:

> Some of these compounds may be potent enough to be many hundreds of times more effective than the traditional chemical warfare agents. Some very important characteristics of new bioregulators that would offer significant military advantages are novel sites of toxic action; rapid and specific effects; penetration of protective filters and equipment; and militarily effective physical incapacitation.

The broad development of understanding is giving investigators in disparate areas of the research the confidence to integrate their different findings in a quite new way. For example, the recent book titled *Neuropsychiatry and Behavioural Neuroscience*[37] includes a chapter on the principles of neuroscience that lists some thirty regularities—predictable brain-behavior relationships—that can be used in understanding and helping to deal with mental illnesses. It is clear that what is being described is a mechanistic science. For example, the first two principles state:

> Brain-behavior relationships underlying neuropsychiatric syndromes are rule-governed and reproducible across individuals . . .
>
> All mental processes derive from brain processes . . .

The third principle in the authors' listing is therefore that "[n]euro-psychiatric symptoms are manifestations of brain dysfunction . . . [that] reflect abnormalities of underlying brain function, whether produced by genetic, structural or environmental influence."

It is not difficult to accept such ideas, for example in regard to language production and comprehension. It has been known for many years that damage to specific areas of the brain produces specific deficiencies in language capability: damage to one region of the cerebral cortex (Broca's area) leads to loss of the ability to generate speech, while damage to a neighboring region (Wernicke's area) leads to a loss of ability to understand language. Similarly, it is clear that damage to specific regions of the frontal lobes of the cerebral cortex can produce specific impairments of human behavior. For example, individuals with damage to the orbitofrontal cortex exhibit disinhibition and impulsiveness. They lack social judgment, have limited insight into their own behavior and are compromised in their ability to empathize with other people. Damage to the medial frontal cortex leads to apathy and akinesia (lack of action).

The principles listed in *Neuropsychiatry and Behavioural Neuroscience* include, in addition to the influence of both genetic and environmental factors, the idea that:

> Neuropsychiatric disorders typically reflect disruption of a system or circuit . . .

and further that;

> Disturbances in transmitters or transmitter systems have specific associated neuropsychiatric symptoms . . .

As we examine a series of specific examples we shall see how claims like those in *Neuropsychiatry and Behavioral Neuroscience* stand up to evidence from recent research.

Examples of Research

By analogy with the research on microbial pathogens described in the introduction to this paper, we are, of course, primarily interested in where particular neuroscience programs are likely to lead rather than with the individual steps along the way.

NEUROTRANSMITTERS

Acetylcholine

Acetylcholine was the first neurotransmitter discovered by Loewi in his 1920s experiment on the heart of the frog. It is a small molecule that is broken down in the synapse by acetylcholinesterase enzyme. The nerve agents discovered in Germany in the 1930s disrupted the normal mechanism by inhibiting this enzyme. The body was therefore unable to clear the acetylcholine from its synapses. Even minute quantities of the nerve agents were sufficient to cause death. Less well known are the considerable efforts to develop incapacitating agents, like BZ, that also disrupted acetylcholine neurotransmission, but by a different mechanism.

When work was being carried out on BZ and other related compounds during the cold war it was known that there were two different types of receptor at the synapses that had acetylcholine as the neurotransmitter chemical. Nicotine mimics the action of acetylcholine at one type and muscarine (an extract from a mushroom) mimics the action at the other. The difficulty for those working during the cold war was that they did not know then, as we know now, that there are some nine sub-types of nicotinic synapse and five sub-types of the muscarinic synapse. Designing a specific chemical to just impact one sub-type to achieve a unique effect was therefore only going to come about by chance and it is no great surprise that no useful chemical incapacitant was developed. BZ, for instance while certainly disrupting memory, just had too many diverse and unpredictable effects.

The muscarinic sub-types of receptor are the most important type in the brain. The sequences of the genes encoding these receptors are strongly conserved in the evolution of the mammals suggesting that they serve vital functions (mutations of the sequence being deleterious). In the central nervous system, "there is evidence that muscarinic receptors are involved in motor control, temperature regulation, cardiovascular regulation and memory."[38] Clearly, this range of functions is of interest to the drug companies, particularly in view of the increasing impact of Alzheimer's disease and memory loss in the aging population of the developed world.

One aspect of the genomics revolution that might not be fully appreciated by those outside of the field of study is that it has been possible to breed mice with specific genes knocked out. These "knock-out" mice are often viable and allow insight into the precise functions of the various sub-types of receptor.[39] From such studies it has become clear that the M2 sub-type of receptor functions as an inhibitory autoreceptor on muscarinic neurons. That is, when the neuron was active and producing neurotransmitter it was also subject to negative feedback reducing its output. Given that it is known that there is a reduction in acetyl-choline neurons in Alzheimer's disease there is every incentive for drug companies to try to find means to block the M2 receptor. Thus it was reported that:[40]

> the high receptor selectivity of SCH72788 [drug candidate chemical], which has a reasonable *in vivo* activity, and, in conscious rats, increases Ach [acetylcholine] concentrations in the striatum and shows positive effects on a rat model of passive avoidance [a widely used relevant behavioral test] . . .

While the details of the degeneration in Alzheimer's disease are complex it clearly might be possible to design a chemical that blocks these receptors and so assists cognitive functions. Equally, it might be possible to find a chemical to enhance the activation of these receptors and thus increase the negative feedback and cut the acetylcholine output to disrupt the brain's memory functions in a rather specific way. Disruption of soldiers' memory capabilities would obviously have a significant negative impact on the warfighting capabilities of modern armies.

Cholecystokinin

An example of a peptide that might appear attractive to those with malign intent is cholecystokinin (CCK). This neuropeptide is found in high concentrations in regions of the brain implicated in the regulation of fear and anxiety. It occurs in a variety of different molecular forms, such as the tetrapeptide cholecystokinin-4 (a string of four amino acids), and these neurotransmitters interact with two different receptor sub-types. It has been known for decades that this peptide causes panic attacks in human beings. As one recent paper noted:[41]

> Intravenous administration of the CCK2 receptor agonist [chemical having the same effect as the natural transmitter], CCK-tetrapeptide (CCK-4), provokes panic attacks in patients with panic disorder (PD) and to a lesser extent in normal controls . . .

This result appears to be rather specific, suggesting a distinct mechanism, as related disorders such as social phobia and obsessive-compulsive disorder are not so affected. Cholecystokinin-4 also produces anxiogenic behaviors in rodents so the effects of drugs that might help those suffering such attacks can be investigated.[42] Moreover, there is accumulating evidence that there is a link between one form of the cholecystokinin-B receptor gene and susceptibility to panic attacks[43] suggesting that further understanding of the causes of panic attacks in humans will shortly become much clearer.

Obviously, again, if a specific drug can be developed to reduce the incidence of panic attacks[44] the reverse may also be possible. While this benignly orientated work involves administration of the drugs by injection it cannot be certain that compounds with similar effects that can be delivered as aerosols will not be discovered by those with malign intent. Clearly it would take only a small percentage of a group of soldiers to be affected by panic attacks to greatly disrupt operations.

Substance P

A rather more recently discovered possibility concerns Substance P. This substance has been known since the early 1930s. It is now understood to be a member of a class of neuropeptides that also includes neurokinin A and neurokinin B. All three have affinities for three receptor sub-types designated as NK1, NK2, and NK3. Substance P has greatest affinity for the NK1 receptor and it is known to have involvement in many of the body's biochemical functions. What effects the substance, or chemical agonists or antagonists (chemicals having the opposite effect) might have will depend on the particular circuit and receptor locations to which a substance is delivered. Substance P has been of concern to biodefense authorities because it can cause very intense bronchoconstriction at low concentrations. A study by a biodefense group noted that "[e]xposure to the substance at extremely low air concentrations may result in incapacitation in humans."[45] The mechanisms involved in this reaction are complex, but synthetic antagonists to NK1 receptors have been tested in clinical trials in an attempt to find ways to alleviate asthma.

What is of more interest here is that there has recently been intense interest in the possibility that Substance P is in some way involved in the mechanism of depression. Mapping of the distribution of the NK1 receptors distribution in the brain showed that they were expressed strongly in regions involved in the regulation of affective (emotional) behavior and stress responses. The development of selective non-peptide Substance P antagonists during the 1990s allowed the role of Substance P to be investigated in detail. One standard method of preclinical testing of antidepressants is to see if they reduce symptoms of anxiety called stress-induced vocalizations in mammalian species. It was discovered that Substance P antagonists did in fact completely inhibit such vocalizations in guinea pig pups separated briefly from their mothers. This led to the initiation of a great deal of work because there is a need for better antidepressants, particularly if they appear to be acting in different ways to the usual drugs.[46] At present the results of clinical trials are unclear.[47] Nevertheless, researchers are now turning to investigate the therapeutic potential of all of the NK receptor system with the possibility that blockage of more than one receptor type could give more dramatic results.[48] Advances in our understanding of the structure of these receptors is greatly assisting the development of new agonists and antagonists of Substance P.[49] Of course, again, as means of relieving depression via this route is elucidated those with malign intent might be able to use the same knowledge in the reverse direction.

A NEUROTRANSMITTER IN A KNOWN BRAIN CIRCUIT

For a long period in the twentieth century there was a huge gap between those who investigated mental illness from a psychiatric or from a behaviorist standpoint. In recent years, a more integrated stance has developed. This more biologically sound approach has allowed greater prominence to be given— correctly—to the function of emotions in behavior.[50] For example, as we have seen, a great deal is now known about the fear circuit in our brain. This is of interest to the medical profession because it may well help them to assist people suffering from problems such as posttraumatic stress disorder (PTSD) in which bad memories are relived in flashbacks and nightmares that significantly disrupt normal living.[51]

The basic elements of the system for responding to fearful events are known to be built into all mammals. Thus if we hear a large explosion humans and other animals will exhibit a startle response and freeze momentarily before the flight-or-fight response kicks in. As one of the main investigators of the fear response, Joseph LeDoux, argued:[52]

> In a situation of danger, a variety of physiological responses occur. Blood is redistributed to the body parts that are more in need (the muscles). This results in changes in blood pressure and heart rate. In addition, the hypothalamic-pituitary-adrenal, or HPA, axis is activated, releasing stress hormones. In general, the body is readied to move quickly. In addition, the brain activates the release of natural opiate peptides, morphine-like substances that block the sensation of pain . . .

Researchers have turned to animal models over which they can exert a certain amount of control, and thus have a simpler problem to analyze, in order to gain a better understanding of the fear system. They have, for example, studied the multiple impacts of fear on the rat through the use of classical fear conditioning (after Pavlov). The rat is repeatedly subjected to a sound (which it does not fear) followed by a mild electric shock (to which it does react with fear). It learns to react to the sound alone in anticipation of the shock. Thus the sound becomes the stimulus triggering the fear response. Investigators like LeDoux knew that sound picked up in the ear is processed in the auditory mid-brain, then the auditory thalamus and finally in the auditory cortex (the highest level). Surprisingly, when lesions were made in the auditory cortex it was found that rats could still associate the shock and sound and were still reacting with fear to the sound alone. The auditory cortex is clearly not required to support such behavior.

Further investigation showed that lesions in either of the sub-cortical levels (auditory thalamus and auditory mid-brain) eliminated the response. The information mediating the fear response was obviously being processed somewhere beyond the thalamus, but not in the auditory cortex. This location was found to be the amygdala—which was not too surprising since the amygdala had been known for years to be important in emotional responses. Such research led LeDoux to the view that in an immediate reaction to any fearful situation:

> The low road, of the thalamo-amygdala pathway, is a quick and dirty system. Because it doesn't involve the cortex at all, it allows us to act first and think later. . . .We freeze first, and that gives us a few seconds to decide what to do: Run away? Hold still? Try to fight?

If we are in a wood and see a stick that might possibly be a snake we are better reacting immediately as if it were indeed a snake. However, "[t]he cortex—the high road, so to speak—also processes the stimulus, but it takes a little longer." While the amygdala pathway prepares for action the cortex pathway is simultaneously processing the information, and if it decides that what we see is actually a stick and not a snake little effort is wasted as it can switch off the emergency response.

In addition to the amygdala's role in the immediate response to any such fearful stimulus, it has been noted also that:[53]

> there is a strong consensus that the amygdala is involved in mediating the effects of emotional arousal on memory. Findings of many studies indicate that the amygdala mediates the consolidation of long-term explicit memories of emotionally arousing experiences by influencing other brain regions involved in memory consolidation.

In other words, in addition to its role in processing information on an immediately fearful situation, the amygdala is also involved in the further process of remembering that particular threat and responding to it in the future. The mechanism by which this is done is complex, but is being elucidated. Under stress the hypothalamus secretes corticotrophin-releasing hormone (CRF) into the pituitary portal blood supply and this causes the anterior pituitary gland to produce adrenocorticotropic hormone that, in turn, enters the general circulation and causes the adrenal cortex to secrete glucocorticoids. At the same time the sympathetic nervous system activates the secretion of adrenaline from the adrenal medulla. These two agents, glucocorticoids and adrenaline, have significant effects on the mobilization of the body, but they also affect the functions of the amygdala. First, there is considerable evidence that adrenaline, which does not pass the blood-brain barrier, still has an indirect impact. Alpha-adrenoreceptors on afferents in the vagal nerve recognize the adrenaline and send information into the central nervous system that leads to enhanced noradrenalin neurotransmitter output in the amygdala.[54] Noradrenalin is also recognized by alpha-adrenoreceptor, and perfusion of the amygdala with alpha-adrenoreceptor agonists after training enhances memory consolidation while antagonism of alpha-adrenoreceptors blocks the enhancement. At the same time, the glucocorticoids released by the adrenal cortex enter the brain freely, where they have multiple effects through specific receptor systems. In particular, glucocorticoid effects on memory consolidation require them to act on the amygdala. Infusion of glucocorticoid agonists into the amygdala after training enhances memory retention whereas infusion of antagonists impairs retention. Again it can be concluded that the amygdala is the location for the impact of glucocorticoid enhancement on memory consolidation.

Details of the neurotransmitter and neuroreceptor systems involved in the various pathways linked to the amygdala's role in memory consolidation are being steadily elucidated. It is the case, for example, that both postsynaptic $alpha_1$-and beta-adrenoceptors are activated in the amygdala cells by the release of noradrenalin.[55] It has also been shown that this noradrenalin-based activation must occur for glucocorticoid enhancement of memory consolidation to happen.[56,57]

In summary then, it is clear that the amygdala is on one of the pathways leading to the initial readiness of the body to respond to danger signals.[58] Subsequently, input from the body leads to noradrenalin and glucocorticoid activation of cells in the amygdala, and output from the activated cells has a considerable impact on the enhancement of memory by other brain structures. Furthermore, enhancement via the amygdala can be interrupted by the use of antagonists that act on the amygdala adrenoceptors. What then does this have to do with treatment of people suffering from PTSD?

Studies on human beings suggest a similar set of roles for the amygdala in dealing with fearful situations.[59] Indeed the idea of a direct relationship between noradrenalin and memory for emotional events has even been tested in humans. Healthy subjects were either given a placebo or propranolol (which passes the blood-brain barriers and antagonizes the action of noradrenalin) one hour before viewing a series of either neutral or emotionally stressful scenes. One week later people who had received the placebo had significantly better memories of the emotional slides but those who had received the propanolol did not remember them any better than the neutral ones.[60]

Such results have led to efforts to prevent people developing PTSD, in one example giving victims of car crashes propranolol quickly after the event. Some observers, however, are concerned that such treatment, if successful, might be used to enable people to carry out dreadful actions and retain no memory of them. Dr. Leon Kass, chairman of the President's Council on Bioethics in the United States has been quoted as saying "[i]t's the morning-after pill for just about anything that produces regret, pain, or guilt."[61] A national coordinator for Vietnam Veterans Against the War agreed and argued that such treatment could "make men and women do anything and think they can get away with it."

A different possibility, of course, is that those with malign intent might find means—through a chemical agent—to induce and enhance PTSD, not prevent it. Given the stress of military operations, PTSD is a frequent outcome for soldiers and the possibility of enhancing that outcome for enemy forces might be seen as advantageous in disrupting operations. Enhancing PTSD might be viewed as even more attractive to interrogators and torturers.

A NEUROTRANSMITTER IN A KNOWN BRAIN CIRCUIT AND WITH A KNOWN GENETIC BASIS

It is clear that another capability that has come about in the genomics revolution is the ability to detect the genetic makeup of individuals. This opens up the prospect of understanding the contribution of a particular genetic makeup to a particular behavior.

A major contribution to this end was published in 2003. In December of that year the journal *Science*, as its "Breakthrough of the Year" featured a study of dark energy and dark matter that gave us a firm age for the universe and a precise speed of expansion. The runner-up was the study of mental illness,[62] and specifically mentioned was an article in *Science* in July of that year.[63] The article was titled "Influence of life stress on depression: moderation by a polymorphism on the 5-HTT gene." A polymorphism is a slight natural variation in a particular gene, and the 5-HTT gene is the gene which codes for the transporter protein for serotonin (5-HT). This protein removes serotonin from the synapse. In the past, many people believed that while a few devastating mental illnesses, such as Huntington's disease, were caused by malfunctions in single genes, the vast majority were caused by the combined actions of many genes with small effects—thus making causal elucidations very difficult. However, this study on depression concluded by stating:

> We speculate that some multifactorial disorders, instead of resulting
> from variations in many genes of small effect, may result from variations

in fewer genes whose effects are conditional on exposure to environmental risks.

In short, if one considers both the genetics and the environmental experience, some mental illnesses may soon be clearly understood because of our new knowledge of the genome.

The polymorphism in the 5-HTT gene concerned the structure of the promoter. This region determines how efficiently the gene is expressed, and therefore the amount of protein produced. In its long form it allows more expression of the gene than the short form. Thus the long form would mean that there was more transporter protein and presumably more precise synaptic action (as the serotonin would be more rapidly removed back into the pre-synaptic neuron). We each carry two copies (or alleles) of the gene so it is possible to separate people into three groups on this basis. We each have either two long forms of the promoter, two short forms, or one of each. Of course, the researchers had good reasons for suspecting that this gene might be involved in depression, because one class of drugs used effectively in treating depression act by inhibiting serotonin reuptake.

The researchers were involved in a long-term assessment of some 1037 children in New Zealand who had been regularly studied as a cohort since birth and ninety-six per cent of the original cohort were still being studied at age 26. Many aspects of their lives could be studied, for example stressful life events occurring between their twenty-first and twenty-sixth birthdays could be carefully catalogued for each individual. These events included employment, finance, housing, health and relationships as types of stressor. Members of the group were also assessed for the occurrence of depression over the year from their twenty-fifth birthday. The results from assessing the interaction of the different forms of the 5-HTT gene and life stressors were very clear-cut. As the authors reported:

> Individuals with one or two copies of the short allele of the 5-HTT promoter polymorphism exhibited more depressive symptoms, diagnosable depression, and suicidality in relation to stressful life events than individuals homozygous for the long allele [i.e., with two long forms] . . .

The impact of life events was clearly shown to have been moderated by the individual's genetic constitution—a quite remarkable discovery only made possible by modern biotechnology capabilities.

The researchers also demonstrated a similar impact of childhood maltreatment on those carrying one or both short versions of the gene. An analogous association has been shown in monkeys,[64] and in other children.[65] However, the latter report also showed that adequate social support could greatly reduce the risk to such maltreated children. This happy result also tends to confirm another principle[66] that "The beneficial effects of psychotherapy are mediated through changes in brain function." Unfortunately, more recent work has again demonstrated the link between the serotonin transporter promoter polymorphism and suicide.[67]

It may be argued, of course, that while it is a breakthrough to show how such gene and environment interactions can affect behavior, that is a long way from the kind of detailed mechanistic understanding that would really allow malign manipulation of the brain and people's behavior. It must be remembered, however, that the genomics revolution has not taken place in isolation. There have been associated major developments in bioinformatics, combinatorial chemistry and in neuroimaging.

ALL THE ABOVE AND NEUROIMAGING

During the 1990s there was a spectacular advance in the technical capabilities allowing investigators to follow what was happening in the brain while it was in operation. This is clear from a paper published in *Science* in 2002. Again it was on the subject of the serotonin transporter gene and was titled "Serotonin transporter genetic variation and the response of the human amygdala." The amygdala makes sense as a target because, as we have seen, it is known to be centrally involved in the processing of threatening inputs and fearful and anxious states.[68] Indeed, as we have noted, if we encounter a potentially threatening situation, a rapid signaling pathway through the amygdala triggers the body's set of reaction that ready it for action—the so-called "fight or flight" response. Only somewhat later will a considered analysis by higher regions of the brain shut down the response if the situation is found not to be threatening. These researchers used a form of functional magnetic resonance imaging to assess subjects' responses to frightening facial images. They divided people into two groups: those with two long alleles and those with one or two copies of the short form of the promoter. The subjects were all healthy but nevertheless there was a clear difference in the responses of the two groups. People with the short form showed greater activity in the amygdala in response to frightening stimuli than those with only the long form. The difference was located in the right amygdala consistent with the right hemisphere's known role in processing facial images.

The 2002 study was published before the work on gene and environment interactions discussed earlier. However, a later, much larger, study involving some ninety people confirmed the 2002 results.[69] This study, "A susceptibility gene for affective disorders and the response of the human amygdala," concluded in part that "heritable variation in 5-HT signaling associated with the 5-HTT . . . results in relatively heightened amygdala responsivity to salient environmental cues." In short, if you have the short version of the promoter you are likely to have a stronger amygdala response to threatening situations. Furthermore, the authors went on to argue that if such threats occur early in life before the full development of the higher centers' control, over-response of the amygdala could bias the system towards over-response. In line with this view, a study of people with social phobia showed that when put under stress, those with the short allele had a stronger response in the right amygdala.[70] It concluded: "the present results support a genetically determined link between serotonergic functions, anxiety proneness and a brain region central for emotional experience and processing." The mechanistic detail of how the system dysfunction arises is being worked out in animal models.[71] Moreover, the serotonin transporter is not the only gene for which this new imaging genomics approach is producing such results.[72]

As this example clearly demonstrates, our understanding of the brain and human behavior is reaching the level at which precise manipulation for beneficial reasons is becoming more and more feasible. Yet such information might also potentially be used for malign purposes, for example to induce anxiety and mood disorders.

Conclusion

None of the forgoing examples would allow the conclusion that a precise irritant chemical agent that would overcome the well-known problems—particularly the small gap between incapacitating and lethal doses—is available at the present time. However, these increasingly complex examples suggest that at least some areas of neuroscience are on a trajectory—have a research program—that is very likely to produce usable beneficial results. Thus it is surely likely that those seeking incapacitating capabilities will argue that these civil research programs should be monitored because there is such rapid progress in civil neuroscience that dual-use capabilities could well come about rather quickly. In short their view is likely to be that the scientific outlook for the development of new incapacitants is good. Preventing such developments will therefore have to be undertaken by means outside of the science and technology.

Notes

1. M. L. Wheelis, L. Rozsa, and M. R. Dando, eds., *Deadly Culture: Biowarfare Programs from 1945 to the Present* (Cambridge, MA: Harvard University Press, 2006).

2. R. J. Jackson, A. J. Ramsey, C. D. Christensen, S. Beaton, and others, "Expression of Mouse Interleukin-4 by a Recombinant Ectromelia Virus Suppresses Cytolytic Lymphocyte Responses and Overcomes Genetic Resistance to Mousepox," *Journal of Virology* 75 (2001): 1205-1210.

3. J. Cello, A. V. Paul, and E. Wimmer, "Chemical Synthesis of Poliovirus cDNA: Generation of Infectious Virus in the Absence of Natural Template," *Science* 297 (2002): 16–18.

4. J. K. Taubenberger, A. H. Reid, A. E. Krafft, K. E. Bijwaard, and others, "Initial Genetic Characterization of the 1918 Spanish Influenza Virus," *Science* 275 (1997): 1793–1796.

5. D. Kobasa, A. Takada, K. Shinya, M. Hatta, and others, "Enhanced Virulence of Influenza A Viruses with Haemagglutinin of the 1918 Pandemic Virus," *Nature* 431 (2004): 703–7.

6. T. M. Tumpey, C. F. Basler, P. V. Aguilar, H. Zeng, and others, "Characterization of the Reconstructed 1918 Spanish Influenza Pandemic Virus," *Science* 310 (2005): 77–80.

7. E. Ghedin, N. A. Sengamalay, M. Shumway, J. Zaborsky, and others, "Large-Scale Sequencing of Human Influenza Reveals the Dynamic Nature of Viral Genome Evolution," *Nature* 437 (2005): 1162–66.

8. M. R. Dando and B. Rappert, "Codes of Conduct for the Life Sciences: Some Insights from UK Academia," *Briefing Paper no. 16*, University of Bradford, 2005.

9. H. O. Smith, C. A. Hutchinson, C. P. Pfannkoch, and J. C. Venter, "Generating a Synthetic Genome by Whole Genome Assembly: OX 174 Bacteriophage from Synthetic Oligonucleotides," *Proceedings of the National Academy of Science* (2004).

10. J. Tian, H. Gong, N. Sheng, and X. Zhou, "Accurate Multiplex Gene Synthesis from Programmable DNA Microchips," *Nature* 432 (2004): 1050–53.

11. M. Meselson, "Averting the Hostile Exploitation of Biotechnology," *The CBW Conventions Bulletin* 48 (2000): 16–19.

12. K. Nixdorff, "Assault on the Immune System," *Disarmament Forum* 1 (2005): 25–37.

13. S. Whitby, *Biological Warfare Against Crops*. (Basingstoke, NH: Palgrave, 2002).

14. G. Cooper and P. Rice, "Centrally Acting Incapacitants," *Journal of the Royal Army Medical Corps* 48 (2002): 388–92.

15. E. Kagan, "Bioregulators as Instruments of Terror," *Clinics in Laboratory Medicine* 21 (2001): 607–18.

16. "Our Uncertain Future: Biosecurity and Globalization of the Life Sciences," National Academies, Washington, D.C., 2006.

17. B. Van Damme, "Moscow Theater Siege: A Deadly Gamble that Nearly Paid Off," *The Pharmaceutical Journal* 269 (2002): 723–24.

18. E. Hammond, "Recent Research, Development, and Use of Biochemical Weapons: What is Publicly Known?" (paper presented at a symposium on incapacitating biochemical weapons, Geneva, Switzerland, 11 June 2005).

19. J. M. Lokoski, W. B. Murray, and J. M. Kenny, "The Advantages and Limitations of Calmatives for Use as a Non-Lethal Technique," Applied Research Laboratory, College of Medicine, The Pennsylvania State University, College Park, 2000.

20. "Chronology," *The Chemical Weapons Convention Bulletin* 27 (15–18 November 1995): 16–17.

21. L. Hess, J. Schreiberova, and J. Fusek, "Pharmacological Non-Lethal Weapons" (paper presented at the Second European Meeting on Non-Lethal Technologies, 2005).

22. It is not just in the area of biochemistry and molecular biology that advances are being made. As we shall see later, technical advances in neuroimaging are beginning to allow investigators to "see" the brain's operations in almost real time.

23. M. L. Wheelis and M. R. Dando, "Neurobiology: A Case Study of the Imminent Militarization of Biology," *International Review of the Red Cross* 87 no. 859 (2005): 553–68.

24. "Mental Health: New Understanding, New Hope," *World Health Report 2001*, (Geneva: World Health Organization, 2001).

25. Leader, "The Future of Mind Control," *The Economist*, 25 May 2002, 11.

26. "The Ethics of Brain Science: Open Your Mind," *The Economist*, 25 May 2002, 93-95.

27. M. Kosfeld, M. Heinrichs, P. J. Zak, U. Fischbacher, and others, "Oxytocin Increases Trust in Humans," *Nature*, 435 (2005): 673–76.

28. J. T. Winslow, "The Social Deficits of the Oxytocin Knockout Mouse," *Neuropeptides* 36 (2002): 221–29.

29. P. Kirsch, C. Esslinger, Q. Chen, D. Mier, and others, "Oxytocin Modulates Neural Circuitry for Social Cognition and Fear in Humans," *Journal of Neuroscience* 25 (2005): 11489–493.

30. D. Huber, P. Vienante, and R. Stoop, "Vasopressin and Oxytocin Excite Distinct Neuronal Populations in the Central Amygdala," *Science* 308 (2005): 245–48.

31. "Neuroscience 2000: A New Era of Discovery," Symposium Organized by the Society of Neuroscience, Washington, D.C., 12–13 April 1999).

32. S. Alexander, J. Peters, A. Mead, and S. Lewis, "TiPS Receptor and Ion Channel Nomenclature Supplement 1999," *Elsevier Trends Journals* (1999).

33. Ion channels are fast acting pores in the cell membrane through which various types of ions (depending on the specificity of the channel) are allowed or enabled to pass, leading to changes in the electrical properties of the postsynaptic cell in response to neurotransmitter release by the pre-synaptic cell.

34. A. D. Howard, G. McAllister, S. D. Feighner, Q. Liu, and others, "Orphan G-Protein-Coupled Receptors and Natural Ligand Discovery," *Trends in the Pharmacological Sciences* 22 (2001): 133–40.

35. One type of receptor, typically slower-acting than ion channels and having more complex effects.

36. S. Bokan, J. G. Breen, and Z. Orehovec, "An Evaluation of Bioregulators as Terrorism and Warfare Agents," *The ASA Newsletter* 90 (2002): 1, 16–19.

37. J. L. Cummings and M. S. Maga, *Neuropsychiatry and Behavioural Neuroscience* (Oxford: Oxford University Press, 2003).

38. M. P. Caulfield and N. J. M Birdsall, "International Union of Pharmacology. XVII. Classification of Muscarinic Acetylcholine Receptors," *Pharmacological Reviews* 50 (1998): 279–90.

39. F. P. Bymaster, "Use of M1-M5 Muscarinic Receptor Knockout Mice as Novel Tools to Delineate the Physiological Roles of the Muscarinic Cholinergic System," *Neurochemical Research* 28 (2003): 437–42.

40. J. E. Lachowicz, "Selective M2 Antagonists Facilitate Acetylcholine Release and Improve Performance in Behavioral Models of Cognition" (presentation 115.2 in the Symposium on Advances in Muscarinic Receptor Research at the International Congress of Pharmacology, San Francisco, 7–12 July 2002).

41. M. A. Katzman, D. Koszycki, and J. Bradwejn, "Effects of CCK–Tetrapeptide in Patients with Social Phobia and Obsessive-Compulsive Disorder," *Depression and Anxiety* 20 (2004): 51–58.

42. J. M. Zanoveli, C. F. Netto, F. S. Guimarares, and H. Zangrossi Jr., "Systemic and Intra-Dorsal Periaqueductal Gray Injections of Cholecytokinin Sulfated Octapeptide (CCK-8s) Induce a Panic-Like Response in Rats Submitted to the Elevated T-Maze," *Peptides* 25 (2004): 1935–1941.

43. V. G. Hosing, A. Schirmacher, G. Kuhlenabaumer, C. Freitag, and others, "Cholecystokinin- and Cholecystokinin-B-Receptor Gene Polymorphisms in Panic Disorder," *Journal of Neural Transmission Supplement* 68 (2004): 147–56.

44. A. S. Kopin, E. W. McBride, K. Schaffer, and M. Beinborn, "CCK Receptor Polymorphisms: An Illustration of Emerging Themes in Pharmacogenomics," *Trends in the Pharmacological Sciences* 21 (2000): 346–53.

45. B. L. Koch, A. A. Edvinsson, L. O. Koskinen, "Inhalation of Substance P and Thiorphan: Acute Toxicity and Effects on Respiration in Conscious Guinea Pigs," *Journal of Applied Toxicology* 19 (1999): 19–23.

46. S. C. Stout, M. J. Owens, and C. B. Nemeroff, "Neurokinin 1 Receptor Antagonists as Potential Antidepressants," *Ann. Rev. Pharmacol. Toxicol.* 41 (2001): 877–906.

47. S. McLean, "Do Substance P and NK1 Receptor Have a Role in Depression and Anxiety?" *Curr Pharm Des* 11 (2005): 1529–47.

48. I. Herpfer and K. Lieb, "Substance P Receptor Antagonists in Psychiatry: Rationale for Development and Therapeutic Potential," *CNS Drugs* 19 (2005): 275–93.

49. P. Datar, S. Srivastava, E. Coutinho, and G. Govil, "Substance P: Structure, Function and Therapeutics," *Curr Top Med Chem* 4 (2004): 75–103.

50. J. Pankesepp, *Textbook of Biological Psychiatry* (New Jersey: Wiley-Liss, 2004).

51. A. Frances and M. B. First, *Your Mental Health: A Layman's Guide to the Psychiatrists' Bible* (New York: Scribner, 1998), 109-116, and Chapter 5, "Exposure to Traumatic Events."

52. J. LeDoux, "The Power of Emotions" in R. Conlon, ed., *States of Mind: New Discoveries About How Our Brains Make Us Who We Are* (New York: John Wiley and Sons, 1999), 123–150.

53. J. L. McGaugh, C. K. McIntyre, and A. E. Power, "Amygdala Modulation of Memory Consolidation: Interaction with Other Brain Systems," *Neurobiology of Learning and Memory* 78 (2002): 539–552.

54. J. L. McGaugh and B. Roozendaal, "Role of Adrenal Stress Hormones in Forming Lasting Memories in the Brain," *Current Opinion in Neurobiology* 12 (2002): 205–210.

55. B. Ferry, B. Roozendaal, and J. L. McGaugh, "Basolateral Amygdala Noradrenergic Influences on Memory Storage are Mediated by an Interaction Between beta- and alpha$_1$-Adrenoceptors," *Journal of Neuroscience* 19, no. 2 (1999): 5119–23.

56. B. Roozendaal, S. Qkuda, E. A. Van der Zee, and J. L. McGaugh, "Glucocorticoid Enhancement of Memory Requires Arousal-Induced Noradrenergic Activation in the Basolateral Amygdala," *Proc. Nat. Acad. Sci.*103 (2006): 6741–46.

57. B. Roozendaal, G. K. Hui, I. R. Hui, D .J. Berlau, and others, "Basolateral Amygdala Noradrenergic Activity Mediates Corticosteroid-Induced Enhancement of Auditory Fear Conditioning," *Neurobiology of Learning and Memory,* 86 (2006): 249–55.

58. E. Vermetten and J. D. Bremner, "Circuits and Systems in Stress: I. Preclinical Studies," *Depression and Anxiety* 15 (2002): 126–47.

59. R. Grossman, M.S. Buchsbaum, and R. Yehuda, "Neuroimaging Studies in Post-Traumatic Stress Disorder," *Psychiatric Clinics of North America* 25 (2002): 317–40.

60. S. M. Southwick, J. D. Bremner, A. Rasmusson, C. A. Morgan, and others, "Role of Norepinephrine in the Pathophysiology and Treatment of Post-Traumatic Stress Disorder," *Biological Psychiatry* 46, no. 9 (1999): 1192–1204.

61. E. Baard, "The Guilt-Free Soldier: New Science Raises the Specter of a World without Regret," *The Village Voice,* 22–28 January 2003.

62. "Breakthrough of the Year: The Runners-Up," *Science* 302 (2003): 2039–40.

63. A. Caspi, K. Sugden, T. E. Moffitt, A. Taylor, and others, "Influence of Life Stress on Depression: Moderation by a Polymorphism in the 5-HTT Gene," *Science* 301(2003): 386–89.

64. C. S. Barr, T. K. Newman, M. Schwardt, C. Shannon, and others, "Sexual Dichotomy of an Interaction between Early Adversity and the Serotonin Transporter Gene Promoter Variant in Rhesus Macaques," *Proc. Nat. Acad. Sci.* 101, no. 33, (2004): 12358–363.

65. J. Kaufman, "Social Supports and Serotonin Transporter Gene Moderate Depression in Maltreated Children," *Proc. Nat. Acad. Sci.* 101 (2004): 17316–321.

66. J. L. Cummings and M. S. Maga, *Neuropsychiatry and Behavioral Neuroscience* (Oxford: Oxford University Press, 2003).

67. P. Y. Lin and G. Tsai, "Association between Serotonin Transporter Gene Promoter Polymorphism and Suicide: Results of a Meta-Analysis," *Biol. Psychiatry* 55 (2004): 1023–w30.

68. A. R. Hariri, V. S. Mattay, A. Tessitore, B. Kolachana, and others, "Serotonin Transporer Genetic Variation and the Response of the Human Amygdala," *Science* 297 (2002): 400–3.

69. A. R. Hariri, E. M. Drabant, V. E. Munoz, B. S. Kolachana, and others, "A Susceptibility Gene for Affective Disorders and the Response of the Human Amygdala," *Arch. Gen. Psychiatry* 62 (2005): 146–52.

70. T. Furmark, M. Tillfors, H. Garpenstrand, I. Marteinsdottir, and others, "Serotonin Transporter Polymorphism Related to Amygdala Excitability and Symptom Severity in Patients with Social Phobia," *Neuroscience Letters* 362 (2004): 189–92.

71. C. S. Barr, T. K. Newman, C. Shannon, C. Parker, and others, "Rearing Conditions and Rh5-HTTLPR Interact to Influence Limbic-Hypothalamic-Pituitary-Adrenal Axis Response to Stress in Infant Macaques," *Biol. Psychiatry* 55 (2004): 733–38.

72. A. R. Hariri and D. R. Weinberger, "Imaging Genomics," *British Medical Bulletin* 65 (2003): 259–70.

CHAPTER 7

Potential Long-Term Physiological Consequences of Exposure to Incapacitating Biochemicals

Kathryn Nixdorff and Jack Melling

Introduction

The past three decades have seen an explosive accumulation of knowledge concerning the mechanisms of pathogenicity of infectious microorganisms and the functions of biological systems. The revolution in biotechnology is continuing on into a revolution in pharmacology with an emphasis on drug discovery and drug delivery. While these advances are essential for the promotion of health security in general, it is clear that this information may also be misused in a malign way to develop new biochemical agents (particularly bioregulators— substances produced by the body in small amounts that regulate biological systems) that can be deployed as weapons.[1,2]

When considering possible long-term consequences of exposure to incapacitating biochemical agents, one has to view their effects within the context of interacting biological (physiological) systems. Traditionally, progress in understanding major physiological systems such as the nervous system, the endocrine system and the immune system has been made by studying each system in isolation. This has been done in an attempt to reduce the enormous complexity involved in biological pathways of interaction. In recent years, however, it has become clear that these three systems interact intricately, and the regulation of their functions by biochemical substances produced within the systems themselves is highly interdependent.[3] All three systems are interconnected through the hypothalamus-pituitary-adrenal (HPA) axis via the action of cytokines, hormones, neurotransmitters, and peptides with their receptors, and also through so-called hardwiring or innervation (the distribution of nerves to a part of the body) of neural and lymphoid organs (figure 7.1). There is a fine network of checks and balances exerted on the operation of all three systems by the elements within them. Accordingly, the modulation or perturbation of the function of one system can have profound effects upon the functions of the others. Biochemical agents used in a malign way therefore pose a particular threat to interacting physiological systems in that they can disrupt the balanced operation of these systems.

To illustrate how one system can affect the others, with possible detrimental effects on all, the interaction of soluble bioregulators of the immune system (cytokines) and the neuroendocrine systems (hormones and neurotransmitters) within the HPA axis will be taken as an example (figure 7.1). Proinflammatory cytokines (substances that cause inflammation) are produced by cells of the immune system after contact with microorganisms or their products.[4] These cytokines gain entry into the circulation from sites of the immune response in tissues and organs. Normally, they are of sufficiently large size that they would not cross the blood-brain barrier. However, there are highly localized areas in the hypothalamus which are devoid of this barrier and through which cytokines can pass.[5,6] The cytokines subsequently bind to receptors on cells in the hypothalamus and trigger reactions that result in what is collectively known as sickness behavior, which is characterized by fever, drowsiness, lethargy and loss of appetite.[7] At the same time, the proinflammatory cytokines induce the production of the hormone corticotropin-releasing factor (CRF),[8] which in turn causes the pituitary gland to produce adenocorticotropic hormone. This hormone enters the circulation and acts on the adrenal cortex to induce the production of glucocorticoids, which have a profound effect in suppressing immune responses, including cytokine production. This negative feedback loop acts to help keep the immune response under control.

However, CRF also has a potentially detrimental effect on the central nervous system. For instance, overproduction of the hormone has been implicated with neurotoxicity and neurodegeneration (damage to nerve cells) in animal studies,[9,10] although this finding has been challenged more recently.[11] A large body of evidence strongly suggests involvement of CRF and its receptors in anxiety behaviors and depression.[12,13,14] Indeed, new drugs that act as CRF receptor antagonists are currently under development and testing, and some have shown promise as antidepressants in clinical trials.[15] Finally, if the proinflammatory cytokines themselves are produced in particularly large amounts or continually during chronic illnesses, this can lead to various systemic disorders such as coronary insufficiency and thrombus formation, and in some cases even to septic shock,[16] the very process that the negative feedback loop described above helps prevent.

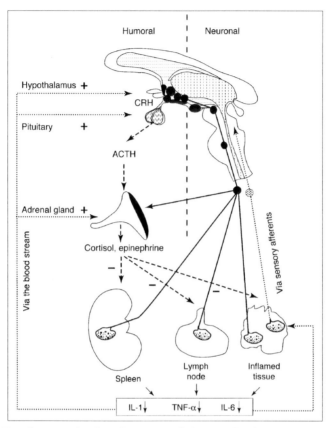

Figure 7.1. Communication Pathways Between the Nervous and Immune Systems. The left side represents the humoral (i.e., based on molecules carried in the blood and other body fluids) hypothalamus-pituitary adrenal gland (HPA) axis regulating the systemic concentration of cortisol and epinephrine (dashed lines). The right side demonstrates the neuronal hypothalamus-autonomic nervous system axis locally influencing immune function via neurotransmitters in lymphoid organs (organs where white blood cells are produced) in inflamed tissue (solid lines). In addition, the cytokines interleukin (IL)-1, IL-6 and tumor necrosis factor alpha (TNF-α) modulate the central nervous system either directly (dotted lines, left) or via receptors on sensory afferents (nerves that carry information to the central nervous system) such as the vagal nerve (feedback mechanisms, for example in inflamed tissue). These afferent sensory nerves are also present in lymphoid organs (not shown). Abbreviations ACTH, adrenocorticotropic hormone; CRH, corticotropin-releasing hormone; HPA, hypothalamus-pituitary-adrenal axis; IL-1, interleukin 1; TNF-α, tumor necrosis factor alpha. Modified from figure 1 in R.H. Straub, et al "Dialogue between the CNS and the Immune System in Lymphoid Organs," Immunology Today 19: 409-413, copyright Elsevier (1998). Used with permission.

It is not difficult to see that a selective overproduction of proinflammatory cytokines could potentially disrupt the normal balance of interactions in these systems and cause several conditions including severely debilitating or incapacitating sickness behavior, major depression, significant immune suppression and septic shock. It is also evident from this description that perturbation of the neuroendocrine system through other means might likewise produce effects on the immune system in the long run.

While some of the reactions briefly outlined in the above model are relatively well established, it must be stressed that the interactions between the neuroendocrine and immune systems are enormously complex and it is generally extremely difficult to predict what the outcome will be if this balanced interaction is perturbed. Furthermore, the effects can be short-term or long-term depending on the biochemical agent and the pathway that is modulated.

Possible Long-Term Effects of Biochemical Incapacitants

This section describes some studies on animals and humans that show possible long-term effects of biochemical incapacitants. While it may be difficult to relate the dosages and means of delivery in every case to a situation in which these incapacitants might be used as biochemical weapons, these studies nevertheless clearly show their potential for inducing long-term effects.

EFFECTS OF PROINFLAMMATORY CYTOKINES

Not only acute but also long-lasting effects have been reported after a single administration of a proinflammatory cytokine. For example, a single intraperitoneal administration of IL-1β to rats caused acute elevations in plasma adrenocorticotropic hormone and cortisone concentrations. At the same time, it produced a long-term (for at least three weeks) increase in the substance arginine vasopressin in CRF neurons of the hypothalamus.[17] Arginine vasopressin is a neuropeptide that strongly potentiates the adrenocorticotropic hormone-releasing effect of CRF, which could contribute to a sustained immunosupression.

A more recent study of the long-term effects of a single administration of IL-1β on the nervous system was carried out by a group of researchers from the same laboratory.[18] Again, rats were given a single intraperitoneal injection of the proinflammatory cytokine IL-1β in a concentration of 5μg/kg. At various time periods thereafter (ten hours to forty-two days), different neuroendocrine responses were measured, such as production of corticosterone and activation of genes controlling the production of CRF or CRF receptors in the hypothalamus and the pituitary gland. Their results showed that a single injection of IL-1β induced biphasic increases in CRF gene and CRF receptor gene activation in the hypothalamus. An early peak occurred at twenty-four hours after IL-1β administration, followed by another peak after twenty-two days. The authors concluded that transient exposure to immune events can induce long-lasting hypothalamus sensitization. This involves at least in part long-term hypothalamic adaptations that enhance central CRF signaling.

Some of the effects of proinflammatory cytokines on the nervous system are achieved through activation of kinases, which are enzymes (catalysts of biochemical reactions) that are essential in the stimulation of cells to become active and carry out their functions.[19,20] They are usually involved in biochemical signaling cascades inside the cell, leading to the activation of genes. Kinases activate components in the signaling cascade by catalyzing biochemical reactions that place phosphate groups on those components and thus increase their reactivity with other, subsequent members in the cascade. One such signaling cascade involves the MAP kinase family of signaling molecules. A very simplified scheme of a MAP kinase cascade in cells of the immune system is presented in figure 7.2.[21] An initial activator of a cell (in the case of a lymphocyte, this would be an antigen) binds specifically to its receptor on the surface of the cell that is to be activated. In an early reaction to this binding event, a kinase called a MAP kinase kinase (MKK) will be activated. This MKK can then activate the MAP kinases, of which there are three kinds, called ERK, JNK/SAPK, and p38. These MAP kinases in turn activate molecules called transcription factors, which are essential for the regulation of gene expression. In immune cells these are the genes controlling, for example, the synthesis of antibodies or cytokines.

Although MKK4 and JNK signaling play a critical role in the activation of immune system cells, they are even more abundantly found in the brain.[22] In studies using mice, Liu et al. showed that forced-swim or immobilization stress selectively induced the activation of MKK4 and JNK in regions of the brain which are involved in learning, memory and stress-related behavioral responses.[23] Although they were abundantly expressed, these kinases were not activated in other regions of the brain.

Proinflammatory cytokines are produced by the immune system in response to vaccination, and these are potent activators of the MKK4-JNK signaling pathway.[24] Given the intricate interactions between the immune system and the nervous system, there is the possibility that vaccination might affect the activation of MAP kinases in the brain. In a continuation of the above studies, the same group of investigators tested their hypothesis that stress, vaccination and

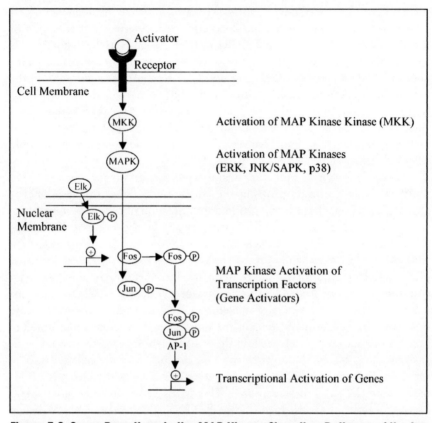

Figure 7.2. Some Reactions in the MAP Kinase Signaling Pathway of the Immune System. An initial activator of a cell (in the case of a lymphocyte, this would be an antigen) binds specifically to its receptor on the surface of the cell that is to be activated. In an early reaction to this binding event, a kinase called a MAP kinase kinase (MKK) will be activated. This MKK can then activate the MAP kinases, of which there are three kinds, called ERK, JNK/SAPK, and p38. These MAP kinases can in turn activate molecules called transcription factors, which are essential for the activation or expression of genes. In immune cells these are the genes controlling, for example, the synthesis of antibodies or cytokines. Modified from figure 10-12 in R.A. Goldsby, et al, Immunology 5th ed., p. 234 (New York: W.H. Freeman & Company, 2003). Used with permission.

the administration of the nerve agent antidote pyridostigmine might synergistically activate MKK4 and JNK in the brain of mice.[25] Such an overactivation of the kinases could possibly lead to neurological disorders. Their theory was tested by examining the effect of immunization alone or in combination with pyridostigmine on the activation of MKK4 and JNK, which were induced by stress.

The immunizing antigen was keyhole limpet hemocyanin, a potent immunogen in mice. For these experiments, mice were immunized on day one and day fourteen with 2 mg/kg of the antigen. On day nineteen, pyridostigmine (10 mg/kg) was administered orally one hour prior to the forced swim stress procedure. This procedure consisted of three ten-minute forced swim sessions with a two-minute rest period after the first two swims. At the end of the forced swim, mice were sacrificed, their brains dissected and MKK4 and JNK were measured in the tissues from different areas in the brain. The results of these experiments showed that immunization of the mice alone had only a slight effect in activating MKK4 and JNK. However, immunization significantly enhanced and prolonged activation of MKK4 and JNK induced by stress. The prolonged effects were seen in animals sacrificed at different times after the forced swim. Effects were evident for up to several days. Treatment with pyridostigmine further enhanced and prolonged kinase activation.

The findings of these studies demonstrate that assault with some combinations of factors can lead to heightened responses that significantly exceed those resulting from exposure to one of those factors alone. Thus stress could lead to activation of MAP kinase signaling cascades in the brain. Vaccination in turn would induce the production of proinflammatory cytokines, which could act peripherally, but also centrally to further activate MAP kinase cascades in the brain, as was determined in the studies reported above. Application of a nerve agent antidote in addition to stress and vaccination produced even greater MAP kinase activation. This points once again to the intricate interaction between the neuroendocrine system and the immune system, and demonstrates that the modulation of one system will have pronounced effects on the other.

EFFECTS OF DRUGS

The Use of an Incapacitant to End the Moscow Theater Crisis

In 2002 the Russian military special forces tried to rescue hostages held at the Moscow Dubrovka Theater Center by Chechen rebels by introducing an unidentified "gas" into the theater ventilation system that was supposed to have incapacitating effects. Of the 800 hostages held in the theater, 127 died and more than 650 of the survivors required hospitalization.[26] At twelve days after the incident, sixty-seven hostages and nine rescuers remained hospitalized, and five were in critical condition. Many of the patients had classic signs of opioid (narcotic) intoxication, and the Russian Health Minister announced several days later that a fentanyl derivative had been used.

There are a large number of fentanyl derivatives that have been developed, and all are potent synthetic narcotics. The precise derivative used in the Moscow crisis and its dosage were never revealed. Several derivatives of fentanyl have a wide therapeutic index (a wide index implies a greater safety margin between effective and lethal dose). For example, carfentanil has been reported to have a particularly wide therapeutic index of 10,000.[27] However, in practice such a wide safety margin has been questioned by animal immobilization studies in which this drug is frequently used. For example, it is significant to note that in these study series, a lethality rate of up to 10 percent has been described for the use of carfentanil, albeit in combination with the muscle relaxant xylazine.[28,29] Other studies on chimpanzees have shown that transmucosal administration of carfentanil alone caused severe respiratory depression,[30] so that this drug alone was not recommended further for immobilization in these animals. Carfentanil was also used in these studies for purposes of euthanasia in gorillas. The dosage needed for killing was quite varied, depending on the health condition of the animals, showing that individuals can respond very differently to the same dosage.

In any case, there were doubts that a fentanyl derivative alone "could have delivered such a hammer blow" in the Moscow theater crisis.[31] Analyses of blood and urine samples from two survivors who returned to Germany showed traces of halothane (an anesthetic), no fentanyl and no evidence of nerve agents.[32] Most reports have come to the conclusion that "collectively, the available evidence strongly suggests that a combination of a potent aerosolized fentanyl derivative, such as carfentanil, and an inhalational anesthetic, such as halothane, was used."[33] In any case, this incident highlights the major problem with so-called non-lethal incapacitants: the effects are not always temporary, and from a scientific and technical viewpoint, these agents are not non-lethal.

Modulators of the Serotonin System of Neurotransmission

Serotonin is a neurotransmitter active in the central nervous system that plays a prominent role in the regulation of such processes as mood, memory and cognition, appetite and sleep. A feeling of well being depends apparently to a large extent on the availability of serotonin in the synaptic cleft or space between cells of the brain (neurons). This is regulated largely by the serotonin transporter that is involved in the reuptake and clearance of serotonin after it has been released from serotonin neurons.[34] The activity of the serotonin transporter has been associated with major depression, and it is the primary target for antidepressants, cocaine, amphetamines and drugs such as 3,4-methylenedioxymethamphetamine (MDMA), better known as Ecstasy. MDMA works by binding to the serotonin transporter. This binding appears to trigger a rapid release of serotonin in the brain, and at the same time reduces its reuptake.

There is, however, compelling evidence that MDMA can damage brain serotonin neurons. Animals treated with MDMA developed long-lasting decreases in regional brain serotonin and transporter density. For example, squirrel monkeys were injected with MDMA subcutaneously at a dose of 5 mg/kg twice daily for four days. Seven years after treatment of the animals, abnormal serotonin innervation patterns (loss of density of serotonin neurons) were still evident, suggesting that these alterations may be permanent. While the authors of this study noted that some serotonin recovery does take place over the seven-year period investigated, this recovery is not always complete and does not occur in several brain regions.[35] While the relevance of the dosage and route of administration used might be questioned, this study did show that MDMA could potentially cause long-term damage.

Other studies in rats showed that MDMA caused a rapid release of serotonin in the brain as expected, but this was followed by a significant decrease in serotonin that persisted at least seven days after administration of the drug.[36] These post-use serotonin depletions may be the cause for the deep depression frequently experienced by MDMA users some days after taking the drug.[37] MDMA users also showed a significant decrease in cognitive performance (verbal recall) even seven days post-drug use. These results may reflect MDMA effects on serotonin, as it is an important neurotransmitter in the hippocampus, one of the most critical brain regions involved in memory formation.[38]

Studies in humans have shown that brain activity changes occur at even moderate doses of MDMA. One group of researchers[39] has used positron emission tomography to measure regional cerebral blood flow, an indicator of which parts of the brain are more active than others at a given time. This study was carried out using sixteen volunteers who had no history of prior MDMA use. Most significantly, results showed that cerebral blood flow was decreased in the amygdala, a change that has been correlated with feelings of euphoria in studies with other mood-altering drugs.

It should be mentioned that proinflammatory cytokines have also been implicated in the pathophysiology of major depression that can be traced to disorders in serotonin neurotransmission. In this regard, IL-1β has been reported to be a potent activator of the expression of the serotonin transporter gene, resulting in the up-regulation of the transporter. This results in enhanced clearance of serotonin from the synaptic cleft, causing a deficiency of the neurotransmitter.[40]

Possible Long-Term Effects of Neurotoxins

A great deal of information concerning possible long-term effects of biochemical incapacitants has come from studies in connection with investigations designed to aid in understanding the illnesses of veterans of the 1990–1991 Gulf War, referred to frequently as the Gulf War Syndrome. Although most of these studies involve effects of nerve agents rather than biochemical incapacitants, they describe long-term neurological effects of low-level exposure to neuroactive agents. Moreover, some biochemical incapacitants (including some toxins) have mechanisms of action similar to those of the nerve agents.

In a study entitled "Scientific Progress in Understanding Gulf War Veteran's Illnesses: Report and Recommendations" by the Research Advisory Committee on Gulf War Veterans' Illnesses (RAC-GWVI) it was concluded that a "substantial proportion of Gulf War veterans are ill with multisymptom conditions not explained by wartime stress or psychiatric illness."[41] It was further reported that "a growing body of evidence indicates that an important component of these conditions appears to be neurological in character."[42]

Above all, there was evidence regarding a probable link between the illnesses and exposures to neurotoxins. In this regard, government reports are cited that have described the extent of exposure of Gulf War veterans to potentially neurotoxic substances during deployment in that region. These include low-level exposures to the chemical nerve agents sarin and cyclosarin, consumption of varying amounts of pyridostigmine bromide tablets as a prophylactic antidote to nerve agents (see below), as well as the use of different amounts and combinations of insect repellents. Many of these neurotoxic substances act by inhibiting the action of acetylcholinesterase, an enzyme that regulates acetylcholine, one of the most important neurotransmitters in the nervous system. Indeed, the RAC-GWVI report concludes that

> Multiple lines of human and animal research indicate that these substances have the potential to cause long-term health effects similar to those experienced by Gulf War Veterans. Animal research has also demonstrated that some combinations of Gulf War-related exposures can lead to adverse effects that significantly exceed those resulting from single exposures.[43]

A brief look at some of the results of these studies will help to demonstrate the significance of the potential of biochemical incapacitants to cause long-term physiological effects.

EFFECTS OF ACETYLCHOLINESTERASE INHIBITORS IN GENERAL

During the normal process of nerve impulse transmission from a nerve to a skeletal muscle cell, the nerve ending releases the neurotransmitter acetylcholine (ACh) into the synapse or space between the ending and a muscle cell. This messenger molecule binds to specific receptors for acetylcholine on the muscle cell and induces that cell to contract or do work. The enzyme acetylcholinesterase, which is also present in the synapse, degrades (destroys) the acetylcholine so that the receptors and the muscle cell return to the resting or relaxed state. However, when acetylcholinesterase inhibitors bind to the enzyme, its ability to degrade acetylcholine is inhibited. As a result, acetylcholine continues to bind to the receptor, over-stimulating the muscle cell to exhaustion and thereby causing it to fail to work.[44]

Acetylcholinesterase is a target for both natural and synthetic toxins that act as inhibitors. Among the natural inhibitors are anatoxin-A(S) of cyanobacteria and green mamba venom, which contains the neurotoxic peptide fasciculin. Synthetic anti-acetylcholinesterases include the highly poisonous organophosphate and carbamate nerve gases (chemical warfare agents) and insecticides.[45] Exposure to toxic levels of organophosphate insecticides or chemical warfare agents can result in the over-stimulation of peripheral organs and central nervous system regulatory centers, both of which receive innervation from acetylcholine-containing nerve cells. Over-stimulation of central cholinergic systems can lead to severe toxicity and death.[46]

The acetylcholinesterase carbamate inhibitor pyridostigmine and particularly its derivative, pyridostigmine bromide (PB), were used during the Gulf War as a prophylactic antidote to organophosphate nerve gas poisons. Although PB itself binds to and inhibits acetylcholinesterase, the enzyme is slowly regenerated to its functional state after binding. With organophosphate poisons such as sarin and particularly soman, regeneration of the acetylcholinesterase enzyme does not occur, and the enzyme remains permanently inhibited. It was reasoned that blocking acetylcholinesterase with pyridostigmine prior to exposure to organophosphate poisons would prevent its reaction with the poison, and that the slow regeneration of acetylcholinesterase activity would occur after the threat of poisoning had passed. Another reason that PB was considered safe is the fact that it (in contrast to pyridostigmine) cannot pass the blood-brain barrier and therefore acts only in the peripheral part of the body and not in the central nervous system, where it might otherwise affect centrally controlled functions. PB also has use as a therapeutic pharmacological drug. For example, it is used routinely in the treatment of the autoimmune disease myasthenia gravis.[47]

LONG-TERM EFFECTS OF LOW-LEVEL EXPOSURE TO ACETYLCHOLINESTERASE INHIBITORS ON THE NERVOUS SYSTEM

While exposure to high doses of organophosphates such as sarin can lead to severe toxicity and even death, little is known about the effects of subclinical amounts. It has been reported that considerable numbers of Gulf War veterans were subjected to low-level exposures to sarin and cyclosarin, and it was suggested that this could be a factor in the development of Gulf War illness.[48]

The possibility that low doses of organophosphates might have subtle effects on brain function came from reports in the 1960s of memory and concentration problems in agricultural and industrial workers after low-level exposure to organophosphate agents.[49]

Studies involving humans have indicated that long-term chronic effects in the central nervous system could be detected in subjects exposed to acute organophosphate pesticide intoxication. In one investigation, 100 individuals with previous acute organophosphate pesticide poisoning were compared to non-poisoned, matched controls. Differences between the two groups were apparent in neurophysiological tests. Differences were noted in intellectual functioning, academic skills, abstraction and flexibility of thinking and simple motor skills. Twice as many cases as controls (twenty-four vs. twelve) had scores in the range characteristic of individuals with cerebral damage or dysfunction.[50] Another study involved thirty-six agricultural workers that had been admitted to a hospital for occupationally related organophosphate poisoning. Testing occurred on an average about two years after the poisoning episode, also using a matched control group. The poisoned group did much worse than the control group on tests that included assessed verbal and visual attention, visual memory, visuomotor speed, problem solving, motor steadiness and dexterity. The authors of the study concluded that "the findings of a persistent decrease in neurophysiological performance among individuals with previous intoxication emphasise the importance of prevention of even single episodes of organophosphate poisoning."[51]

The results of such studies suggested to Kaufer and coworkers[52] that exposure to acetylcholinesterase inhibitors could lead to persistent changes in key cholinergic brain proteins. In order to investigate this, these researchers developed an in vitro system (tissue culture system) of mouse brain slices bathed in a physiological solution, with which they could perform molecular biological analyses of the effects of diisopropylfluorophosphate, pyridostigmine or other acetylcholinesterase inhibitors. These analyses consisted of the test for the induction of the expression of genes controlling the production of brain proteins. The production of messenger ribonucleic acid (mRNA) by a specific gene in response to treatment of the tissues with organophosphate (diisopropylfluorophosphate) or carbamate (pyridostigmine) anti-acetylcholinesterases was used as a measure of protein gene activation. The expression of the genes controlling the production of key cholinergic proteins (e.g., acetylcholinesterase) was of particular interest. As early as ten minutes after exposure to the anti-acetylcholinesterase agents, dramatic increases were detected in the levels of the mRNA specific for the transcription factor cFos, which is involved in the expression of the acetylcholinesterase gene. Accordingly, twenty minutes later a pronounced increase in acetylcholinesterase mRNA was seen. Thus, the acetyl-cholinesterase gene responded rapidly and dramatically after exposure to acetyl-cholinesterase inhibitors.

Most significantly, their findings indicated that even moderate nerve cell ex-citation could lead to overt changes in the expression of brain protein genes. This suggested to them that a feedback process involving acetylcholinesterase inhibi-tion was initiated by exposure to the anti-acetylcholinesterase agents. While this might be an attempt to reach homeostasis again, the result was apparently an overproduction of acetylcholinesterase. This in turn could lead to a deficiency in acetylcholine availability for neurotransmission, which might result in long-term deleterious changes in cognitive functions. The key here is balance. If the balance is disrupted, either too much or too little acetylcholine would be deleterious, leading to overstimulation or understimulation. Earlier studies in mice by the same group using stress as the assault showed similar changes in gene activity in mice. These changes were shown to be persistent for at least eighty hours fol-lowing stress, the length of the period of observation.[53]

Recent studies in rats using gene profiling techniques to examine the effects of sublethal doses of sarin on all known genes related to brain and nervous sys-tem function have shown that the expression of some genes remained altered even three months after administration of the acetylcholinesterase inhibitor.[54] Expression patterns measured at an early time point (fifteen minutes) after ad-ministration of a sub-lethal dose ($0.5 \times LD_{50}$) of sarin identified sixty-five genes with significantly altered expression. One of these, *Cam Kinase II*, was identified as a primary gene responsible for immediate neuronal cell death following expo-sure to sarin. The expression of some thirty-eight genes remained altered three months after administration of a higher dosage ($1 \times LD_{50}$), which some animals survived. Alterations were particularly prominent in genes involved in signaling and neurotransmission.

EFFECTS OF LOW-LEVEL EXPOSURE TO ACETYLCHOLINESTERASE INHIBITORS ON THE IMMUNE SYSTEM

As indicated in the introduction of this paper, the brain communicates with the immune system in an intricate fashion. Therefore, it would be expected that acetyl-cholinesterase inhibitors would also affect the function of the immune system. Sev-eral investigations show that this is indeed so. Before looking at these studies more closely, a brief description of the components and functions of the immune system that are relevant to these investigations will be presented, in order to provide a bet-ter basis for understanding the impact of the results of those studies.

The hallmark of the immune system is its ability to respond to an invasion of the body by microorganisms or toxic components in ways that afford protection against disease. The responses of the immune system include both non-specific (innate immune system) and specific (adaptive immune system) components. These react in different ways to antigens (chemical compounds—mainly proteins and polysaccharides), which are substances that can elicit an immune response if they are foreign to the body. Many antigens are not harmful by themselves, the exception being toxins. Microorganisms are composed of a mosaic of many different antigens.

The innate immune system represents the all-important first line of defence against pathogens and is absolutely essential for keeping an infection in check before adaptive immunity can be induced. It includes components that are present and ready for action even before an antigen challenge is encountered. These are cellular and molecular components that are less specific than those of the adaptive system. The innate system is essential to defence, but it cannot sustain a prolonged fight against microorganisms, especially if those invaders are highly pathogenic.

The adaptive immune system is composed of specific humoral and cellular components. The cellular components (white blood cells called *lymphocytes*) must be driven by antigens to go through different phases of activation, maturation and proliferation (multiplication) in order to carry out their functions. The function of B lymphocytes is to produce antibodies while the function of T lymphocytes is to help regulate immune responses (T helper cells) or to initiate the death of infected cells (cytotoxic T cells). T and B cells are able to react to an antigen challenge with a high degree of specificity. As a result, immunity is afforded against one specific infectious agent carrying those antigens. However, adaptive immunity takes several days to be induced.

Animal studies have been carried out to investigate possible effects of low doses of sarin on immune system function. Kalra et al.[55] exposed rats to sub-clinical doses (0.2 and 0.4 mg/m^3) of sarin that do not cause acute symptoms through inhalation for one hour per day for five or ten days. Following this treatment, the animals were immunized with a specific antigen, and four days thereafter the animals were sacrificed and their spleens were removed as a source of lymphocytes to test for antibody responses. The results showed that the antibody-producing cell responses of animals exposed to 0.4 mg/m^3 sarin were reduced approximately threefold over those of animals receiving an injection of a solution without sarin. In addition, T cells from the spleen were tested for their ability to proliferate in response to different T cell specific stimuli. According to these results T cell proliferative responses of animals exposed to 0.4 mg/m^3 sarin for one hour a day for ten days were reduced somewhat more than threefold over those of the controls. Even for animals receiving the very low dose of 0.2 mg/m^3

sarin, the spleen cell proliferative responses to a T cell agonist were reduced more than twofold over the responses of the control animals.

Other neuroactive compounds including opiates[56] and nicotine[57] have also been shown to affect the immune system through the central nervous system.

Stress Increases Permeability of the Blood-Brain Barrier

Stress seems to precipitate or worsen a number of neurological inflammatory conditions, possibly by increasing the permeability of the blood-brain barrier and allowing the entry of incapacitating substances that normally would be excluded, and of the immune system cells that can elicit a heightened inflammatory response or otherwise cause damage to tissues.[58]

The blood-brain barrier consists of very tight junctions between the cells making up the walls of blood vessels leading to the brain. Under normal conditions this barrier regulates entry of any compound or cell into the brain, thus protecting brain tissue from assault by substances that could be harmful. The integrity of the blood-brain barrier can be disrupted under certain circumstances. Alteration of the protective function of this structure is apparently important in the pathophysiology of various inflammatory diseases of the central nervous system, such as multiple sclerosis. Similarly, there is evidence that the blood-brain barrier becomes more penetrable with an increasing immune response, and that activated T cells of the immune system can readily enter the brain, whereas nonactivated T cells are excluded under normal conditions.[59]

The question as to whether stress could be a factor in allowing pyridostigmine bromide to penetrate the blood-brain barrier, which might then affect centrally controlled systems, was investigated in studies using mice as experimental animals.[60] In these studies, mice were stressed by two four-minute swim sessions with a four-minute rest period in between. Ten minutes following the forced swim the mice were injected with a physiological saline solution as a control, or with different doses (0.5 or 1.0 mg/kg of body weight) of pyridostigmine. Ten minutes after these injections, the mice were sacrificed and the brains dissected, homogenized, and the tissues measured for acetylcholinesterase activity. Permeability of the blood-brain barrier was determined by anesthetizing the mice and injecting them in the heart with a dye solution that normally does not penetrate appreciably into the brain from the circulation. The results of these studies indicated that after mice were subjected to the stress of the force swim protocol, an increase in the blood-brain barrier permeability reduced the dosage of pyridostigmine required to inhibit 50 percent of brain acetylcholinesterase activity from 1.50 to 0.01 mg/kg body weight.

The findings suggested that peripherally acting drugs that normally are excluded by the blood-brain barrier may reach the brain if administered under stress or during activation of the immune system and thus affect centrally controlled functions. The work outlined above did not directly test the long-term effects under this regime. However, it was noted that the responses they measured of acetylcholinesterase gene activation "predict the induction of secondary and tertiary processes with unknown consequences, depending on complex and variable elements."[61]

Esposito and his colleagues[62] also tested whether acute stress increases the permeability of the blood-brain barrier in rats. Stress was induced by immobilizing the rats in a special plexiglass apparatus for thirty minutes, immediately following the injection of a radioactive substance that could not normally pass the blood-brain barrier. After the stress period, animals were anesthetized and their circulation flushed out with solutions to remove any traces of the radioactive material from the circulation. The rats were then sacrificed and any radioactive substance that might have penetrated the blood-brain barrier was measured in various parts of the brain. Results of these tests indicated that stress could cause disruption of the blood-brain barrier, and this was most likely mediated by the activation of mast cells, which are found in areas adjacent to the blood vessels in the brain. These cells are, for example, critical for the development of allergic reactions. Upon activation, mast cells release substances such as histamine, which can cause blood vessels in the area to dilate.

Delivery of Biochemical Incapacitants

The ability to attack biological systems through the use of biochemical incapacitants is intimately related to developments in targeting technology. This technology is being intensively developed for use in cancer and gene therapy, and is still mainly in the experimental stage. Nevertheless, it is evident that cytokines as bioregulators can be delivered quite effectively by viruses engineered to carry cytokine genes, as was illustrated in the mousepox experiment with the cytokine interleukin 4.[63] Aerosols represent another potential method for delivering biochemical agents. Aerosols are particles in the form of a liquid or a powder that are suspended in air and can be inhaled. In the late 1980s the U.S. Army, within its biodefense research program, investigated the ability of endogenous bioregulators to be absorbed through the aerosol route. This was done in order to determine how effectively such substances can be taken up by inhalation. It was reported, for example, that the hormone insulin and the proinflammatory cytokine interleukin 1 were effective in aerosol form in basic pulmonary absorption studies.[64]

The potential of this route is being extensively investigated in connection with interests in drug delivery. Indeed, it has been stated that the greatest potential for delivering drugs is through the pulmonary route by inhalation of particles of a particular size.[65] In this regard, the production of defined nanoparticles combined with new methods for making substances absorbable through the nasal and respiratory tracts represent advances that could create a potential for greatly improved delivery of bioactive compounds.[66] The nasal route has emerged as being of particular choice for delivery of drugs. This route provides rapid absorption into the circulation with little or no degradation, particularly if the substances have characteristics that promote their ability to dissolve in lipids (fats). Nasal delivery also has the potential of providing direct access of drugs to the brain via the olfactory region.[67]

Summary

Numerous human and animal studies have shown that exposure to incapacitating biochemical agents may induce heterogeneous cognitive and physiological impairments and lead to long-term health effects. This is even more pronounced when exposures to incapacitating agents are combined with other factors such as stress or activation of the immune system. The immune system interacts intricately through biochemical bioregulators with the nervous system and the endocrine system. This interaction is highly interdependent so that the modulation of the function of one system with a biologically active biochemical agent will profoundly affect the function of the others. Each one of these systems is in itself extremely complex in the regulatory processes that control and assure its proper function. The interaction of these systems with each other raises this complexity to enormous proportions. In the light of this complexity, it is extremely difficult to predict exactly what the consequences of exposure to incapacitating biochemical agents might be. This uncertainty emphasizes the importance of the prevention of any exposure to such agents.

Notes

1. M. Dando, "Genomics, Bioregulators, Cell Receptors and Potential Biological Weapons," *Defense Analysis* 17 (2001): 239–58.

2. M. Wheelis, "Biotechnology and Biochemical Weapons," *The Nonproliferation Review* 9 (2002): 9.

166   KATHRYN NIXDORFF AND JACK MELLING

3. R. H. Straub, J. Westermann, J. Schölmerich, and W. Falk, "Dialogue between the CNS and the Immune System in Lymphoid Organs," *Immunology Today* 19 (1998): 409–13.

4. L. Steinman, "Elaborate Interactions between the Immune and Nervous Systems," *Nature Immunology* 5 (2004): 575–81.

5. N. P. Turrin and S. Rivest, "Unravelling the Molecular Details Involved in the Intimate Link Between the Immune and the Neuroendocrine Systems," *Experimental Biology and Medicine* 229 (2004): 996–1006.

6. J. Licinio and P. Frost, "The Neuroimmune-Endocrine Axis: Pathophysiological Implications for the Central Nervous System Cytokines and Hypothalamus-Pituitary-Adrenal Hormone Dynamics," *Brazilian Journal of Medical and Biological Research* 33 (2000): 1141–48.

7. A. Inui, "Cytokines and Sickness Behaviour: Implications from Knockout Animal Models," *Trends in Immunology* 22 (2001): 469–73.

8. Straub, Westermann, Schölmerich, and Falk, "Dialogue Between the CNS and the Immune System."

9. P. J. Strijbos, J. K. Relton, and N. J. Rothwell, "Corticotropin-Releasing Factor Antagonist Inhibits Neuronal Damage Induced by Focal Cerebral Ischemia or Activation of NMDA Receptors in the Rat Brain," *Brain Research* 656 (1994): 405–8.

10. M. K Lyons, R. E. Anderson, and F. B. Meyer, "Corticotropin-Releasing Factor Antagonist Reduces Ischemic Hippocampal Neuronal Injury," *Brain Research* 545 (1991): 339–42.

11. H. Plamondon and S. Khan, "The CRH1 Antagonist CP154,526 Failed to Alter Ischemia-Induced Neurodegeneration and Spatial Memory Deficits in Rats but Inhibited Behavioural Activity in the Novel Open Field," *Behavioural Brain Research* 166 (2006): 85–92.

12. T. L. Bale and W. W. Vale, "CRF and CRF Receptors: Role in Stress Responsivity and Other Behaviours," *Annual Review of Pharmacology and Toxicology* 44 (2004): 525–57.

13. T. Kaneta and A. W. Kusnecov, "The Role of Central Corticotropin-Releasing Hormone in the Anorexic and Endocrine Effects of the Bacterial T Cell Superantigen, Staphylococcal Enterotoxin A," *Brain, Behaviour and Immunity* 19 (2005): 138–46.

14. A. W. Zobel, T. Nickel, H. E. Kunzel, N. Ackl, A. Sonntag, M. Ising, and F. Holsboer, "Effects of the High-Affinity Corticotropin-Releasing Hormone Receptor 1 Antagonist R121919 in Major Depression: The First 20 Patients Tested," *Journal of Psychiatric Research* 34 (2000): 171–81.

15. M. F. Bear, B. W. Connors, and M. A. Paradiso, "Chapter 22: Mental Illness" in *Neuroscience. Exploring the Brain*, 3rd ed. (Philadelphia, PA: Lippincott, Williams & Wilkins, 2006): 677.

16. E. T. Rietschel and H. Brade, "Bacterial Endotoxins," *Scientific American* 267 (1992): 54–61.

17. E. D. Schmidt, A. W. Janszen, F. G.Wouterlood, and F. J. H. Tilders, "Interleukin-1-Induced Long-Lasting Changes in Hypothalamic Corticotropin-Releasing Hormone (CRH)-Neurons and Hyperresponsiveness of the Hypothalamus-Pituitary-Adrenal Axis," *Journal of Neuroscience* 15 (1995): 7417–26.

18. E. D. Schmidt, G. Aguilera, R. Binnekade, and F. J. H. Tilders, "Single Administration of Interleukin-1 Increased Corticotropin-Releasing Hormone and Corticotropin Releasing Hormone-Receptor mRNA in the Hypothalamic Paraventricular Nucleus which Paralleled Long-Lasting (Weeks) Sensitization to Emotional Stressors," *Neuroscience* 116 (2003): 275–83.

19. Turrin and Rivest, "Unravelling the Molecular Details."

20. B. Conti, I. Tabarean, C. Andrei, and T. Bartfai, "Cytokines and Fever," *Frontiers in Biosciences* 9 (2004): 1433–49.

21. R. A. Goldsby, T. J. Kindt, B. A. Osborne, and J. Kuby, *Immunology* 5th ed. (New York: W.H. Freeman & Company, 2003).

22. Y. F. Liu, K. Bertram, G. Perides, B. S. McEwen, and D. Wang, "Stress Induces Activation of Stress-Activated Kinase in the Mouse Brain," *Journal of Neurochemistry* 89 (2004): 1034–43.

23. Liu, Bertram, Perides, McEwen, and Wang, "Stress Induces Activation."

24. C. Dong, R. J. Davis, and R. A. Flavell, "MAP Kinases in the Immune Response," *Annual Review of Immunology* 20 (2002): 55–72.

25. D. Wang, G. Perides, and Y. F. Liu, "Vaccination Alone or in Combination with Pyridostigmine Promotes and Prolongs Activation of Stress-Activated Kinases Induced by Stress in the Mouse Brain," *Journal of Neurochemistry* 93 (2005): 1010–20.

26. P. M. Wax, C. E. Becker, and S. C. Curry, "Unexpected 'Gas' Casualties in Moscow: A Medical Toxicology Perspective," *Annals of Emergency Medicine* 41(2003): 700–5.

27. Wax, Becker, and Curry, "Unexpected 'Gas' Casualties."

28. U. S. Seal, S. M. Schmitt, and R. O. Peterson, "Carfentanil and Xylazine for Immobilization of Moose (Alces alces) on Isle Royale," *Journal of Wildlife Diseases* 21 (1985): 48–51.

29. H. Delvaux, R. Courtois, L. Breton, and R. Patenaude, "Relative Efficiency of Succinylcholine, Xylazine, and Carfentanil/Xylazine Mixtures to Immobilize Free-Ranging Moose," *Journal of Wildlife Diseases* 35 (1999): 38–48.

30. K. S. Kearns, B. Swenson, and E. C. Ramsay, "Dosage Trials with Transmucosal Carfentanil Citrate in Non-Human Primates," *Zoo Biology* 18 (1999): 397–402.

31. M. Enserink and R. Stone, "Toxicology. Questions Swirl Over Knockout Gas Used in Hostage Crisis," *Science* 298 (2002): 1150–51.

32. Enserik and Stone, "Toxicology. Questions Swirl."

33. Wax, Becker, and Curry, "Unexpected 'Gas' Casualties in Moscow."

34. M. Kubera and M. Maes, "Serotonin-Immune Interactions in Major Depression," in P. Patterson, C. Kordon, and Y. Christen, eds., *Neuro-Immune Interactions in Neurologic and Psychiatric Disorders* (Berlin: Springer Press, 2000): 79–87.

35. G. Hatzidimitriou, U. N. McCann, and G. A. Ricaurte, "Altered Serotonin Innervation Patterns in the Forebrain of Monkeys Treated with (±)3,4-Methylenedioxymethamphetamine Seven Years Previously: Factors Influencing Abnormal Recovery," *Journal of Neuroscience* 19 (1999): 5096–107.

36. B. K. Yamamoto, "Neurochemical Mediators and Neurophysiological Consequences of Acute MDMA Exposure in Rats," (Presentation at MDMA/Ecstasy Research:

Advances, Challenges and Future Directions. Workshop organized by National Institutes of Health and National Institute of Drug Abuse, Bethesda, MD. 19–20 July 2001, <http://www.drugabuse.gov/Meetings/MDMA/MDMAVideo/MDMA14.ram> (25 February 2007)).

37. A. C. Parrot and J. Lasky, "Ecstasy (MDMA) Effect upon Mood and Cognition: Before, During and After a Saturday Night Dance," *Psychopharmacology* 139 (1998): 261–68.

38. National Institutes of Health and National Institute of Drug Abuse, "Ecstasy: What We Know and Don't Know About MDMA," *A Scientific Review* 26 (presentation at MDMA/Ecstasy Research: Advances, Challenges and Future Directions; workshop organized by National Institutes of Health and National Institute of Drug Abuse, Bethesda, MD. 19–20 July 2001).

39. A. Gamma, A. Buck, T. Berthold, D. Held, and F.X. Vollenweider, "3,4-Methyl-enedioxymethamphetamine (MDMA) Modulates Cortical and Limbic Brain Activity as Measured by [H215O]-PET in Healthy Humans," *Neuropsychopharmacology* 23 (2000): 388–95.

40. A. I. Cztonkowska, M. Zienowicz, A. Bidzinski, P. Maciejak, M. Lehner, E. Taracha, A. Wislowska, and A. Plaznik, "The Role of Neurosteroids in the Anxiolytic, Antidepressive and Anticonvulsive Effects of Selective Serotonin Reuptake Inhibitors," *Medical Science Monitor* 9 (2003): RA270-RA275.

41. Research Advisory Committee on Gulf War Veterans' Illnesses (hereinafter RAC-GWVI), "Scientific Progress in Understanding Gulf War Veterans' Illnesses: Report and Recommendations," U.S. Department of Veterans Affairs (September 2004): 2. Available at <RAC@med.va.gov> or <http://www.va.gov/RAC-GWVI> (25 February 2007).

42. RAC-GWVI, "Scientific Progress," 18.

43. RAC-GWVI, "Scientific Progress," 65.

44. W. W. Carmichael, "The Toxins of Cyanobacteria," *Scientific American* 270 (1994): 78–86.

45. H. Soreq and S. Seidman, "Acetylcholinesterase – New Roles for an Old Actor," *Nature Reviews Neuroscience* 2 (2001): 294–302.

46. M. A. Prendergast, A. V. Terry Jr., and J. J. Buccafusco, "Chronic, Low-Level Exposure to Diisopropylfluorophosphate Causes Protracted Impairment of Spatial Navigation Learning," *Psychopharmacology* 129 (1997): 183–91.

47. Soreq and Seidman, "Acetylcholinesterase."

48. M. B. Abou-Donia, K. R. Wilmarth, K. F. Jensen, F. W. Oehme, and T. L. Kurt, "Neurotoxicity Resulting from Co-exposure to Pyridostigmine Bromide, Deet, and Permethrin: Implications of Gulf War Chemical Exposures," *Journal of Toxicology and Environmental Health* 48 (1996): 35–56.

49. I. Wickelgren, "The Big Easy Serves up a Feast to Visiting Neuroscientists," *Science* 278 (1997): 1404.

50. E. P. Savage, T J. Keefe, L. M. Mounce, R. K. Heaton, J.A. Lewin, and P. J. Burcar, "Chronic Neurological Sequelae of Acute Organophosphate Pesticide Poisoning," *Archives of Environmental Health* 43 (1988): 38–45.

51. L. Rosenstock, M. Keifer, W.E. Daniell, R. McConnell, and K. Claypoole, "Chronic Central Nervous System Effects of Acute Organophosphate Pesticide Intoxication," *Lancet* 338 (1991): 223–27.

52. D. Kaufer, A. Friedman, S. Seidman, and H. Soreq, "Anticholinesterases Induce Multigenic Transcriptional Feedback Response Suppressing Cholinergic Neurotransmission," *Chemico-Biological Interactions* 119–20 (1999): 349–60.

53. D. Kaufer, A. Friedman, S. Seidman, and H. Soreq, "Acute Stress Facilitates Long-Lasting Changes in Cholinergic Gene Expression," *Nature* 393 (1998): 373–77.

54. T. V. Damodaran, A. G. Patel, S.T. Greenfield, H. K. Dressman, S. M. Lin, and M. B. Abou-Donia, "Gene Expression Profiles of the Rat Brain Both Immediately and 3 Months Following Acute Sarin Exposure," *Biochemical Pharmacology* 71 (2006): 497–520.

55. R. Kalra, S. P. Singh, S. Razani-Boroujerdi, R. J. Langley, W. B. Blackwell, R. F. Henderson, and M. L. Sopori, "Subclinical Doses of the Nerve Gas Sarin Impair T Cell Responses Through the Autonomic Nervous System," *Toxicology and Applied Pharmacology* 184 (2002): 82–87.

56. C. J. Nelson and D. T. Lysle, "Involvement of Substance P and Central Opioid Receptors in Morphine Modulation of the CHS Response," *Journal of Neuroimmunology* 115 (2001): 101–10.

57. M. Sopori, "Effects of Cigarette Smoke on the Immune System," *Nature Reviews Immunology* 2 (2002): 372–77.

58. P. Esposito, D. Gheorghe, K. Kandere, X. Pang, and others, "Acute Stress Increases Permeability of the Blood-Brain Barrier Through Activation of Brain Mast Cells," *Brain Research* 888 (2001): 117–27.

59. L. M. Boulanger and C. J. Shatz, "Immune Signaling in Neural Development, Synaptic Plasticity and Disease," *Nature Reviews Neuroscience* 5 (2004): 521–31.

60. A. Friedman, D. Kaufer, J. Shemer, I. Hendler, H. Soreq, and I. Tur-Kaspa, "Pyridostigmine Brain Penetration under Stress Enhances Neuronal Excitability and Induces Early Immediate Transcriptional Response," *Nature Medicine* 2 (1996): 382–85.

61. Friedman, Kaufer, Shemar, Hendler, Soreq and Tur-Kaspa, "Pyridostigmine Brain Penetration."

62. Esposito, Gheorghe, Kandere, Pang, and others, "Acute Stress Increases Permeability."

63. R. J. Jackson, A. J. Ramsay, C. Christensen, S. Beaton, D. F. R. Hall, and I. A. Ramshaw, "Expression of Mouse Interleukin-4 by a Recombinant Ectromelia Virus Suppresses Cytolytic Lymphocyte Responses and Overcomes Genetic Resistance to Mousepox," *Journal of Virology* 75 (2001): 1205–10.

64. USAMRIID, "Basic Studies Seeking Generic Medical Countermeasures Against Agents of Biological Origin," *Annual Report for Fiscal Year 1987*, 19.

65. S. Shohet and G. Wood, "Delivering Biotherapeutics—Technical Opportunities and Strategic Trends," *Journal of Commercial Biotechnology* 9 (2002): 59–66.

66. Shohet and Wood, "Developing Biotherapeutics."

67. L. Illum, "Transport of Drugs from the Nasal Cavity to the Central Nervous System," *European Journal of Pharmaceutical Sciences* 11 (2000): 1–18. C. L. Graff and G. M. Pollack, "Nasal Drug Administration: Potential for Targeted Central Nervous System Delivery," *Journal of Pharmaceutical Sciences* 94 (2005): 1187–95.

CHAPTER 8

Incapacitating Chemical and Biochemical Weapons and Law Enforcement Under the Chemical Weapons Convention

David P. Fidler

Introduction

Following September 11, 2001, the United States asserted that one of its greatest national security threats involved the convergence of global terrorism and the dissemination of technologies related to weapons of mass destruction.[1] This assertion represented yet another concern about the harm that can emerge from the malevolent exploitation of scientific and technological developments. Anxiety about research in, and development of, incapacitating chemical and biochemical weapons also reveals growing fears about the potential misuse of science and technology.[2,3]

Historically, arms control and disarmament mechanisms have been used to ban or regulate the development and use of new weapons. A central international legal issue in the emerging controversy about biochemical weapons is how the Biological Weapons Convention (BWC)[4] and the Chemical Weapons Convention (CWC)[5] apply to such weapons. This chapter focuses primarily on the provision of the CWC that allows states parties to use toxic chemicals for law enforcement, including domestic riot control, as a purpose not prohibited by the treaty (CWC, Article II.9[d]). The law enforcement provision was controversial

Aspects of this chapter's analysis were first published in "The Meaning of Moscow: 'Non-Lethal' Weapons and International Law in the Early Twenty-first Century," *International Review of the Red Cross* 87, no. 859 (2005).

during the CWC's negotiation, and it has raised questions since the treaty was completed. This chapter interprets Article II.9(d) and then analyzes this interpretation's implications for concerns that Article II.9(d) constitutes a threat to the CWC and the BWC.

A 1994 editorial in the *Chemical Weapons Convention Bulletin* asked, "What is 'law enforcement'? . . . Whose law? What law? Enforced where? By whom?"[6] The editorial feared that Article II.9(d) constituted "a grave weakness . . . [at] the core of the Convention" that made the treaty vulnerable to "advancing science and technology."[7]

The use of a chemical agent by Russian law enforcement and military forces in a hostage rescue operation in October 2002 reopened questions about the meaning of Article II.9(d) and its potential implications for control of incapacitating chemicals and biochemicals as weapons.[8,9] Experts have debated whether Russia's use of a chemical incapacitating agent, identified as an opioid of the fentanyl group, fell within Article II.9(d). In the wake of the Moscow incident, a *CBW Conventions Bulletin* editorial raised again the question "what in the context of the Convention is 'law enforcement'?"[10]

The debate over Article II.9(d) connected with growing concerns about military and law enforcement interest in "non-lethal" chemical weapons, including both riot control agents (RCAs) and incapacitating agents, displayed by countries during the 1990s and early 2000s.[11] In addition, so-called "biochemical" weapons represent a new potential class of weapons that could affect the CWC's law enforcement provision. Biochemical agents differ from more traditional toxic chemicals in that they could fall within both the CWC and the BWC. This overlap has raised concerns that Article II.9(d) may affect the BWC's prohibition on biological weapons. These developments suggest that Article II.9(d)'s importance has grown with each passing year.

The questions concerning the meaning of the law enforcement provision have focused on two main issues. First, can toxic chemicals that are not riot control agents be used for law enforcement purposes? Second, does the term "law enforcement" cover enforcement of not only domestic but also international law? This chapter answers both these questions.

This chapter focuses on whether this interpretation of Article II.9(d) encourages what many experts fear most, namely the (1) development of incapacitating chemical and biochemical weapons for law enforcement purposes; (2) spill-over of such weapons development into military use; and (3) spread of such weapons to terrorists, criminals, and repressive governments. This analysis addresses both the CWC and the BWC because of concerns that biochemical weapons straddle both these arms control regimes.

Interpreting Article II.9(d) of the CWC

TOXIC CHEMICALS COVERED BY ARTICLE II.9(D)

Toxic Chemicals for Law Enforcement: Limited to Riot Control Agents?

Article II.9(d) of the CWC provides: "'Purposes Not Prohibited Under this Convention' means: . . . (d) Law enforcement including domestic riot control purposes." The first question this provision raises is what range of toxic chemicals can states parties use for law enforcement purposes.

Some experts have claimed that any toxic chemical used for law enforcement has to have the same properties as a riot control agent—a chemical "not listed in a Schedule, which can produce rapidly in humans sensory irritation or disabling physical effects which disappear within a short period of time following termination of exposure" (CWC, Article II.7). Chayes and Meselson argued that "[a] toxic chemical used by virtue of its toxic properties is only of a type consistent with the purpose of law enforcement . . . if it meets the Convention's definition of a 'riot control agent' in Article II(7)."[12] Krutzsch made the same argument.[13]

This interpretation is wrong for four reasons. First, Article II.9(d) allows countries to use toxic chemicals for capital punishment; and chemicals used for this law enforcement purpose are clearly not riot control agents. Even those advocating for restricting the range of toxic chemicals for law enforcement to those that meet the riot control agent definition admit that lethal doses of toxic chemicals can be used in capital punishment.[14]

Second, international law on treaty interpretation does not support interpreting Article II.9(d) as restricting toxic chemicals used for law enforcement purposes only to riot control agents. Under international law, a treaty must be interpreted "in good faith in accordance with the ordinary meaning to be given to the terms of the treaty in their context and in the light of its object and purpose."[15] Article II.1(a) of the CWC states: "'Chemical Weapons' means the following, together or separately: (a) Toxic chemicals and their precursors, except where intended for purposes not prohibited under this Convention, as long as the types and quantities are consistent with such purposes." Thus, "toxic chemicals" are chemical weapons except where intended for purposes not prohibited by the CWC, such as law enforcement. The law enforcement provision applies, therefore, to "toxic chemicals," which constitute a much broader category of chemicals than riot control agents (Article II.2). Article II.1(a) does not mention riot control agents as a restriction on the "toxic chemicals" that states parties can use for purposes not prohibited under the CWC.

Third, the CWC defines riot control agents as chemicals that are not listed on any Schedule to the CWC (Article II.7). Toxic chemicals that states parties can use for purposes not prohibited, including law enforcement purposes, can be listed on Schedules 2 and 3 of the CWC's Schedules of Chemicals. The CWC's Verification Annex makes this clear: CWC states parties may not produce, acquire, retain, or use Schedule 1 chemicals unless, among other things, "[t]he chemicals are applied to research, medical, pharmaceutical or protective purposes" (Verification Annex, Part VI, A.2[a]).

Law enforcement is not listed anywhere as a purpose for which states parties may produce, acquire, retain, or use Schedule 1 chemicals. As Krutzsch and Trapp correctly observed, the Verification Annex relating to Schedule 1 chemicals is more restrictive in terms of the purposes not prohibited than Article II.9, which means that "a Schedule 1 chemical cannot be used for any other purposes than those listed even if such a purpose were a peaceful one not related to the development, production or use of a chemical weapon."[16] The Verification Annex means that CWC states parties cannot produce, acquire, retain, or use Schedule 1 chemicals for law enforcement purposes. By contrast, the Verification Annex on Schedule 2 and 3 chemicals does not restrict in the same manner the purposes not prohibited, meaning that toxic chemicals listed on Schedules 2 or 3 (which cannot be riot control agents) may be employed for law enforcement purposes—at least under some circumstances.

Fourth, in the Moscow hostage incident, Russian use of a toxic chemical that is not a riot control agent for a law enforcement purpose provides some evidence of state practice that the CWC does not limit the chemicals that can be used under Article II.9(d) to riot control agents. Under international law, subsequent state practice under a treaty can be used when determining the meaning of the treaty's provisions.[17] The state practice generated by the Moscow tragedy involves Russia's use of the toxic chemical and the acquiescence of other CWC states parties to such use. As Wheelis commented, "most analysts consider the Russian use of a fentanyl derivative to have been legal" under Article II.9(d).[18] Thus, international law on treaty interpretation indicates that the CWC does not limit the range of toxic chemicals that can be used for law enforcement purposes to riot control agents.

Disciplines on Development and Use of Toxic Chemicals for Law Enforcement

Even though the CWC does not restrict law enforcement use of toxic chemicals only to riot control agents, use of a toxic chemical for law enforcement purposes is still subject to the CWC requirement that the types and quantities of chemicals developed, produced, acquired, stockpiled, retained, transferred, or used must be consistent with such permitted purposes (Article II.1[a]). These disciplines ensure that development, possession, and use of toxic chemicals for law enforcement purposes do not undermine the CWC's prohibition on the development and use of toxic chemicals for military purposes. These rules must also be interpreted in good faith to ascertain their ordinary meaning in light of their context and of the treaty's object and purpose.

The "types and quantities" discipline requires scrutiny of the relationship between the chemical or biochemical agent and the law enforcement objective in question. The more difficult it is to control the effects of the use of a chemical or biochemical in a law enforcement operation, the more suspect such use becomes in terms of the agent being of a type or quantity consistent with a law enforcement purpose. This interpretation resonates with concerns raised about the deaths caused in Moscow by use of an incapacitating chemical.[19]

Use of incapacitating chemicals or biochemicals when the government can control neither individual dosage nor exposure conditions is not legitimate except in extreme situations. Extreme law enforcement situations are those in which public authorities confront the need to resort to potentially lethal force to resolve urgent, life threatening situations because less violent and dangerous means of resolving the problems have failed. The Moscow hostage crisis was an extreme law enforcement situation.[20] Absent such an extreme situation, a government is not using a chemical or biochemical agent of a type, or in a quantity, consistent with law enforcement purposes when it cannot control dosage or exposure conditions.

International human rights law supports this interpretation. In extreme law enforcement situations, governments contemplating use of incapacitating chemicals or biochemicals confront their obligation to protect the right to life.[21] This obligation prohibits governments from arbitrarily taking the lives of persons subject to their jurisdictions.[22] International human rights law permits no derogation from this obligation, even in time of public emergency.[23]

Human rights organizations have accused the Russian Federation of violating the right to life by failing to provide adequate medical services to rescued hostages who succumbed to the fentanyl gas.[24] The inability to control dosage or exposure environment in extreme law enforcement emergencies heightens governmental responsibility to ensure all precautions are taken to minimize harm to innocent people and to provide immediate and adequate medical attention to those exposed and perhaps adversely affected.[25]

This interpretation means the "types and quantities" restraint on use of incapacitating chemicals or biochemicals for non-extreme law enforcement situations requires CWC states parties to maintain strict control over the dosage and exposure environment.[26] Such control would mean that law enforcement authorities have to have physical custody over the individual in question. A law enforcement situation involving physical custody of persons brings international law on human rights into play. International law on civil and political rights addresses the spectrum of law enforcement activities, from initial custody through criminal trial to incarceration. Reading the "types and quantities" rule in light of international human rights law severely limits when law enforcement authorities could use incapacitating chemical or biochemicals against detained persons.

International human rights law prohibits torture or other cruel, inhuman, or degrading treatment or punishment and permits no derogations from this prohibition.[27] Non-consensual, non-therapeutic use of any chemical or biochemical against detained individuals would constitute degrading treatment and could, depending on the severity of the substance's physiological or psychological effects, constitute cruel or inhuman treatment and perhaps even torture.[28] The international community has long condemned the non-consensual, non-therapeutic use of psychotropic drugs and other types of chemicals against detained persons. The only contexts in which non-consensual, non-therapeutic use of a chemical or biochemical substance against a detained person might be compatible with international human rights law involve situations in which the detained person poses an immediate, violent threat to himself (e.g., attempting suicide) or to safety and order in the detention facility (e.g., attacking guards or participating in riots).

The above interpretation of the "types and quantities" rule significantly restrains a CWC state party's ability to develop and use incapacitating chemicals or biochemicals for law enforcement purposes. The Article II.9(d) legal "loophole" may not, in fact, be as serious as some experts have feared. Such a conclusion does not, of course, mean that all states parties will properly interpret these provisions of the CWC or follow the correct interpretation in their actual behavior.

MEANING OF "LAW ENFORCEMENT" IN ARTICLE II.9(D)

Interpreting "Law Enforcement"

The second major question to arise in connection with the interpretation of Article II.9(d) is the meaning of the term "law enforcement." What activities fall within "law enforcement"? As Dando asked, "when . . . does law enforcement end and a method of warfare begin?"[29] The CWC does not define "law enforcement," which requires again turning to international legal principles on treaty interpretation. The basic interpretive question is whether "law enforcement" should be interpreted narrowly or broadly. As discussed below, the choice involves deciding whether "law enforcement" includes activities relating to international law.

In legal opinions on proposed chemical-based "non-lethal" weapons and on oleoresin capsicum (OC) spray, the Judge Advocate General of the U.S. Department of the Navy (U.S. Navy JAG) argued that the meaning of "law enforcement" in Article II.9(d) was unclear and that "[t]he nature of activities permitted under article II.9(d) is one that will be determined by the practice of states."[30,31] Although state practice informs treaty interpretation, state practice is secondary to the first principle of treaty interpretation. That principle, as stated in the previous section, is to interpret at treaty "in good faith in accordance with the ordinary meaning to be given to the terms of the treaty in their context and in the light of its object and purpose."[32]

U.S. Navy JAG did not apply this fundamental rule of treaty interpretation. Rather, it appears to have assumed that this rule would not provide a clear answer. Thus the U.S. Navy JAG argued that state practice would determine the meaning of "law enforcement." Despite this assumption, an examination of the "ordinary meaning" of law enforcement is both relevant and worthwhile.

Enforcement of Domestic Law

What does "law enforcement" mean? The ordinary meaning of "enforcement" is to compel observance or obedience.[33] The ordinary meaning of "law" clearly refers to *domestic law*, or the law that applies to activities within the territory, or subject to the jurisdiction, of a sovereign state. Article II.9(d) contemplates, therefore, the enforcement of domestic law.

Article II.9(d) allows states parties to use lethal doses of toxic chemicals for capital punishment—a law enforcement function that takes place within a state's jurisdiction. In addition, Article II.9(d) allows toxic chemicals to be used for "[l]aw enforcement including domestic riot control purposes." The phrase "including domestic riot control" illustrates a permitted law enforcement activity and focuses attention on domestic law enforcement within a state's borders or jurisdiction. Although Article II.9(d) covers the enforcement of domestic law within a state's sovereign territory, two questions remain: Does Article II.9(d) permit the use of toxic chemicals to enforce domestic law extrajurisdictionally and to enforce international law?

Use of Toxic Chemicals in Extrajurisdictional Enforcement of Domestic Law

Another treaty interpretation principle is that states shall take into account any relevant rules of international law applicable to the treaty's subject matter.[34] Pursuant to this rule, analyzing whether Article II.9(d) allows states parties to use toxic chemicals in the extrajurisdictional enforcement of domestic law must take into account international law on extrajurisdictional enforcement of domestic law. Applying these rules makes clear that Article II.9(d) cannot authorize the use of toxic chemicals to enforce domestic law extrajurisdictionally.

Under international law, a state may *enforce* a law only if it has jurisdiction to *prescribe* the law.[35] The rules on prescriptive jurisdiction allow a state to prescribe law with respect to (1) conduct, persons, or activities wholly or in substantial part within its territory or areas subject to its jurisdiction; (2) the activities, interests, status, or relations of its nationals outside as well as within its territory and areas subject to its jurisdiction; and (3) conduct outside its territory or areas subject to its jurisdiction (a) that has or is intended to have substantial effect within its territory, and (b) by persons not its nationals that is directed against the security of the state or against a limited class of other state interests.[36] The international legal rules on prescriptive jurisdiction demonstrate that a state may exercise jurisdiction to *prescribe* domestic law beyond its jurisdictional boundaries.

International law on jurisdiction to *enforce* law is, however, stricter: "It is universally recognized, as a corollary of state sovereignty, that officials of one state may not exercise their functions in the territory of another state without the latter's consent."[37] Two fundamental principles of international law support this position: first, the principle of sovereignty and sovereign equality of states;[38] and second, the principle prohibiting intervention into the domestic affairs of other states.[39] A state cannot enforce its domestic law in the territory or jurisdiction of another state without that state's consent.

These rules mean that Article II.9(d) only permits a state party to use toxic chemicals for law enforcement purposes within areas subject to its jurisdiction. Under international law on enforcement jurisdiction, Article II.9(d) cannot be interpreted as allowing a state party to use a toxic chemical to enforce its domestic law inside areas subject to the jurisdiction of another state. Such use would only be legitimate when (1) the CWC state party with jurisdiction permits toxic chemicals to be used; (2) the permission relates to a law enforcement purpose; and (3) the use complies with the "types and quantities" rule.

The rules on jurisdiction to enforce law demonstrate that the ordinary meaning of "law enforcement" in Article II.9(d) incorporates the *enforcement of domestic law within the state's own territory or areas subject to its jurisdiction.* The ordinary meaning of "law enforcement" does not include the extrajurisdictional enforcement of domestic law because such enforcement depends entirely on the consent of another state.

Use of Toxic Chemicals to Enforce International Law

a. Toxic Chemicals and Enforcing International Law   Whether Article II.9(d) allows states parties to use toxic chemicals to enforce international law is another question that has arisen.[40] The CWC negotiating record indicates lack of agreement on this point.[41] The negotiators changed "domestic law enforcement and domestic riot control" in earlier drafts to "law enforcement including domestic riot control" in the final draft, leaving open whether this change creates the possibility of legitimate use of toxic chemicals for non-domestic law enforcement. Does the ordinary meaning of "law enforcement" in light of the CWC's object and purpose include enforcement of international law?

To consider international law within the scope of "law enforcement" would require an unconventional approach to the relationship between international law and enforcement. Whether international law is enforceable is a perennial debate that makes including international law within the ordinary meaning of "law enforcement" dubious. The decentralized and anarchic nature of the international system complicates enforcement of international law. International law contains few centralized mechanisms under which states can compel other states to obey rules of international law. As stated in *Oppenheim's International Law*, international law suffers deficiencies in the means available for enforcement of its rules.[42] Thus, arguing that the ordinary meaning of "law enforcement" encompasses international law lacks credibility given the controversial relationship between enforcement and international law.

Enforcement of international law is also subject to principles regulating how states should handle their disputes. Peaceful dispute settlement is a generally applicable principle,[43] according to which states must settle disputes amicably without resort to force, violence, and weaponry. States can take peaceful countermeasures, such as diplomatic or economic sanctions, to try to compel another state to comply with its international legal duties. Peaceful dispute settlement does not, however, contemplate use of toxic chemicals to compel obedience with international law. In fact, nothing in international law justifies one state using toxic chemicals to compel another state to comply with international law.

b. Law Enforcement and the Right to Use Force in Self-Defense
Could a CWC state party use toxic chemicals, pursuant to the law enforcement provision, in the exercise of its inherent right of self-defense against an armed attack or other form of illegal aggression by state or non-state actors? In other words, a state's use of the toxic chemicals might form part of the enforcement of international legal rules prohibiting the use of force. This argument lacks any support in international law. Self-defense against aggression is an inherent right that states possess;[44] it is not a "law enforcement" mechanism.

Further, the CWC's text, context, object, and purpose seek the elimination of the use of toxic chemicals in armed conflict. Allowing toxic chemicals to be used as part of the right of self-defense would permit chemical weapons to be used in armed conflict—the very thing the CWC prohibits. The same reasoning applies to armed conflict conducted by the armed forces of a state outside its jurisdiction, whether such operations involve UN Security Council-authorized collective security responses, humanitarian intervention, or anticipatory or preemptive self-defense.

Extraterritorial Law Enforcement Activities Undertaken by Military Forces and Permitted by International Law

The change from "domestic law enforcement" to "law enforcement" during the CWC negotiations does not mean the CWC permits states parties to enforce international law by using toxic chemicals. This interpretation still leaves unanswered the significance of the change from "domestic law enforcement" to "law enforcement" that occurred during the negotiations. This change implies that negotiating states believed that some law enforcement activities could be conducted extraterritorially. International law does permit certain extraterritorial law enforcement activities by military forces in both traditional and nontraditional military operations. These activities fall within the scope of Article II.9(d).

   a. Law Enforcement Activities in Connection with Traditional Military Operations: Occupation and Control of Prisoners of War   International law recognizes a number of contexts in which military forces legitimately engage in law enforcement activities in connection with traditional military operations. These contexts generally relate to the preservation of public order and safety in areas subject to the control of military forces. First, international humanitarian law acknowledges the responsibility of an occupying power "to maintain the orderly government of the territory."[45] The International Committee of the Red Cross (ICRC) observed that this provision empowers the occupying power "in its capacity as the Power responsible for public law and order."[46] Fulfilling this responsibility includes activities such as controlling civilian crowds in order to prevent disorder in the occupied territory.

   Second, international humanitarian law also allows occupying military forces to ensure the security of their members and property, of the occupying administration, and of the establishments and lines of communication used by them.[47] According to the ICRC, "[t]his power has long been recognized by international law."[48] This right gives occupying forces permission to enact and implement penal legislation in order to protect their soldiers, administrators, buildings, lines of communication, equipment, and other forms of property from problems created or threats posed by noncombatants in the occupied territory.

   Third, international humanitarian law recognizes that the occupying power may enforce the laws of the occupied territory and the laws it promulgates pursuant to its responsibilities under the international law of occupation.[49] Such powers include law enforcement techniques and weapons used to control civilian crowds and to protect public order and safety.

   Fourth, international humanitarian law allows military forces to regulate the behavior of prisoners of war (POWs).[50] Military forces can enforce laws, regulations, and orders against POWs[51] and may use weapons against POWs in extreme circumstances, such as escape attempts.[52] According to the ICRC, the detaining power may use force against POWs engaged in rebellious or mutinous behavior: "Before resorting to weapons of war, sentries can use others which do not cause fatal injury and may even be considered as warnings—tear gas, truncheons, etc."[53] These four contexts in which international law recognizes the legitimacy of extraterritorial law enforcement activities by military forces indicate that Article II.9(d) includes these activities. This interpretation covers some of the circumstances in which the United States claims the ability to use riot control agents in military situations, namely: (1) in areas under direct and distinct US military control, including the control of rioting prisoners of war; and (2) in rear echelon areas outside the zone of immediate combat to secure convoys from civil disturbances.[54]

b. Law Enforcement Activities and Nontraditional Military Operations: Peacekeeping   The foregoing analysis also applies to nontraditional military operations, such as peacekeeping operations, recognized as legitimate under international law. Nontraditional military operations have legitimacy under international law if they are conducted pursuant to: (1) a request for peacekeeping forces from a sovereign state; and (2) the authorization of peacekeeping operations by the UN Security Council under Chapter VII of the UN Charter.

Military forces conducting peacekeeping operations often find themselves in control of and responsible for the security of, and public order and safety within, civilian populations. They get involved in law enforcement operations (e.g., arresting suspected war criminals, rescuing hostages); and face threats to the security of their personnel and equipment from noncombatants. For example, after being unable to prevent violent mobs from attacking monasteries in Kosovo in March 2004, Germany announced its intention to equip its peacekeepers with riot control agents.[55] Similarly, French military forces used riot control agents against rioting civilians in the aftermath of French military intervention following an attack on French peacekeepers by the air force of the Ivory Coast.[56] Indeed, the challenges military forces face handling civilian populations in peacekeeping operations have partly fueled military interest in "nonlethal" weapons.[57]

Thus, the CWC permits the use of riot control agents for law enforcement purposes undertaken by military forces during nontraditional military operations sanctioned by international law. This interpretation is consistent with claims by the United States that its military forces may lawfully use riot control agents in (1) the conduct of peacetime military operations within an area of ongoing armed conflict when the United States is not a party to the conflict; (2) peacekeeping operations authorized by the receiving state, including peacekeeping operations pursuant to Chapter VI of the UN Charter; and (3) peacekeeping operations where force is authorized by the UN Security Council under Chapter VII of the UN Charter.[58]

This interpretation of Article II.9(d) does not support, however, the U.S. position that it may use riot control agents against combatant forces in the above-listed nontraditional military operations.[59] The types of law enforcement activities that international law allows military forces to undertake in traditional and nontraditional military operations address the interaction of military troops and noncombatants, in the form of either POWs or civilians, not the engagement of combatant forces.

Interpreting Article II.9(d) as presented above has two implications that deserve brief mention. First, this interpretation might suggest that military forces conducting extraterritorial law enforcement activities permitted by international law might not be limited to the use of riot control agents in extreme law enforcement situations. State practice suggests, however, that the CWC is more restrictive in connection with the use of toxic chemicals by military forces in extraterritorial law enforcement activities. CWC states parties, including the United States, have never claimed the ability to use, or actually have used, toxic chemicals other than riot control agents for the types of law enforcement activities permitted by international law in traditional and nontraditional military operations. President Bush authorized U.S. military forces to use riot control agents in Iraq in 2003, for example, under the circumstances described in Executive Order 11850.[60] Likewise, the UK military indicated in March 2003 that it would only use riot control agents in Iraq for riot control purposes (Davison and Lewer 2004: 34).[61]

This more restrictive interpretation of Article II.9(d) has two sources: first, the law enforcement activities are extraterritorial and thus do not benefit from the wider discretion international law generally recognizes that governments have within their own territories; and second, military forces undertake the extraterritorial law enforcement activities. The CWC's object and purpose of prohibiting military use of chemical weapons in armed conflict means that heightened scrutiny, and extra safeguards, are appropriate when extraterritorial military activities involving toxic chemicals are at issue.

The second implication of the interpretation of Article II.9(d) found above is that it covers many, but not all, of the uses of riot control agents the United States claims are legal under the CWC. It does not cover two situations in which the United States believes riot control agents are legally permissible: (1) contexts in which civilians are used to mask or screen attacks and civilian casualties can be reduced or avoided; and (2) rescue missions in remote areas of downed aircrew and passengers, and of escaping POWs.[62] Neither of these situations resembles the law enforcement activities sanctioned by international law in which military forces may engage. Riot control agent use against enemy combatants who are attempting to capture downed aircrew and passengers or escaping POWs or who are using civilians as shields against attack or masks for attacks is more akin to a method of warfare than a law enforcement purpose. Interpreting Article II.9(d) in this manner is consistent with treaty interpretation principles because it distinguishes between law enforcement purposes permitted by Article II.9(d) and methods of warfare prohibited by Article I.5.

c. Law Enforcement and Fighting Insurgencies   The war in Iraq has raised the question whether military forces can use riot control agents or incapacitating chemicals in counter-insurgency operations. In other words, can counter-insurgency operations mounted by military forces be considered a law enforcement purpose under Article II.9(d)? The insurgency context presents difficulties because it falls between armed conflict between states and law enforcement within a state. Environments involving insurgencies and large-scale, organized civil violence have presented international humanitarian law with problems in the past, as evidenced by the controversies that surround Additional Protocol II (1977) on non-international armed conflict. Thus, one should not be surprised that the insurgency context creates problems for interpreting Article II.9(d).

International humanitarian law on non-international armed conflict applies to conflicts in the territory of a state between its armed forces and dissident armed forces or other organized armed groups that exercise such control over a part of the state's territory as to enable them to carry out sustained and concerted military operations.[63] This threshold provides a demarcation point between armed conflict and law enforcement within a state. Thus, Additional Protocol II is a relevant source of applicable rules that should inform the interpretation of Article II.9(d).

Military action taken against insurgents who exercise control over part of a state's territory and carry out sustained and concerted military operations constitutes armed conflict rather than law enforcement, and thus falls outside Article II.9(d). The CWC's prohibition of the use of chemical weapons "under any circumstance" (Article I.1) encompasses civil armed conflict as well as international armed conflict. This reasoning also holds that riot control agent use in counter-insurgency operations would be a method of warfare prohibited by Article I.5 of the CWC. The state practice of military forces in Iraq to date supports this interpretation because such forces have not used riot control agents or incapacitating chemicals in counter-insurgency operations.

CONCLUSION ON THE INTERPRETATION OF ARTICLE II.9(D)

The controversy about the CWC's law enforcement provision, and its intensification in the wake of the Moscow incident and growing fears about new types of incapacitating chemical and biochemical agents, has put Article II.9(d) in the arms control spotlight. The interpretation of Article II.9(d) presented above answers many questions raised about this provision and perhaps addresses worries that it constitutes a grave weakness and renders the CWC vulnerable to advances in science and technology. Clarification of the provision is important; but, as the next part explores, determining the meaning of the law enforcement provision constitutes only part of the larger debate about the threat posed by incapacitating chemical and biochemical agents.

Implications of the Interpretation of Article II.9(d) for the CWC and BWC

The overarching fear about Article II.9(d) is that its increased utilization by states will undermine the prohibitions against development and use of chemical and biological weapons enshrined in the CWC and BWC respectively. This fear divides into three distinct but interdependent concerns. First, Article II.9(d) provides incentives for states to pursue development of new, incapacitating chemical and biochemical agents, which do not fit within the definition of a riot control agent, under the guise of law enforcement. Second, such development will spill-over into military use in armed conflict. Third, the development and any use of such incapacitating agents will cause these new technologies to disseminate, raising the specter that repressive governments, terrorists, and criminals will have their arsenals enhanced at the expense of human rights, national security, and domestic law and order.

STIMULATING DEVELOPMENT OF THE NEXT GENERATION OF CHEMICAL AND BIOCHEMICAL WEAPONS

Overview of the Concerns

As indicated in the Introduction, Article II.9(d) has been the source of anxiety since states completed the negotiation of the CWC, especially with regard to the "loophole" it might provide for development of new chemical and biochemical weapons technologies. The dangers states perceive from terrorism as a threat to homeland security and law enforcement may drive some states to explore more vigorously the potential of incapacitating chemical and biochemical agents.

The possible emergence of biochemical agents, which have characteristics that might place them simultaneously under the CWC and BWC, also creates the possibility that Article II.9(d) may provide cover for the development of technologies previously considered banned under the BWC. Lewer and Davison note the development of biochemicals could "exploit the loophole in the CWC that permits the use of certain chemicals for 'law enforcement including domestic riot control purposes.'"[64] In essence, any "pull" generated by Article II.9(d) for those interested in biochemical development might create a *de facto* law enforcement exception in the BWC, which does not exist in its actual text. Or, more likely, proponents of biochemical development will interpret the permitted "peaceful purposes" in Article I of the BWC to include law enforcement as interpreted in Article II.9(d) of the CWC. These concerns are significant and require examination.

Incapacitating Chemicals and Biochemicals and Law Enforcement under the CWC

Will Article II.9(d) produce increasing law enforcement interest in incapacitating chemicals and biochemicals, particularly in the age of terrorism? Whether Article II.9(d) creates strong incentives for CWC states parties to develop incapacitating chemical and biochemical agents depends, of course, on the scope of this permitted purpose. The interpretation of Article II.9(d) provided earlier suggests that this provision does not constitute a gaping loophole in the CWC or a material threat to the BWC.

For domestic law enforcement, use of incapacitating agents in contexts in which the government could control neither dosage nor the exposure environment would only be legitimate in extreme law enforcement situations. In addition, such use would trigger significant obligations for governments concerning medical treatment for those exposed to the incapacitating agents. For extraterritorial law enforcement activities undertaken by military forces and sanctioned by international law, states can at present only legitimately use riot control agents, not incapacitating agents. These interpretations do not provide a foundation on which states could build extensive programs investigating incapacitating chemical or biochemical agents for law enforcement purposes.

The rise of terrorism has fueled the "loophole" fears because the terrorist threat requires vigorous law enforcement responses. Terrorists, after all, perpetrated the hostage crisis that led to Russian forces using an incapacitating toxic chemical. Terrorism does not, however, affect, or require abandoning, the interpretations of Article II.9(d) presented above.

As the aftermath of the Moscow incident showed, law enforcement use of incapacitating chemicals or biochemicals in situations in which authorities can control neither dosage nor the exposure environment is illegitimate except in extreme circumstances. Terrorist acts do not always involve mass hostage taking or create other extreme law enforcement circumstances. In addition, whether terrorism, organized crime interests, or a "lone wolf" criminal causes extreme law enforcement events is not analytically relevant to the choices that governments have to make under international law concerning the use of incapacitating agents.

In contexts in which governments have physical custody over suspected terrorists, the rules on the use of incapacitating agents for law enforcement purposes also do not change because the detained persons are suspected terrorists. Governments are not allowed to use chemicals or biochemicals against detained persons in non-consensual, non-therapeutic ways except in very limited contexts, as explored earlier. Whether the detained person is a terrorist or an ordinary criminal has no bearing on the application of the relevant rules of international law.

These observations suggest that terrorism does not change how Article II.9(d) should be interpreted and applied and thus does not enlarge any "loophole" associated with this provision.

Article II.9(d) of the CWC and the BWC

This chapter's interpretation means that Article II.9(d) does not invite states to develop large and diverse stockpiles of chemical and biochemical incapacitating agents for law enforcement purposes. Perceiving an exploitable "loophole" in Article II.9(d) partakes of interpretive approaches to the meaning of treaty provisions that are incomplete. The CWC does not contain a *laissez faire* attitude about the development and use of chemicals or biochemicals for law enforcement purposes.

The strict scrutiny required for any law enforcement use of incapacitating toxic chemicals prevents Article II.9(d) from undermining the BWC's prohibitions. Arguments that the BWC allows the development and use of incapacitating biochemicals for law enforcement purposes because such purposes are "peaceful purposes" (Article I.1(a)) and are not "hostile purposes" (Article I.1(b)) would be subject to the same level of scrutiny required by the CWC in terms of its Article II.9(d). This approach reinforces the interdependence between the CWC and BWC and the importance of Article II.9(d) in that relationship.

Use of an incapacitating biochemical when the law enforcement authorities can control neither dosage nor the exposure environment is not "a peaceful purpose," except in extreme law enforcement situations. Deliberate non-consensual, non-therapeutic use of an incapacitating biochemical against a detained person would be a hostile act, except in extreme situations directly involving the immediate physical safety of the detained person, law enforcement authorities, and other individuals in detention. Even in these situations, law enforcement authorities have options available that do not require resort to the use of incapacitating biochemical agents.

SPILL-OVER FROM LAW ENFORCEMENT PURPOSES INTO MILITARY USES

The second major fear about Article II.9(d) is that law enforcement uses of chemicals or biochemicals might spill-over into military contexts. If chemicals and biochemicals show promise as incapacitating agents in law enforcement contexts, pressure might develop for military forces to use such agents in non-law enforcement activities. Commentators have expressed concern that research being conducted in the United States by civilian agencies is really being conducted at the behest of the Department of Defense because of military interest in the capabilities of the chemical and biochemical agents in question.

The spill-over fear sometimes flows from a misinterpretation of Article II.9(d), a misinterpretation this chapter attempted to correct. This concern deserves, however, to be addressed directly. Without question, the moment military forces develop and use incapacitating chemicals or biochemicals in armed conflict, the fundamental norms of the CWC and BWC will be in jeopardy. This possibility means that the very limited room Article II.9(d) leaves open for use of incapacitating toxic chemicals should be carefully monitored to ensure that spill-over into military capabilities does not occur.

Analyzing the spill-over fear requires assessing whether military interest in incapacitating chemicals and biochemicals poses a direct threat to the objects and purposes of the CWC and BWC. Admittedly, such an assessment is difficult when military interest in such chemicals and biochemicals is shrouded in secrecy and non-transparent national security politics.[65] Before such interest manifests itself in real military capabilities, however, governments would have to decide to violate either or both the CWC and BWC or amend the treaties to permit military use of incapacitating chemicals and biochemicals. Such steps would represent a far more serious challenge to the CWC than U.S. deployment of riot control agents with military forces for purposes listed in Executive Order 11850 even though such deployment remains controversial.

Some indications are emerging that military interest in incapacitating chemicals and biochemicals might not mature to the point that generates serious interest in amending or violating the treaties. A shift in opinion among leading U.S. experts on "non-lethal" weapons (NLWs) concerning incapacitating chemical and biochemical weapons can be detected in two reports sponsored by the influential Council on Foreign Relations in the United States. In 1999, a Council-sponsored Independent Task Force discussed the CWC and BWC in connection with "non-lethal" chemical and biological weapons and argued that "[o]n occasion, U.S. security might be improved by a modification to a treaty."[66] This argument clearly revealed a willingness on the part of NLW opinion leaders to contemplate amendments to the CWC and BWC.

In 2004, a new Council-sponsored Independent Task Force on NLWs "considered the benefits that would accrue and the problems that would be posed by either a U.S. attempt to interpret the CWC or by a U.S. move to amend or to renounce the CWC in order to be able to use chemicals as non-lethal weapons against enemy combatants."[67] This consideration led the Task Force to conclude:

> The Task Force believes that to press for an amendment to the CWC or even to assert a right to use RCAs as a method of warfare risks impairing the legitimacy of all NLW. This would also free others to openly and legitimately conduct focused governmental R&D that could more readily yield advanced lethal agents than improved non-lethal capabilities. . . . Accordingly, the Task Force judges that on balance the best course for the United States is to reaffirm its commitment to the CWC and the BWC and to be a leader in ensuring that other nations comply with the treaties.[68]

The shift from the position in the 1999 report to the conclusion reached in the 2004 report indicates a growing awareness among those involved in thinking about NLWs generally and "non-lethal" biological and chemical weapons specifically that loosening the strictures of the CWC and BWC would harm U.S. national security. U.S. national security interests in opposing the spread of weapons of mass destruction also play a role in heightened sensibilities about the dangers of military use of chemical and biochemical agents. Although the Council on Foreign Relations-sponsored task forces did not speak for the U.S. Department of Defense, and although other evidence exists of a continuing military interest in incapacitating chemical and biochemical agents,[69] sensitivity about, and opposition to, crossing the line from interest to capability has grown among opinion leaders in the United States.

Any spill-over from law enforcement to military capability is, thus, unlikely to happen through innocuous, unintentional "mission creep" but would have to involve deliberate decisions by governments to flout the CWC and BWC. In other words, any spill-over would have to result from a treaty-busting exercise. As the 2004 Council on Foreign Relations-sponsored Independent Task Force concluded, such a dramatic step would have adverse ramifications for national and international security that would far outweigh any benefit military forces could achieve through using incapacitating chemical and biochemical agents on twenty-first century battlefields. As Koplow has argued, "[c]hemical and biolog-

ical weapons are among the few areas where international law has been labori-
ously installed to restrict combat violence; those taboos should not be relaxed."[70]

BAD GUYS AND INCAPACITATING CHEMICALS
AND BIOCHEMICALS

The third major concern about Article II.9(d) involves worries that development
and use of incapacitating chemical and biochemical agents by law enforcement
or military authorities would lead, inevitably, to those agents being available to,
and misused by, repressive governments, terrorists, and criminal interests.[71] This
chapter's interpretation of Article II.9(d) demonstrates that this provision does
not provide a broad platform from which governments can develop robust
chemical and biochemical capabilities. The "bad guy" warning deserves, however, to be treated on its own terms because it represents a serious concern about
the implications of moving in the incapacitating chemical and biochemical direction for any reason.

Fears about catastrophic terrorism involving weapons of mass destruction
would only be deepened if governments made terrorist use of "non-lethal"
chemical and biochemical agents easier by developing incapacitating chemical
and biochemical capabilities for the very limited law enforcement contexts in
which they could legitimately use such capabilities. The prospects of terrorists
or criminal interests successfully developing incapacitating chemical and biochemical capabilities on their own are remote. The most likely dissemination
routes would be (1) repressive governments developing these technologies and
not controlling their spread to malevolent non-state actors; or (2) accountable
governments developing incapacitating chemical and biochemical capabilities,
which nefarious individuals or groups then exploit to harm such governments
and their populations.

This dynamic makes pursuit of incapacitating chemical and biochemical
agents for law enforcement purposes questionable not only legally but also as a
policy matter. The "bad guy" argument reinforces the appropriateness of interpreting Article II.9(d) in the manner presented in this chapter. But the "bad
guy" argument accentuates the policy ramifications of the decisions that have
to be made about incapacitating chemical and biochemical agents and law
enforcement.

In short, the "bad guy" argument presents a challenge that implicates but
goes beyond Article II.9(d)'s meaning. Strict compliance with the law enforcement provision by states does not guarantee that the bad guys will refrain from
trying to exploit emerging new chemical and biochemical possibilities. The

objective is to ensure that Article II.9(d) does not create a Pandora's Box for the bad guys to pilfer.

Conclusion

Developments in the biological and chemical sciences promise tremendous benefits for human knowledge, industry, health, and well being. But, as with every other transformative scientific phenomenon, the promise comes with peril. Governments, groups, and individuals will try to exploit these developments for ends that undermine security and debase the human condition. Harvesting the promise and weeding out the peril in the husbandry of chemical and biochemical advances involve operating the normative and legal structures in place for regulating chemical and biological weapons correctly and vigilantly.

For reasons this chapter explored, successful management of rapidly advancing biological and chemical capabilities requires the proper interpretation and application of Article II.9(d) of the CWC. This chapter interpreted this provision of the CWC and argued that Article II.9(d) is not, and should not be considered, a grave threat to the core object and purpose of either the CWC or the BWC. This chapter's approach to Article II.9(d) also indicates that many fears associated with this provision are overstated or unfounded.

Proper treaty interpretation does not, however, make the world go round, especially if powerful countries decide to act in ways contrary to their treaty commitments. The challenges presented by revolutions in the biological and chemical sciences go beyond treaties and stimulate a struggle between the best and the worst humanity has to offer. As Coupland argued, preventing the malign use of advances in sciences and biotechnology "will lack a vital strand if the politicians, diplomats, lawyers and scientists working on the BWC and CWC do not feel accountable to humanity and adapt their beliefs and behavior accordingly."[72] Article II.9(d) of the CWC plays a role in this struggle, but the contest will be decided ultimately outside the boundaries of the principles of treaty interpretation.

Notes

1. *National Security Strategy of the United States*, Washington, D.C.: White House, 2002, <http://www.whitehouse.gov/nsc/nss.pdf> (26 February, 2007).

2. Mark Wheelis, "Will the New Biology Lead to New Weapons?" *Arms Control Today* (July/August 2004): 6–13.

3. Mark Wheelis and Malcolm Dando, "Neurobiology: A Case Study of the Imminent Militarization of Biology," *International Review of the Red Cross* 87, no. 859 (2005): 553–68.

4. "Convention on the Prohibition of the Development, Production, and Stockpiling of Bacteriological (Biological) and Toxin Weapons and on Their Destruction, 1972," in M. Cherif Bassiouni, ed., *A Manual on International Humanitarian Law and Arms Control Agreements* (Transnational Publishers, 2000): 379–84.

5. "Convention on the Prohibition of the Development, Production, Stockpiling, and Use of Chemical Weapons and on Their Destruction, 1993," in M. Cherif Bassiouni, ed., *A Manual on International Humanitarian Law and Arms Control Agreements* (Transnational Publishers, 2000): 385–432.

6. Editorial, "New Technologies and the Loophole in the Convention," *Chemical Weapons Convention Bulletin* no. 23, (March 1994): 1–2.

7. Editorial, "New Technologies and the Loophole in the Convention," *Chemical Weapons Convention Bulletin* no. 23, (March 1994): 1–2.

8. David A. Koplow, "Tangled Up in Khaki and Blue: Lethal and Non-Lethal Weapons in Recent Confrontations," *Georgetown Journal of International Law* 36, no. 3 (2005): 703–808.

9. David P. Fidler, "The Meaning of Moscow: 'Non-Lethal' Weapons and International Law in the Early 21st Century," *International Review of the Red Cross* 87, no. 859 (2005): 525–52.

10. Editorial, "Law Enforcement and the CWC," *CBW Conventions Bulletin*, no. 58 (December 2002): 1–2.

11. *Biotechnology, Weapons and Humanity II*, British Medical Association (2004): 31-32.

12. Abram Chayes and Matthew Meselson, "Proposed Guidelines on the Status of Riot Control Agents and Other Toxic Chemicals under the Chemical Weapons Convention," *Chemical Weapons Convention Bulletin*, no. 35, (March 1997), 13–18.

13. Walter Krutzsch, *"Non-Lethal" Chemicals for Law Enforcement?* Berlin Information Center for Transatlantic Security, Research Note 03.2, (April 2003), 4.

14. Chayes and Meselson, "Proposed Guidelines," 13.

15. Article 31.1 of "Vienna Convention on the Law of Treaties, 1969," in I. Brownlie, ed., *Basic Documents in International Law*, 4th ed. (London: Clarendon Press, 1995): 388–425.

16. Walter Krutzch and Ralf Trapp, *A Commentary on the Chemical Weapons Convention* (Martinus Nijhoff Publishers, 1994): 418.

17. "Article 31.3(b) in the Vienna Convention on the Law of Treaties, 1969," in I. Brownlie, ed., *Basic Documents in International Law*, 4th ed. (Clarendon Press, 1995), 388–425.

18. Wheelis, "Will the New Biology."

19. Malcolm Dando notes the following: "As with any chemical incapacitants, the concentration of fentanyl in any particular part of the building will have been difficult to control, the effects of any given concentration of fentanyl on any particularly susceptible individual would not have been known, and achievement of a certain separation between

the incapacitating and lethal effects of the drug—in other words, discriminating between making people unconscious without stopping them breathing—is very difficult." See Malcolm Dando, "The Danger to the Chemical Weapons Convention from Incapacitating Chemicals," *First CWC Review Conference Paper* no. 4 (March 2003).

20. As Human Rights Watch commented on the Moscow incident: "International law does not prohibit the use of potentially lethal force in operations to liberate hostages, but it requires that such force be 'absolutely necessary' and that all precautions be taken in both the planning and execution of such operations to minimize the loss of civilian life." See "Independent Commission of Inquiry Must Investigate Raid on Moscow Theater: Inadequate Protection for Consequences of Gas Violates Obligation to Protect Life," Published by the Human Rights Watch, 30 October 2002, <http://www.hrw.org/press/2002/10/russia1030.htm> (25 February 2007).

21. Article 3 in "Universal Declaration of Human Rights, 1948," in Ian Brownlie, ed., *Basic Documents on Human Rights*, 3rd. ed. (London: Clarendon Press, 1992): 21–27; Article 6 in "International Covenant on Civil and Political Rights" in Brownlie, ed. *Basic Documents on Human Rights*, 125–43.

22. Human Rights Committee, "General Comment no. 6, art. 6, 1982, para. 3" in *Compilation of General Comments and General Recommendations Adopted by Human Rights Treaty Bodies, UN Doc. HRI/GEN/1/Rev.1*, at 6 (1994).

23. See Article 4 in the "International Covenant on Civil and Political Rights, 1966," in Brownlie, ed., *Basic Documents on Human Rights*, 3rd ed. 125–43.

24. Human Rights Watch, "Independent Commission of Inquiry," 2002.

25. Commenting on the possible use of incapacitating chemicals for law enforcement purposes, the British government argued: "The decision to use any drug whether intended to induce a state of calm or complete unconsciousness requires knowledge of a subject's medical history, particularly the use of any prescribed or non-prescribed medication and any relevant medical conditions. There would also be considerable responsibility in terms of immediate and post-incident aftercare." This can be found at: Nick Lewer and Neil Davison, "Non-Lethal Technologies—An Overview," *Disarmament Forum* (2005): 37–51.

26. "To elicit the desired level of mood alteration without causing a dangerous level of respiratory depression (i.e., calming while maintaining consciousness) requires a tight control on dose level," in Committee for an Assessment of Non-Lethal Weapons Science and Technology, (*An Assessment of Non-Lethal Weapons Science and Technology* (National Academics Press, 2003): 27.

27. Article 5 in the "Universal Declaration of Human Rights," 1948; Articles 4.2 and 7 in the "International Covenant on Civil and Political Rights," 1966.

28. For more detailed analysis of these international human rights issues, see the chapters by William Aceves and Françoise Hampson in this volume.

29. Malcolm Dando, "Scientific and Technological Change and the Future of the CWC: The Problem of Non-Lethal Weapons," *Disarmament Forum* (2002): 33-34.

30. U.S. Navy Judge Advocate General, *Preliminary Legal Review of Proposed Chemical-Based Non-Lethal Weapons*, (30 November 1997): 12.

31. U.S. Navy Judge Advocate General, *Legal Review of Oleoresin Capsicum (OC) Pepper Spray*, (19 May 1998), 13.

32. Article 31.1 in "Vienna Convention on the Law of Treaties 1969."

33. *New Shorter Oxford English Dictionary.* (Oxford: Oxford University Press, 1993): 820; Sir Robert Jennings and Sir Arthur Watts, *Oppenheim's International Law* 9th ed. (Essex, England: Longmans, 1992).

34. Article 31 (c) in "Vienna Convention 1969."

35. American Law Institute, *Restatement of the Law Third, Foreign Relations Law of the United States*, (Philadelphia:1986), §431(1).

36. American Law Institute, *Restatement* 402.

37. American Law Institute, *Restatement* 329.

38. Article 2.1 in the *United Nations Charter, 1945.*

39. "Article 2.7 in the United Nations Charter, 1945," in I. Brownlie, ed. *Basic Documents in International Law* 4th ed., (London: Clarendon Press, 1995): 1–35.

40. Chayes and Meselson, "Proposed Guidelines," 15.

41. J. P. Perry Robinson and Matthew S. Meselson, "Background Note on Agendum 2, 2nd Workshop of the Pugwash Study Group on the Implementation of the Chemical and Biological Weapons Conventions," 1–2 May 1994.

42. Jennings and Watts, *Oppenheim's International Law*, 11.

43. Articles 2.3, 2.4 and 33.1 in *United Nations Charter, 1945.*

44. Article 51 in *United Nations Charter, 1945.*

45. Article 64 in the Geneva Convention IV, "Relative to the Protection of Civilian Persons in Time of War, 1949," *United Nations Treaty Series* 75, 287.

46. International Committee of the Red Cross, Commentary on Geneva Convention IV Relative to the Protection of Civilian Persons in Time of War, (1958), 337.

47. Article 61 in the "Geneva Convention *IV, 1949.*"

48. International Committee of the Red Cross Commentary on "Geneva Convention *IV, 1958, 337.*"

49. Articles 64-78 in the "Geneva Convention *IV, 1949.*"

50. Articles 41 and 82 in the "Geneva Convention *III, 1949.*"

51. Article 92 in the "Geneva Convention III, Relative to the Treatment of Prisoners of War, 1949," *United Nations Treaty Series* 75, 135.

52. Article 42 in the *Geneva Convention III, 1949.*

53. International Committee of the Red Cross, "Commentary on Geneva Convention III: Relative to the Treatment of Prisoners of War," (1960) 247.

54. Executive Office of the President, *Executive Order 11850—Renunciation of Certain Uses in War of Chemical Herbicides and Riot Control Agents* (Washington, D.C., 8 April 1975 ¶¶ [a] [d]) appears at 40 FR 16187, 3 CFR, 1971–1975 Comp., 980 <http://www.armscontrolcenter.org/archives/001943.php> (13 July 2006).

55. Neil Davison and Nick Lewer, *Bradford Non-Lethal Weapons Research Project Report No. 6*, (West Yorkshire, England: Bradford University, 2004):34.

56. Neil Davison and Nick Lewer, *Bradford Non-Lethal Weapons Research Project Report No. 7* (West Yorkshire, England: Bradford University, 2005): 53.

57. David P. Fidler, "The International Legal Implications of 'Non-Lethal' Weapons," *Michigan Journal of International Law* 21 (1999): 58.

58. U.S. Senate Executive Resolution no. 7—Relative to the Chemical Weapons Convention, ¶ 26A *Congressional Record* vol. 143, S3373-01, 17 April 1997, 143.

59. U.S. Senate Resolution no. 75: ¶ 26A.

60. Neil Davison and Nick Lewer, *Bradford Non-Lethal Weapons Research Project Report No. 4* (West Yorkshire, England: Bradford University, 2003): 13.

61. This situation has produced incentives for trying to fit new chemical compounds, such as malodorants, within the definition of a RCA, as the United States has done (N. Davison and N. Lewer *Bradford Non-Lethal Weapons,* (2003): 10). Such an approach will not, however, work for stronger irritant chemical agents and possible biochemical agents. As a National Research Council report observed, "[t]he use of calmatives had . . . been envisioned in connection with hostage situations and for use with 'unmanageable' prisoners, but not for riot situations in which incapacitated individuals might be trampled or crushed in the rioting." See: Committee for an Assessment of Non-Lethal Weapons Science and Technology, *An Assessment of Non-Lethal Weapons Science and Technology,* 27.

62. Executive Order 11850, 1975, ¶¶: b-c.

63. "Additional Protocol II, 1977: Article 1," *Additional Protocol to the Geneva Conventions of August 12, 1949, and Relating to the Protection of Victims of Non-International Armed Conflicts,* Protocol II, (1977) Article 1, <http://www.unhchr.ch/html/menu3/b/94.htm> (25 February 2007).

64. Lewer and Davidson, *Non-Lethal Technologies—An Overview,* 44–45.

65. Wheelis, "Will the New Biology," 8–9.

66. Council on Foreign Relations, *Non-Lethal Technologies and Prospects: Independent Task Force,* (Council on Foreign Relations, 1999) 1999.

67. Council on Foreign Relations, *Non-Lethal Weapons and Capabilities, Independent Task Force,* 2004, 31.

68. Council on Foreign Relations, Independent Task Force 2004, 32.

69. Dando, "The Danger to the Chemical Weapons Convention," 17.

70. Koplow, "Tangled Up in Khaki and Blue," 2005, 804.

71. Mark Wheelis, "'Non-Lethal' Chemical Weapons: A Faustian Bargain?" *Issues in Science and Technology,* (Spring 2003).

72. Robin Coupland, "Special Comment," *Disarmament Forum* (2005): 6.

CHAPTER 9

Toxic Chemicals for Law Enforcement Including Domestic Riot Control Purposes Under the Chemical Weapons Convention

Adolf von Wagner

The Chemical Weapons Convention (CWC) was negotiated and concluded in the firm resolve to prohibit forever all chemical weapons and to make sure that no loopholes in the Convention allow for an evasion of this prohibition. Keeping this undisputed purpose in mind makes it easier to interpret and apply the provisions of the Convention that, deplorably, are not as unequivocal in their language as would have been desirable. With this in mind, it should be feasible to determine the borderline between what is prohibited and what is not prohibited for law enforcement, including domestic riot control purposes, under the Chemical Weapons Convention.

This chapter begins with establishing the legal basis for the prohibitions of the Convention in order to set the stage for the discussion of the clauses that deal with riot control and domestic law enforcement. It goes on to discuss relevant CWC prohibitions that are not in dispute as well as those that could be described as in the "gray area." The chapter also discusses the negotiating history of the CWC and the relevance of the 1925 Geneva Protocol in interpreting the CWC.

This paper was drafted for oral delivery. It, therefore, does not contain any footnotes but gives the sources of quotations in the text. In addition, most factual statements are based on practical experiences during negotiations, in the Ad-hoc Committee of the Conference on Disarmament without any records, i.e., without any quotable sources.

The Legal Basis

The basic rule is contained in Article I, paragraph 1 CWC:

Each State Party to this Convention undertakes never under any circumstances:

(a) To develop, produce, otherwise acquire, stockpile or retain chemical weapons, or transfer, directly or indirectly, chemical weapons to anyone;
(b) To use chemical weapons;
(c) To engage in any military preparations to use chemical weapons;
(d) To assist, encourage or induce, in any way, anyone to engage in any activity prohibited to a State Party under this Convention.

This fundamental commitment of each State Party to the CWC, however, requires a definition of what is a "chemical weapon." The definition is contained in Article II, paragraph 1 of the CWC:

"Chemical Weapons" means the following, together or separately:

(a) Toxic chemicals and their precursors, except where intended for purposes not prohibited under this Convention, as long as the types and quantities are consistent with such purposes;
(b) Munitions and devices, specifically designed to cause death or other harm through the toxic properties of those toxic chemicals specified in subparagraph (a), which would be released as a result of the employment of such munitions and devices;
(c) Any equipment specifically designed for use directly in connection with the employment of munitions and devices specified in subparagraph (b).

Article II, paragraph 2 of the CWC contains the definition of toxic chemical:

"Toxic Chemical" means:

> Any chemical that through its chemical action on life processes can cause death, temporary incapacitation or permanent harm to humans or animals. This includes all such chemicals, regardless of their origin or of their method of production, and regardless of whether they are produced in facilities, in munitions or elsewhere.

> (For the purpose of implementing this Convention, toxic chemicals which have been identified for the application of verification measures are listed in Schedules contained in the Annex on Chemicals.)

This logical sequence of provisions defines both legally and practically which chemical substances, in general, are considered to be chemical weapons and, as such, are covered by the CWC's prohibitions and which are not.

Toxicity, and not lethal effect, as a material-oriented criterion, is the first prerequisite for qualifying a chemical as a chemical weapon. The second criterion is the intent of its use; that is, its purpose. The purpose makes the ultimate difference whether a toxic chemical is a chemical weapon or not. Toxicity and purpose are linked together and phrased as an exception to make clear that any toxic chemical is a chemical weapon unless it is used for a non-prohibited purpose. Thus, the purpose-oriented criterion is dependent on a material condition as quoted above in Article II, paragraph 1, subparagraph (a)—which reads as follows:

> *Toxic chemicals and their precursors* are not considered to be chemical weapons *where intended for purposes not prohibited under this Convention*, but only under the condition that *the types and quantities* of such toxic chemicals and their precursors *are consistent with such purposes.* (emphasis added)

Those "Purposes Not Prohibited Under this Convention" are listed in Article II, paragraph 9. Of the four different purposes listed in subparagraph 9, the fourth, "(d) law enforcement including domestic riot control," has a different character than the first three. The relationship between purpose and toxicity distinguishes the purpose in (d) from those that precede it. The first three purposes defined under subparagraphs 9 are

(a) Industrial, agricultural, research, medical, pharmaceutical or other peaceful purposes;
(b) Protective purposes, namely those purposes directly related to protection against toxic chemicals and to protection against chemical weapons;
(c) Military purposes not connected with the use of chemical weapons and not dependent on the use of the toxic properties of chemicals as a method of warfare;

(A) to (c) are uses that are not prohibited because the purposes exclude the application of the toxic properties of these agents against human beings and animals. In contrast, the provision in subparagraph 9 (d) says that the harmful effects of the toxic properties of these agents against human beings are deliberately meant for this purpose. In other words, there is no difference, in principle, between riot control agents and chemical weapons.

The exceptional character of this purpose must be read in conjunction with the definition in Article II, paragraph 7. It reads "'Riot Control Agent' means: Any chemical not listed in a Schedule, which can produce rapidly in humans sensory irritation or disabling physical effects which disappear within a short time following termination of exposure." The legal effect of this definition for subparagraph 9 (d) is to specify the meaning of the limiting condition contained in Article II, paragraph 1., subparagraph (a) . . . *as long as types and quantities are consistent with such purpose.*

But the Convention omits law enforcement agents from this definition of riot control agent, nor does it provide for a separate definition of law enforcement agents. This omission has been taken by some as an argument for an extensive interpretation. The advocates of an extensive interpretation have tried to create a loophole to justify certain activities that stand in sharp contrast to the overarching purpose of the Convention. According to them, domestic riot control and law enforcement purposes are two separate perceptions: domestic riot control—well defined and tightly limited—must be taken to be just one aspect of law enforcement. Law enforcement alone as the other aspect, therefore, might justify the use of toxic chemicals without being restricted by any definition or other tight limits valid for riot control agents. A closer and more objective examination of the Convention, however, shows that the word "law" refers to the limits of what may be enforced—namely laws based on national legislation and on accepted principles of international law, democracy and human rights. On the other hand, "riot control" refers to the executive measures within the legal limits of law enforcement. In other words, law enforcement qualifies the conditions under which riot control measures shall be applied. This understanding assumes further that riot control measures can be taken only within the territory or under the jurisdiction of the State or in any other place under its legitimate control and by its constitutionally empowered organs.

U.S.-British consultations on this topic in the year 2000 showed a distinct difference of opinion. The relevant Assessment Report on these consultations says "the United States and UK interpret the Chemical Weapons Convention differently regarding Riot Control Agents. The UK interpretation considers them to be chemical weapons under the CWC, and thus proscribed; the U.S. view is that they are not banned under that agreement."

The above mentioned understanding specifies that "law enforcement" qualifies the conditions under which "riot control" measures shall be applied. It follows then that the two terms are not identical. The word "including" indicates that *law enforcement* purposes might contain more than just *riot control purposes.* Such an understanding would be in line with practical needs in the field of domestic law enforcement, i.e., for capital punishment.

It was undisputed during negotiations and also in later academic discussions that the understanding related to the special case of capital punishment cannot serve as a tool for a wider interpretation of the term law enforcement as a purpose that disqualifies toxic chemicals as chemical weapons.

Thus, toxic chemicals and their precursors are not considered to be chemical weapons if they are intended for purposes of "law enforcement including domestic riot control." This legal exception from what is prohibited under the Convention does, by no means, allow for an interpretation according to which, in general, toxic chemicals prohibited for domestic riot control purposes could be used freely for law enforcement purposes.

Article II, paragraph 1 (a) of the CWC also helps to find the correct relationship between *law enforcement* and *domestic riot control purposes*. This provision says that toxic chemicals and their precursors are not considered to be chemical weapons if they are "intended for purposes not prohibited under this Convention," but only *as long as types and quantities are consistent with such purposes*. This limitation of the legal exception is valid for law enforcement and domestic riot control purposes. If types and quantities of toxic chemicals and their precursors are not consistent with the purpose, these toxic agents are prohibited for riot control purposes and equally for any other law enforcement purposes. For example, types and quantities not consistent with the purpose would be toxic chemicals filled into artillery ammunition, spray tanks, bombs or the like or stored in military facilities. These types and quantities would rather indicate that such toxic chemicals are not likely to be used for law enforcement including domestic riot control purposes, even if they would otherwise qualify for such purposes.

Despite all these legal indications that seem to show in sufficient clarity that there is no legal loophole between the terms *law enforcement* and *domestic riot control,* some analysts continue to challenge this position. They conclude that "the use of toxic chemicals for law enforcement purposes under the CWC is not limited to RCAs."[1] There is little doubt that their interpretation rather quickly would destroy the CWC.

During the final weeks of negotiations, in summer 1992, such a risk suddenly emerged when issues—already dealt with—reappeared on the agenda. This prompted an Explanatory Note by the Chairman of the negotiating body of the Conference on Disarmament (CD/CW/WP 414, 26 June 1992) stating, among other things:

> 4. Particularly riot control agents constitute a real problem. These irritants, physically disabling agents are used around the world in law enforcement and riot control, by police and other organs responsible for maintaining law and order. The same agents, however, would

constitute an immediate risk and danger if they were allowed to develop into a new generation of non-lethal but nonetheless effective
chemical agents of warfare, causing insurmountable problems in trying to distinguish in the ensuing grey area between "real" and "non-
lethal" chemical weapons as well as between "real" and "non-lethal"
chemical warfare units.

This language became part of a compromise solution for this problem. It
was never challenged during negotiations, it did not hinder any Conference on
Disarmament delegation to approve the draft CWC, thus safeguarding the necessary consensus. Neither was it an obstacle for more than 130 co-sponsors for
the UN-resolution endorsing the CWC nor for more than 175 States that have
become Parties to the Convention.

"Undisputed Limits"

There are no doubts as to a number of undisputed limits and interpretations of
what is prohibited under the Convention and how the Convention should be
read:

- only chemicals not listed in any Schedule may be used for domestic riot control purposes (Article II, paragraph 7 CWC);
- riot control agents may not be used as a method of warfare (Article I, paragraph 5 CWC);
- the expression "method of warfare" has been used in Protocol I to the Geneva
  Convention Relating to the Protection of Victims of International Armed
  Conflict of 12 August 1949. Article 43 of this Protocol reads as follows: "The
  armed forces of a Party to the conflict consist of organized armed forces,
  groups and units which are under a command responsible to that Party for the
  conduct of its subordinates, even if that Party is represented by a government
  or an authority not recognized by an adverse Party." Thus, "method of warfare" refers not only to armed conflict between sovereign states, but also to internal armed conflicts which may be local and relatively small-scale outbreaks
  of military or paramilitary violence.
- riot control agents must be declared in detail to the Organization (Article III,
  paragraph 1 (e) CWC); this obligation indicates that chemicals for riot control purposes, as defined by the Convention, belong in the category of chemical weapons;
- lethal or non-lethal agents or weapons are nowhere mentioned in the CWC;
  both terms, lethal and non-lethal, were contained in papers used during the

negotiations. All these terms were voluntarily deleted since a technical differentiation between lethal and non-lethal is not feasible and, therefore, not foreseen by the Convention. These terms are, hence, not relevant in its context.

"Grey Areas"

One grey area already touched upon must be mentioned again: chemicals listed in CWC schedules as well as others not covered by the CWC's definition of riot control agents are prohibited for riot control purposes. The argument that those chemicals, however, may be used for law enforcement has been disposed of above. Nevertheless, as the two terms are not identical, there is room for one exception: the exception for capital punishment. The capital punishment exception was agreed to during negotiations in Geneva and, therefore, seems to be the only acceptable exception.

No doubt seems to exist that the use of any toxic agent for law enforcement is prohibited as a method of warfare, although Article 1, paragraph 5 CWC mentions only riot control agents. When dealing with the Geneva Protocol of 1925, this will be explained more in depth.

However, States Parties are not required to declare agents for law enforcement to the Organization for the Prevention of Chemical Weapons (OPCW) as long as they are not listed in Schedules, as the declaration requirement is expressly limited to riot control agents, this seems to be a theoretical distinction, as there are, for practical purposes, no non-prohibited law enforcement agents beyond those for domestic riot control purposes.

Besides these acknowledged legal grey areas, there are actual or imaginative scenarios that raise doubts as to whether certain agents could be employed in accordance with the CWC. Such scenarios can exemplify the theoretical borderline between what is not prohibited and what is indeed prohibited.

The storming of the theater in Moscow on 26 October 2002 where Chechen militants held around 800 hostages, of which more than 100 were killed when Russian security forces pumped a fentanyl derivate into the theater, is an illustrative example. As shown, this fentanyl derivate can cause death. It is, therefore, according to Article II, paragraph 2 of the Convention a toxic chemical. If it had been a chemical, produced and stored for medical purposes, which are not prohibited under the Convention, it would not have been considered to be a chemical weapon. Nevertheless, as the agent was used—or, better, misused—for a different purpose, namely domestic law enforcement, it cannot be considered as "not prohibited under this Convention." In addition, this exception, as stated above, is permissible only *as long as the types and quantities* of the toxic chemical *are consistent with such purpose.* In order to rapidly disable the terrorists, large quantities of the substance were needed, causing many deaths, permanent harm, and long lasting disabling effects. Therefore, as the substance used has properties that exclude its use as an agent for law enforcement including domestic riot control, Russian security forces in Moscow acted in violation of the Chemical Weapons Convention and the Geneva Protocol. The Russian Federation is a Party to both international agreements.

It was argued during the CWC negotiations, that States Parties to the Convention should be entitled to use agents that are not permissible under the Convention for law enforcement including riot control purposes for rescuing a downed pilot from behind enemy lines in a war or war-like situation. Such an argument was not acceptable as it clearly would contradict Article I, paragraph 5, stipulating that "Each State Party undertakes not to use riot control agents as a method of warfare." On the other hand, it was uncontradicted that such agents could well be used in cases of a riot, for example, in a prisoner of war camp or in similar situations.

In March 2004 the German Bundeswehr was confronted with a severe upheaval in Kosovo in which rioting Albanians burned and destroyed Serbian houses and churches. German soldiers, on the basis of the German law with which the Chemical Weapons Convention was implemented, were not allowed to use riot control agents against the rioters, although the CWC itself would have permitted such use in a police or peacekeeping action. Therefore, the German law was applied in a way that—beyond the actual case—might be helpful to interpret the provisions on "law enforcement including domestic riot control purposes" of the CWC. In setting forth the reasons for the CWC implementation legislation, the text says that the German army, when involved in military activities mandated or led by systems of mutual collective security or being in the interest of such systems, must have adequate means to maintain safety and order. The text further defines systems of mutual collective security as being mainly those of the United Nations, of NATO and of the European Union.

It may be deduced from such language that riot control agents may be used in extraterritorial activities, be it by military or by police authorities, if these activities are founded on an internationally accepted legal basis, for example a UN-resolution. At the same time, it seems to be clear from this language but also in view of the undisputed consensus during negotiations and the text of the Convention that riot control agents may not be used as a method of warfare and that the limited and conditional use of riot control agents in extraterritorial activities, by no means, allows for the use of agents other than riot control agents.

Admittedly, to draw the borderline between a civil upheaval in which agents for law enforcement are not prohibited and paramilitary violence in which they are prohibited as a method of warfare will not always be easy in practice. But it must be kept in mind that the CWC was not meant to define legally and practically the difference between a freedom fighter and a terrorist.

If, however, careful and objective analysis comes to the conclusion that the use of toxic chemicals constituted a violation of the Convention or other legal instruments, state practice in breach of international law cannot heal the illegality of such violation. This is true and in accordance with international customary law, even if such illegal state practice is repeated several times and by several states.

Other Legal Instruments

Even the above mentioned rules and tools might not suffice to interpret the Chemical Weapons Convention in all its aspects as regards the exception for "law enforcement including domestic riot control purposes" which are "Purposes Not Prohibited Under this Convention." The specifications and limitations of this complicated exception may be elucidated further in drawing upon other international legal instruments which are either mentioned in the Convention itself, such as the Geneva Protocol for the Prohibition of the Use in War of Asphyxiating, Poisonous or other Gases, and of Bacteriological Methods of Warfare of 1925, or form a legal framework for it, such as the Vienna Convention on the Law of Treaties of 1969.

THE GENEVA PROTOCOL

Throughout the negotiation of the Chemical Weapons Convention, the achievement of a comprehensive chemical weapons ban with the broadest possible scope, like the Geneva Protocol, was the generally-shared objective. The entire negotiating process of more than twenty years was a constant affirmation of this objective. All toxic agents, including non-lethal chemical weapons, tear gas and other irritants are within the scope of the prohibition of the Geneva Protocol. Important evidence for this is the United Nations General Assembly Resolution 2603 A (XXIV) that affirmed the comprehensive character of this prohibition in its only operational paragraph by saying:

> Declares as contrary to the generally recognized rules of international law, as embodied in the Protocol for the Prohibition of the Use in War of Asphyxiating, Poisonous or Other Gases, and of Bacteriological Methods of Warfare, signed in Geneva on 17 June 1925, the use in international armed conflicts of:
>> (a) Any chemical agents of warfare—chemical substances, whether gaseous, liquid or solid—which might be employed, because of their direct toxic effects on man, animals or plants;

The Preamble to the CWC refers to the Geneva Protocol in three of its paragraphs: paragraph 3 recalls that the United Nations General Assembly condemned all actions contrary to the principles and objectives of the Geneva Protocol; paragraph 4 recognizes that the CWC reaffirms principles and objectives of and obligations assumed under the Geneva Protocol; paragraph 6 states the resolve that the CWC, by excluding completely the possibility of the use of chemical weapons through implementing its provisions, complements the obligations assumed under the Geneva Protocol.

Beyond these preambular paragraphs, Article XIII of the Chemical Weapons Convention states with total clarity that "Nothing in this Convention shall be interpreted as in any way limiting or detracting from the obligations assumed by any State under the Protocol . . . signed at Geneva on 17 June 1925, . . . "

The Geneva Protocol, indeed, is very comprehensive and does not allow for any exception for law enforcement or riot control purposes. It is generally accepted, however, that Article XIII of the Convention referring to the Geneva Protocol does not overrule the exception contained in Article II, paragraph 1 (a) of the Convention, namely the one expressed for purposes not prohibited. This is all the more true as the Geneva Protocol is limited to prohibit *the use* of toxic chemicals *in war* and as it was developed further by customary international law in all other armed conflicts.

On the other hand, it seems clear that the Convention in referring to the Geneva Protocol and its comprehensive prohibition, strives for a narrow interpretation of the exception contained in Article II, paragraph 1 (a).

In all cases that might be considered to be grey areas, the Geneva Protocol renders valuable assistance in confirming the narrow interpretation of the accepted exceptions to the general rules of the Convention. Should there exist any doubt concerning the prohibition of the use of law enforcement agents as a method of warfare just because such agents are not expressly mentioned in Article I, paragraph 5 of the Convention, the Geneva Protocol, referred to in Article XIII of the Convention, in its first paragraph states without room for any doubt or exception that "the use in war of asphyxiating, poisonous or other gases, and of all analogous liquids, materials or devices has been justly condemned by the general opinion of the civilized world."

This conclusion, furthermore, is confirmed by the previously quoted United Nations General Assembly Resolution 2603 A (XXIV) that reads in one of its preambular paragraphs:

> Recognizing therefore, in the light of all the above circumstances, that the Geneva Protocol embodies the generally recognized rules of international law prohibiting the use in international armed conflicts of all biological and chemical methods of warfare, *regardless of any technical developments* (emphasis by the author).

On these grounds, the Geneva Protocol renders valuable assistance in interpreting the Chemical Weapons Convention. Such an interpretation will conclude that the comprehensive ban of chemical weapons should not be watered down, regardless of short-lived national interests.

THE VIENNA CONVENTION ON THE LAW OF TREATIES

The Vienna Convention on the Law of Treaties of 23 May 1969 in its Article 31, paragraph 1 stipulates that "a treaty shall be interpreted in good faith in accordance with the ordinary meaning to be given to the terms of the treaty in their context and in the light of its object and purpose." As a supplementary means of interpretation, Article 32 of the Treaty offers the statement: "Recourse may be had to supplementary means of interpretation, including the preparatory work of the treaty and the circumstances of its conclusion . . . "

Taking into account the tools provided by the Chemical Weapons Convention itself, shedding light on the meaning of the non-prohibited use of toxic chemicals for "law enforcement including domestic riot control purposes," and screening the relevant provisions of the Convention with the help of the Geneva Protocol of 1925 in the spirit prescribed by the Vienna Convention on the Law of Treaties, confirms that the specific term *domestic riot control* is contained in the general one, namely *law enforcement*. This relationship is clearly expressed by the word *including*, making both terms parts of a coherent statement. As shown above, any interpretation considering *law enforcement* to be a purpose of its own and, therefore, allowing differentiation between toxic chemicals not prohibited for law enforcement and toxic chemicals not prohibited for domestic riot control purposes—from a purely legal standpoint—is simply false. It would be an interpretation out of context and inconsistent with the object and purpose of the CWC.

Were the differentiation of the two coherent parts of the statement in Article II, paragraph 9 (d) admissible, toxic chemicals listed in Schedules would be prohibited only for domestic riot control purposes but not for law enforcement. Furthermore, the differentiation would lead to the absurd result that *Each Party undertakes not to use riot control agents as a method of warfare*, whereas the use of law enforcement agents would not be prohibited as a method of warfare by the Convention but only by the Geneva Protocol.

In such case, any State Party, without any restrictions, could develop, produce, acquire, stockpile, retain or use listed toxic chemicals claiming they are intended for law enforcement purposes. The door would be wide open for any State Party to the Convention to enter into the development and production of a third generation of chemical weapons under the guise of law enforcement purposes. This would give rise to a legal turmoil between an existing prohibition in the Geneva Protocol and an artificially construed permission in the Convention. Such a false interpretation could give rise to gross violations with far reaching consequences. It would doom the CWC to meaninglessness.

Reading the provisions of the CWC, accepting the philosophy and the resolve which prevailed during the entire duration of the painstaking negotiations, shared by all parties, and viewed in the common spirit when it was unanimously adopted by the General Assembly of the United Nations and finally signed, it must be concluded that the Convention with regard to "law enforcement including domestic riot control" allows only for a very narrow exception from the rule (Article I CWC) that

Each Party to this Convention undertakes never under any circumstances:

(a) To develop, produce, otherwise acquire, stockpile or retain chemical weapons, or transfer, directly or indirectly, chemical weapons to anyone;
(b) To use chemical weapons; . . .

Conclusions

An international legal instrument on arms control and disarmament like the CWC needs a sound common understanding on its interpretation for its viable implementation. Substantive agreements reached through protracted negotiations are reflected in the text of the treaty and are binding for all Parties. Nevertheless, ambiguous wording can never be completely excluded. To resolve ambiguities, there are rules for the interpretation of treaties. For example, such interpretation must be based on the substance of the agreement. By no means can subsequent interpretation change the contents of what had been agreed upon during negotiations. It clearly is a misperception that interpretation can change the contents of an agreement by reading something into a text that had not been previously agreed to. Any attempt to this end is undertaken in bad faith, as it is intended to achieve an anticipated result, in disregard of the object and purpose of the CWC.

Therefore, any interpretation that could dilute the general rule quoted above by expanding the very narrow exception constitutes a clear and severe violation of the Convention—a violation that should duly be handled by the Organs of the Organization for the Prohibition of Chemical Weapons in accordance with the provisions of the CWC.

Note

1. David Fidler, "Memorandum on the Interpretation of Article II 9 (d) of the Chemical Weapons Convention in Regard to the Use of Toxic Chemicals for Law Enforcement Purposes," 16 April 2003.

CHAPTER 10

Incapacitating Biochemicals and the Biological Weapons Convention

Marie Isabelle Chevrier and James F. Leonard

Introduction

This chapter addresses the relevance of the Biological Weapons Convention (BWC) to incapacitating biochemical weapons. Technical discussions of incapacitating biochemical agents and how they might be used in armed conflict or hostile situations are covered elsewhere in this volume. It is useful nevertheless to introduce some common definitions of the substances under discussion. Biochemicals include all the substances that are produced by chemical reactions in living organisms as well as their synthetic analogs. Toxins are biochemicals produced by some living organisms, typically plants, animals or bacteria that can cause death, disease, incapacitation or other deleterious consequences. Many toxins can also be produced through chemical synthesis. Incapacitating biochemicals, as we have used the term throughout the book, describes those biochemicals that do not typically lead to death or permanent injury. While these biochemicals are described as incapacitating, some individuals could suffer permanent injury or death following exposure to them as a consequence of individual sensitivity or exposure to higher than intended doses. Many biochemicals are harmless or even beneficial at low doses, but incapacitating or lethal at a higher dose.

Thus a question arises regarding the extent to which the BWC prohibits the development and production of incapacitating biochemicals and biochemicals that have harmful effects in some, but not all, circumstances for a hostile purpose or in armed conflict. Is the development and production of these biochemicals for a purpose that is not permitted under the Convention, i.e., for the purpose of deliberately altering the mental or physical functions of human beings in an adverse fashion without their consent, prohibited under the category of toxins, under the category of other biological agents or do they fall outside the scope of the BWC?[1]

The answer to these questions in part relies on Section 3, Article 31 of The Vienna Convention on the Law of Treaties, which sets forth the manner in which international treaties are to be interpreted. The general rule is to interpret the treaty "with the ordinary meaning to be given to the terms of the treaty in their context and in the light of its object and purpose." If the ordinary meaning of the treaty language is "ambiguous or obscure" supplementary means may be used to interpret the treaty. The supplementary means to interpret a treaty include "the preparatory work of the treaty and the circumstances of its conclusion." The supplementary material may be used in order to confirm the meaning of treaty language as well as to determine the meaning.[2] The Vienna Convention also states that "any subsequent agreement between the parties regarding the interpretation of the treaty or the application of its provisions" shall be taken into account as part of the general rule of interpretation.

In this chapter we consider the ordinary meaning of the language of the specific prohibitions under Article I of the BWC. We then examine the treaty as a whole to better understand the terms in context and in light of the BWC's object and purpose. We then proceed to the historical record of the development and drafting of the Convention, to further build on the context, object and purpose of the Convention, and to confirm the interpretation of the treaty reached in the first section. Finally, we look at interpretations of the BWC prohibitions since its entry into force, principally through documents from the Review Conferences of the Convention.

The Ordinary Meaning of Relevant Prohibitions of the BWC

Article I of the BWC sets forth the principle obligations and prohibitions. It states:

Each State Party to the Convention undertakes never in any circumstances to develop, produce, stockpile or otherwise acquire or retain:

(1) Microbial or other biological agents, or toxins, whatever their origin or method of production, of types and in quantities that have no justification for prophylactic, protective or other peaceful purposes:

(2) Weapons, equipment or means of delivery designed to use such agents or toxins for hostile purposes or in armed conflict.

Several types of agent thus fall under the purview of this article: microbial and other biological agents, and toxins. The ordinary meaning of microbe is commonly understood to describe microscopic living organisms, capable of self-replication, mutation, and evolution. Bacteria, viruses, protozoa, and many fungi and algae fall into this category. Biochemical agents would not.

The ordinary meaning of the term "other biological agents" includes biological agents that are larger than microbes, insects for example, and also includes biological agents that are not living. The latter category for instance, includes prions—infectious agents that do not reproduce in the manner of living organisms. It also includes biochemical agents, because they are the product of living organisms and can cause harmful effects in other living organisms, most particularly humans, animals and plants. If "other biological agents" pertained only to larger living agents, or only to nonliving agents, specific language that conveyed this narrower meaning could have been used. The ordinary meaning of "other biological agents," unmodified by any restricting adjectives or clauses, implies a very broad scope, provided that broad scope is consistent with the object and purpose of the Convention, as discussed below. This broad scope encompasses living biological agents larger than microbes and nonliving biological agents, including biochemicals. We thus conclude that development and production of incapacitating biochemical agents for hostile purposes are prohibited by the BWC.

The development and production of incapacitating biochemical agents may also be prohibited by treaty language pertaining to toxins. The term "toxin" does not have a specific technical meaning, but is commonly used to denote chemical compounds produced by a living organism that are toxic—harmful—to another living organism. Toxins include a range of chemical types, modes of action, and extent of harm; botulinum toxin (a protein produced by a particular bacterium) and saxitoxin (a biochemical produced by certain marine algae) are both lethal in small amounts, whereas bee sting toxin causes only local and temporary painful effects. The ordinary meaning of "toxins" includes incapacitating as well as lethal toxins, and their possession and development is prohibited under the BWC unless it can be justified for a prophylactic, protective or other peaceful purpose. The fact that some toxic chemicals of biological origin have beneficial uses at certain dosages does not exclude them from the general category of toxins. Botulinum toxin, for example, is widely used in medicine for a number of beneficial effects, but no one would dispute that it remains a toxin, whose possession and development for hostile purposes is prohibited by the BWC. Thus, incapacitating biochemical weapons are prohibited under the ordinary meaning of both "other biological agents" and "toxins," again provided that the context and purpose of the Convention do not contradict this interpretation.

The purpose of the BWC is clearly stated in the Preamble: "[d]etermined, for the sake of all mankind to exclude completely the possibility of bacteriological (biological) agents and toxins being used as weapons . . . " The preamble goes on to state that "no effort should be spared to minimize this risk." Thus the object and purpose of the Convention support the broad interpretation of the terms of Article I put forth in this section. The supplementary material of the Convention also supports this interpretation of the BWC in reference to incapacitating biochemical agents. Now we turn to the origins of the Convention and interpretations of its prohibitions since entry into force.

Origins of the BWC

Several significant developments fostered the development of the BWC and influenced its final language. Principal documents include the 1968 UK Working Paper on Microbiological Warfare, the 1969 UK Biological Warfare Draft Convention, the 1969 report of the Secretary General of the United Nations *Chemical and Bacteriological (Biological) Weapons and the Effects of Their Possible Use,* and the Communist Draft Biological Weapons Convention of 1971. In addition, the 1969 decision by the United States to unilaterally renounce the possession of biological weapons and its subsequent decision to renounce the possession of toxin weapons influenced the final language of the Convention. Each of these will be discussed herein.[3]

In 1968 the UK delegation tabled a Working Paper on Microbiological Warfare at the Eighteen Nation Disarmament Committee (ENDC) in Geneva that described the principal elements of a new Convention that would ban the development, possession and use of biological, but not chemical, weapons. The first element would be a prohibition of any use of microbiological warfare in any circumstances based on a common understanding that such use was contrary to international law and a crime against humanity. A second element would be a ban on the production of agents for hostile purposes while recognizing the necessity of production of agents for peaceful purposes.[4] The UK tabled this working paper despite a lack of enthusiasm for the endeavor by either the Soviet Union or the United States. A May 1969 UK paper included talking points for an informal meeting at the ENDC in which the rationale for what became the general purpose criterion of Article I of the BWC, was explained. It states:

Will the Proposed Convention specify precisely what is prohibited?

The trouble with listing exactly what is prohibited is that any agents of biological warfare subsequently developed remain outside the prohibition, at any rate for some time. We therefore favour a general prohibition, covering something on the lines of "microbial agents causing death or disease by infection in man, other animals, or crops.[5]

The quoted passage unequivocally demonstrates that the originators of the treaty intended to draft the Convention in such a way as to include restrictions on biological agents that were unknown in 1968, such as prions.

When the UK tabled its "Biological Warfare Draft Convention" in 1969 Articles I and II embodied these two elements. Article I read as follows:

Each of the Parties to the Convention undertakes never in any circumstances, by making use for hostile purposes of microbial or other biological agents causing death or disease by infection or infestation in man, other animals or crops, to engage in biological methods of warfare.

Article II of the UK Draft Convention contained the prohibition on production and acquisition and read as follows:

Each of the Parties to the Convention undertakes:

(a) not to produce or otherwise acquire, or assist in or permit the production or acquisition of
   (i) microbial or other biological agents of types and in quantities that have no independent peaceful justification for prophylactic or other purposes;
   (ii) ancillary equipment or vectors the purpose of which is to facilitate the use of such agents for hostile purposes;
(b) not to conduct, assist or permit research aimed at production of the kind prohibited in sub-paragraph (a) of this article; and to destroy, or divert to peaceful purposes, within three months after the Convention comes into force for that Party, any stocks in its possession of such agents or ancillary equipment or vectors as have been produced or otherwise acquired for hostile purposes.

Article I of the UK Draft, banning the *use* of "microbial or other biological agents" did not survive criticism from some States that believed a new Convention banning the *use* of biological weapons would undermine the 1925 Geneva

Protocol. The sense of this operative article, banning *use of biological weapons in any circumstances* was ultimately relegated to a preambulatory rather than an operative clause and forms the purpose of the Convention as discussed in the previous section.

It is worthwhile to describe the changes to the language of Article II of the UK Draft Convention that ultimately were embodied in Article I of the BWC and the reasoning behind those changes insofar as is possible from open sources. Of critical importance in terms of the coverage of biochemicals in the BWC is the expansion of the prohibition from "microbial or other biological agents" to "microbial or other biological agents, or toxins whatever their origin or method of production . . . " The change in the language indicates that the drafters sought to broaden the category of agents that the Convention prohibited.

Lethal and Incapacitating Weapons

In late 1968, the UN General Assembly, upon the recommendation of the ENDC, asked the Secretary General to issue a report with the assistance of a group of experts on the effects of chemical and biological weapons.[6] In a telegram the U.S. Mission in Geneva demonstrated its understanding of the differences between lethal and incapacitating biological and chemical agents in a discussion of the terms of reference of that report. The Mission reported that Cromartie of the UK delegation provided the following comments:

> We [the UK] would much prefer the report to cover not only "lethal" but "incapacitating" agents as well. Limiting the study to "lethal" agents would seriously reduce its value . . . There is also the scientific point that what may be incapacitating in some circumstances may be lethal in others. As a last resort, it would be better to omit the word "lethal" altogether. [7]

The drafters of the language of the BWC understood that both lethal and non-lethal or incapacitating agents could be used for hostile purposes or in armed conflict, and the Convention was drafted to cover all microbial and other biological agents, rather than restricting the prohibitions to lethal agents.

The U.S. abandonment of its offensive biological weapons programs is also pertinent and instructive. In November 1969 U.S. President Richard Nixon renounced the use of biological weapons, announced that the U.S. biological program would be "confined to research and development for defensive purposes," and announced the U.S. government's intention to destroy existing stocks of biological weapons. In doing so, the President included separate subparagraphs on lethal biological agents and incapacitating agents. The decision memorandum stated:

(a) The United States will renounce the use of lethal methods of bacteriological/biological warfare.
(b) The United States will similarly renounce the use of all other methods of bacteriological/biological warfare (for example, incapacitating agents.)[8]

When President Nixon made this announcement the U.S. classified the weapons in its biological arsenal as lethal biologicals, incapacitating biologicals, lethal toxins and incapacitating toxins.[9]

U.S. Policy Review on Toxins

Following the U.S. renunciation of biological weapons, the United States undertook a separate policy review of toxins. At the time toxins in the U.S. arsenal were classified separately as lethal (e.g., botulinum toxin) or incapacitating (e.g., staphylococcal enterotoxin).[10] Participants in the review acknowledged that toxins were classified as chemicals by the Secretary General's Report on chemical and biological weapons and concurred with that definition.[11] Despite their chemical designation, toxins were part of the U.S. biological program because of the "origin of toxins and the technology of production."[12]

A vexing issue regarding toxins in 1970 was that although toxins were chemicals, their production involved the propagation of living biological agents (i.e., *Clostridium botulinum* bacteria) that produced the toxins in quantities that were not consistent with a prophylactic purpose. Accordingly, the UK had publicly stated that the manufacture of toxins would be prohibited by their 1969 Draft Convention.[13] Once again this is evidence that the language of the UK Draft Convention "microbial or other biological agents" was intended to include non-living, biochemical agents. However, at the time of the policy review the process of producing some toxins through chemical synthesis had already had some success, and the review foresaw that toxin production techniques in the future would not necessarily require the production of large quantities of biological agents.[14]

The policy review elicited different recommendations from relevant U.S. government departments. The Joint Chiefs of Staff recommended that the U.S. "[r]eserve the option to develop and stockpile toxins produced by either biological processes or chemical synthesis and thereby retain maximum flexibility in chemical retaliation."[15] The Secretary of Defense, however, recommended that the U.S. toxin policy be limited to "research and development program for the development of chemically-synthesized toxins and related delivery systems/ weapons."[16] The U.S. did not then have the ability to chemically synthesize toxins of military interest, but expected to have that capability in three to five years.[17] The Department of State, however, recommended that the U.S. "should renounce the use of toxins regardless of the method of production and limit its efforts in this field to research and development for defensive purposes only and to protect against technological surprise."[18] In defending this recommendation the State Department argued that any policy to retain toxins "would make it more difficult for us to achieve international support for the UK draft Convention."[19] The National Security Council review concurred with the recommendation of the State Department and President Nixon made the policy decision to forgo possession of all toxin weapons, both lethal and incapacitating, whether produced through biological or chemical processes.[20]

It is critical to note that U.S. sources conclude that natural biochemicals that are toxic at abnormal doses are included in the category of "toxins." In a section on "Types of Studies Conducted Using Toxins," a Department of Defense document on U.S. biological defense research explains that "physiologically active compounds, particularly peptide hormones and neuromodulators, are included for consideration in the toxin category because excesses of these compounds can cause physiological imbalances similar to those caused by some toxins."[21]

Development of the Language of the BWC

The U.S. decision on toxins paved the way for the UK to accept a friendly amendment to its Draft Convention and specify that its prohibitions pertained to toxins even if they were produced through chemical synthesis. In introducing the amendment, U.S. Ambassador James Leonard stated that "although toxins are chemical substances, their characteristics from the view point of arms control are so closely related to those of biological agents that the treatment of these two categories in the same convention would be not only feasible but highly desirable."[22] At the same time the U.S. proposed amendment deleted the qualifying phrase "by infection or infestation" because, according to Leonard, "we believe that the emphasis of the prohibition should be on the agents themselves rather than on the manner in which a disease is introduced."[23]

In March 1971 the Soviet Union along with many of its allies tabled a "Communist Draft Convention on the Prohibition of the Development, Production, and Stockpiling of Bacteriological (Biological) Weapons and Toxins and on Their Destruction."[24] Article I of the Soviet Draft contained language similar to that ultimately adopted. It read,

Each State Party to this Convention undertakes not to develop, produce, stockpile or otherwise acquire:

(1) Microbiological or other biological agents or toxins of such types and in such quantities as are not designed for the prevention of disease or for other peaceful purposes;
(2) Auxiliary equipment or means of delivery designed to facilitate the use of such agents or toxins for hostile purposes.[25]

In introducing the Draft Convention the Soviet representative stated that "the basic aim of the agreement is to preclude completely the possibility of the use in war of bacteriological weapons and toxins."[26] It is worthwhile to observe how the final text of the BWC expands the prohibition in important ways. To do so we have rewritten the text of Article 1 as it first appeared in the Communist Draft with additions to the text that appear in the BWC in italics and deletions in brackets.

Each State Party to this Convention undertakes [not] *never in any circumstances* to develop, produce, stockpile or otherwise acquire *or retain*:

(1) *Microbial* [microbiological] or other biological agents or toxins *whatever their origin or method of production* of such types and in such quantities [as are not designed for the prevention of disease] *that have no justification for prophylactic, protective* or [for] other peaceful purposes;
(2) [auxiliary] *weapons*, equipment or means of delivery designed to [facilitate the] use [of] such agents or toxins for hostile purposes *or in armed conflict.*

Each change in language extends the prohibition in significant ways. Many states contributed to the language that expanded the prohibition. The United Arab Republic, for instance, added the terms "never in any circumstances" which first appeared in the British Draft Convention of July 10, 1969 and Sweden proposed the addition of the phrase defining toxins "whatever their origin or method of production."

All of the previous discussion tends to confirm that the ordinary meaning of the term "other biological agents" in Article I of the BWC was written to have the broadest possible interpretation, and to cover biological agents not yet discovered. Additionally, it is clear that the term "toxins" was meant to cover incapacitating biochemical substances as well as lethal ones. Finally, the addition of the phrase "or in armed conflict" to subsection (2) of Article I is explicit in making the possession of any delivery system designed to use biological agents or toxins for any type of hostile purpose or in armed conflict was also an expansion of the language. Its inclusion was to underscore that the purpose of the Convention was very broad, to prevent the use of biological agents for all hostile purposes, including, but not limited to armed conflict. That is in contrast to the more restrictive term "warfare" used in the Geneva Protocol of 1925.

Subsequent Agreements Regarding the Interpretation of the BWC

Review Conferences of the BWC occurring at five year intervals have continued to reinforce the broadest interpretation of the prohibitions of Article I of the Convention.[27] The Final Declaration of the Second Review conference in 1986 stated that Article I covered "toxins (both proteinaceous and non-proteinaceous) of a microbial, animal or vegetable nature and their synthetically produced analogues."[28]

The Final Declaration of the Fourth BWC Review Conference in 1996 affirms that the BWC ban includes components of microbial or other biological agents and toxins as well as natural and "artificially created or altered" forms. The pertinent sections read:

5. The Conference also reaffirms that the Convention unequivocally covers all microbial or other biological agents or toxins, naturally or artificially created or altered, as well as their components, whatever their origin or method of production, of types and in quantities that have no justification for prophylactic, protective or other peaceful purposes.
6. The Conference, conscious of apprehensions arising from relevant scientific and technological developments, inter alia, in the fields of microbiology, biotechnology, molecular biology, genetic engineering, and any applications resulting from genome studies, and the possibilities of their use for purposes inconsistent with the objectives and the provisions of the Convention, reaffirms that the undertaking given by the States Parties in Article I applies to all such developments.[29]

The States Parties have repeatedly recognized that bioregulator substances and their analogs are relevant to the BWC as shown by recurring reference to them at BWC review conferences. An extensive review was issued by Canada at the third BWC Review Conference in September 1991, entitled "Novel Toxins and Bioregulators: The Emerging Scientific and Technological Issues Relating to Verification and the Biological and Toxin Weapons Convention." A paper entitled "Technological developments of relevance to the BWC," submitted by the United States for the Fourth Review Conference in 1996, discusses peptides that can be modified as agonists or antagonists. Agonists are compounds that bind to and activate cell receptors that are normally stimulated by naturally occurring bioregulators, while antagonists are compounds that bind to cell receptors and prevent them from being activated by the natural bioregulators.[30] The U.S. paper states that the range of the activity of the peptides "covers the entire living system, from mental processes (e.g., endorphins) to . . . mood, consciousness, temperature control, sleep or emotions . . . These substances would be extremely difficult to detect but could cause serious consequences or even death if used improperly."[31] A similar paper submitted by Sweden in 1996 ends a discussion of drug design with "The worldwide increase in knowledge in this area of research increases the risk of hostile use of biological [sic] active agents, whether naturally occurring or not."[32]

A contribution by Sweden to a Background Paper on New Scientific and Technological Developments Relevant to the BWC, prepared by the Secretariat for the Fifth BWC Review Conference in 2001, cites pharmaceutical research on "modulators of the immune system and bioregulators" as potentially of compliance concern.[33] In the same Background Paper, the UK wrote of the "enormous increase in knowledge about the structure of cellular receptors in man, animals and plants, and about the molecular basis of bioregulation, including immunomodulation [the ability to influence the immune system]. Many of the small bioactive molecules are proteins or peptides that in principle could be easily produced in recombinant microorganisms or in transgenic animals or plants, making production on weapon scales increasingly feasible."[34]

Conclusion

The BWC is consistently recognized as the first international agreement to ban an entire class of weapons. The phrase "biochemical agents" does not appear in the text of the BWC. Nevertheless, that does not mean that the BWC is silent on the issue of the development and production of biochemical agents to create incapacitating or temporary detrimental effects.

The drafters of the BWC had the wisdom to recognize that its provisions would need to stand the test of time. They, therefore, wrote the general purpose criterion so as to prohibit the development of all biological agents and all toxins as weapons. This foresight is reflected in the ordinary meaning of the term "microbial and other biological agents" in Article I of the Convention. The drafters of the BWC knew that unforeseen developments in the biological sciences could affect the prohibitions contained in the Convention and therefore included the phrase "whatever their origin or means of production" in broadening the category of toxins to include those which might be synthetically synthesized. They drafted the Convention to have the widest possible ban against any and all biological and toxin warfare agents and delivery devices, while permitting the production of biological substances for prophylactic, protective or other peaceful purposes.

Based on this review, we conclude that the drafters of the BWC clearly understood the differences between self-replicating agents such as bacteria and viruses and non-replicating biochemical agents and toxins. They understood that toxins were a subset of chemicals. The drafters also clearly understood the spectrum of effects of chemical agents (whether or not they were of biological origin) and biological agents ranging from lethal agents at one end, to harassing agents at the other. Within the spectrum are incapacitating agents, which could be physical chemicals or biochemicals. The record also shows that the drafters of the Convention expanded the definition of the prohibition over time to unambiguously include all biological agents and all toxins, even if their synthesis did not involve the propagation of biological agents. Moreover, the drafters of the Convention anticipated the advance of the biosciences. They sought to draft the prohibition of the possession of incapacitating, as well as lethal, biological agents and toxins to cover future discoveries in the field. The widest possible application of the prohibition has been reinforced since the BWC entered into force in 1975 through explicit understandings achieved at Review Conferences of the Convention.

As we have demonstrated, incapacitating toxins were well recognized by the treaty drafters; incapacitating toxins had already been developed as weapons. The intentions of the drafters of the treaty are clear that the prohibition was not limited to agents or toxins that had already been developed as weapons or that existed in the arsenals of any state. They intended to ban the future development of any biological agent or any chemical of biological origin that could produce toxic effects for hostile use or in armed conflict. The examples in the paper are drawn not only from the long available diplomatic record of the negotiations but also from once classified internal government documents in the United Kingdom and the United States that demonstrate the intentions of these two governments. After the BWC entered into force, its States Parties continued to reinforce a broad interpretation of the ban through statements in background papers and in Final Declarations at BWC Review Conferences.

Nothing in this chapter precludes incapacitating biochemical weapons from being simultaneously prohibited by other treaties and international laws. As discussed in other chapters of this volume, the Chemical Weapons Convention (CWC) applies to all toxic chemicals, including biochemicals. Indeed two toxins are explicitly listed on the schedules to the CWC.

As for the treaty's objective and purpose one can find no clearer statement of the treaty's purpose than that contained in the preamble:

Determined, for the sake of all mankind, to exclude completely the possibility of bacteriological (biological) agents and toxins being used as weapons, . . . Convinced that such use would be repugnant to the conscience of mankind and that no effort should be spared to minimize this risk, . . .

We conclude that the development of biochemicals for deliberate hostile use to impair the physical or mental functions of humans without their consent would be a violation of the Convention. Any attempt to reconcile the prohibitions of the BWC with an interpretation that would allow the development, production or use of such biochemical weapons would not be credible given the historical record.

Acknowledgements: The authors wish to thank Jonathan B. Tucker for his assistance in obtaining documents on the U.S. toxin policy review. They also thank the other members of the Scientists Working Group on Biological and Chemical Weapons, Julian Perry Robinson and Paul A. Jargowsky for their helpful comments on an earlier draft.

Notes

1. This paper does not address the simultaneous or overlapping coverage of the Chemical Weapons Convention on these substances under the category of "other toxic chemicals." Nevertheless the drafters of the CWC created overlapping obligations with the BWC by including ricin and saxitoxin Schedule 1 Toxic Chemicals. Full text of the Convention can be found at <http://www.opcw.org> (25 January 2007).

2. *Vienna Convention on the Law of Treaties*, 1155 U.N.T.S. 331, 8 I.L.M. 679. University of Minnesota Human Rights Library, <http://umn.edu/humanrts/instree/vienna-convention.html> (25 May 2006).

3. This is not meant to discount the contributions by, among others, the governments of Sweden and Malta to BTW disarmament efforts. However, on the specific topic of biochemicals and the BWC the aforementioned developments are believed to be the most influential. For further discussion of the diplomatic history of the BWC see Marie Isabelle Chevrier "The Politics of Biological Disarmament" in Mark Wheelis, Lajos Rozsa, and Malcolm Dando, eds. *Deadly Cultures: Biological Weapons Since 1945* (Cambridge, MA: Harvard University Press, 2006): 304–28.

4. Arms Control and Disarmament Agency, "British Working Paper on Microbiological Warfare," *Documents on Disarmament, 1968* (Washington, D.C: U.S. Government Printing Office, 1969): 569–71.

5. "Talking Points on Biological Warfare for E.N.D.C.: Informal Meeting on 14 May 1969," FCO 73/114, Public Records Office (PRO) Kew, UK.

6. "Questions of General and Complete Disarmament" in *United Nations General Assembly Resolution 2454 (XXIII)*, 20 December 1968, <http://www.un.org/documents/ga/res/23/ares23.htm> (25 January 2007).

7. "Department of State Telegram From U.S. Mission in Geneva to Secretary of State Washington D.C. Confidential, Subject: UK comments on CBW Study Terms of Reference, 21 August 1968," Box 2879, POL 27-10, General Records of the Department of State, Central Foreign Policy Files, National Archives and Records Administration (hereinafter NARA), College Park, MD. Declassified 5 February 2003.

8. "National Security Decision Memorandum 35, November 25, 1969, Subject: United States Policy on Chemical Warfare Program and Bacteriological/Biological Research Program," Vol. 1, National Security Council Files: Subject Files, Chemical, Biological Warfare (Toxins, etc.), Box 310, Richard M. Nixon Presidential Materials Staff, NARA.

9. Lethal biological agents are listed as "P. Tularense (rabbit fever bacteria)," "B. Anthracis (anthrax bacteria)" and "Tularemia"; incapacitating biological agents are listed as "Venezuelan Equine Encephalymyelitis Virus (VEE)" and Q fever; lethal toxins are listed as "Clostridium Botulinum" and "Toxin (Botulinum/Shellfish)"; Staphylococcus Aureus Enterotoxin is listed as an incapacitating toxin. Attachment to "Memorandum for the President from Secretary of Defense Melvin Laird, Subject: National Security Decision Memoranda 35 and 44, July 6, 1970," Secret NSC Files, NARA.

10. Michael A. Guhin, "Memorandum for Dr. Kissinger. Subject: The Toxins Issue, December 18, 1969," Top Secret NSC Files, NARA.

11. Guhin, "Memorandum."

12. Guhin, "Memorandum."

13. Guhin, "Memorandum."

14. Guhin, "Memorandum."

15. David Packard, "Memorandum for the Assistant to the President for National Security Affairs. Subject: Program Options on Toxins, February 12, 1970," NSC Files, NARA.

16. Packard, "Memorandum."

17. Packard, "Memorandum."

18. "Memorandum for the President from Acting Secretary of State. Subject: U.S. Policy on Toxins, February 10, 1970," Secret. NSC Files, NARA.

19. "Memorandum for the President," 1970.

20. For a more lengthy treatment of the toxin policy review see Jonathan B. Tucker, "A Farewell to Germs: The U.S. Renunciation of Biological and Toxin Warfare, 1969–1970," *International Security* 27, no.1 (Summer 2002): 136–39.

21. Programmatic Environmental Impact Statement on the Biological Defense Research Program, April 1989, Appendix 4, section 3.2, page 9.

22. Statement by the United States Representative (Leonard) to the Conference of the Committee on Disarmament: "Toxin Amendment to British Draft Convention on Biological Weapons," 30 June 1970, CCD/PV.474, 8–9; U.S. Arms Control and Disarmament Agency, *Documents on Disarmament, 1970* (Washington, D.C.: U.S. Government Printing Office, 1971): 276.

23. Statement by United States Representative (Leonard), "Toxin Amendment."

24. "Communist Draft Convention on the Prohibition of the Development, Production, and Stockpiling of Bacteriological (Biological) Weapons and Toxins and on Their Destruction, March 30, 1971." CCD/325; U.S. Arms Control and Disarmament Agency, *Documents on Disarmament, 1971*, (Washington, D.C.: U.S. GPO, 1972): 190–93.

25. "Communist Draft Convention," 192.

26. Statement by the Soviet Representative (Roshchin) to the Conference of the Committee on Disarmament: Chemical and Bacteriological Weapons, 30 March 1971. CCD/PV.505, 11–19. U.S. Arms Control and Disarmament Agency, *Documents on Disarmament, 1971* (Washington, D.C.: US GPO, 1972): 187.

27. One of the purposes of review conferences is to take account of scientific developments occurring between conferences.

28. "Final Declaration of the Second Review Conference of the Parties to the Convention on the Prohibition of the Development, Production and Stockpiling of Bacteriological (Biological) and Toxin Weapons and on their Destruction," 8–26 September 1986, BWC/CONF.II/13/II.

29. "Fourth Review Conference of the Parties to the Convention on the Prohibition of the Development, Production and Stockpiling of Bacteriological (Biological) and Toxin Weapons and on Their Destruction," 26 November–6 December 1996, Final Declaration, BWC/CONF.IV/9.

30. Definitions of agonists and antagonists are found at Online Medical Dictionary at <http://cancerweb.ncl.ac.uk/omd/> (7 June 2005).

31. "Background Paper On New Scientific And Technological Developments Relevant To The Convention On The Prohibition of the Development, Production and Stockpiling of Bacteriological (Biological) and Toxin Weapons and on Their Destruction," 30 October 1996: 18 et seq., BWC/CONF.IV/4*.

32. "Background Paper On New Scientific And Technological Developments Relevant To The Convention On The Prohibition of the Development, Production and Stockpiling of Bacteriological (Biological) and Toxin Weapons and on Their Destruction," Addendum 1 21 November 1996, BWC/CONF.IV/4/Add.I,

33. "Background Paper On New Scientific And Technological Developments Relevant To The Convention On The Prohibition of the Development, Production and Stockpiling of Bacteriological (Biological) and Toxin Weapons and on Their Destruction," 14 September 2001, BWC/CONF.V/4. (Prepared by the Secretariat; the Swedish submission (no title) begins on page 8.)

34. "Background Paper On New Scientific And Technological Developments Relevant To The Convention On The Prohibition of the Development, Production and Stockpiling of Bacteriological (Biological) and Toxin Weapons and on Their Destruction," Addendum 1 26 October 2001, par. 43, BWC/CONF.V/4/Add.I.

CHAPTER 11

Incapacitating Biochemical Weapons: Risks and Uncertainties

Robin M. Coupland

The starting point for this discussion is that when weapons are used, they have an impact on health; this is a function of their design.[1] However, weapons can only make this impact on the human body by one or more of a limited number of mechanisms. These are: physical force (penetrating or crushing by impact of blunt objects, projectiles, explosive blast or laceration); changing body chemistry (poison or the deliberate spread of disease); changing body temperature (burning or freezing); or by electromagnetic energy or irradiation (lasers, or nuclear irradiation).

Most societies accept that within them, designated actors are permitted to carry weapons for defense or law enforcement. The idea that careful regulation of these capacities for armed violence is necessary for humans' continued successful collaboration and existence is both intuitive and widely accepted. This acceptance, however, extends only to weapons that injure by physical force. Poisoning has always been viewed as abhorrent in warfare and has never been seen as compatible with the idea of reasonable use of force. In other words, there is something fundamental in human psychology, culture and even morality that has generated a general abhorrence of the use of poison. The 1925 Geneva Protocol, the 1972 Biological Weapons Convention (BWC) and the 1993 Chemical Weapons Convention (CWC) are recent codifications of this taboo in formal international law. (The BWC and the CWC extend the prohibition from use to the development, production, stockpiling and transfer of these weapons.) This taboo and the legal regimes that have flowed from it are pertinent to any debate about *any* weapon which exerts its effect by changing body chemistry.

225

"Incapacitating biochemical weapons" is the best term to date for chemicals the use of which as weapons carries a purported low lethality. They are also referred to as "calmatives." They are rendered more acceptable by the fact that they are promoted as simply another application of pharmaceutical agents originally designed for medical use.[2] The use of these weapons is foreseen by proponents for the full spectrum of tactical situations, including both police and military activities; that is, from riot control to hostage release to international armed conflict. This is the case even though most would argue that such use in armed conflict would violate the CWC and possibly the BWC as well. My arguments here address primarily the theoretical use of incapacitating biochemical weapons in armed conflict. From this, many principles and questions can be extrapolated to other situations.

A number of pharmaceutical agents—mainly anesthetics and analgesics—have been assessed as having potential for use as incapacitating biochemical weapons. The most likely mode of delivery in a tactical situation would be by inhalation. (Other chemicals which might be used as "weapons" but which are not considered here are "malodorants" and lachrymatory agents such as the riot control agent, CS.) A primary consideration of the effects of weapons on health permits a "victim-orientated" analysis of the issues surrounding the use of such weapons. In relation to incapacitating biochemical weapons, it is only by such an analysis that the risks and uncertainties become apparent and objective. While the risks and uncertainties can be ascertained through a process of logical deduction, many have already been highlighted by the use of a fentanyl derivative in vapor form to end the Moscow theater siege in October 2002.[3]

My early work with the International Committee of the Red Cross (ICRC) was as a field surgeon. I know that thousands of colleagues, whether doctors, nurses or physiotherapists, have a similar working familiarity with the effects of weapons resulting from physical force. This vast experience of health professionals is recorded and reflected in hundreds of publications in the medical literature over more than a hundred years. Therefore, one might be able to predict the effects on the civilian population when a new munition that employs a particularly large or widespread explosion is used in a populated area. One might also be able to predict the effects on an individual combatant of an antipersonnel mine, a bullet that carries an explosive charge or a new rifle that fires more bullets at higher velocity. Likewise, it becomes obvious and comprehensible how whole populations become vulnerable to the widespread availability of small arms. I would propose that the effects of weapons that injure by physical force serve as a kind of reference point for consideration of any new weapon that might exert its effects by a different mechanism.[4]

The reality is that the effects on people of a new weapon or method of warfare may be neither understood nor recognized by health professionals. If they are not understood by health professionals, are they likely to be understood by soldiers or, for that matter, design engineers, diplomats or even lawyers? If these effects are not well understood, how are judgments about legality to be made?

In relation to incapacitating biochemical weapons, there are questions that should be answered before they are deployed. These are:

- What will the real lethality be when used?
- What is the speed of onset of incapacitation?
- What are the short, medium and long-term effects?
- How long will the effects last?
- Will the effects be recognizable by health professionals?
- Will the effects be treatable?
- Will the effects be recognizable by the users (e.g., soldiers)?

The complexity of assessing the utility of incapacitating biochemical weapons together with the risks and uncertainties can be demonstrated by considering the first and last of the above questions. Demonstrating the complexity and then unraveling it are logical prerequisites for any legal assessment.

No weapon, whatever its design, carries a zero risk of mortality among the victims. The same could be said for "lethal" weapons; no existing weapon, when used in battle and as a function of its design causes a 100 percent mortality. Lethality is a function of not only the design of a weapon but also how that weapon is used and the vulnerability of the victims.[5] About 20 percent of people injured in battle by a Kalashnikov eventually die. The mortality associated with being injured by a hand grenade in an open area is about 10 percent. So when people talk about "non-lethal" weapons, it is not clear what is being referred to because it is not clear what a lethal weapon is. Any weapon has the capacity to kill; much depends on the context in which that weapon is used. It is pertinent to this paper that fourteen people died in the sarin gas attack on the Tokyo subway while forty-five survivors were proven to have been intoxicated (a "lethality" of 23.7 percent). These figures provide comparable mortality figures to the use of a fentanyl derivative in Moscow in which, purportedly, 120 people died of the 800 exposed to the vapor (a "lethality" of 15 percent). In brief, there is no evidence that any currently existing pharmaceutical agent, when used as an incapacitating weapon, will consistently result in a lower lethality than when other weapons are used.

It is critical to the tactical and legal discussion about this issue that, as a principle of pharmacology, the only difference between a drug and a poison is the dose. This means the effects of an incapacitating biochemical weapon will also depend on its means of delivery together with the environment in which it is delivered. Furthermore, delivering a rapidly effective dose from a tactical perspective means some people will inevitably receive a dangerous if not lethal dose. There is no equivalent of this phenomenon with respect to weapons that injure by physical force. There exists little information about how the dose might be regulated in a tactical situation. There is no evidence that the dose *can* be regulated to the degree necessary to ensure it is consistently "non-lethal" in such situations especially given the variation in vulnerability of potential victims brought by extremes of age, small body mass or preexisting health problems.

With regard to the real lethality, it is of concern to the ICRC that incapacitating biochemical weapons are discussed under the umbrella of "non-lethal" weapons. The ICRC has a policy of referring to "non-lethal" weapons in quotation marks and to "so-called non-lethal weapons" in speech. The reason for this is that this class of weapon has not been adequately defined. The ICRC is of the opinion that a "non-lethal" weapon, from the perspective of international humanitarian law (IHL)[6], should be considered as any other weapon whatever its technology or its purported effect and whether or not it is labeled "non-lethal." There is nothing in IHL or any other branch of international law that says that "non-lethal" weapons fall into their own distinct category that excuses them from individual legal scrutiny. Apart from incapacitating biochemical weapons, two other "non-lethal" weapons have already been prohibited in warfare; namely, blinding laser weapons and riot control agents.

The health-related, tactical and legal issues multiply in complexity if one asks whether a soldier will be able to recognize when an opponent is "incapacitated." This question is the core concern of the ICRC in this area because once combatants become wounded or sick or intend to surrender, they are protected under IHL. A useful approach is to consider what would happen if the perfect incapacitating biochemical weapon really existed: that is, an agent which could be deployed without risk of any permanent effect and which can incapacitate its victim by simply eliminating all movement of the body for, approximately thirty minutes from the instant of attack. Putting aside the fact that, in armed conflict this would constitute use of a chemical weapon, this nonetheless throws up other critical questions pertinent to IHL. Imagine a soldier entering an area in which enemy combatants have been incapacitated; they are standing or lying still with their weapons at hand and with their eyes fixed on the sky. There is limited visibility. How will the attacking soldier, when rushing into attack, know his enemy has been incapacitated? The most likely scenario is that the soldier will shoot because he or she is trained to do so reflexively in battle. Being incapacitated could simply serve to increase the vulnerability to attack by conventional weapons. In other words, even the "best" incapacitating biochemical weapons could cause increased mortality because of increased vulnerability. This is not such an unrealistic projection. It is likely that, as a result of any "non-lethal" weapons being used on the battlefield, the battlefield would become more lethal. All military personnel to whom I have spoken about this recognize that such a scenario raises a formidable, if not insurmountable, challenge in terms of training.

An absolute prerequisite for protection under IHL of combatants who are *hors de combat* is soldiers' ability to recognize when enemy soldiers are wounded, sick or laying down their weapons. But is the incapacitated enemy soldier wounded or sick? There would be no obvious sign of injury; he or she would not be bleeding from a gaping wound. The "sickness" would be difficult to recognize. Does the incapacitated soldier intend to surrender? He or she will be unable to show signs of such an intention to anyone approaching. Therefore, the deployment of incapacitating biochemical weapons on the battlefield is a question which requires serious consideration in terms of IHL; not only because of the prohibition on use of chemical weapons but also because first, it would not be clear if a combatant was *hors de combat;* and second, it could generate confusion about the legal protection of this new category of vulnerable person. Another major concern is that the proponents of these weapons propose that they be used by soldiers when the enemy is integrated in the civilian population, or even when necessary directly against civilians. Does this not risk undermining two other fundamentals of IHL: that civilians shall be spared from deliberate attack, and that attacks which do not distinguish between military objectives and civilians are prohibited?

States have an obligation under Article 36 of the 1977 Additional Protocol I to the 1949 Geneva Conventions to undertake a review of the legality of any "new weapon, means or method of warfare." Therefore, a baseline question for any lawyer undertaking a legal review of an incapacitating biochemical weapon is this: Even if the weapon in question is not prohibited and is labeled "non-lethal," have I really thought through *all* the implications of its deployment?

There are, inevitably, many other linked issues that should be considered prior to deployment of incapacitating biochemical weapons, each of which carries its own set of risks and uncertainties. Examples are: the proliferation of such weapons; an "arms race of countermeasures;" the possibility of a lower threshold of use; and the perceptions of those attacked with new chemical or biological weapons and their most likely response.

I would not deny that incapacitating biochemical weapons offer, at least theoretically, advantages in certain tactical situations. I have argued here for an objective approach to the use of incapacitating biochemical weapons beginning with an evidence-based consideration of the foreseeable effects on the victims. The analysis of their use in armed conflict permits identification of certain risks and uncertainties that can be extrapolated and need to be addressed in relation to all tactical situations including law enforcement.

In terms of risks, deployment of incapacitating biochemical weapons represents a step towards legitimizing the use of poison in tactical situations. It would represent a very dangerous step back toward the use of toxicity on the battlefield. It could increase the overall lethality of any tactical situation. The effects might be neither recognizable nor treatable. The deployment might undermine fundamental tenets of IHL. There are, for me at least, many uncertainties. What is the state of development of such weapons? What would be the public perception of their use? How would such issues be handled in the mainstream media? What would be the reaction of those targeted with such weapons in a tactical situation? Would they react in kind or with other chemical weapons? How does the tactical situation play out if those initially targeted have effective countermeasures such as protective masks? What will be the international, political, and diplomatic reaction given the obvious threat to the CWC, the BWC and IHL? Lastly, how does the use of incapacitating biochemical weapons for law enforcement, with all its inherent risks, correlate with the notion of reasonable use of force or the prohibition on cruel, inhuman or degrading treatment?

In his "Art of War," written 2000 years ago, Sun Tsu said "Those who are not thoroughly aware of the disadvantages in the use of arms cannot be thoroughly aware of the advantages in the use of arms." This paper is a call for objective consideration of both the advantages and the disadvantages of incapacitating biochemical weapons.

Notes

1. Robin M. Coupland, "The Effect of Weapons on Health," *Lancet* 347 (1996): 450–51. See also "Weapons and their Relation to Life and Health," World Medical Association 48th General Assembly, 1996.

2. Joan M. Lakoski, W. Bosseau Murray, and John M. Kenney, "The Advantages and Limitations of Calmatives for Use as a Non-Lethal Technique," Applied Research Laboratory, College of Medicine of The Pennsylvania State University, 2000.

3. In medical practice, fentanyl is used primarily as an analgesic in both injection and inhalational form. Other related compounds such as remifentanil, carfentanil, and sufentanil have been used in veterinary practice for large animal anesthesia but only by injection. See also Robin M. Coupland, "Incapacitating Chemical Weapons: A Year after the Moscow Theatre Siege," *Lancet* 361 (2003): 1346.

4. Robin M. Coupland, "Abhorrent Weapons and 'Superfluous Injury or Unnecessary Suffering': From Field Surgery to Law," *British Medical Journal* 315 (1997): 1450–52.

5. Robin M. Coupland and David Meddings, "Mortality Associated with the Use of Weapons in Armed Conflict, Wartime Atrocities and Civilian Mass Shootings: Literature Review," *British Medical Journal* 319 (1999): 407–10.

6. The major part of this body of law comprises the 1949 Geneva Conventions and their 1977 Additional Protocols.

CHAPTER 12

International Law and the Regulation of Weapons

Françoise J. Hampson

Introduction

This chapter attempts to explain how international law addresses issues relating to biochemical weapons. It does not seek to provide answers, except in a few instances, since at present there are no easy answers. The text is designed principally for non-lawyers, or non-international lawyers. There is a risk that people concerned about an issue find a legal text that appears to address the matter and treat it as though it were not a technical text or in the same way as they would treat domestic or national law. This is not special pleading by an international lawyer. In order to construct potentially effective arguments, it is essential to work within the constraints of the accepted framework of rules. To do otherwise is not only wasted effort. It is to betray those who might have been helped by legitimate arguments. For this reason, it is necessary first to address certain features of the international legal system relevant to the regulation of weapons. Constraints of space mean that the issues need to be presented in the most cursory fashion. The three ways in which international law handles the regulation of weapons in general will then be considered, before the specific issues concerning biochemical weapons.

Features of Public International Law Relevant to the Regulation of Weapons

International law addresses principally the relations between States. Historically, it followed that it dealt generally with what States did outside their borders and only with what occurred within national territory to the extent that it affected other States.[1] That is why the recent development of human rights law, which concerns the relationship between a State and those within its jurisdiction, including its own citizens, represented such a significant development.

For the most part, international law is civil, as opposed to criminal, in character. The International Court of Justice (ICJ), for example, hears disputes between States and does not have the power to jail anyone. There is an exception regarding international crimes, a category which includes aggression, genocide, war crimes and crimes against humanity. In the case of international crimes, any State is free to try a suspected perpetrator, subject to national law providing for the requisite jurisdiction,[2] and subject to sovereign immunity.[3] International criminal courts have been in existence only since the 1990s. They are limited by the terms of their constituent instruments with regard to the crimes they can try; moreover, their jurisdiction may be limited geographically and to certain time periods.[4] The international Criminal Court (ICC) is not limited geographically but its jurisdiction is limited to nationals of States and territories that have ratified its Statute and to situations referred to the court by the Security Council.[5] It is limited to crimes committed after the entry into force of the Statute and it only has jurisdiction over a defined category of international crimes. These include war crimes and crimes against humanity, the crimes most likely to be relevant in relation to weapons. The possibility of trial before an international court exists alongside the possibility of trials under domestic law.

International law is law but it does not function in the same way as domestic law. In particular, there is no way of compelling a State to submit a dispute to the ICJ, unless it has chosen to accept such a jurisdiction on the part of the ICJ, and no way of enforcing the Court's judgments, other than by Security Council action. This does not mean that States are free to violate international law with impunity. Consequences will flow from such violations but they may not be judicial consequences. Powerful States can "get away with" more than weaker States but even they suffer adverse effects.[6]

The rules of international law are found principally in treaties and in customary international law.[7] A treaty is only binding on a State if it has ratified it. Mere signature, indicating a future intent to be bound, is not sufficient but a State that has signed a treaty is not free to undermine its objects and purposes.[8] It is up to the State to amend its domestic law to bring it into line with its international obligations. It cannot plead its domestic law as an excuse for the violations of its international commitments.[9] It is not enough to determine whether a State has ratified a treaty. It is essential to examine whether it has made any relevant reservations or statements of understanding. Reservations potentially modify the scope of the treaty obligations accepted by the ratifying State.[10] It is necessary to examine the treaty to see whether reservations are permitted.

Generally speaking, in the case of multilateral treaties, a State is free to make reservations unless the treaty expressly prohibits all reservations or only permits specific reservations.[11] Where reservations are, in principle, permitted, there is a further limitation. No reservation can be made which is inconsistent with the objects and purposes of the treaty.[12] It is not clear whether such a provision does not constitute a reservation at all or whether it is a reservation but it is invalid and/or ineffective.[13]

Where a State is a party to a treaty, it may dispute the interpretation to be given to a particular provision or contend that it is not applicable on the facts but it cannot claim not to be bound by the formulation of the norm found in the treaty.

The other principal source of international law is customary international law.[14] In order to establish that a norm is binding as a matter of customary law, it is necessary to show widespread State practice, combined with evidence that the principle is followed because it is considered binding.[15] There are a variety of problems in establishing that a norm has the status of a legal rule, particularly with regard to the regulation of weapons. In part, that is attributable to the significant amount of treaty law in the field. It makes it difficult to distinguish between practice based on the treaty and that based on a possible customary rule. Another difficulty results from the fact that, in this area, any norm often takes the form of a prohibition. It is not easy to establish practice or *opinion juris* based on what States do *not* do.

The relationship between international law and domestic or national law needs to be considered from two different perspectives. According to international law, as already seen, it is up to the State to amend its domestic law to ensure that it is in accordance with its international obligations. Also of importance is what domestic law has to say about the status of international law. Broadly speaking, there is a spectrum in the practice of national legal systems. At one end, domestic law may treat any ratified treaty as having a higher status than any domestic law, including the constitution.[16] Further along the spectrum, domestic law may treat a ratified treaty as having the same status as the constitution and therefore a higher status than ordinary legislation. Civil law jurisdictions commonly take the position that a ratified treaty has the same status as ordinary national law. In certain cases, while national law takes this position in theory, it appears that, in practice, domestic measures are needed to make at least some international legal provisions enforceable by the courts. At the other end of the spectrum, treaty provisions have no effect on the law of the land within the State unless they are transformed or incorporated into national law. This is frequently the position in common law jurisdictions.

The discussion of the relationship between international law and domestic law has so far focused on treaty provisions. As far as the status of customary international law at the national level is concerned, the position is more uncertain.[17] In particular, it is not clear how civil law jurisdictions treat customary international law in either theory or practice. Custom as a source of law is much less problematical for common law jurisdictions. In England, for example, in theory the common law includes within it the customary law of nations. The impact in practice is much reduced nowadays because legislation prevails over the common law and most matters are in practice dealt with by legislation.

A breach by a State of its international legal obligations entails state responsibility.[18] This can be discharged in a variety of ways, including but not limited to compensation. In certain cases, the international obligation may require a State to take effective domestic enforcement action. If it fails to do so, at the international level it will bear civil responsibility for the failure. One of the most common examples is in the area of human rights law. A violation of human rights law, for example torture, is committed by an individual acting in the name of the State. The international obligation may require the State to bring national criminal proceedings against a suspect. Failure to do so may require the State, at the international level, to provide compensation to the victim. In many cases, the act in question may be an international crime. That is not, however, always the case.[19]

When addressing issues concerning the regulation of weapon use, it is essential to remember that they arise within this general international law framework. It is not enough, for example, to know that a treaty exists. In addition, one must consider whether State X has ratified the treaty and, if so, whether it has attached a valid reservation to its ratification.

International Law and the Regulation of Weapons

International law addresses the regulation of weapons in three different ways. Weapons of mass destruction (WMD) are handled through the UN Committee on Disarmament. Conventional weapons are dealt with in the context of the law of armed conflict. Finally, certain consequences of weapon use are indirectly the concern of human rights law. These categories may overlap.

THE COMMITTEE ON DISARMAMENT AND WMD

The nature of the problems posed by WMD has an important effect on the process by which international law is made in this field and on the law itself. Unlike other treaties, where like-minded States can reach an agreement and try to persuade other States to ratify,[20] in the case of WMD it is vital that all relevant players be brought on board. This means that what is being sought is a consensus. There is a risk that this represents the lowest common denominator, rather than the highest common factor. Whilst in other areas consensus negotiations might have net advantages, there is a real difficulty in the case of WMD. The nature of the threat posed by such weapons requires the highest possible level of obligation, in terms of the scope and clarity of the provisions, the intrusiveness of the monitoring and the rigor of the enforcement provisions. On the other hand, it is vital to get all States to join in the regime established. It is not surprising that the result can be deliberately ambiguous provisions to paper over disagreement.

In the case of WMD, what is being sought is an absolute prohibition of use. Where any and every possible use of a weapon is unlawful, it is possible also to prohibit the manufacture and stockpiling of the weapon. That would not be possible where use might be lawful in limited circumstances. In that case, the use of the weapon would be regulated.

The Committee on Disarmament has been unable to conclude a treaty prohibiting the use of nuclear weapons. Atomic energy is regulated under the supervision of the International Atomic Energy Agency (IAEA), with a view to preventing the proliferation of nuclear weapons. Whilst there have been some successes, such as South Africa's abandonment of its nuclear weapons program, the acquisition and testing of nuclear weapons by India and Pakistan, without undue adverse consequences for those States, shows the limitations of the process.

The Committee on Disarmament has concluded two treaties prohibiting categories of weapons. In 1972, during the Cold War, it concluded the Convention on the Prohibition of the Development, Production and Stockpiling of Bacteriological (Biological) and Toxin Weapons and on their Destruction, hereinafter referred to as the Biological Weapons Convention (BWC).[21] In 1993, during a brief period of openness to collective international action following the end of the Cold War, it was possible to conclude the Chemical Weapons Convention (CWC).[22] The marked difference in the two treaty regimes is, to a significant extent, the product of the time at which they were concluded. One may question whether it would be possible to reach an agreement as intrusive as the Chemical Weapons Convention today. This has important implications for the regulation of biochemical weapons. Treaties typically take a very long time to negotiate. That is one of the reasons why international law, even more than national law, has a problem keeping up-to-date with scientific developments.

The BWC deals with "microbial or other biological agents, or toxins whatever their origin or method of production, of types and in quantities that have no justification for prophylactic, protective or other peaceful purposes" and weapons or the means of delivery of such agents for hostile purposes.[23] Ratifying States undertake not to develop, produce, stockpile, acquire or retain prohibited items. The general purpose criterion of the Convention distinguishes between biological agents and toxins when used for hostile purposes and when used for peaceful purposes, rather than identifying any particular agents as coming into one category or the other. The treaty does not provide a regulatory framework for biological agents and toxins, most if not all of which are capable of coming into either category. There are no provisions on the right of inspection of another State's facilities, beyond an obligation to cooperate with an investigation ordered by the Security Council following a complaint of noncompliance.[24] Using the Security Council as a means of enforcement exposes such a complaint to the risk of the exercise of the veto. This is a potential problem if the State complained against is a veto power. The treaty does require States both not to manufacture such weapons themselves and also requires them to prohibit any manufacture within their territory.[25] Thus, there is a legislative prohibition, but a danger exists that without effective enforcement the prohibition won't be implemented in practice. This weakness of the treaty is reflected in the fact that the former Soviet Union is alleged to have had a biological weapons program long after it ratified the treaty in 1975. There have been recent attempts to negotiate a Protocol providing for the effective monitoring of the implementation and enforcement of the Convention but the United States withdrew its support at the point where agreement appeared to be possible.

The CWC is an altogether different proposition.[26] The treaty is applicable to toxic chemicals and their precursors and equipment used to deliver such chemicals.[27] The terms are defined and separate annexes provide lists of, for example, toxic chemicals and precursors. States are required to indicate what toxic chemicals are present in their territory and to provide a plan for their destruction.[28] The treaty provides for elaborate verification measures. Unlike the BWC, verification is part of the implementation of the Convention, rather than part of the process for investigating alleged violations. For present purposes, the most important provisions are those defining the prohibited chemicals and determining the scope of applicability. A toxic chemical is "[a]ny chemical which through its chemical action on life processes can cause death, temporary incapacitation or permanent harm to humans or animals. This includes all such chemicals, regardless of their origin or of their method of production, and regardless of whether they are produced in facilities, in munitions or elsewhere."[29] A precursor is "[a]ny chemical reactant which takes part at any stage in the production by whatever method of a toxic chemical. This includes any key component of a binary or multicomponent chemical system."[30] States undertake, amongst other things, never to use chemical weapons and never to use riot control agents as weapons of warfare.[31] A riot control agent is "[a]ny chemical not listed in a

Schedule, which can produce rapidly in humans sensory irritation or disabling physical effects which disappear within a short time following termination of exposure."[32] However, purposes *not* prohibited under the Convention include "[l]aw enforcement including domestic riot control purposes."[33] This implies that riot control agents, as defined, can be used for law enforcement purposes but not during conflict. If that includes internal conflict, it is essential to be able to determine when an activity is part of an armed conflict and when it is law enforcement.

A very real problem posed by chemical agents, including biochemical agents, is that they may be used for both useful and sinister purposes. The law needed to find a way to enable the former activities to be continued, while ensuring that effective measures were in place to prevent the latter. Such measures will inevitably have some impact on the lawful activities. They will have to be subject to regulation and control that will make certain operations more time-consuming. There is no reason why it should impede commercial secrecy as far as competitors are concerned, on condition that information given to regulatory bodies is kept confidential.

The Committee on Disarmament has not elaborated a treaty on biochemical weapons. Insofar as a biochemical agent comes within the definition of a toxic chemical or precursor within the Chemical Weapons Convention, its use as a weapon is already prohibited, and its possession is regulated even if not listed in a schedule.[34] If it does not come within that definition and is not a biological weapon, the only other basis on which it could be said to be prohibited by a specific treaty provision is if it comes within the 1925 Geneva Gas Protocol.[35]

THE LAW OF ARMED CONFLICT (LOAC) AND THE REGULATION OF WEAPONS

The law of armed conflict (LOAC) is also known as international humanitarian law. It takes no position on the lawfulness of the resort to armed force. That is the province of the *jus ad bellum*, regulated principally by the UN Charter and customary international law. LOAC is the body of rules applicable during situations of armed conflict. It deals with how the fighting is carried out and with the protection of victims of the conflict. The rules are *only* applicable to armed conflict.[36]

It is significant that the rules are applicable to armed conflicts rather than to war, in a technical legal sense. The rules apply by virtue of a factual situation of armed conflict, whether or not it has been recognized as such, which has been defined as "a resort to armed force between States or protracted armed violence between governmental authorities and organized armed groups or between such groups within a State."[37]

Treaty law distinguishes between international conflicts, defined as conflicts between two or more contracting parties, and non-international conflicts, with the former being subject to both more rules and more precise rules than the latter, particularly with regard to the conduct of hostilities.[38] In the past fifteen years, especially as a result of the judgments of the *ad hoc* criminal tribunals for the former Yugoslavia and Rwanda and the terms of the Statute of the International Criminal Court, it has become clear that there is a significant body of customary law regulating non-international conflicts.[39]

The treaty regime for the enforcement of LOAC is unusual. Whilst the possibility of inter-State civil complaints exists,[40] that is not the only or even the principal means of enforcement. The law, above all, seeks to prevent violations. That requires measures to be taken within the armed forces, rather than action after the event by the other side. The treaties also provide for criminal proceedings in the event of violations. It is envisaged that these will usually be brought by the national authorities of the suspected perpetrator, either by court martial or ordinary criminal proceedings.[41] Many violations constitute war crimes, with regard to which any State is free to prosecute. In international conflicts, there is also a category of "grave breaches," defined in the four Geneva Conventions of 1949 and Protocol I of 1977. A State is required to seek out suspected perpetrators of grave breaches in its territory and to prosecute them, unless they are transferred to another state for trial.

LOAC is a legal hybrid. Like any other inter-State obligation, it binds States. Additionally, insofar as it creates international crimes, it binds individuals. War crimes may be committed by anyone.[42] Most importantly, non-State fighters in a non-international armed conflict are bound by the rules. They can be prosecuted for violations. It is less clear whether non-State fighting groups can be held liable under civil law. The ICJ only has jurisdiction over States. It may be possible to bring proceedings against such groups in national courts, if domestic law makes that possible.[43]

The regulation of weapons as part of LOAC predates the multilateral treaty regime, which started in the nineteenth century. The law in this area is based on the notion that "[i]n any armed conflict, the right of the Parties to the conflict to choose methods or means of warfare is not unlimited."[44] The law is based on four fundamental principles. A weapon will be *prohibited* if it is inherently indiscriminate, causes "superfluous injury or unnecessary suffering" (SIRUS) or is perfidious. In addition, no weapons can be *used* in such a way as to cause disproportionate harm to civilians. In other words, a weapon will be banned if *any* use of it is objectionable on certain specific grounds and its use will be regulated where it can be used in a legitimate way but there is a real risk of its being used in a way that causes disproportionate harm to civilians.

Whilst these principles are reflected in both treaty law and customary law, there is a real difficulty in determining that a weapon is banned solely on the basis of customary law.[45] There are two examples of weapons or adaptations to weapons whose use is banned on this basis but they go back a century.[46] The author is aware of no weapon the use of which has been banned in the past fifty years without a treaty provision to that effect. The development of customary law is still significant for those States not party to a treaty prohibiting a particular weapon.

Until recently, the treaty rules regulating weapons were only applicable in international armed conflicts. The Appeal Chamber of the International Criminal Tribunal for the former Yugoslavia stated that

> Indeed, elementary considerations of humanity and common sense make it preposterous that the use by States of weapons prohibited in armed conflicts between themselves be allowed when States try to put down rebellion by their own nationals on their own territory. What is inhuman, and consequently proscribed, in international wars cannot but be inhumane and inadmissible in civil strife."[47]

This paved the way for the extension of the Certain Conventional Weapons Convention (CCWC) and its Protocols to non-international conflicts.[48]

Whilst this is both a helpful and a logical development, it makes it all the more important to be able to distinguish between armed conflicts and policing operations.[49]

What Constitutes a Weapon?

There is no definition of the term weapon in treaty law but it is clear that the concept applies to anything in the possession of one party used to inflict harm on the other party. It is clearly not limited to traditional battlefield munitions.[50]

Inherently Indiscriminate

It is vital, and not always easy, to distinguish between a weapon which is inherently indiscriminate and one which is used in an indiscriminate way. In order to be inherently indiscriminate, it must be designed in such a way as to be incapable of being used in a discriminate way. A well-established example is remotely-delivered lethal gas. By virtue of the characteristics of the weapon, once it is used, its effects cannot be restricted or controlled so as to avoid harm to civilians or even to the forces using it.[51] Antipersonnel landmines have sometimes been claimed to be indiscriminate, on the grounds that the trigger to detonation does not distinguish between a military foot and a civilian foot. It is submitted that this represents a misunderstanding of the concept of indiscriminate harm and/or of the principle of distinction. Just because a weapon is not aimed does not necessarily make its use indiscriminate. It is, however, the case that in the majority of cases antipersonnel landmines have been and are used in an indiscriminate way. That is a reason for regulating, rather than banning, their use. All parties to the Ottawa Convention undertake not to use antipersonnel landmines as defined. Those States not party to that Convention may be bound by treaty provisions regulating their use, notably the amended second Protocol to the CCWC.[52]

"Superfluous Injury or Unnecessary Suffering" (SIRUS)

At first sight, this prohibition is little short of extraordinary. It is lawful to kill a member of the opposing armed forces but not to cause him certain types of injury. In fact, an analogous distinction is found in human rights law, where all forms of inhuman treatment are prohibited but not all killings.

What the principle means is best illustrated by an example, the most famous being expanding bullets, also known as "dum-dum" bullets.[53] It is lawful to fire at opposing fighters but it is not lawful to cause injuries over and above those necessary to render them *hors de combat*—incapable of continuing to fight. The injuries caused by expanding bullets not only have the lawful effect of stopping the person from fighting but also give rise to injuries that are much more difficult to treat.

This example also illustrates the problem of making what was designed as a battlefield ban applicable in non-international conflicts, which often take a very different form. There are circumstances in which the use of expanding bullets poses less of a risk to others in the vicinity than conventional ammunition. This is particularly likely to be the case where the target is surrounded by civilians. On account of their characteristics, expanding bullets are less likely to exit the person hit, thereby avoiding the risk of also hitting someone else.

Whilst it is possible to identify weapons which have been banned on the basis of SIRUS, it is more difficult to identify the criteria which determine that an injury is superfluous or suffering unnecessary, so as to apply them in advance of the first use of a weapon. Could it be argued, for example, that the injuries caused to soldiers by antipersonnel landmines have these characteristics? The injuries make significant demands on blood supplies and surgical time and require forces to be diverted to deal with the wounded. The International Committee of the Red Cross (ICRC) tried to establish benchmarks for a "normal" battlefield injury, with a view to arguing that anything that caused more harm was *prima facie* unlawful, unless it could be shown in the circumstances to have been necessary.[54] They encountered methodological objections, including from military medical personnel.

The prohibition applies not only to weapons or means of combat but also to tactics or methods.[55] Two examples illustrate the possible significance of this extension. During the Gulf War 1990–1991, certain U.S. tanks were fitted with devices that functioned a little like ploughs. They picked up sand in front of the tanks and dumped it to the side. This was a way of removing antitank mines but it also buried Iraqi forces alive in trenches. A more recent example concerns the use of white phosphorous in Fallujah, Iraq. It had the effect of flushing out insurgents but it also caused extremely dangerous burns. In both cases, it may be relevant to know what the primary purpose of the tactic was. Armed forces are not well served by the tendency to use pithy and dramatic phrases. The use of "shake and bake" might suggest that the object of the use of white phosphorous was to cause serious burns. It is not clear that that was in fact the case.

Other Prohibited Weapons

Certain other weapons are the subject of specific treaty bans. It is not always clear on what the ban is based. In some cases, it appears to be the risk to civilians. That is presumably the objection to making toys and domestic appliances into weapons.[56] The ban could also be explained by the prohibition of perfidy. That might also be the objection to the poisoning of wells and water supplies.[57]

That does not explain certain prohibitions that apply to weapons used against armed forces, such as the prohibition of the use of poison on spears.[58] A modern equivalent might be the use of a poisonous coating on ammunition.

It appears that certain weapons are prohibited because, in effect, they are seen as unfair or unchivalrous. Soldiers have historically objected to weapons they cannot see (e.g., poison and gas) or to weapons that mutilate (e.g., lasers designed to blind).[59] It would appear that weapons banned on this somewhat nebulous basis are the subject of express treaty provision. The prohibition may also become part of customary law. The reference to lasers designed to blind suggests that this category may still be of contemporary relevance.

Restrictions on the Use of Certain Weapons

Clearly, any weapon is capable of being used in an unlawful way. The law provides for that general risk by setting out what can and cannot be targeted and the precautions that need to be taken before and during an attack.[60]

Certain weapons, however, carry with them a particular risk to civilians if they are misused. The treaty provisions regulating such weapons represent a more detailed articulation of the application of the general principles. The most notable examples are antipersonnel landmines, antitank or antivehicle mines and incendiary weapons.[61]

Enforcement

The treaty provisions banning and regulating weapon use contain no special enforcement provisions, other than those generally applicable to LOAC and international law generally, with the exception of the Ottawa Convention on antipersonnel landmines. Where the rules on weapon use are contained in a general LOAC treaty, the lack of enforcement provisions specific to weapons is not surprising. It is a more noteworthy omission in the case of the CCWC. Certain of the crimes within the jurisdiction of the International Criminal Court are weapons related but only in relation to international conflicts.[62]

Development of Future Weapons

A party to Protocol I of 1977 to the Geneva Conventions of 1949 is under an obligation to determine whether the employment of a new method or means of warfare would, in some or all circumstances, be prohibited by the Protocol or by any other rule of international law applicable to that State.[63] It is not clear whether this principle applies to means and methods of warfare used in non-international conflicts.[64] It has been suggested that under a dozen States in fact have a system in place for the conduct of such weapons reviews.[65] The rules do not establish whether a State can rely on a review conducted by another State, from which it purchased or obtained the weapon. What has to be known regarding the effects of a weapon in order to carry out such a review will be examined further below.

LOAC rules on weapons focus on the effects of weapons that arise as a result of their design features. It is only on that basis that the use of a weapon may be banned in all circumstances. Other LOAC rules, such as those prohibiting indiscriminate attacks, are based on the responsibility for the foreseeable effects of actions determined at the time the action is decided upon, and not with the benefit of hindsight. Insofar as the second group of issues involves questions attributable to the weapon chosen to carry out a particular attack, it is concerned with weapons the use of which needs to be regulated.

HUMAN RIGHTS LAW

Human rights law does not, on the face of it, specifically address weapon use. It is clear, however, from the caselaw of human rights bodies that the effects of certain uses of weapons may give rise to human rights concerns.

Human rights law consists of treaty provisions and of what might be termed UN Charter law. The former UN Commission on Human Rights has established Special Procedures that have a given mandate.[66] In this context, the most relevant Special Procedures are the Special Rapporteur on Torture and the Special Rapporteur on Extrajudicial, Summary or Arbitrary Executions.[67] The individuals holding these mandates can scrutinize relevant conduct of any UN member. They are not limited to those that have ratified a particular treaty. In addition, certain Special Procedures are appointed to address the situation within a particular State. It is not clear whether the standards applied by the Special Procedures should be called customary law or whether it is in a special category of UN law.

The advantage of human rights law is that there is a plethora of monitoring and enforcement mechanisms but it is far from being the case that all States are subject to the latter. The two Special Rapporteurs mentioned and two of the international treaty bodies could monitor the use of unlawful weapons or the unlawful use of potentially lawful weapons.[68]

By enforcement bodies, in this context, is meant not only those that deliver a legally binding result but also those that reach a decision on the particular facts. Generally speaking, where there is a dispute on the facts, the Special Procedures are not in a position to reach a conclusion. It is different where a State agrees with the facts presented by another party but claims they do not represent a violation of the law. For example, if individuals claim that a State has used unlawful weapons and the State denies the claim, the Special Procedures do not have the investigatory and forensic resources to establish the facts. If, however, the claim is that a State used "dum-dum" bullets during an armed conflict and the State agrees that it did so but asserts that their use was lawful, the Special Procedures may, subject to a major constraint considered shortly, be able to make a legal determination.

In the context of the right of individual petition, the Human Rights Committee has to reach non-binding conclusions.[69] The European and Inter-American Courts of Human Rights and the new African Court on Human and Peoples' Rights deliver legally binding judgments.[70] They only have jurisdiction over those States that have ratified the relevant Conventions and Protocols and there are various other significant limitations on their jurisdiction. An important feature of these enforcement mechanisms is that, almost uniquely in international law, they can be directly or indirectly triggered by individuals.[71] They are far more likely to bring such complaints than are foreign States, particularly where the claim concerns something that the State has done in its own territory.

There are two important preliminary questions that need to be considered before one can examine the substantive rules of human rights law. The first is whether human rights law applies during armed conflict and, if so, to what extent. The second is the extent to which human rights law applies outside national territory.

It appears to be now well established that at least some human rights law remains applicable even during armed conflict.[72] It is not clear, however, which matters are exclusively regulated by human rights law or by LOAC and which by both. To take a specific example, it would seem obvious that LOAC applies during an international armed conflict so as to render lawful detention as a prisoner of war, if it would not otherwise be lawful under human rights law. It is not certain, however, whether the human rights law requirement of the possibility of review of the lawfulness of detention by an independent body (*habeas corpus*) continues to be applicable, at least in the case of the detention of civilians.[73]

Customary international law has long recognized the possibility of a "persistent objector" to the application of a norm to itself.[74] Such objection does not prevent a norm evolving and acquiring the status of a customary rule but it would not be applicable to a State that has persistently objected. It is not clear whether the principle can apply to the application of treaty law, at least absent a relevant reservation by the objecting State.[75] The application of the principle to human rights law also raises particular difficulties. It is unlikely that a State could avoid responsibility by claiming to be a persistent objector to the prohibition of genocide. This raises the relationship between the persistent objector principle and the *jus cogens* doctrine. Rules of *jus cogens* are said to be of such a fundamental character that they prevail over incompatible treaty law and arguably persistent objections. The doctrine is controversial and its scope uncertain.

Israel has long maintained that human rights law is not applicable when LOAC is applicable. The ICJ, in its Advisory Opinion on the "wall" being constructed in Occupied Territory, assumed that Israel was bound by its human rights treaty obligations in such territory, as does the Human Rights Committee, but it did not address the question of whether Israel can claim to be a persistent objector. The United States has erratically maintained a similar position before the Inter-American Commission of Human Rights and more recently before the Human Rights Committee, which calls into question the persistence of any objection. When the United States ratified the International Covenant on Civil and Political Rights, the position of the Human Rights Committee was well known but the United States did not make a reservation with regard to the Covenant's applicability in situations of armed conflict.

It will be recalled that States frequently refuse to characterize an internal armed conflict as such, preferring to call it criminal or terrorist activity. In such a situation, they can hardly challenge the applicability of human rights law. Nevertheless, it is submitted that enforcement bodies should characterize the situation for themselves. If they fail to do so, they may find a State in breach of its human rights obligations for doing something not only permitted but required by LOAC.[76] This is most likely to be a problem under the European Convention on Human Rights, on account of the way in which the provisions on the use of potentially lethal force and detention are drafted.[77] The fact that a State can derogate in such a situation and has chosen not to do so is relevant but, it is submitted, not decisive.

The second major issue is the extent to which human rights law is applicable outside national territory.[78] If it is not so applicable, human rights law would be applicable to domestic policing operations, to non-international conflicts, whether or not the State recognized it as such, and to those aspects of an international conflict occurring in national territory. In other words, human rights law would not apply to what the United States and other States have done in Afghanistan, Iraq or Yemen.

The law on some aspects of this question is at present totally confused. There is significant case law to the effect that human rights law is applicable outside national territory where foreign territory is occupied and it is also applicable to persons in the physical control of another State, albeit outside that State's territory.[79] It is not clear whether human rights law is applicable to the acts of State agents outside national territory where the State controls the infliction of the alleged violation.[80] If, for example, the armed forces of State A detain X in State B and torture and kill him in State B, there is consistent human rights caselaw that he was within State A's jurisdiction, which will be liable for his ill-treatment and death. The caselaw suggests, however, that if State A deliberately bombs a building in which X is located, in order to kill him, and does so kill him, he may not be regarded as within State A's jurisdiction for the purpose of human rights law. These two contrasting positions appear to be incoherent but it is not clear how or when the situation will be clarified.

The question of the applicability of human rights law in situations of conflict and the problem of the extent of its extraterritorial application must be borne in mind when considering whether the use of biochemical weapons may give rise to a human rights violation.

To date, it would appear that the only issues relating to weapon use that have formed the basis of the decision of a human rights body are questions concerning the choice of weapon. Unsuccessful challenges have been mounted to the use of plastic baton rounds.[81] Successful challenges have been made to the use of live ammunition from armored personnel carriers as an agent of riot control.[82] The European Court of Human Rights (ECHR) said that the forces should have had other weapons at their disposal, such as tear gas. Whilst not necessarily inappropriate on the particular facts, that does suggest that the ECHR adopts a law enforcement approach, rather than one based on LOAC. The danger is that they will fail to recognize that the State is prohibited from using a particular weapon under LOAC. If a State uses "dum-dum" bullets during a military operation against insurgents, there is an argument that such use is unlawful, unless possibly they were used to protect civilians. The case law to date of the ECHR suggests that the judges might not recognize the issue themselves and might not accept such an argument raised by applicants. The Inter-American Commission and Court of Human Rights have shown a much greater willingness to consider the relevance of LOAC.[83]

One argument that has not yet been raised in a case in which it was decisive is the human rights law equivalent of SIRUS. During the course of a non-international armed conflict, the next-of-kin of insurgents might wish to challenge not the fact of their being killed but the manner in which they died, particularly if it offended religious susceptibilities. The use of incendiary weapons as antipersonnel weapons might be argued to give rise to inhuman treatment, both in relation to those killed and in relation to the next-of-kin, who have to deal with an incinerated corpse.

Applying the Legal Frameworks to Biochemical Weapons

CREATING A SPECIAL TREATY REGIME

Each of the three legal regimes considered is self-contained. It is not possible, for example, to argue for compulsory weapons reviews outside the context of LOAC.

Those concerned about the development and use of biochemical weapons need to use the law for two quite distinct purposes. The first is to create a framework for the regulation of such weapons. That involves creating new law. The second is to use existing law to challenge particular uses or practices.

To the extent to which biochemical weapons come within the definitions of the 1925 Geneva Protocol, the BWC or the CWC, their use is already regulated or prohibited. The most effective of the three treaties is the CWC, on account of its elaborate regulation of dual use agents. The advantage of clarifying the extent to which biochemical weapons may be covered by the other two conventions is less clear, given their weak or nonexistent regulatory or enforcement frameworks.

The major problem in attempting to create a new legal regime specifically for biochemical weapons is the evident reluctance of at least one major player to elaborate an enforcement mechanism for a treaty which is already in existence. If the United States is unwilling to conclude a Protocol to the BWC, it is unlikely to be any keener on a biochemical weapons treaty. In that case, serious consideration needs to be given to whether it would be worthwhile to proceed without U.S. participation.

The attitude of the United States illustrates a paradox of wider applicability. States in the forefront of weapon development appear not to have mechanisms or tools for evaluating the overall net usefulness of a new weapon. They appear to think only in terms of their use of the weapon against an enemy and not of their vulnerability to its use against them, whether by State or non-State actors. An example is the use of computer network attacks.[84] In view of the U.S. vulnerability to such attack, it might have made more sense for the United States to seek to protect itself from such attacks by joining in the creation of a multilateral treaty defining unlawful targets of attack and providing for judicial cooperation to identify suspected perpetrators. States cannot expect to ban the use by others of weapons they themselves wish to use. Their interests might better be served by ensuring that no one can obtain the weapon in question. There is no evidence of this type of analysis of net benefit having been undertaken in the field of biochemical weapons.

Comprehensive regulation of the type found in the CWC would be difficult to obtain in the case of biochemical weapons, even though it would seem to be the best solution. Nevertheless, the use of other legal tools may have a certain nuisance value and might, in the longer term, persuade States to seek a more comprehensive solution.

The big disadvantage of the other legal regimes, including the LOAC and human rights law, is that they only address certain of the issues raised by biochemical weapons. They do not deal with the field as a whole.

LAW OF ARMED CONFLICT

The LOAC regime is capable of addressing the issue of the lawfulness of weapon use in the development stage but only if the weapon is inherently indiscriminate or designed in such a way as to give rise to injuries which are superfluous or suffering which is unnecessary. One cannot say that biochemical weapons *per se*, or incapacitating biochemicals in particular, fall foul of these proscriptions, although a particular biochemical weapon might do so.

One of the labels frequently applied to at least some biochemical weapons is "non-lethal".[85] This is a misnomer. Less lethal would be a more appropriate designation. The lethality of a weapon is not the only test for its unlawfulness under LOAC.[86] Where a weapon is designed to incapacitate a person who could lawfully be killed, the weapon is unlikely to be prohibited unless its effects cannot be confined to lawful targets or unless it gives rise to SIRUS.

Both LOAC generally and the requirement of weapon review assume that one knows the consequences of the use of a weapon. A problem arises where a new type of weapon has not been tested against humans. Enough is known about the human body to use appropriate substitutes to determine the effect of new ammunition. It may be more difficult to determine with sufficient precision the likely effects, in both the short-term and long-term, of incapacitating biochemical weapons. It is not enough to consider the effects of individual biochemical agents. It is also necessary to consider their effects in combination. To that general problem may be added concerns about different responses to different "doses" and varying responses on the part of different members of the population. In addition to variations based on age and size, some people may simply be more susceptible than others to such agents. The location in which a weapon is used may also affect the reaction.

This highlights a potential problem with weapons reviews. The reviewer is faced with a weapon designed for a particular use. He may determine that, used for that purpose, it would be lawful. It is less clear whether the reviewer signals circumstances in which it should not be used. If a soldier is given a weapon, he ought to be able to rely on its lawfulness when used as he has been trained to use it. In that case, he may need to be trained in how *not* to use it. An example would be the use of tear gas in confined spaces. It is not clear that weapons reviews indicate limitations on the use of a weapon.

It may be possible to mount a challenge to the weapons review of a biochemical weapon either on general grounds regarding such reviews or specifically because it is not possible to determine short- and long-term effects on a variety of people without testing on humans. Soldiers would be required to give informed consent before being made to act as guineapigs. How could the consent be informed when the tests are necessary precisely because the consequences are not known? It could also be argued that soldiers do not represent an adequate crossection of the population, since they are generally young and unusually fit.

A further concern is the wider context in which it is envisaged that such weapons would be used. If the biochemical weapon is to be used to disable an individual or group, what then happens to those so disabled? If the disablement of the group was undertaken so as to kill some or all of them, additional considerations would apply. Whilst it is lawful, during armed conflict, to kill opposing fighters, by virtue of their disablement they would have been rendered *hors de combat*. If unconscious, they cannot surrender but they can be detained. If suspected wrongdoers are detained, the adverse effect on the whole group might be thought to be justified, at least if the group was being threatened by the wrongdoers and the harm to the others was short-term and not serious. Where the weapon is used to disable a group which is not being threatened by the wrongdoer but simply as a means of reaching him, one must again consider whether the harm done to the others was proportionate, in terms of the seriousness of the effect, the number affected and the length of time for which the effects lasted. When evaluating the proportionality of the harm suffered by the others, it is not to be assessed solely in comparison to taking no action at all. One measure of assessment would be the proportionality of the harm in the comparison to what would be suffered if other means were used to kill the target, such as live ammunition. That said, according to LOAC, where a lawful military objective cannot be targeted without causing disproportionate civilian casualties, there is a requirement that the attack be called off.[87] In other words, there are three choices for the military commander and not two. In a situation in which fighters are known to be in a group of civilians, the choices would be, first, to use an incapacitating biochemical weapon to disable the group and detain the fighters; second, to use a sniper or some other conventional means to kill the fighter, with some risk to others in the group from a possible ricochet and, third, to do nothing at present on account of the risk to the group but to wait for the fighter to leave the group. If the actual effects of the use of a biochemical weapon on a group of people are not known, it is difficult to see how the commander will be able to choose between the three options. It is not likely to be enough to advocate a precautionary principle. It may be more successful to argue that existing law requires that the effects be known before a weapon can be approved. It is therefore essential that it be tested in the types of situation in which it is likely to be used.

It must be remembered that the LOAC regime, including the requirement of weapons reviews, only applies in situations of armed conflict. As a matter of international law, there is no such requirement for weapons used in policing operations, unless it can be regarded as implicit in the human rights obligation to protect the right to life. Policing operations arise at the national level where there is no armed conflict, at the national level alongside an armed conflict or where the State denies that the situation constitutes an armed conflict and also internationally, during the very varied range of peace support operations.

HUMAN RIGHTS LAW

It would be theoretically possible for human rights monitoring mechanisms to take a position on biochemical weapons *per se*. Any such pronouncement would have to be based on the effects of such weapons. If those effects are unknown or are dependent upon the precise weapon used and the particular way in which it is used, it is most unlikely that they would in fact be able to take such a position.

It is more likely that both monitoring and enforcement mechanisms will be called upon to determine whether a particular use of such a weapon constitutes a violation of human rights norms. This can only arise after the event. Such an issue might be raised by an injured victim or the next-of-kin of a dead victim. A claim would be based on one or more of three arguments. First, it might be argued that the use of such weapons gave rise to inhuman treatment. Any delay in providing medical treatment might be combined with the effects of the weapon to strengthen the claim.[88] A second argument, only applicable in the case of death, would be that the particular form taken by the resort to potentially lethal force was disproportionate. This is assessed not by the LOAC standard of proportionality in relation to the military advantage anticipated but by a different and stricter standard. Under human rights law the force has to be proportionate to the threat posed by the person against whom the force was used, taking into account the need to protect others in the vicinity from any harm and in the light of the other means available.[89] The standard in the European Convention on Human Rights is particularly strict, requiring that the force used was "no more than absolutely necessary."[90] The final argument is potentially applicable to lifethreatening situations not resulting in death. States are required to *protect* the right to life. This obliges States not to engage in lifethreatening activities.[91] The use of a weapon which was potentially lethal but whose precise effects were unknown might be regarded as life threatening. An enforcement body may determine that the forces on the ground did not act unlawfully but that not enough was done in the planning of the operation to protect those in the vicinity or even to make it possible to detain the suspects.[92]

The advantages of human rights law are that it is not limited to armed conflict situations and that, at least in relation to some States, the enforcement mechanisms can be accessed by individuals. A disadvantage is that, generally speaking, it only comes into play after the event. Whilst it is theoretically possible for an individual to bring a complaint alleging that they are potentially vulnerable to such a violation, it would be extremely difficult to do so in this type of situation.[93]

A PRACTICAL EXAMPLE OF THE OPERATION OF THE THREE LEGAL REGIMES

The means by which the Moscow theater siege was ended provides an example of how the legal regimes can be applied to a particular situation.[94]

If the substance used constituted a chemical weapon within the definition of the Chemical Weapons Convention, its use was unlawful.[95] That would open the way to the use of inter-State enforcement mechanisms. That would be of no practical benefit to the survivors or the next-of-kin, apart from the case of foreigners whose home State might be able to support the case under the rules of state responsibility.

Before considering the application of LOAC, it would be necessary to determine whether the act occurred as part of an armed conflict. Whilst the hostage-takers were allegedly Chechens, that might not be sufficient to regard the act as part of a conflict taking place elsewhere. Furthermore, at the international level, the Russian Federation denies the applicability of LOAC to the situation, even though the Russian constitutional court has characterized the situation as coming within Protocol II of 1977 to the four Geneva Conventions of 1949.[96] If LOAC were applicable, it would be necessary to determine which treaty rules originally applicable only in international conflicts are now applicable in non-international conflicts as a matter of customary law. That would be important with regard to weapons prohibited by the 1925 Geneva Gas Protocol.[97] If that was potentially applicable, it would be necessary to determine whether the substance used came within its provisions. That might require an assessment of whether the substance was known or ought to have been known to be potentially lethal. It is not clear how much needs to be known. Would it be unlawful to use a weapon that was not expected to be lethal but which had not been tested to determine the appropriate concentration for a non-lethal effect?

An argument based on the 1925 Protocol could be combined with one under general LOAC provisions. It might be argued that the weapon caused disproportionate civilian casualties. It must be remembered that the enforcement provisions in relation to non-international conflicts are much more limited than those available for conduct in international conflicts. It is difficult to imagine a third State being able to bring inter-State proceedings, unless one of its nationals was harmed. Civil claims before the courts of third States would be met by a claim of sovereign immunity. Civil claims in Russia would depend on Russian domestic law.[98] The act would not appear to come within the limited list of crimes in non-international conflicts within the jurisdiction of the ICC. If it were argued that the act nevertheless represented an international crime, third States would be able to exercise jurisdiction, provided that their domestic law so provided. At the national level there might be a further requirement that the perpetrator or the victim be within the jurisdiction of the State concerned, which would be unlikely unless responsibility could be pursued up the chain of command. Clearly Russia cannot be expected to exercise criminal jurisdiction in relation to an officially authorized attack. The position would have been very different if the attack had occurred in the context of an international armed conflict. There would then have been the possibility of an inter-State complaint and a greater possibility of an international court or the domestic courts of third States exercising criminal jurisdiction.

Under human rights law, the Special Procedures could raise the issue but would be unlikely to be able to reach a conclusion.[99] Two treaty bodies could address the question, the Human Rights Committee and the European Court of

Human Rights. In its concluding observations, following the presentation of Russia's fifth periodic report, the Human Rights Committee referred to the rescue operation principally in relation to the need for an independent and impartial investigation of what happened.[100] This suggests that, without the means to carry out their own investigations, human rights bodies are often unable to determine whether an incident violated human rights law. They can only comment upon the need for a proper investigation to determine the facts. Were such an investigation to be conducted, it would determine whether human rights law had been violated and what remedial action might be necessary.

It is not known whether those who unsuccessfully sought legal redress from the Russian courts have submitted individual complaints to the Human Rights Committee or the European Court of Human Rights. The procedures before those two bodies inevitably take a certain time and it may be too soon to know. The European Court of Human Rights has the ability to undertake fact-finding, which would suggest that it would be better placed to handle such a case. The strongest arguments would appear to be that the Russian security forces used a weapon the effects of which they did not know or that they used a potentially lethal weapon without taking adequate measures to protect against its lethality. Alternatively, the failure to ensure that there were an adequate number of appropriately trained personnel on hand and a sufficient quantity of the antidote meant that they did not take sufficient steps to protect people from the effects of the weapon. The alternative argument covers the possibility that the use of the weapon, in the particular circumstances, was potentially lawful.

It is therefore clear that there are major legal and political difficulties in enforcing the rules, particularly in the case of non-international conflicts. Whilst more avenues are available in the case of international conflicts, their applicability does depend on whether the potential defendant has accepted the jurisdiction in question. The United States, for example, no longer accepts the compulsory jurisdiction of the ICJ and has gone to remarkable lengths to protect its citizens from ever being brought before the International Criminal Court.[101]

Conclusion

Any legal strategy to address biochemical weapons needs to take three forms. There is, first, a need to examine the extent to which biochemical weapons are within the scope of the CWC.[102] Second, existing law can be used both to challenge the adequacy of weapons reviews, if the effects of the weapon are not sufficiently known, and also to challenge particular instances of the use of such weapons. Human rights law provides effective tools for engaging in the latter type of activity but not the ideal norms. LOAC provides more appropriate standards but very inadequate tools for enabling effective challenges to be mounted. The third strategy would be to seek a multilateral regulatory framework for the handling of biochemical agents that could be used as weapons, along the lines of the Chemical Weapons Convention. Whilst this would be the most effective solution to the problems posed by such agents, it could be expected to take well over a decade to obtain an agreed text, if it were achievable at all. To that would have to be added the time necessary for ratification and domestic implementation. It would be foolhardy to put all the biochemical eggs into the one, very problematic, basket. The only realistic strategy is to pursue all three strategies at the same time, in the hope that the pursuit of the first two will lessen State resistance to the third. For such a campaign to have any chance of success, it is vital that the argument should not be left to scientists and lawyers. The public needs to be mobilized.[103] If the public represents the foot soldiers, they need tools to wage the various battles ahead of them. Those tools can only be provided by the scientific community.

Notes

1. For example, a foreign sovereign cannot be brought before the courts of another State without the consent of the former, since that would diminish it as a sovereign. A State might be responsible for how it treats a foreign national, the latter being treated in some sense as the property of their home State. A State cannot use its territory in such a way as to cause harm to another State.

2. Just because international law allows a State to try a suspect does not mean that domestic law provides for it. In practice, States have been reluctant to try foreigners for acts committed abroad against foreigners, particularly States from a common law tradition.

3. Certain individuals, while exercising high State functions, cannot be prosecuted by the courts of other States. That does not prevent their being tried by an international court. Also see *Case Concerning the Arrest Warrant of 11 April 2000, (DRC v. Belgium)*, International Court of Justice (hereafter ICJ), judgment of 14 February 2002.

4. Examples include the *ad hoc* tribunals for the former Yugoslavia and Rwanda and the hybrid (national/international) special court in Sierra Leone. The Nuremberg and Tokyo trials are not included as they were established by victors, rather than by the international community as a whole.

5. See <http://www.icc-cpi.int/home.html> The Security Council has referred the situation in Darfur to the International Criminal Court (ICC).

6. For example, the impact on the perception of the United States resulting from the invasion of Iraq, the abuse of detainees and extraordinary rendition.

7. Statute of ICJ, Article 38.1, <http://www.icj-cij.org> (25 February 2007).

8. Vienna Convention on the Law of Treaties, 1155 U.N.T.S. 331, Article18, <http://www.oas.org/legal/english/docs/Vienna%20Convention%20Treaties.htm> (25 February 2007). This is presumably one reason why the administration of President George W. Bush "de-signed" the Statute of the International Criminal Court. Concluding agree-

ments with States party to the Statute not to allow U.S. citizens to be brought before the ICC might be thought to undermine its objects and purposes.

9. Vienna Convention on the Law of Treaties, Article 27.

10. Vienna Convention on the Law of Treaties, Article 2.1. (d).

11. Vienna Convention on the Law of Treaties, Article 19; Convention on the Prohibition of the Development, Production, Stockpiling and Use of Chemical Weapons and on their Destruction, 13 January 1993, 1974 U.N.T.S. 317. (hereinafter the Chemical Weapons Convention). Article XXII, for example, prohibits the making of reservations to the provisions of the treaty and only allows reservations to the annexes if they are compatible with the object and purpose of the treaty. For treaties in the field of the law of armed conflict, see the treaty database of the International Committee of the Red Cross (ICRC) at <http://www.icrc.org/ihl> (25 February 2007).

12. Vienna Convention on the Law of Treaties, Article 19 (c).

13. This could be important where a State does not indicate its objection to a reservation within the time limits defined in Article 20.5 of the Vienna Convention on the Law of Treaties but subsequently claimed that it was not required to notify its objection, since the instrument in question did not constitute a reservation by virtue of its conflict with the objects and purposes of the treaty.

14. For an introduction to the topic, see J.-M. Henckaerts and L. Doswald-Beck, *Customary International Humanitarian Law* 1 (Cambridge: Cambridge University Press, 2005): xxxi–xlv.

15. The second requirement is known by its Latin tag, *opinion juris (sive necessitatis)*.

16. This position is unusual. It is said to be the case in the Netherlands.

17. Traditionally, communist States did not recognize customary international law as a source of international law. The sovereignty of a State could only be restricted by obligations to which it had given express consent, i.e., ratified treaties. While customary international law is now recognized in theory as a source of law by former Communist States, it is not clear what impact this has in practice.

18. *Responsibility of States for Internationally Wrongful Acts*, ILC, Official Records of the General Assembly, Fifty-sixth Session, Supplement no. 10 (A/56/10), <http://www.un.org/law/ilc> (25 February 2007).

19. For example, under the European Convention on Human Rights (ECHR), a State is required to bring to trial state agents suspected of having committed an unlawful killing. Such a killing will only constitute an international crime if it is in furtherance of genocide or a crime against humanity, a war crime or prohibited under Conventions dealing with terrorist attacks. An unlawful killing by a policeman in the course of his duties would not normally be an international crime.

20. For example, the process by which Convention on the Prohibition of the Use, Stockpiling, Production and Transfer of Anti-Personnel Mines and on their Destruction, 1997 (the Ottawa Convention) came into being; see also note 11.

21. Convention on the Prohibition of the Development, Production and Stockpiling of Bacteriological and Toxin Weapons and on their Destruction, 10 April 1972, 1015 U.N.T.S.163 (hereinafter Biological and Toxin Weapons Convention).

22. Chemical Weapons Convention.

23. Biological and Toxin Weapons Convention, Article I. See the chapter by Marie I. Chevrier and Ambassador James F. Leonard in this volume.

24. Biological and Toxin Weapons Convention, Article VI.

25. Biological and Toxin Weapons Convention, Article IV.

26. Chemical Weapons Convention.

27. Chemical Weapons Convention, Article II.

28. Chemical Weapons Convention, Article III.

29. Chemical Weapons Convention, Article II, 2.

30. Chemical Weapons Convention, Article II, 3.

31. Chemical Weapons Convention, Article I, 5.

32. Chemical Weapons Convention, Article II, 7.

33. Chemical Weapons Convention, Article II, 8.

34. Following the definition of a toxic chemical, the Convention continues: "For the purpose of implementing this Convention, toxic chemicals which have been identified for the application of verification measures are listed in Schedules contained in the Annex on Chemicals." See also Chemical Weapons Convention, Article II, 2. This suggests that chemicals not listed in the annex may still be prohibited. It is simply that they will not be chemicals in relation to which the verification processes apply.

35. See further below as well as the chapters in this volume by David Fidler, Ambassador Adolf von Wagner, and Marie I. Chevrier and Ambassador James F. Leonard.

36. In order to apply the rules during armed conflict, certain measures need to be taken in time of peace. (For example on weapons reviews, see further below.)

37. *Tadic Case,* (IT-94-1), Interlocutory Appeal on Jurisdiction, ICTY Appeal Chamber, decision of 2 October 1995, paragraph 70.

38. In addition, the occupation of the whole or part of the territory of another State, even without armed resistance, is subjected to the regime applicable to international conflicts; see Geneva Conventions of 1949, Article 2. For parties to Additional Protocol I of 1977 to the Geneva Conventions of 1949, Article 1.4 all indicates that a further limited category of conflicts are to be treated as international. Since a right of self-determination does not apply to groups within existing sovereign States, this is of limited applicability.

39. Henckaerts and Doswald-Beck, *Customary International Humanitarian Law.*

40. India instituted proceedings against Pakistan before the ICJ concerning the treatment of prisoners of war during the conflict surrounding the birth of Bangladesh. Those proceedings were discontinued.

41. The trial of Lt. Calley for the My Lai massacre was conducted under the U.C.M.J. but was, in effect, a trial for war crimes.

42. For example, if civilians shoot a person who is *hors de combat* or who parachutes out of an aircraft in distress, they commit a war crime.

43. There are currently proceedings in the United States brought by the next-of-kin of persons killed in Al-Qaeda attacks.

44. Protocol Additional to the Geneva Conventions of 12 August 1949, and Relating to the Protection of Victims of International Armed Conflicts (Protocol I), 1977, 1125 U.N.T.S. 3 (hereinafter Protocol I of 1977), Article 35.1. This principle appears also to be applicable as customary law in both international and non-international conflicts;

256 FRANÇOISE J. HAMPSON

Chapter 20, Henckaerts and Doswald-Beck, *Customary International Humanitarian Law* 1 (Cambridge: Cambridge University Press, 2005).

45. A. Cassese, "Weapons Causing Unnecessary Suffering: Are They Prohibited?" *Rivista Di Diritto Internazionale* 48, no. 1 (1975).

46. Lances with barbed heads and serrated-edged bayonets; see Jean-Marie Henckaerts and Louise Doswald-Beck, *Customary International Humanitarian Law* 1 (Cambridge: Cambridge University Press, 2005): 240–44.

47. *Tadic Case*, (IT-94-1), Interlocutory Appeal on Jurisdiction, paragraph 119.

48. Convention on Prohibitions or Restrictions on the Use of Certain Conventional Weapons Which May be Deemed to be Excessively Injurious or to Have Indiscriminate Effects (CCWC), held in Geneva 10 October 1980, Amendment Article 1, 21. The Convention on the Prohibition of the Use, Stockpiling, Production and Transfer of Anti-Personnel Mines and on their Destruction (the Ottawa Convention), 18 September 1997, has been applicable to both international and non-international conflicts from the outset.

49. For example, into which category does the Moscow theater siege come? See further below.

50. For example, electronic attacks against computer networks would appear to qualify. See also: Michael N. Schmitt and Brian T. O'Donnell, eds., *Computer Network Attack and International Law: International Law Studies, vol. 76* (Newport, RI: Naval War College, 2002): 568.

51. Such weapons are also the subject of a treaty ban—the 1925 Geneva Gas Protocol. Their use is therefore prohibited even if, in the circumstances, it could be used in such a way as to avoid dispersal. See: The Protocol for the Prohibition of the Use of Asphyxiating, Poisonous or Other Gases, and of Bacteriological Methods of Warfare, 17 June 1925, 94 L.N.T.S. 65. The Geneva Gas Protocol of 1925 applies to poisonous or other gases, and to all analogous liquids, materials or devices and bacteriological methods of warfare. States simply undertake not to use such weapons in warfare. Many States have entered reservations only accepting that they would not be the first to use such weapons. If a possible use is envisaged by way of reprisal, it must be lawful for States to manufacture and stockpile such weapons. The treaty contains no enforcement provisions.

52. Protocol on Prohibitions or Restrictions on the Use of Mines, Booby-Traps and Other Devices (Protocol II), as amended on 3 May 1996, 1342 U.N.T.S. 168, 35 I.L.M. 1206 (hereinafter Protocol on Prohibitions or Restrictions on the Use of Mines).

53. "Hague Declaration (IV, 3) Concerning Expanding Bullets," *The Hague* 29 (July 1899).

54. R. M. Coupland and P. Herby, "Review of the Legality of Weapons: A New Approach to the SIRUS Project," *International Review of the Red Cross*, no.835 (1999): 583–92, <http://www.icrc.org/Web/Eng/siteeng0.nsf/iwpList136/CF3D4E11317B8AE2C1256B66005D8927>.

55. Protocol Additional to the Geneva Conventions of 12 August 1949, and Relating to the Protection of Victims of International Armed Conflicts (Protocol I), 1977, 1125 U.N.T.S. 3 (hereinafter Protocol I of 1977), Article 35.

56. Protocol on Prohibitions or Restrictions on the Use of Mines, Article 7.

57. Protocol I of 1977, Article 54.2.

58. Hague Convention IV of 1907, respecting the laws and customs of war on land, Annex, Article23.

59. Protocol on Blinding Laser Weapons (Protocol IV), Additional to the Convention on Prohibitions or Restrictions on the Use of Certain Conventional Weapons, 13 October 1995.

60. Protocol I of 1977, Articles 51–58.

61. In addition to the treaties on landmines previously referred to, see Protocol on Prohibitions or Restrictions on the Use of Incendiary Weapons (Protocol III), 10 October 1980, 1342 U.N.T.S. 171.

62. Rome Statute of the International Criminal Court, Article 8.2 (b), xvii–xx. That simply means that this particular court does not have the jurisdiction to determine a charge based on the unlawfulness of a weapon used in non-international conflict. If the use of such weapons in non-international conflicts is an international crime under customary international law, any State whose courts give effect to universal jurisdiction will be free to try a suspect for such a crime.

63. Protocol I of 1977, Article 36.

64. The customary law study by Henckaerts and Doswald-Beck contains no such rule note 46.

65. See *A Guide to the Legal Review of New Weapons, Means and Methods of Warfare*, International Committee of the Red Cross, 2006, < http://www.icrc.org/Web/Eng/siteeng0.nsf/html/new-weapons-publication-190106> (8 March 2007).

66. The Commission has recently been replaced by a Human Rights Council, which met for the first time in June 2006.

67. For material on the special procedures and on international human rights treaties, see the website of the Office of the UN High Commissioner for Human Rights at: <http://www.ohchr.org> (8 March 2007).

68. The Human Rights Committee, established under the International Covenant on Civil and Political Rights, and the Committee against Torture, under the Convention against Torture.

69. In order to have jurisdiction to hear a complaint brought by an individual, the State against which the claim is brought must have ratified both the International Covenant on Civil and Political Rights and the first Optional Protocol.

70. *European Convention on Human Rights* at: <http://www.echr.coe.int/echr> (8 March 2007); American Convention on Human Rights at: <http://www.cidh.org/Basicos/basic3.htm> (8 March 2007); Protocol to the African Charter on Human and Peoples' Rights on the Establishment of an African Court on Human and Peoples' Rights at: <http://www.africa-union.org/organs/orgCourt_of_Justice.htm> (8 March 2007).

71. Individuals have direct access to the European Court of Human Rights. In the case of the other two bodies, individuals have access to the relevant Commission, which in turn can refer a case to the Court.

72. In addition to a large number of UN General Assembly resolutions, two judgments of the ICJ confirm this position; the Advisory Opinion on the "Legality or Threat of Use of Nuclear Weapons," ICJ, 8 July 1996, paragraph 25 and the Advisory Opinion on "The Legal Consequences of the Construction of a Wall in the Occupied Palestinian Territory," ICJ, 9 July 2004, paragraphs 90 and 93.

73. For the views of international human rights bodies, see Human Rights Committee, General Comment No.29 on States of Emergency, CCPR/C/21/Rev.1/Add.11 and reports of the Working Group on Arbitrary Detention e.g. Report of the Working Group on Arbitrary Detention, (E/CN.4/2003/8), 16 December 2002, paras. 61–64.

74. For an example of its application, see *Anglo-Norwegian Fisheries Case*, ICJ, judgment of 18 December 1951.

75. Where a State knows of the prevailing interpretation at the time of ratification, it might be expected to enter a reservation. Where the interpretation only arises subsequent to the ratification, it would not be reasonable to deny the effectiveness of an objection by a State party on this basis but the State would be expected to indicate its objection at the earliest opportunity.

76. Such a situation arose before the former European Commission of Human Rights following the Turkish invasion of Cyprus. Since Turkey had not derogated from the Convention (a means established by the treaty for modifying, within limits, the scope of its obligations), the Commission applied the detention provision without modification. That meant that the detention of POWs was unlawful, because it was not a ground of detention recognized by the treaty. Had Turkey invoked the derogation clause, there is no doubt that the Commission would have accepted as lawful the detention of POWs. See generally 6780174 and 6950175, Report of the European Commission of Human Rights, adopted on 10 July 1976.

77. European Convention on Human Rights, Articles 2 and 5.

78. See Annex I to the third U.S. periodic report to the Human Rights Committee, CCPR/C/USA/3, 28 November 2005.

79. On occupied territory, see earlier references to Israel and the Occupied Territory and *Loizidou v. Turkey*, 15318/89, ECHR, judgment of 18 December 18 1996. On extra-territorial detention, see *Ocalan v. Turkey*, 46221/99, ECHR, Grand Chamber judgment of 12 May 2005.

80. For example, the attack on the RTS television station in Belgrade during the conflict between NATO and Serbia/Montenegro in relation to Kosovo; *Bankovic & Others v. Belgium & 16 Other Members of NATO*, 52207/99, ECHR, admissibility decision of 12 December 2001.

81. *Stewart v. United Kingdom*, 10044/82, European Commission of Human Rights, admissibility decision of 10 July 1984, 39 D & R 162.

82. *Güleç v. Turkey*, 54/1997/838/1044, ECHR, judgment of 27 July 1998, paragraph 71.

83. For example, *Abella v. Argentina, Case 11.137*, Report no. 55/97, Inter-Am.C.H.R., OEA/Ser.L/V/II.95 doc. 7 rev. at 271 (1997); *Bámaca Velásquez Case*, judgment of 25 November 2000, Inter-Am Ct. H.R. (Ser. C) no. 70 (2000).

84. For example, electronic attacks against computer networks would appear to qualify; Michael N. Schmitt and Brian T. O'Donnell, eds., *Computer Network Attack and International Law: International Law Studies, vol. 76* (Newport, RI: Naval War College, 2002): 568.

85. Nick Lewer and Steven Schofield, *Non-lethal Weapons: A Fatal Attraction?* (London: Zed Books, 1997).

86. Weapons which render death inevitable are prohibited according to the St. Petersburg Declaration of 1868.

87. Protocol I of 1977, Article 57.2.b.

88. *Ilhan v. Turkey*, 22277/93, ECHR, judgment of 27 June 2000. See also the discussion of the Moscow theater siege below.

89. For example, *Güleç*, see note 83. See also *Ergi v. Turkey*, 23818/94, ECHR, judgment of 28 July 1998, which would appear to have violated both the human rights and the LOAC prohibition of indiscriminate attacks. In *Isayeva, Yusupova and Bazayeva v. Russia*, 57947-49/00, ECHR, judgment of 24 February 2005, the Court did not consider the potential applicability of LOAC to killings during military operations in Chechnya. On the relationship between LOAC and human rights law, see Lubell, "Challenges in applying human rights law to armed conflicts" *International Review of the Red Cross* 860 (2005): 737.

90. European Convention on Human Rights, Article 2.

91. *Acar and others v. Turkey*, 36088/97 & 38417/97, ECHR, judgment of 24 May 2005; contrast *Ilhan*, note 89.

92. *McCann & others v. United Kingdom*, 18984/91, ECHR, judgment of 27 September 1995; see also *Ergi*, and European Convention on Human Rights, Article 2.

93. Where an applicant comes into a category of persons who are potentially affected by legislation, the applicant may challenge the legislation; e.g. a woman of childbearing age would be potentially affected by legislation prohibiting abortion, even if not pregnant at the time of the application. It is not clear whether this principle is only applicable in relation to legislation, or whether it can also be applied to the use of an allegedly unlawful weapon. Even if the argument could be made, it would probably only be applicable to a weapon whose use would be unlawful in all circumstances.

94. For an account of what occurred, see: <http://en.wikipedia.org/wiki/Moscow_Theatre_Siege>.

95. It has been claimed that the gas was an opiate, not a nerve agent, and most probably BMU8 added to a fentanyl derivative; see: <http://www.bbc.co.uk/science/horizon/2004/moscowtheatretrans.shtml>. A different report, from the head pharmacist in the Belgian armed forces, suggests that the substance was aerosolized fentanyl and gaseous halothane; See also *The Pharmaceutical Journal 269*, no.7224 (2002): 723. Also accessed at: <http://www.pjonline.com/Editorial/20021116/articles/moscow.html>. Whether the substance was in gaseous form or not would not be decisive to the application of the two conventions.

96. Protocol II applies to non-international armed conflicts between the State and non-State fighters in which the latter have such control over territory as to enable the conduct of sustained and concerted military operations. Judgment of the Constitutional Court of the Russian Federation of July 31, 1995 on the constitutionality of the Presidential Decrees and the Resolutions of the Federal Government concerning the situation in Chechnya, European Commission for Democracy through Law of the Council of Europe, CDL-INF (96), 1.

97. Henckaerts and Doswald-Beck, *Customary International Humanitarian Law* 1, 262. This suggests that the use of weapons prohibited by the Protocol would probably be regarded as unlawful in non-international conflicts.

98. It has been suggested that claims are precluded against the State in such circumstances; see: <http://www.chinadaily.com.cn/en/doc/2003-10/24/content_275270.htm>.

99. The Special Rapporteur on Extra-Judicial, Summary or Arbitrary Executions raised the matter: "Concern is also expressed about the actions by Russian police/security forces in the October 2002 incident in a Moscow theater where Chechen separatists were holding several hundred civilians hostage. During the attack against the separatists more than 100 civilians died, allegedly because of a gas deployed by the Russian forces to disable the hostage takers. The Special Rapporteur has been collecting information from various sources about the incident and plans to take the issue up in 2003 with the Government of the Russian Federation." Report E/CN.4/2003/3, 13 January 2003, paragraph 34, but there appears to be no reference to the incident in subsequent reports.

100. "Concluding Observations of the Human Rights Committee, Russian Federation, on June 11, 2003," CCPR/CO/79/RUS, paragraph 14.

101. This does not protect U.S. citizens from the exercise of the jurisdiction of national courts in the United States, whether state, federal or military.

102. See, in particular, the chapters by David Fidler and Adolf von Wagner in this volume.

103. It is highly unlikely that without the global campaign on antipersonnel landmines, the Ottawa Convention banning their acquisition, transfer or use would have been concluded or come into effect.

CHAPTER 13

Human Rights Law and the Use of Incapacitating Biochemical Weapons

William J. Aceves

Introduction

The debate over the development, production, and use of biochemical weapons has traditionally occurred within two distinct legal frameworks: international humanitarian law and the *lex specialis* regulating biochemical weapons.[1]

International humanitarian law, or *jus in bello*, regulates the treatment of civilians and combatants in times of armed conflict.[2] It also regulates the use of weapons and military tactics. Its norms are established through numerous international instruments as well as through the customary laws of war. The cornerstones of humanitarian law are set forth in the four Geneva Conventions of 1949 and the two 1977 Protocols.[3] These treaties are recognized as codifying customary international law with respect to international humanitarian law.[4] According to the International Court of Justice, these treaties "are to be observed by all States whether or not they have ratified the conventions that contain them, because they constitute intransgressible principles of international customary law."[5] Much of the debate over biochemical weapons has occurred within the strictures of international humanitarian law.[6]

The *lex specialis* regulating biochemical weapons consists of several international instruments, including the Biological Weapons Convention (BWC) and the Chemical Weapons Convention (CWC).[7] The BWC prohibits the development, production, stockpiling, acquisition, or retention of microbial or other biological agents or toxins.[8] The CWC prohibits the development, production, acquisition, stockpiling, retention, or use of chemical weapons.[9] The *lex specialis* regulating biochemical weapons is broader in nature than international humanitarian law because it is not limited to armed conflict situations. It regulates these weapons in times of peace and war.

While most of the debate over biochemical weapons has occurred within the confines of international humanitarian law and the *lex specialis* regulating biochemical weapons, there is another applicable regulatory framework: international criminal law.[10] The use of biochemical weapons can give rise to international criminal liability as a war crime, as a crime against humanity, or as an act of genocide.[11] In *The Zyklon B Case*, for example, a British military tribunal convicted German industrialists Bruno Tesch and Karl Weinbacher of war crimes for their role in supplying Zyklon B gas to Nazi Germany.[12] Zyklon B was an industrial pesticide used to kill thousands of prisoners in Nazi concentration camps during the Second World War.[13] More recent developments codify the prohibition against the use of biochemical weapons in the context of international criminal law. For example, the Rome Statute of the International Criminal Court asserts jurisdiction over war crimes, crimes against humanity, and genocide.[14] The use of "asphyxiating, poisonous or other gases, and all analogous liquids, materials or devices" is specifically listed as a war crime.[15] "Employing weapons, projectiles and material and methods of warfare which are of a nature to cause superfluous injury or unnecessary suffering or which are inherently indiscriminate in violation of the international law of armed conflict" also constitutes a war crime.[16]

This chapter suggests yet another legal framework that applies to biochemical weapons: human rights law.[17] Human rights law developed after the Second World War in response to the atrocities of that brutal conflict, particularly to those atrocities committed against civilians.[18] It is founded on the inherent dignity of the individual and the right of all people to be treated humanely and with respect. Human rights law is based on multiple international instruments, both multilateral and regional, and customary international law. It differs from international humanitarian law, international criminal law, and the *lex specialis* regulating biochemical weapons in several respects. Unlike international humanitarian law, human rights law is not limited to situations of armed conflict. Unlike international criminal law, human rights law regulates behavior that may not give rise to criminal liability. And unlike the *lex specialis* regulating biochemical weapons, human rights law is not limited to any particular weapon. Rather, it applies to all forms of state conduct and regulates all uses of official force. Thus, human rights law provides extensive protections for civilians and combatants, in times of peace and war.

In recent years, concern over the development and use of incapacitating biochemical weapons has increased. These weapons—from riot control agents to military munitions—are designed to incapacitate rather than kill.[19] Despite their stated objective, these weapons are capable of causing serious injury or even death. The purpose of this chapter, therefore, is to provide a brief overview of human rights law and consider its applicability to incapacitating biochemical weapons. While several human rights norms may be implicated, the right to life norm and the prohibition against cruel, inhuman, or degrading treatment are perhaps the most relevant norms for addressing these weapons. Both these norms protect the physical and mental integrity of the person. Both these norms also include a corollary obligation on the lawful use of force. Thus, principles of necessity, distinction, and proportionality are relevant considerations for gauging the lawful use of force and whether such force violates the right to life norm or the prohibition against cruel, inhuman, or degrading treatment.[20] In addition, human rights law represents an important regulatory framework because it promotes accountability for violations.[21] Accordingly, this chapter first examines the right to life norm as set forth in human rights law and considers its applicability to incapacitating biochemical weapons. The chapter then examines the prohibition against cruel, inhuman, or degrading treatment and considers its applicability. Finally, the relationship between human rights law and other regulatory norms involving incapacitating biochemical weapons is considered. It suggests that human rights law should play an important role in regulating these weapons.

The Right to Life Norm

The right to life norm, and its attendant restriction on the use of force, is perhaps the most firmly established human rights norm. It is enshrined in every major human rights instrument, including multilateral and regional agreements. Indeed, it is recognized as a *jus cogens* norm, a peremptory norm that allows for no derogation.[22]

The right to life norm is recognized in the International Covenant on Civil and Political Rights (ICCPR).[23] Article 6 of the ICCPR provides that "[e]very human being has the inherent right to life. This right shall be protected by law. No one shall be arbitrarily deprived of his life." The meaning of "arbitrarily" was discussed extensively throughout the negotiating process for the ICCPR. According to the *travaux préparatores*, delegates defined the word "arbitrarily" in various ways: "done capriciously or at pleasure; without adequate determining principle; depending on the will alone; tyrannical; despotic; without cause upon law; not governed by any fixed rule or standard."[24] They also found the term synonymous with the expression "without due process of law."[25]

The Human Rights Committee, which was established by the ICCPR to monitor compliance with the treaty, has clarified the meaning of the right to life norm on several occasions. In General Comment No. 6, the Human Rights

Committee indicated that the right to life is "the supreme right from which no derogation is permitted even in time of public emergency which threatens the life of the nation."[26] The Committee further noted that the deprivation of life "is a matter of the utmost gravity."[27] Therefore, states "have the supreme duty to prevent wars, acts of genocide and other acts of mass violence causing arbitrary loss of life."[28] While the Human Rights Committee has issued numerous statements regarding the right to life, it has seldom addressed the application of this norm to biochemical weapons. In its 2003 Concluding Observations to the Russian Federation, for example, the Committee referenced the October 2002 Moscow theater hostage crisis, where fentanyl gas was used to incapacitate the hostage takers but eventually killed 130 of the approximately 800 hostages:[29]

> While acknowledging the serious nature of the hostage-taking situation, the Committee cannot but be concerned at the outcome of the rescue operation in the Dubrovka theatre in Moscow on 26 October 2002. The Committee notes that various attempts to investigate the situation are still under way but expresses its concern that there has been no independent and impartial assessment of the circumstances, regarding medical care of the hostages after their liberation and the killing of the hostage-takers.[30]

The Committee requested that the Russian Federation investigate the incident, initiate prosecutions where appropriate, and offer compensation to victims. "The State party should ensure that the circumstances of the rescue operation in the Dubrovka theater are subject to an independent, in depth investigation, the results of which are made public, and, if appropriate, prosecutions are initiated and compensation paid to the victims and their families."[31]

The Commission on Human Rights and its subsidiary body, the Sub-Commission on the Promotion and Protection of Human Rights, have also addressed biochemical weapons, albeit briefly.[32] In 1996, for example, the Sub-Commission adopted a resolution expressing concern about the use of weapons with indiscriminate effects.[33] The Sub-Commission urged all states "to be guided in their national policies by the need to curb the production and spread of weapons of mass destruction or with indiscriminate effect, in particular nuclear weapons, chemical weapons, fuel-air bombs, napalm, cluster bombs, biological weaponry and weaponry containing depleted uranium."[34] In 1997, the Sub-Commission reiterated its concerns over the "use of weapons of mass or indiscriminate destruction or of a nature to cause superfluous injury or unnecessary suffering, both against members of the armed forces and against civilian populations, resulting in death, pain, misery and disability."[35] It also expressed concern over "repeated reports of the long-term consequences of the use of such weapons upon human life and health."[36] Even the Special Rapporteur on Extrajudicial, Summary or Arbitrary Executions, which was established by the Commission on Human Rights, has expressed concerns about excessive use of force by states, including the use of tear gas that lead to unexplained deaths.[37]

An integral feature of the right to life norm is the necessary restriction on the use of force. Several international instruments seek to clarify those situations where use of force is appropriate and these instruments have been applied in the context of the right to life norm.[38] For example, the UN Code of Conduct for Law Enforcement Officials was adopted by the UN General Assembly and describes the conditions for the lawful use of force by law enforcement officials.[39] It provides that law enforcement officials "shall respect and protect human dignity and maintain and uphold the human rights of all persons."[40] It then provides that "[l]aw enforcement officials may use force only when strictly necessary and to the extent required for the performance of their duty."[41] This provision is explained further by the accompanying commentary to the UN Code of Conduct.

(a) This provision emphasizes that the use of force by law enforcement officials should be exceptional; while it implies that law enforcement officials may be authorized to use force as is reasonably necessary under the circumstances for the prevention of crime or in effecting or assisting in the lawful arrest of offenders or suspected offenders, no force going beyond that may be used.

(b) National law ordinarily restricts the use of force by law enforcement officials in accordance with a principle of proportionality . . . In no case should this provision be interpreted to authorize the use of force which is disproportionate to the legitimate objective to be achieved.

(c) The use of firearms is considered an extreme measure. Every effort should be made to exclude the use of firearms, especially against children. In general, firearms should not be used except when a suspected offender offers armed resistance or otherwise jeopardizes the lives of others and less extreme measures are not sufficient to restrain or apprehend the suspected offender. In every instance in which a firearm is discharged, a report should be made promptly to the competent authorities.[42]

The UN Basic Principles on the Use of Force and Firearms by Law Enforcement Officials impose similar restrictions on the use of force by law enforcement officials.[43] In general, law enforcement officials may use force "only if other means remain ineffective or without any promise of achieving the intended result."[44] When the lawful use of force is unavoidable, the Basic Principles require that law enforcement officials:

(a) Exercise restraint in such use and act in proportion to the seriousness of the offence and the legitimate objective to be achieved;

(b) Minimize damage and injury, and respect and preserve human life;
(c) Ensure that assistance and medical aid are rendered to any injured or affected persons at the earliest possible moment;
(d) Ensure that relatives or close friends of the injured or affected person are notified at the earliest possible moment.[45]

The Basic Principles also contain specific provisions regarding non-lethal weapons. Governments and law enforcement agencies are encouraged to develop a range of weapons and ammunition that would allow for a differentiated use of force and firearms. "These should include the development of non-lethal incapacitating weapons for use in appropriate situations, with a view to increasingly restraining the application of means capable of causing death or injury to persons."[46] However, "[t]he development and deployment of non-lethal incapacitating weapons should be carefully evaluated in order to minimize the risk of endangering uninvolved persons, and the use of such weapons should be carefully controlled."[47]

The right to life norm and its attendant restrictions on the use of force are also recognized in regional agreements. Article 4(1) of the American Convention on Human Rights provides that "[e]very person has the right to have his life respected. This right shall be protected by law and, in general, from the moment of conception. No one shall be arbitrarily deprived of his life."[48] In *Neira Alegría*, the Inter-American Court of Human Rights considered whether Peru violated the right to life norm set forth in the American Convention when military personnel killed several prison inmates following a prison uprising.[49] While the Inter-American Court acknowledged the right of Peru to use force in the maintenance of state security, it also found that such action must be proportionate and must always comport with the obligations set forth in the American Convention, including the right to life set forth in Article 4.[50] Given that the Peruvian authorities used disproportionate force, the Inter-American Court held that "it may reasonably be concluded that [the victims] were arbitrarily deprived of their lives by the Peruvian forces in violation of Article 4(1) of the Convention."[51] In *Velásquez Rodríguez*, the Inter-American Court made similar references to the limitations on the power of the state to take action that may threaten the safety or well being of individuals.[52]

> Without question, the State has the right and duty to guarantee its security. It is also indisputable that all societies suffer some deficiencies in their legal orders. However, regardless of the seriousness of certain actions and the culpability of the perpetrators of certain crimes, the power of the State is not unlimited, nor may the State resort to any means to attain its ends. The State is subject to law and morality. Disrespect for human dignity cannot serve as the basis for any State action.[53]

The European human rights system also recognizes the right to life norm and its attendant restrictions on the use of force. Article 2(1) of the European Convention on the Protection of Human Rights and Fundamental Freedoms provides that "[e]veryone's right to life shall be protected by law. No one shall be deprived of his life intentionally save in the execution of a sentence of a court following his conviction of a crime for which this penalty is provided by law."[54] Article 2(2) then adds that "[d]eprivation of life shall not be regarded as inflicted in contravention of this article when it results from the use of force which is no more than absolutely necessary: (a) in defence of any person from unlawful violence; (b) in order to effect a lawful arrest or to prevent escape of a person lawfully detained; (c) in action lawfully taken for the purpose of quelling a riot or insurrection." In *McCann v. United Kingdom*, the European Court of Human Rights considered whether the United Kingdom violated Article 2 of the European Convention when British military personnel killed three Irish Republican Army terrorists in Gibraltar.[55] While the European Court acknowledged that states have a right and an obligation to protect against terrorist violence, it also established that there are strict limits on the use of force. Specifically, the use of force must be no more than absolutely necessary and must be strictly proportionate in order to comply with Article 2. Alternatives to lethal force must always be considered. In addition, law enforcement personnel must be adequately trained in the use of lethal force.

> [H]aving regard to the decision not to prevent the suspects from travelling into Gibraltar, to the failure of the authorities to make sufficient allowances for the possibility that their intelligence assessments might, in some respects at least, be erroneous and to the automatic recourse to lethal force when the soldiers opened fire, the Court is not persuaded that the killing of the three terrorists constituted the use of force which was no more than absolutely necessary in defence of persons from unlawful violence within the meaning of Article 2 . . . of the Convention.[56]

The European Court reiterated these principles regarding the right to life in *Akkum v. Turkey*, which involved the death of several individuals at the hands of Turkish security forces.[57]

> The text of Article 2, read as a whole, demonstrates that it covers not only intentional killing but also the situations where it is permitted to "use force" which may result, as an unintended outcome, in the deprivation of life. The deliberate or intended use of lethal force is only one factor, however, to be taken into account in assessing its necessity. Any use of force must be no more than "absolutely necessary" for the achievement of one or more of the purposes set out in sub-paragraphs

(a) to (c). .... In the light of the importance of the protection afforded by Article 2, the Court must subject deprivations of life to the most careful scrutiny, taking into consideration not only the actions of State agents but also all the surrounding circumstances. Use of force by State agents in pursuit of one of the aims delineated in paragraph 2 of Article 2 may be justified where it is based on an honest belief which is perceived for good reasons to be valid at the time but which subsequently turns out to be mistaken.[58]

In sum, the right to life norm places strict limits on the use of force, which includes the use of incapacitating biochemical weapons. As the October 2002 Moscow theater hostage crisis reveals, incapacitating weapons can cause loss of life. States must, therefore, act with due diligence in all cases involving these weapons. The use of these weapons must be carefully regulated and cannot cause indiscriminate harm. Their use must be proportionate to the perceived threat and must be justified under the circumstances. Thus, the right to life norm places significant restrictions on the use of incapacitating biochemical weapons.

The Prohibition against Cruel, Inhuman, or Degrading Treatment

The prohibition against cruel, inhuman, or degrading treatment is also firmly established in international law.[59] It is recognized as a *jus cogens* norm, applicable in times of peace and war and which allows for no derogation.

The prohibition against cruel, inhuman, or degrading treatment is recognized in all of the major multilateral human rights instruments.[60] The International Covenant on Civil and Political Rights provides that "[n]o one shall be subjected to torture or to cruel, inhuman, or degrading treatment or punishment."[61] The Human Rights Committee has indicated that the purpose of this provision is "to protect both the dignity and the physical and mental integrity of the individual."[62] Furthermore, the prohibition against cruel, inhuman or degrading treatment encompasses a wide variety of actions. Accordingly, the Committee has indicated that it is unnecessary "to draw up a list of prohibited acts or to establish sharp distinctions between the different kinds of punishment or treatment; these distinctions depend on the nature, purpose and severity of the treatment applied."[63]

The Convention against Torture and other Cruel, Inhuman or Degrading Treatment or Punishment (CAT) provides the most detailed definition of cruel, inhuman, or degrading treatment.[64] The definition of cruel, inhuman, or degrading treatment requires an initial reference to the definition of torture. Article 1 of the Convention against Torture provides:

For the purposes of this Convention, the term "torture" means any act by which severe pain or suffering, whether physical or mental, is intentionally inflicted on a person for such purposes as obtaining from him or a third person information or a confession, punishing him for an act he or a third person has committed or is suspected of having committed, or intimidating or coercing him or a third person, or for any reason based on discrimination of any kind, when such pain or suffering is inflicted by or at the instigation of or with the consent or acquiescence of a public official or other person acting in an official capacity. It does not include pain or suffering arising only from, inherent in or incidental to lawful sanctions.[65]

Article 16 then provides that "[e]ach State Party shall undertake to prevent in any territory under its jurisdiction other acts of cruel, inhuman or degrading treatment or punishment which do not amount to torture as defined in article 1, when such acts are committed by or at the instigation of or with the consent or acquiescence of a public official or other person acting in an official capacity."[66] The Committee against Torture, which was established to oversee implementation of the Convention against Torture, has indicated that the prohibition against cruel, inhuman, or degrading treatment is a fundamental principle of international law. It has also indicated that this norm applies even in times of war or national emergency.[67] The Committee against Torture has seldom addressed the application of the norm against cruel, inhuman, or degrading treatment to biochemical weapons. In 2005, for example, the Committee against Torture expressed concerns over Canada's use of incapacitating chemical weapons by law enforcement. The Committee expressed concern over "continued allegations of inappropriate use of chemical, irritant, incapacitating and mechanical weapons by law-enforcement authorities in the context of crowd control."[68] The concerns expressed by the Committee suggest that the use of incapacitating weapons may violate the prohibition against cruel, inhuman, or degrading treatment in some cases.

The prohibition against cruel, inhuman, or degrading treatment and its restrictions on the use of force are recognized in numerous international instruments. For example, the UN Code of Conduct for Law Enforcement Officials provides that: "[n]o law enforcement official may inflict, instigate or tolerate any act of torture or other cruel, inhuman or degrading treatment or punishment, nor may any law enforcement official invoke superior orders or exceptional circumstances such as a state of war or a threat of war, a threat to national security, internal political instability or any other public emergency as a justification of torture or other cruel, inhuman or degrading treatment or punishment."[69] The UN Special Rapporteur on the Question of Torture has also indicated that the prohibition on cruel, inhuman, or degrading treatment places limits upon the lawful use of force.[70] The Special Rapporteur has emphasized that the use of force must be regulated by principles of proportionality and that the disproportionate exercise of police powers might constitute cruel, inhuman, or degrading treatment.[71]

> In other words, since the enforcement of the law against suspected criminals, rioters or terrorists may legitimately require the use of force, and even of lethal weapons, by the police and other security forces, only if such use of force is disproportionate in relation to the purpose to be achieved and results in pain or suffering meeting a certain threshold, will it amount to cruel or inhuman treatment or punishment. Whether the use of force is to be qualified as lawful, in terms of article 16 of CAT or article 7 of ICCPR, or excessive depends on the proportionality of the force applied in a particular situation. Disproportionate or excessive exercise of police powers amounts to CIDT [cruel, inhuman, or degrading treatment] and is always prohibited.[72]

In establishing whether the use of force is disproportionate and violates the prohibition against cruel, inhuman, or degrading treatment, the Special Rapporteur has indicated that law enforcement officials must balance several factors, including: (1) the type of weapon used and the intensity of the force applied; (2) the effects on personal integrity; and (3) the objective that is sought.[73]

The prohibition against cruel, inhuman, or degrading treatment and its restrictions on the use of force are also recognized in regional agreements. For example, the European Convention provides that "[n]o one shall be subjected to torture or to inhuman or degrading treatment or punishment."[74] The European Court of Human Rights has indicated that this provision extends to acts that cause intense physical or mental suffering.[75] In *Selmouni v. France*, the European Court stressed that the prohibition against inhuman or degrading treatment is non-derogable (i.e., cannot be suspended) even in the most difficult circumstances, including the fight against terrorism.[76] In *Ribitsch v. Austria*, the European Court held that "in respect of a person deprived of his liberty, any recourse to physical force which has not been made strictly necessary by his own conduct diminishes human dignity and is in principle an infringement of the right set forth in Article 3 . . . of the Convention."[77]

Similarly, the American Convention on Human Rights provides that "[n]o one shall be subjected to torture or to cruel, inhuman, or degrading punishment or treatment."[78] In *Loayza-Tamayo v. Peru*, the Inter-American Court of Human Rights acknowledged that multiple factors are relevant in considering whether the prohibition against cruel, inhuman, or degrading treatment has been breached.

> The violation of the right to physical and psychological integrity of persons is a category of violation that has several gradations and em-

braces treatment ranging from torture to other types of humiliation or cruel, inhuman or degrading treatment with varying degrees of physical and psychological effects caused by endogenous and exogenous factors which must be proven in each specific situation.[79]

Referencing the case law of the European Court of Human Rights, the Inter-American Court indicated, "[a]ny use of force that is not strictly necessary to ensure proper behavior on the part of the detainee constitutes an assault on the dignity of the person . . . in violation of Article 5 of the American Convention."

In sum, international law prohibits cruel, inhuman, or degrading treatment. Determinations of whether such treatment has occurred require an assessment of all the circumstances in the case, including the form and duration of mistreatment, the level of suffering, the physical and mental status of the victim, and the purpose of the perpetrator.[80] While international law does not enumerate every form of conduct that would violate this fundamental prohibition, it remains a universal, definable, and obligatory norm. Any act of cruel, inhuman, or degrading treatment violates international law, and no circumstances whatsoever may be invoked to justify derogation. States can also be held accountable for violations of this fundamental norm. Thus, the prohibition against cruel, inhuman or degrading treatment places significant restrictions on the use of incapacitating biochemical weapons. These weapons are designed to impair the physical and mental integrity of the individual. Depending on the nature, duration, and long-term effects of this impairment, the use of incapacitating biochemical weapons can give rise to a claim of cruel, inhuman, or degrading treatment.

The Status of Human Rights Law

Human rights law, including the right to life norm and the prohibition against cruel, inhuman, or degrading treatment, has broad applicability. It is not limited to situations of armed conflict or to any particular weapon. Rather, it applies to all forms of state conduct and regulates all uses of official force, including actions of military personnel and law enforcement officials. It regulates state action in times of peace and war and protects combatants and civilians. The broad coverage of human rights law stands in contrast to the narrow parameters offered by other legal frameworks. Because of its broad applicability, the status of human rights law as an overarching legal framework, and its relationship to other regulatory frameworks, merits clarification.[81]

In the *Nuclear Weapons* case, the International Court of Justice (ICJ) examined whether the threat or use of nuclear weapons in any circumstance is permitted under international law. In its analysis, the Court examined the relationship between two legal frameworks: human rights law and international humanitarian law. It observed that the right to life norm as set forth in the International Covenant on Civil and Political Rights applies even in time of war.[82]

> The Court observes that the protection of the International Covenant of Civil and Political Rights does not cease in times of war, except by operation of Article 4 of the Covenant whereby certain provisions may be derogated from in a time of national emergency. Respect for the right to life is not, however, such a provision. In principle, the right not arbitrarily to be deprived of one's life applies also in hostilities. The test of what is an arbitrary deprivation of life, however, then falls to be determined by the applicable *lex specialis*, namely, the law applicable in armed conflict that is designed to regulate the conduct of hostilities.[83]

The ICJ indicated that the test of what constitutes an arbitrary deprivation of life in time of armed conflict must be determined by reference to international humanitarian law, which is designed to regulate the conduct of hostilities.

> Thus whether a particular loss of life, through the use of a certain weapon in warfare, is to be considered an arbitrary deprivation of life contrary to Article 6 of the Covenant [on Civil and Political Rights], can only be decided by reference to the law applicable in armed conflict and not deduced from the terms of the Covenant itself.[84]

In *Legal Consequences of the Construction of a Wall in the Occupied Palestinian Territories*, the ICJ examined the legal consequences arising from the construction of a wall being built by Israel in the Occupied Territories.[85] It was asked to examine this question in light of international law, including the 1949 Geneva Conventions as well as relevant UN Security Council and General Assembly resolutions. Israel asserted that human rights law, including the provisions of the International Covenant on Civil and Political Rights, did not apply to the Occupied Territories because "human rights treaties were intended for the protection of citizens from their own Government in times of peace."[86] The ICJ rejected this assertion, reiterating its position on the relationship between human rights law and humanitarian law.

> More generally, the Court considers that the protection offered by human rights conventions does not cease in case of armed conflict, save through the effect of provisions for derogation of the kind to be found in Article 4 of the International Covenant on Civil and Political Rights. As regards the relationship between international humanitarian law and human rights law, there are thus three possible

situations: some rights may be exclusively matters of international humanitarian law; others may be exclusively matters of human rights law; yet others may be matters of both these branches of international law. In order to answer the question put to it, the Court will have to take into consideration both these branches of international law, namely human rights law and, as *lex specialis*, international humanitarian law.[87]

The UN Human Rights Committee has made similar findings about the relationship between human rights law and humanitarian law. In its General Comment No. 31, the Committee examined the nature of the legal obligations established under the International Covenant on Civil and Political Rights.[88] According to the Committee:

> the Covenant applies also in situations of armed conflict to which the rules of international humanitarian law are applicable. While, in respect of certain Covenant rights, more specific rules of international humanitarian law may be especially relevant for the purpose of the interpretation of the Covenant rights, both spheres of law are complementary, not mutually exclusive.[89]

The Inter-American Commission on Human Rights has also discussed the relationship between human rights law and other international norms. In its 2002 report on Terrorism and Human Rights, the Commission offered an extensive analysis of the relationship between human rights law and humanitarian law.[90] It noted that the applicability of human rights law in the context of terrorist violence depends on the context of such violence.[91] In situations of peace, human rights law is fully applicable. In situations that threaten the independence or security of the state, human rights law is still applicable, but it is subject to the limited derogations recognized by law. In situations of armed conflict, human rights law applies in conjunction with humanitarian law.

> Nevertheless, the American Convention and other universal and regional human rights instruments were not designed specifically to regulate armed conflict situations and do not contain specific rules governing the use of force and the means and methods of warfare in that context. Accordingly, in situations of armed conflict, international humanitarian law may serve as *lex specialis* in interpreting and applying international human rights instruments. For example, both Article 4 of the American Convention and humanitarian law applicable to armed conflicts protect the right to life and, thus, prohibit summary executions in all circumstances. However, reference to Article 4 of the Convention alone may be insufficient to assess whether,

in situations of armed conflicts, the right to life has been infringed. This is in part because the Convention is devoid of rules that either define or distinguish civilians from combatants and other military targets. Nor does the Convention specify the circumstances under which it is not illegal, in the context of an armed conflict, to attack a combatant or civilian or when civilian casualties as a consequence of military operations do not imply a violation of international law. Consequently, in such circumstances, one must necessarily look to and apply definitional standards and relevant rules of international humanitarian law as sources of authoritative guidance in the assessment of the respect of the inter-American Instruments in combat situations.[92]

The Inter-American Commission has echoed these views in several cases.[93] In *Abella v. Argentina*, for example, the Commission stated that "[t]he American Convention, as well as other universal and regional human rights instruments, and the 1949 Geneva Conventions share a common nucleus of non-derogable rights and a common purpose of protecting human life and dignity. These human rights treaties apply both in peacetime, and during situations of armed conflict."[94] In situations where both human rights law and humanitarian law apply, the most favorable provisions should regulate treatment. Thus, "the Commission is duty bound to give legal effort to the provision(s) of that treaty with the higher standard(s) applicable to the right(s) or freedom(s) in question. If that higher standard is a rule of humanitarian law, the Commission should apply it."[95]

Finally, the International Committee of the Red Cross (ICRC) has noted the important relationship between human rights law and humanitarian law. In a speech by ICRC President Jacob Kellenberger to the UN Commission on Human Rights, he reiterated that human rights law and humanitarian law serve complementary functions.

> International humanitarian and human rights law are distinct bodies of law but complementary. Their complementary nature is evidenced, among other things, by their common underlying purpose, which is to protect the life, health and dignity of the individual. While one of the specific aims of international humanitarian law is to ensure the protection of persons affected by armed conflict and, in particular, of those who find themselves in the hands of the adversary, the purpose of human rights law is to govern the relationship between States and individuals. In either case, the guiding principle is that, because they are human, individuals have the right to be protected from arbitrary action and abuse.[96]

The relationship between human rights law and humanitarian law is indicative of how human rights law can interact with other regulatory frameworks. Human rights law does not replace humanitarian law in gauging the lawful use of force in situations of armed conflict. Rather, it functions alongside humanitarian law, providing guidance to the international community on the most effective manner to promote respect for human dignity in situations of armed conflict.[97] Theodor Meron has referred to this process as the "humanization of humanitarian law."[98] According to Meron, human rights law has already influenced the development of humanitarian law. To proceed, it will require even greater integration into the public consciousness. "Education, training, persuasion, and emphasis on values that lie outside the law, such as ethics, honor, mercy, and shame, must be vigorously pursued."[99]

A similar phenomenon, where human rights law informs other regulatory frameworks, can apply to international criminal law and the *lex specialis* regulating biochemical weapons. If there are differences between human rights law and these other regulatory frameworks, states should give legal effect to the provisions that offer the highest level of protection to individuals. The infusion of a human rights law framework into discussions on incapacitating biochemical weapons can highlight the importance of human dignity, foster accountability, and promote "innovations in the formation, formulation, and interpretation of rules."[100] For example, a human rights framework counsels against the use of weapons that are indiscriminate and that endanger innocent people. It counsels against the use of weapons that can cause superfluous injuries or suffering. Because incapacitating biochemical weapons impair the physical and mental integrity of the individual, their effects on human dignity and autonomy must be proportionate to the perceived harm their use seeks to avoid. Incapacitating weapons that can cause death must be subject to particularly stringent controls. Violations of these human rights norms should be subject to sanctions, both civil and criminal. And, these conditions apply in times of peace and war.

Conclusion

Incapacitating weapons were developed to incapacitate rather than kill. In principle, therefore, human rights law would support the use of incapacitating biochemical weapons as an alternative to the use of lethal weapons. This approach is preferable under human rights law, which places the right to life norm at the top of the hierarchy of protected norms.[101]

But the use of incapacitating biochemical weapons must also comport with the requirements of human rights law. Principles of necessity, distinction, and proportionality are relevant considerations for gauging the legitimacy of these weapons. Failure to comply with these requirements may violate human rights law, including the right to life norm as well as the prohibition against cruel, inhuman, or degrading treatment, and give rise to legal liability.

In 2003, Amnesty International expressed concerns about how weapons "ostensibly designed and promoted for security purposes" and designated as non-lethal could easily violate international human rights standards.[102] Amnesty International called on states to ensure that non-lethal weapons are properly tested to ensure compliance with human rights law. It also issued recommendations regarding the use of irritant chemical agents (although these principles would also apply to the use of incapacitating biological agents).

> Establish laws and regulations based upon international human rights standards to strictly control the use of chemical irritants in law enforcement, and establish effective monitoring mechanisms to ensure such laws and regulations are adhered to, and kept under review; prohibit the indiscriminate or arbitrary use of riot control irritants such as tear gas on people in confined spaces;
>
> Refrain from using irritant chemical agents designed to sedate people for law enforcement purposes unless it can be demonstrated impartially that the agent has been proven to have legitimate use with a suitable margin of safety which will ensure that individuals are only exposed to incapacitating and not lethal concentrations, and will be protected from indiscriminate or arbitrary effects as required by international human rights standards;
>
> Suspend the deployment and transfer of those types of pepper spray or other chemical irritants, which have revealed a substantial risk of abuse, unwarranted injury or death, pending a rigorous and independent inquiry into its effects in each case by appropriate medical, legal, police and other experts. Publish the results of the inquiry on each type and sub-type of such weapons and demonstrate before the legislature/parliament in each case that the effects are consistent with international human rights standards before making any decision on deployment.[103]

Other human rights organizations have expressed similar concerns.[104]

Because incapacitating biochemical weapons offer both promise and peril to human rights, their development and use should be regulated by human rights law. Otherwise, the dominant legal framework on human dignity is excluded from the debate over weapons that can cause human suffering and death through their impairment of the physical and mental integrity of the individual.

Acknowledgements: Lauren Bortolotti, Shaun Dunning, Kevin Gupta, Victor Herrera, and Melissa Robbins provided excellent research assistance.

Notes

1. *Lex specialis* is Latin for "specific law."

2. See Jean-Marie Henckaerts, "Study on Customary International Humanitarian Law: A Contribution to the Understanding and Respect for the Rule of Law in Armed Conflict," *International Review of the Red Cross* 87, no. 857 (March 2005): 175–212; Mary Ellen O'Connell, *International Law and the Use of Force* (Eagan, MN: Foundation Press, 2004); William V. Dunlap, R. John Pritchard and John Carey, eds., *International Humanitarian Law: Origins* (Ardsley, NY: Transnational Publishers, 2003); Frits Kalshoven and Liesbeth Zegveld, *Constraints on the Waging of War: An Introduction to International Humanitarian Law*, 3rd Edition (Geneva: International Committee of the Red Cross, 2003).

3. "Convention for the Amelioration of the Condition of the Wounded and Sick in Armed Forces in the Field, August 12, 1949," 75 *United Nations Treaty Series* 31 (hereafter *UNTS*); "Convention for the Amelioration of the Condition of the Wounded, Sick and Shipwrecked Members of the Armed Forces at Sea, August 12, 1949," 75 *UNTS* 85; "Convention Relative to the Treatment of Prisoners of War, August 12, 1949," 75 *UNTS* 135; "Convention Relative to the Protection of Civilian Persons in Time of War, August 12, 1949," 75 *UNTS* 287; "Protocol Additional to the Geneva Conventions of 12 August 1949, and Relating to the Protection of Victims of International Armed Conflicts, December 12, 1977," 1125 *UNTS* 3; "Protocol Additional to the Geneva Conventions of 12 August 1949, and Relating to the Protection of Victims of Non-International Armed Conflicts, June 8, 1977," 1125 *UNTS* 609.

4. Other humanitarian law agreements include the Convention for the Protection of Cultural Property in the Event of Armed Conflict, the Conventional Weapons Convention, and the Ottawa Convention on Anti-Personnel Mines. See "Convention for the Protection of Cultural Property in the Event of Armed Conflict, May 14, 1954," 249 *UNTS* 240; "Convention on Prohibitions or Restrictions on the Use of Certain Conventional Weapons Which May Be Deemed to Be Excessively Injurious or to Have Indiscriminate Effects, April 10, 1981," 1342 *UNTS* 7; "Convention on the Prohibition of the Use, Stockpiling, Production and Transfer of Anti-Personnel Mines and on Their Destruction, September 18, 1997," 2056 *UNTS* 211.

5. "Legality of the Threat or Use of Nuclear Weapons," Advisory Opinion, 1996, *International Court of Justice (ICJ)* 226 (3 July 1996): paragraph 79.

6. See, for example, David Fidler, "International Law and Weapons of Mass Destruction: End of the Arms Control Approach?" *Duke Journal of Comparative and International Law* 14, no. 1 (Winter/Spring 2004): 39–88; M. Cherif Bassiouni, ed., *A Manual on International Humanitarian Law and Arms Control Agreements* (Ardsley, NY: Transnational Publishers, 2000); Cf. Mark Wheelis and Malcom Dando, "Neurobiology: A Case

Study of the Imminent Militarization of Biology," *International Review of the Red Cross* 87, no. 859 (September 2005): 553-572.

7. See Walter Krutzsch, ed., *A Commentary on the Chemical Weapons Convention* (Berlin: Springer, 1994); Erhard Geissler, ed., *Strengthening the Biological Weapons Convention by Confidence-Building Measures* (Oxford: Oxford University Press, 1990); Victoria Sutton, *Law and Bioterrorism* (Durham, NC: Carolina Academic Press, 2003).

8. "Convention on the Prohibition of the Development, Production and Stockpiling of Bacteriological and Toxin Weapons and on their Destruction, Apr. 10, 1972," 163 *UNTS* 1015.

9. "Convention on the Prohibition of the Development, Production, Stockpiling and Use of Chemical Weapons and on their Destruction, Jan. 13, 1993," 1974 *UNTS* 317.

10. See Barry Kellman, "Responses to the September 11 Attacks: An International Criminal Law Approach to Bioterrorism," *Harvard Journal of Law and Public Policy* 25, no. 2 (Spring 2002): 721-742; John Dugard, "Bridging the Gap Between Human Rights and Humanitarian Law: The Punishment of Offenders," *International Review of the Red Cross* 80, no. 324 (1998): 445–53.

11. See John C. Watkins, Jr. and John Paul Weber, *War Crimes and War Crime Trials: From Leipzig to the ICC and Beyond* (Durham: Carolina Academic Press, 2006); Jordan J. Paust and others, *International Criminal Law: Cases and Materials*, 2nd edition (Durham: Carolina Academic Press, 2000).

12. See British Military Court Hamburg, "Trial of Bruno Tesch and Two Others (The Zyklon B Case)," in *Law Reports of War Criminals, United National War Crimes Commission, Volume 1* (London: HMSO, 1947): 93–103. See also *United States v. Carl Krauch*, in *Trials of War Criminals Before the Nuremberg Military Tribunals Under Control Council Law No. 10*, VIII (Mazal Library, 1950), 1081.

13. In contrast, atrocities committed by the Japanese army's bacteriological weapons program did not lead to war crimes prosecution. See Yves Beigbeder, *Judging War Criminals: The Politics of International Justice* (New York: St. Martin's Press, 1999), 72–75.

14. "Rome Statute of the International Criminal Court, July 17, 1998," 2187 *UNTS* 3. The Iraqi Special Tribunal, which was established to prosecute perpetrators of atrocities committed during the Saddam Hussein era, contains similar provisions regarding genocide, war crimes, and crimes against humanity. "Statute of the Iraqi Special Tribunal, Coalition Provisional Authority Order No. 48 of 2003," *Iraqi Official Gazette*, December 10, 2003, Article 127. Significantly, Hussein and several other defendants were charged by the Special Tribunal with genocide and crimes against humanity for atrocities committed against Iraqi Kurds, which includes the 1988 chemical attacks on the town of Halabja that killed 5,000 people and injured 10,000. See Edward Wong, "Hussein Charged with Genocide in 50,000 Deaths," *New York Times*, 5 April 2006, at A1; Aamer Madhani, "Hussein Charged with '80s Genocide," *Chicago Tribune*, 5 April 2006, at 1. See Margaret Sewell, "Freedom from Fear: Prosecuting the Iraqi Regime for the Use of Chemical Weapons," *St. Thomas Law Review* 16, no.2 (2004): 365.

15. "Rome Statute of the International Criminal Court," Article 8(2)(b) (xviii).

16. "Rome Statute of the International Criminal Court," Article 8(2)(b) (xx).

17. See Kenneth Watkin, "Controlling the Use of Force: A Role for Human Rights Norms in Contemporary Armed Conflict," *American Journal of International Law* 98 (2004): 1; Peter Weiss & John Burroughs, "Weapons of Mass Destruction and Human Rights," *Disarmament Forum* 25 (2004); Jordan Paust, "The Right to Life in Human Rights Law and the Laws of War," *Saskatchewan Law Review* 65 (2002): 411.

18. See Henry J. Steiner and Philip Alston, *International Human Rights in Context*, 2nd ed. (Oxford: Oxford University Press, 1996); Louis Henkin, ed. *Human Rights* (Eagan, MN: Foundation Press, 1999).

19. See Nick Lewer & Neil Davison, "Non-Lethal Technologies: An Overview," *Disarmament Forum* 37 (2005); David Fidler, "The Meaning of Moscow: 'Non-Lethal' Weapons and International Law in the Early 21st Century," *International Review of the Red Cross* 87 (2005): 525.

20. Gabriel Swiney, "Saving Lives: The Principle of Distinction and the Realities of Modern War," *International Law* 39 (2005): 733; Michael N. Schmitt, "The Principle of Discrimination in 21st Century Warfare," *Yale Human Rights & Development Law Journal* 2 (1999): 143; Judith Gail Gardam, "Proportionality and Force in International Law," *American Journal of International Law* 87 (1993): 391.

21. Dinah Shelton, *Remedies in International Human Rights Law*, 2nd ed., (Oxford, New York: Oxford University Press, 2005).

22. No multilateral or regional human rights instrument allows derogation from the right to life norm. See Thomas Buergenthal & Dinah Shelton, *Protecting Human Rights in the Americas*, 4th ed., (Arlington: N. P. Engel, 1995); Joan Fitzpatrick, *Human Rights in Crisis: The International System for Protecting Rights During States of Emergency*, (Philadelphia: University of Philadelphia Press, 1994).

23. "International Covenant on Civil and Political Rights, Mar. 23, 1976," 999 *UNTS* 171. As of 1 April 2006, there are 156 States Parties to the ICCPR.

24. Marc J. Bossuyt, *Guide to the Travaux Préparatoires of the International Covenant on Civil and Political Rights*, 123 (Dordrecht: Martinus Nijhoff, 1987).

25. Bossuyt, *Guide to the Travaux Préparatoires*, 124.

26. Human Rights Committee, "General Comment No. 6," paragraph 1 (1982), Compilation of General Comments and General Recommendations Adopted by Human Rights Treaty Bodies," *U.N. Doc. HRI/GEN/1/Rev.7* at 128 (2004).

27. Human Rights Committee, "General Comment No. 6," paragraph 3

28. Human Rights Committee, "General Comment No. 6," paragraph 2.

29. See John Daniszewski & David Holley, "At Least 90 Captives Die in Moscow Raid," *Los Angeles Times*, 27 October 2002, at A1; Michael Wines, "Hostage Drama in Moscow," *New York Times*, 27 October 2002, at A1.

30. Russian Federation, "Concluding Observations of the Human Rights Committee: Russian Federation, *U.N. Doc. CCPR/CO/79/RUS*, 2003," paragraph 14.

31. Russian Federation, "Concluding Observations."

32. Both the Commission on Human Rights and the Sub-Commission have undergone significant structural changes in recent years. In 2006, the Commission on Human Rights was replaced by the Human Rights Council. In 1999, the Sub-Commission on the Prevention of Discrimination and Protection of Minorities was renamed the Sub-Commission on the Promotion and Protection of Human Rights.

33. "U.N. Sub-Commission on Prevention of Discrimination and Protection of Minorities, International Peace and Security as an Essential Condition for the Enjoyment of Human Rights, Above All the Right to Life, Res. 1996/16," *U.N. Doc. E/CN.4/SUB.2/RES/1996/16* (1996).

34. "U.N. Sub-Commission on Prevention of Discrimination, 1996/16" paragraph 1.

35. "U.N. Sub-Commission on Prevention of Discrimination and Protection of Minorities, International Peace and Security as an Essential Condition for the Enjoyment of Human Rights, Above All the Right to Life, Res. 1997/36," *U.N. Doc. E/CN.4/SUB.2/RES/1997/36* (1997).

36. "U.N. Sub-Commission on Prevention of Discrimination, 1997/36."

37. See "Commission on Human Rights, Report of the Special Rapporteur, Philip Alston," *U.N. Doc. E/CN.4/2006/53 Add.1* (2005), 317-319 (expressing concern regarding deaths possibly caused by use of tear gas).

38. See International Committee of the Red Cross, "Guide for Police Conduct and Behavior" (Geneva: International Committee of the Red Cross, 2004); Ralph Crawshaw, Barry Devlin, and Tom Williamson, *Human Rights and Policing*, (Boston: Springer, 1998).

39. "U.N. Code of Conduct for Law Enforcement Officials, G.A. Res. 34/169," *U.N. Doc. A/34/46*, (1979).

40. "U.N. Code of Conduct," Article 2.

41. "U.N. Code of Conduct," Article 3.

42. "U.N. Code of Conduct," Article 3 (commentary).

43. "Basic Principles on the Use of Force and Firearms by Law Enforcement Officials," *U.N. Doc. A/CONF.144/28Rev. 1* at 112 (1990).

44. "Basic Principles on the Use of Force," paragraph 4.

45. "Basic Principles on the Use of Force," paragraph 5.

46. "Basic Principles on the Use of Force," paragraph 2.

47. "Basic Principles on the Use of Force," paragraph 3.

48. "American Convention on Human Rights, Article 4(1), Nov. 22, 1969," *O.A.S.T.S.* no. 36, at 1.

49. *Neira Alegría*, 1995 Inter-Am. Ct. H.R. (ser. C) No. 20 (19 January 1995).

50. *Neira Alegría*, paragraph 74.

51. *Neira Alegría*, paragraph 76.

52. *Velásquez Rodríguez*, 1988 Inter-Am. Ct. H.R. (ser. C) No. 4 (29 July 1988).

53. *Velásquez Rodríguez*, paragraph 154 (emphasis added); *Godinez Cruz*, 1989 Inter-Am. Ct. H.R. (ser. C) No. 5 (20 January 1989), paragraph 162; Gangaram Panday, 1994 Inter-Am. Ct. H.R. (ser. C) No. 16 (21 January 1994), paragraph 4 (dissenting opinion).

54. "European Convention for the Protection of Human Rights and Fundamental Freedoms, Article 2(1), Sept. 3, 1953," 213 *UNTS* 222.

55. *McCann v. United Kingdom*, 21 European Human Rights Report 97 (1996).

56. *McCann v. United Kingdom*, 176–77. See also *Andronicou and Constantinou v. Cyprus*, 25 European Human Rights Report 491, 545 (1998). ("[T]he Court must, in making its assessment, subject deprivations of life to the most careful scrutiny, particularly where deliberate lethal force is used, taking into consideration not only the actions of the agents of the state who actually administer the force but also all the surrounding

circumstances, including such matters as the planning and control of the actions under examination."); *K.H.W. v. Germany,* 36 European Human Rights Report 59 (2003).

57. *Akkum v. Turkey,* Human Rights Law Journal 26 (2005): 352.

58. *Akkum v. Turkey,* 368.

59. See Nigel S. Rodley, *The Treatment of Prisoners under International Law* 2nd ed., (Oxford: Clarendon Press, 1999); J. Herman Burgers & Hans Danelius, *The United Nations Convention Against Torture: A Handbook on the Convention against Torture and Other Cruel, Inhuman or Degrading Treatment or Punishment,* Dordrecht: Martinus Nijhoff, 1988).

60. See, "Universal Declaration of Human Rights, G.A. Res. 217A (III), Article 5," *U.N Doc. A/810* at 71, Dec. 12, 1948 ("No one shall be subjected to torture or to cruel, inhuman or degrading treatment or punishment"); "International Covenant on Civil and Political Rights," Article 7 ("No one shall be subjected to torture or to cruel, inhuman or degrading treatment or punishment").

61. "International Covenant on Civil and Political Rights," Article 7.

62. "Human Rights Committee, General Comment No. 20," paragraph 2 (1992), Compilation of General Comments and General Recommendations Adopted by Human Rights Treaty Bodies, U.N. Doc. HRI/GEN/1/Rev.7 at 150 (2004).

63. "Human Rights Committee, General Comment No. 20," paragraph 4; "Human Rights Committee, General Comment No. 7, paragraph 2 (1982): Compilation of General Comments and General Recommendations Adopted by Human Rights Treaty Bodies," *U.N. Doc. HRI/GEN/1/Rev.7* at 129 (2004).

64. "Convention against Torture and Other Cruel, Inhuman or Degrading Treatment or Punishment," Dec. 10, 1984, 1465 *UNTS* 85. As of 1 April 2006, there are 141 States Parties to the Convention.

65. "Convention against Torture," Article 1.

66. "Convention against Torture," Article 16.

67. Following the attacks of 11 September 2001, for example, the Committee against Torture reiterated that the prohibition allows for no derogation and must be observed in all circumstances; U.N. Committee against Torture, "Statement of the U.N. Committee against Torture," *U.N. Doc. CAT/C/XXVII/Misc.7* (22 November 2001).

68. "Conclusions and Recommendations of the Committee against Torture: Canada," *U.N. Doc. CAT/C/CO/34/CAN,* (2005): paragraph 4(i).

69. UN Code of Conduct for Law Enforcement Officials, supra note 39, at Article 5.

70. The Special Rapporteur was established by the Commission on Human Rights in 1985 to consider the question of torture and other cruel, inhuman, or degrading treatment. "Commission on Human Rights, Torture and Other Cruel, Inhuman or Degrading Treatment or Punishment: Report by the Special Rapporteur, Mr. P. Kooijmans Appointed Pursuant to Commission on Human Rights Resolution 1985/33," *U.N. Doc. E/CN.4/1986/15* (1986).

71. "U.N. Commission on Human Rights, Civil and Political Rights, Including the Questions of Torture and Detention, Report of the Special Rapporteur on the Question of Torture," *U.N. Doc. E/CN.4/2006/6* (2005).

72. "U.N. Commission on Human Rights," 12-13.

73. "U.N. Commission on Human Rights," 14.

74. European Convention, Article 3.

75. *Ireland v. United Kingdom*, 2 European Human Rights Report 25, 80 (1979-1980).

76. *Selmouni v. France*, 29 European Human Rights Report 403, 440 (2000).

77. *Ribitsch v. Austria*, 21 European Human Rights Report 573, 603 (1996).

78. American Convention, Article 5.

79. *Loayza-Tamayo v. Peru*, 1997 Inter-American Court Human Rights (Ser. C) No. 33 (17 September 1997), paragraph 57 (citing *Ribitsch v. Austria*).

80. For example, acts are considered cruel if they "cause [. . .] serious mental or physical suffering or injury or constitute [. . .] a serious attack on human dignity." *Prosecutor v. Kordic and Cerkez*, Case No. IT-95-14/2, Judgment, paragraph 265 (26 February 2001); *Prosecutor v. Blaskic*, Case No. IT-95-14-T, Judgment, paragraphs 186, 700 (3 March 2000); *Prosecutor v. Jelisic*, Case No. IT-95-10, Judgment, paragraphs 34, 41 (14 December 1999). Inhuman treatment covers treatment that "deliberately causes severe suffering, mental or physical, which, in the particular situation, is unjustifiable." *The Greek Case*, 12 Y.B. European Convention on Human Rights 1, 186 (1969) (European Commission on Human Rights); See also *Prosecutor v. Delalic*, Case No. IT-96-21-T, ICTY (Trial Chamber), Nov. 16, 1998, paragraph 543. Inhuman treatment also covers conduct that "constitutes a serious attack on human dignity." *Prosecutor v. Delalic*, Case No. IT-96/21-T, Judgment, paragraph 543 (16 November 1998). Degrading treatment includes actions meant "to arouse in their victims feelings of fear, anguish and inferiority capable of humiliating and debasing them and possibly breaking their physical or moral resistance." *Ireland v. United Kingdom*, 80, European Human Rights Report.

81. Hans-Joachim Heintze, "On the Relationship Between Human Rights Law Protection and International Humanitarian Law," *International Review of the Red Cross* 86, 789 (2004); Robert Kolb, "The Relationship Between International Humanitarian Law and Human Rights Law: A Brief History of the 1948 Universal Declaration of Human Rights and the 1949 Geneva Conventions," *International Review of the Red Cross* 80 (1998): 409; Françoise J. Hampson, "Using International Human Rights Machinery to Enforce the International Law of Armed Conflicts," *Revue de droit militaire et de droit de la guerre* 31 (1992): 119.

82. "Legality of the Threat or Use of Nuclear Weapons," paragraph 25.

83. "Legality of the Threat or Use of Nuclear Weapons," paragraph 25.

84. "Legality of the Threat or Use of Nuclear Weapons," paragraph 25; "Special Issue: The Advisory Opinion of the International Court of Justice on the Legality of Nuclear Weapons and International Humanitarian Law," *International Review of the Red Cross* 79 (1997): 3.

85. "Legal Consequences of the Construction of a Wall in the Occupied Palestinian Territories," Advisory Opinion, 2004 *ICJ* (9 July 2004).

86. "Legal Consequences of the Construction," paragraph 102.

87. "Legal Consequences of the Construction," paragraph 106.

88. UN Human Rights Committee, "General Comment No. 31," *U.N. Doc. CCPR/C/21/Rev.1/Add.13* (2004).

89. UN Human Rights Committee, "General Comment No. 31," paragraph 11.
90. Inter-American Commission on Human Rights, "Report on Terrorism and Human Rights," OEA/Ser.L/V/II.116 Doc. 5 rev. 1 corr. (22 October 2002).
91. Inter-American Commission on Human Rights, "Report on Terrorism and Human Rights," paragraph 18.
92. Inter-American Commission on Human Rights, "Report on Terrorism and Human Rights," paragraph 61.
93. See, e.g., *Abella v. Argentina*, Case 11.137, Inter-Am. C.H.R., Report No. 55/97, OEA/Ser.L/V/II.95 doc.7 rev. (1997); *Avilan v. Colombia*, Case 11.142, Inter-Am. C.H.R., Report No. 26/97, OEA/Ser.L/V/II.98 doc. 6 rev. (1998).
94. *Abella v. Argentina*, paragraph 158; Liesbeth Zegveld, "The Inter-American Commission on Human Rights and Humanitarian Law: A Comment on the Tablada Case," *International Review of the Red Cross* 90 (1998): 505.
95. *Abella v. Argentina*, at paragraph 165.
96. See President of the International Committee of the Red Cross Jacob Kellenberger's speech to the UN Commission on Human Rights, delivered 17 March 2004.
97. Cf. *Prosecutor v. Furundzija*, Case No. IT-95-17/1-T, Judgment, paragraph 183, 10 December 1998; "The general principle of respect for human dignity is . . . of such paramount importance as to permeate the whole body of international law."
98. Theodor Meron, "The Humanization of Humanitarian Law," *American Journal International Law* 94 (2000): 239; Robin Coupland, "Humanity: What Is It and How Does It Influence International Law?" *International Review of the Red Cross* 83 (2001): 969.
99. Meron, "Humanization of Humanitarian Law," 278.
100. Meron, "Humanization of Humanitarian Law," 239.
101. See Laura S. Ziemer, "Application in Tibet of the Principles on Human Rights and the Environment," *Harvard Human Rights Journal* 14 (2001): 233, 245 ("The right to life is the most important of all human rights legally guaranteed and protected by contemporary international law."); Roger Normand & Christoph Wilcke, "Human Rights, Sanctions, and Terrorist Threats: The United Nations Sanctions Against Iraq," *Transnational Law & Contemporary Problems* 11 (2001): 339 ("The right to life is the most important human right, which the UN Human Rights Committee considers to be 'the supreme right from which no derogation is permitted even in time of public emergency.'" See "General Comments Under Article 40, Paragraph 4, of the Covenant, U.N. GAOR, Human Rights Committee, 40th Session, Supp. No. 40," *U.N. Doc. A/40/40* (1984)). See also Dinah Shelton, "Normative Hierarchy in International Law," *American Journal of International Law* 100 (2006): 291; Dinah Shelton, "Hierarchy of Norms and Human Rights: Of Trumps and Winners," *Saskatchewan Law Review* 65 (2002): 299; Francisco Forrest Martin, "Delineating a Hierarchical Outline of International Law Sources and Norms," *Saskatchewan Law Review* 65 (2002): 333; Theodor Meron, "On a Hierarchy of International Human Rights," *American Journal of International Law* 80 (1986): 1. See also Prosper Weil, "Towards Relative Normativity in International Law?" *American Journal of International Law* 77 (1983): 413.

102. Amnesty International, "The Pain Merchants: Security Equipment and its Use in Torture and Other Ill-Treatment," 73 (2 December 2003).

103. Amnesty International, "The Pain Merchants," 76–77.

104. See "Human Rights Watch, Independent Commission of Inquiry Must Investigate Raid on Moscow Theater: Inadequate Preparation for Consequences of Gas Violates Obligation to Protect Life," (30 October 2002).

CHAPTER 14

Protecting and Reinforcing Humanitarian Norms: The Way Forward

Peter Herby

Discussions about the use of weapons labelled "non-lethal" for riot control, hostage rescue, peace keeping and peace enforcement operations as well as in "traditional" battlefield situations have focused mainly on the technology and engagement doctrine of these new weapons. "Biochemical weapons" are increasingly being talked about as a possible "non-lethal" option for armed forces.

While there may be debate about the effects, utility and legality of some other types of weapons being promoted as "non-lethal," for the International Committee of the Red Cross (ICRC), the use in armed conflict of any biological or chemical weapon, whatever its purported lethality, would represent a clear violation of the 1925 Geneva Protocol, the 1993 Chemical Weapons Convention (CWC), the 1972 Biological Weapons Convention (BWC) and Customary International Law. Nonetheless, these important norms are under pressure today as never before as a result of advances in medical knowledge, chemistry and the life sciences. Yielding to the temptation to gain tactical advantage from technological advances, to bend or rewrite the rules and to ignore age-old taboos in this field may bring short term gain for some. But this is also the most likely path back to chemical and biological warfare—the complete prohibition of which was one of the important achievements of the twentieth century.

There is an understandable desire to consider the use of certain new biochemical technologies in a domestic law enforcement context. However even in that domain it is essential to proceed cautiously and to carefully consider issues such as: the short- and long-term health consequences, human rights issues and, perhaps most importantly, the implications of the entirely predictable proliferation of such weapons and their use by non-State actors. Whatever one's analysis of implications for domestic law enforcement, it is clear that there is pressure from many quarters to also equip military forces with chemical incapacitants. There is a small but growing body of opinion that both the BWC and the CWC will need to be revised to permit use of such weapons. The ICRC is totally opposed to permitting the use of any chemical or biological weapons, whatever their mode of action, as a means of warfare.

It is not only the prohibition on the use of poison in warfare that risks being undermined by the introduction of biochemical incapacitants. Several of the most fundamental rules of international humanitarian law are also at stake. Among these are:

1. The absolute prohibition of attacks on civilians and of attacks which do not distinguish between civilians and military objectives. In discussions of potential scenarios for the use of incapacitants in situations in which civilians are interspersed with combatants are consistently mentioned. Yet under international humanitarian law indiscriminate attacks are illegal. It is likely that the use of incapacitants will lower the threshold for attacks that affect civilians and combatants without distinction, with an inherent risk that this rule will be undermined.

2. The protection of soldiers who are no longer participating in hostilities. The law of war prohibits attacks on fighters who are out of combat when they have been rendered unconscious or have otherwise been incapacitated by wound or sickness and are therefore incapable of defending themselves. It also protects those who have clearly signalled their intention to surrender.

    But how will a soldier, in the heat of battle, recognize that their opponent is rendered *hors de combat* by an incapacitant especially if the incapacitation is partial and so it may appear that the person is still capable of using his or her weapons? And how will a soldier who has been incapacitated be in a position to signal his or her intention to surrender?

3. The prohibition of weapons which are of a nature to cause superfluous injury or unnecessary suffering or, in lay terms, which cause injury that is more severe than that needed to take a soldier out of action. We cannot assume that "non-lethal" biochemical weapons would merely incapacitate by making a person sleep. Would not lifelong epileptic convulsions, permanent damage to internal organs, long-term and severe vomiting, or an extended coma risk violating the prohibition on "superfluous injury or unnecessary suffering?" Indeed one "non-lethal" weapon, namely blinding lasers, has already been prohibited due to the permanent and severe nature of the injury it was designed to inflict.

In addition to these specific rules there is considerable risk that the overall objective of international humanitarian law, to reduce the "human cost" of warfare, could also be threatened. The use of biochemical incapacitants in combination with conventional weapons could have just such an effect by disabling soldiers who are then more exposed to lethal force. If soldiers are unable to determine who is out of action and who is not, and military officers tell us this would be extremely difficult with incapacitants, then both types of force are likely to be used in combination. The result could be just the opposite of what the term "non-lethal" means: an overall increase in the lethality of warfare.

It is also important to consider the subtle messages that are being reinforced in every conference and article on so-called "non-lethal weapons" (and we are thankful that this symposium did not use that label). The messages are:

- that a new type of weapon exists which is "non-lethal";
- that any injury sustained by a soldier will be less serious than an injury from a conventional weapon;
- that as a result of these new weapons, the technical means exists to inflict a level of injury on civilians—either intentionally or unintentionally—that is acceptable;
- that due to the above factors, international humanitarian law does not need to be applied in the same way to the use of this type of weapon;
- that disarmament agreements, such as the Biological and Chemical Weapons Conventions, which were negotiated before the emergence of "non-lethal" weapons, are outdated and need to be revisited; and
- that in targeting decisions the requirement to distinguish between civilians and soldiers does not need to be applied as rigorously when "non-lethal" weapons are being used.

It is also important to recall the "Marten's Clause," enshrined in several international humanitarian law treaties, in which it is stated that warfare is governed not only by specific rules but by the "principles of humanity" and the "dictates of the public conscience." It is just this principle that the International Court of Justice has judged to have been "an effective means of addressing the rapid development of military technology." Weapons that are abhorrent to the public conscience may be prohibited on this basis alone. It is arguable that this, more than other specific rules, is the basis of the complete prohibition of chemical and biological weapons, of blinding laser weapons (a truly non-lethal technology) and of antipersonnel landmines.

Public conscience is of particular relevance to the prohibition of chemical or biological incapacitants. The prohibition of poisoning and the deliberate spread of disease is based not only on the fine points of a treaty among governments; it is based on a taboo which goes back several millennia and to diverse cultural and ethical traditions. It is among the tools with which humanity has engaged in an age-old struggle against germs and disease. A future in which scientific developments mean that people must fear remote and hostile interference with their own bodily processes such as sleep, consciousness, memory or fertility would indeed be pretty bleak and quite disturbing. It is highly likely that most reasonable people would cringe if they thought that knowledge from biomedical research could be used to control or incapacitate them from a distance. Is this innate consciousness of what is "inhuman" or "beyond the pale" not central to what lawyers have called "the dictates of the public conscience?" It is precisely that "public conscience" which the International Court of Justice has pointed to as being one of our best hopes of preventing the employment of military technologies that are unacceptable.

Having considered the humanitarian norms that are at stake and why they need protection it is perhaps time to turn to how they might be reinforced.

An obvious but necessary element is awareness of both the existence and relevance of these norms, among the public, policymakers, weapon bearers and diplomats involved in arms negotiations. Discussions about chemical and biological weapons and their elimination have all too often been treated only as the domain of experts and the result of security tradeoffs among States; as a concession that States make to others. But this view restricts options for defending these norms and disempowers those whom the norms exist to protect.

Reinforcing these norms should also involve States undertaking a rigorous review of every new weapon under consideration in light of existing international law obligations. There is an existing obligation in Protocol I of 1977 Additional to the Geneva Conventions requiring States to determine in "the study, development, acquisition or adopting of a new weapon, means or method of warfare" whether "its employment would, in some or all circumstances, be prohibited by this Protocol or any other rule of international law . . . ."[1] Yet less than ten States have systematic mechanisms for such reviews in place. At the 2003 International Conference of the Red Cross and Red Crescent, States Parties to the Geneva Conventions agreed that such reviews should "involve a multidisciplinary approach, including military, legal, environmental and health-related considerations" and furthermore, that States should "review with particular scrutiny all new weapons . . . that cause health effects with which medical personnel are not familiar." This requirement applies both to those States manufacturing weapons and to those purchasing them.

Another way to reinforce the norm against the use of poison and deliberate spread of disease is to actively engage pertinent scientists, industry and those who fund scientific research. This means building a "culture of responsibility" in and demanding vigilance among scientists. It also means integrating into scientific education knowledge of and respect for legal and ethical norms. Without this element of prevention it is difficult to see how a State-centered legal regime alone can survive the pressures implicit in the globalization of knowledge, the proliferation of dual-use technologies and access to these by would-be perpetrators. Yet it is just such an approach that we have relied on as our primary protection in recent decades.

Reinforcing the norms also means avoiding misleading terms such as "nonlethal" in relation to weapons. We should have a clear understanding of the likely effects on people, both short- and long-term, of each proposed weapon.

It is also essential that the legal and policy implications of a world in which the weapon being considered will inevitably become available to a variety of actors are soberly addressed. Above all, we should resist, in the strongest terms, any implication that new technologies have made intentional poisoning, the deliberate spread of disease or attacks on civilians permissible.

And finally, let's reflect on history. In the last century several of the large scale uses of chemical weapons began with the use of irritants or incapacitants which then escalated. This was the case in the First World War, in Ethiopia in 1936, in China between 1937 and 1945, in Yemen between 1963 and 1967 and in the Iran-Iraq War of 1980 to 1989. It was with these vivid memories as background that the Biological and Chemical Weapons Conventions were adopted in 1972 and 1993 respectively. The complete prohibition of all chemical and biological weapons, whether intended to be lethal or incapacitating, was not an accident.

In conclusion, protecting and reinforcing humanitarian norms in this field requires an approach based not only on knowledge of tactical objectives and technological possibilities, but also of the real effects on people of biological and chemical weapons. The dictates of the public conscience and the objectives of international humanitarian law need to be understood and respected. But in the final analysis, it is not the norms that must be protected: it is humanity. Past generations for several millennia have consistently deemed poisoning and the deliberate spread of disease on the battlefield abhorrent and totally rejected this option. So should we.

Note

1. "Additional Protocol I to the 1949 Geneva Conventions, art. 36," *Geneva Conventions of August 12, 1949,* (Geneva, Switzerland: 1997).

Conclusion
and Recommendations

Alan M. Pearson, Marie Isabelle Chevrier
and Mark Wheelis

In this volume we have attempted to present a thorough discussion of the many historical, scientific, military, and legal issues surrounding the development and use of incapacitating biochemical weapons. The contributing authors hold a range of views on these issues. In this chapter we offer some conclusions and recommendations. These represent the opinions of the editors only.

Incapacitating biochemical weapons could provide military commanders with more humane and effective options in certain situations. But in our view their potential benefits in these specific, and possibly rare, situations are outweighed by their potential for abuse and the potentially large negative effects their development could have on arms control regimes and international law. The importance of averting the hostile exploitation of biotechnology, with all of the negative consequences that could follow, outweighs the occasional benefits that might be gained from the use of incapacitating biochemical weapons. To quote the Council on Foreign Relations Task Force on Non-Lethal Weapons:

> Expanding and strengthening the...commitment to the prohibitions on the use of chemicals and biological and toxic agents in warfare is essential if we are not to see such weapons developed by states and used by them or others to devastating effect.[1]

A partial ban that allows some chemicals to be used for hostile military purposes but not others would be fraught with ambiguity. As the editors of the *CBW Conventions Bulletin* have noted, "what is being lost sight of here are the grave risks inherent in *any* blanket exemption for *any* toxic chemical."[2] Absent efforts aimed at control, it is likely that advances in science and technology will eventually lead to the development and use of incapacitating or other biochemical weapons, even if they don't work as well as expected.

The Biological Weapons Convention (BWC) and especially the Chemical Weapons Convention (CWC) provide frameworks and mechanisms for action, if their States Parties decide to use them. Together with the 1925 Geneva Protocol, these treaties effectively outlaw the development, production, stockpiling or use of the full spectrum of biological and chemical weapons, whether lethal or incapacitating. In addition, the use of incapacitating chemical weapons could violate international humanitarian and human rights law. Discussion of the complex issues involved and multilateral clarification of current legal and political uncertainties is essential to avoid an erosion of the norms and goals embodied in the CWC and the BWC and expressed in their preambles:

Determined for the sake of all mankind, to exclude completely the possibility of the use of chemical weapons. [CWC]

Determined for the sake of all mankind, to exclude completely the possibility of bacteriological (biological) agents and toxins being used as weapons. [BWC]

Governments will have an opportunity to begin discussing incapacitating biochemical weapons at the Second Review Conference of the CWC in 2008. We believe that it is urgent that States Parties do so. The failure of States Parties to discuss the issue at the first Review Conference (despite substantial pressure from several nongovernmental and intergovernmental organizations), and the failure of any State Party to question the Russian use of incapacitating biochemical weapons in Moscow and Nalchik, already conveys an impression of permissiveness. In the continued absence of discussion, the barriers to development, production, stockpiling and use in armed conflict of incapacitating biochemical weapons are likely to erode until discussion becomes moot.

In addition to opening a formal discussion of the appropriate role (if any) of incapacitating biochemical weapons in military operations and law enforcement, there are a series of specific actions that the Review Conference could take. Perhaps most feasible at present would be for States Parties to set in motion a process for arriving at a common understanding of the meaning of the term "law enforcement" as a purpose not prohibited by the convention. Such a process would bring in considerations of international humanitarian law and human rights law in order to narrow uncertainties in the application of the law enforcement exemption as much as possible before state practice establishes new norms that run counter to those embodied in the Convention. At a minimum States

Parties should confirm that all toxic chemicals, including riot control agents, used for law enforcement are prohibited as a method of warfare.

A second step that States Parties could take that would be most helpful would be to agree to develop a procedure for declaring all agents they hold for law enforcement purposes, and their amounts. Currently, the CWC requires States Parties to declare the identity (although not the amount) of all riot control agents held for riot control purposes (Article III.1.e), but it does not require declarations of other agents that may be held for law enforcement purposes. Such declarations would greatly facilitate transparency and confidence in treaty compliance. Since amending the treaty would not likely be a palatable or effective mechanism for achieving declarations of law enforcement agents, a supplemental agreement could be explored, perhaps structured similarly to the Confidence Building Measures adopted by the States Parties to the BWC. Agreement by the States Parties to institute such a Confidence Building Measure could be achieved by consensus at the Review Conference. Although the record of State Party submission of Confidence Building Measures under the BWC has not been good,[3] the presence of an administering organization for the CWC (unlike the situation with the BWC until very recently) would likely allow for much better performance, as the organization could remind States Parties that failed to submit, and assist those that needed it. Alternatively, States Parties could agree that the only chemicals that may be used for law enforcement under the Convention are riot control agents, and agents for judicial execution. Such an agreement would make unnecessary a Confidence Building Measure for chemicals other than riot control agents held for law enforcement.

States Parties could additionally strive for a consensus that the term "riot control agent" encompasses only those riot control agents already in common police use around the world.[4] By effectively banning the development of new riot control agents, such an agreement would avoid the problem that military development of biochemical incapacitants could be pursued under the guise of development of better riot control agents.

In addition to these discussions that could clarify the legal position of incapacitating biochemical weapons and increase transparency, individual States Parties, or a group of States Parties, could (under Article IX) request that the Russian Federation clarify the situation with regard to its presumptive stockpile of incapacitating biochemical agents, the anticipated uses to which they might be put, and the political and legal controls on their deployment and use. If these discussions are not satisfactory, the Convention provides that the parties can request the assistance of the Executive Council in clarification.

Actions taken to strengthen the treaties will not be effective unless they are complemented by other actions taken outside of, but in concert with, the formal treaty regimes. States should take steps to greatly increase the transparency and strengthen the oversight of relevant areas of research and development, most particularly of military and law enforcement activities in the life sciences and the area of "non-lethal" weapons. Of particular importance would be maximal transparency about any activities involving development of incapacitating agents for possible use for law enforcement. Such activities, arguably permitted by the CWC (see the chapters by Fidler and von Wagner for conflicting views), could nevertheless be quite provocative and destabilizing if it is not clear that they are truly intended only for domestic law enforcement.

In the interests of confidence in the CWC and support for the norm it embodies, we recommend that such development be eschewed. However, if any State Party elects to go ahead, it should do so in as transparent a fashion as possible. In order to foster confidence in treaty compliance, any such program should have the following properties: it should be unclassified; it should be administered and funded by a ministry of justice, not defense; it should be conducted by civilian or law enforcement laboratories, not by military laboratories or by civilian laboratories that do substantial military contracting; its justification should cite domestic law enforcement goals only; munitions and delivery devices should be ones appropriate for police, rather than military, tactics; and safety criteria should be consistent with domestic use.[5] States Parties should pursue clarification under the CWC of any programs of incapacitating biochemical weapon development that do not fully meet these criteria.

More generally, increased dialogue about incapacitating biochemical weapons between the scientific, medical, legal, military, and policy communities, and those concerned with questions of human rights and humanitarian law is essential, both to identify potential problems and to develop and implement effective solutions. The science and technology required for the development of incapacitating biochemical weapons, and of other weapons that target specific physiological mechanisms and systems, will come from academia, medicine, and industry. Academia develops most of the basic knowledge that underlies drug discovery and development. The biotechnology and pharmaceutical industries identify and develop new therapeutic compounds, and industry has historically been the major source of compounds for military researchers attempting to develop incapacitating biochemical weapons. Medical researchers gather clinical data critical for the successful development of such weapons. If a useful biochemical incapacitant is discovered, it will most likely come from one or more of these sectors rather than from a military laboratory. Each of these sectors thus has a particular responsibility for the future. Biologists, chemists, toxicologists, pharmacologists and doctors can and should bring their special expertise to bear on efforts to strengthen both the treaty regimes and, even more, the norms enshrined within them.

The world may be witnessing a renaissance of military research into bio-chemical incapacitants.[6] Until the States Parties to the CWC and BWC clarify any uncertainties in the application of these conventions, and until practices and procedures designed to prevent application of the life sciences for hostile pur-poses are put into place, the development of incapacitating biochemical weapons is likely to continue, albeit under a cloud of military, legal, political and scien-tific uncertainty. It will take a concerted effort, from the local to the national to the international, to ensure that biotechnology does not become the next mili-tary technology, with incapacitating biochemical weapons leading the way.

Notes

1. Graham T. Allison, Paul X. Kelley, and Richard L. Garwin, *Non-lethal Weapons and Capabilities*, Report of an Independent Task Force sponsored by the Council on Foreign Relations (New York: Council on Foreign Relations Press, 2004): 62–63.

2. CBW Conventions Bulletin Editors, "'Non-lethal' weapons, the CWC and the BWC," *CBW Conventions Bulletin* 61 (Harvard Sussex Program on CBW Armament and Arms Limitation, September 2003): 2.

3. Iris Hunger and Nicolas Isla, "Confidence-building needs transparency: an analysis of the BTWC's confidence-building measures," *Disarmament Forum* 3 (2006): 27–36.

4. Mark Wheelis "Biotechnology and Biochemical Weapons," *Nonproliferation Review* 9 (Spring 2002): 48–53.

5. Mark Wheelis, "'Non-Lethal' Chemical Weapons: A Faustian Bargain," *Issues in Science and Technology* (Spring 2003): 74–78.

6. Tobias Feakin, *Bradford Non-Lethal Weapons Research Project, Research Report 3* (Brad-ford: Department of Peace Studies, University of Bradford, August 2001), <http://www.brad.ac.uk/acad/nlw/research_reports/researchreport3.php> (14 July 2006).

Index

3-quinuclidinyl benzilate. *See* BZ

acetylcholine, 130, 133–34, 158
acetylcholinesterase inhibitors: effects on
    immune system, 162–63; effects on
    nervous system, 159–61; mechanism
    of, 158–59
Advanced Riot Control Agent Device
    (ARCAD), xxii, 71, 73, 80
Al Qaeda, 11
American Convention on Human Rights,
    266, 270–71
Amnesty International, 276
amygdala, 129–30, 137–38
antipersonnel landmines, 239, 240
ARCAD. *See* Advanced Riot Control
    Agent Device

Beslan school hostage crisis, 6
biochemical threat spectrum, 125, *126*
Biological and Toxin Weapons
    Convention. *See* Biological Weapons
    Convention
Biological Weapons Convention (BWC),
    xxix, 13, 225, 235–36, 285–86, 289,
    292; draft conventions, 213–14,

216–17; impact of CWC law
    enforcement exemption on, 184–86;
    incapacitating biochemical weapons
    and, xxvi–xxvii, 6; object and
    purpose, 212, 220–21; permitted
    purposes under, 209–10; range of
    biological agents and toxins covered
    by, xxvi–xxvii, 210–11, 217, 218,
    219–20
bioregulators, 150; Biological Weapons
    Convention and, xxvii, 218–19;
    defined, xvi, 1; as incapacitating
    biochemical weapons, 125–26, 131,
    149; military exploitation of, 131;
    relation to toxins, xxvii, 125, 216
blinding laser weapons, xxviii, 228, 241,
    286
blood-brain barrier, 76, 138, 150,
    163–64
botulinum toxin, xvi
brain, 2; growth in understanding of xviii,
    129; manipulating function of, xxiv,
    2–3, 129, 134, 141, 142
Branch Davidians, 115–16
BWC. *See* Biological Weapons
    Convention

About the Contributors

William J. Aceves is professor of law and associate dean for academic affairs at California Western School of Law. He has represented human rights and civil liberties organizations as *amicus curiae* counsel in U.S. courts, including the U.S. Supreme Court. Aceves is the author of *The Anatomy of Torture* (Brill, 2007) and the Amnesty International USA report *A Safe Haven for Torturers* (2002). He regularly works with the American Civil Liberties Union, Amnesty International, the Center for Constitutional Rights, the Center for Justice & Accountability, and the International Law Association on projects involving the domestic application of international law.

Marie Isabelle Chevrier is associate professor of public policy and political economy at the University of Texas at Dallas and Chair of the Scientists Working Group on Biological and Chemical Weapons at the Center for Arms Control and Non-Proliferation. She served as associate director of the Harvard Sussex Program on Chemical and Biological Armaments and Arms Limitation at Harvard University, and on the faculty of two NATO Advanced Study Institutes. She is a member of the Pugwash Study Group on the Chemical and Biological Weapons Conventions. In 2004 she was a Fulbright Scholar at Jamia Millia Islamia University, New Delhi, India.

Robin M. Coupland is the adviser on armed violence and the effects of weapons for the International Committee of the Red Cross (ICRC). He joined the ICRC in 1987 and worked as a field surgeon in Thailand, Cambodia, Pakistan, Afghanistan, Yemen, Angola, Somalia, Kenya and Sudan. His work has since focused on the health aspects of the design and use of weapons. He graduated from the Cambridge University School of Clinical Medicine, UK and trained as a surgeon at the University College Hospital, London. He became a Fellow of the Royal College of Surgeons in 1985.

Malcolm R. Dando is professor of international security in the Department of Peace Studies at the University of Bradford. Trained originally as a biologist, his research interests center on preventing the hostile misuse of modern biology. His publications include *Deadly Cultures: Biological Weapons Since* 1945 (Harvard, 2006) which he edited with Mark Wheelis and Lajos Rozsa.

George P. Fenton is a retired U.S. Marine Corps Colonel. He was the Director of the Department of Defense Joint Non-Lethal Weapons Directorate from 1998 to 2002. He is currently serving as the Vice President of Government and Military Programs at TASER International.

David P. Fidler is the Calamaras Professor of Law and director of the Center on American and Global Security at Indiana University. A leading expert on international law and public health, his publications include *International Law and Infectious Diseases* (Clarendon Press, 1999), *SARS, Governance, and the Globalization of Disease* (Palgrave, 2004), and *Biosecurity in the Global Age: Biological Weapons, Public Health, and the Rule of Law* (with Lawrence O. Gostin, forthcoming, Stanford University Press). He has served as a consultant to the World Health Organization, World Bank, U.S. Centers for Disease Control and Prevention, U.S. Department of Defense's Defense Science Board, and various nongovernmental organizations.

Martin Furmanski is a member of the Scientist's Working Group on Chemical and Biological Weapons at the Center for Arms Control and Nonproliferation. He has participated in field investigations with the late Sheldon Harris on biological attacks in China during the Sino-Japanese war, and has authored chapters in several histories of chemical and biological weapons, including *Deadly Cultures* (Harvard, 2006), and *Blood Weeping Accusations* (Beijing, 2005). His medical and scientific training is in medical microbiology, anatomic pathology, and clinical pathology including clinical toxicology.

Alan Goldhammer is deputy vice president for regulatory affairs at the Pharmaceutical Research and Manufacturers of America (PhRMA). Previously, he was executive director, Technical Affairs for the Biotechnology Industry Organization (BIO), and earlier was a senior staff fellow in the Clinical Endocrinology Branch at the National Institutes of Health. He has served as a regulatory affairs consultant to the International Food Biotechnology Council in Washington, D.C. and as an expert adviser to the U.S. government on issues related to Biological Weapons Convention. Goldhammer is a member of the American Chemical Society and the American Association for the Advancement of Science.

Françoise J. Hampson is professor of law at the Human Rights Center, University of Essex. She has taught, researched and published widely on armed conflict, international humanitarian law and human rights. She has served as an independent expert member of the UN Sub-Commission on the Promotion and Protection of Human Rights (1998–2007) and has successfully litigated many cases before the European Court of Human Rights, particularly involving the protection of human rights in situations of armed conflict. She has been involved in various projects of the International Committee of the Red Cross, including serving on the Steering Committee and Group of Experts for the Study on Customary International Humanitarian Law.

Peter Herby is head of the Arms Unit in the Legal Division of the International Committee of the Red Cross (ICRC). He has written and spoken extensively on the norms of humanitarian law applicable to the use of arms, and has represented the ICRC in all arms-related negotiations since 1994. He is co-author of the ICRC study *Arms Availability and the Situation of Civilians in Armed Conflict* (1999), and is responsible for the development of the ICRC's initiative on "Biotechnology, Weapons and Humanity." Previously, he directed the disarmament and arms control program of the Quaker United Nations Office in Geneva.

James F. Leonard was chief U.S. negotiator for the Biological Weapons Convention as Assistant Director of the U.S. Arms Control and Disarmament Agency (ACDA) from 1969 to 1973. After serving as President of the United Nations Association (1973–1977), he returned to government service, first as U.S. deputy permanent representative to the United Nations, then as deputy special representative to the Middle East peace negotiations from 1979 to 1981. Prior to joining ACDA, he spent twenty years as a Foreign Service Officer in Damascus, Moscow, Paris, Taipei and Washington, D.C. He works with a number of non-governmental organizations focused on arms control, non-proliferation and security issues.

Jack Melling is a senior science fellow at the Center for Arms Control and Non-Proliferation, a consultant to the U.S. Government Accountability Office, and Senior Scientific Advisor to the International AIDS Vaccine Initiative. Previously, he served as chief executive and director of the Microbiological Research Authority, Porton Down, UK Department of Health. Melling has also held executive positions at the Center for Applied Microbiology and Research at Porton Down, the Salk Institute Biologicals Development Center in Pennsylvania, and the Karl Landsteiner Institute for Vaccine Development in Vienna. He has worked as a Senior Project Manager at the Battelle Memorial Institute, Columbus, Ohio.

Kathryn Nixdorff is a professor in the Department of Microbiology and Genetics at Darmstadt University of Technology, Germany, where she has served as department chairman and dean of the School of Biology. She is a founding member of the university's interdisciplinary research group concerned with science, technology and security (IANUS). She represents the International Network of Engineers and Scientists for Global Responsibility (INES) on the Board of Directors of the BioWeapons Prevention Project. She served as a scientific expert for Germany at the Meeting of Experts to the Biological and Toxin Weapons Convention in June 2005.

Alan M. Pearson is the director of the Biological and Chemical Weapons Control Program at the Center for Arms Control and Non-Proliferation in Washington, D.C. Previously, he was a global security science and technology fellow for the American Association for the Advancement of Science and the Nuclear Threat Initiative, serving as an advisor to the Biological and Chemical Countermeasures Portfolio in the U.S. Department of Homeland Security. He was an American Cancer Society post-doctoral research fellow at Harvard University Medical School.

Adolf von Wagner served in the German Foreign Service for nearly forty years before his retirement in 2000, including postings in Marseille, Santiago de Chile, Washington, D.C. and Moscow. He served as the Head of Delegation to the Fourth Review Conference of the Nuclear Non-Proliferation Treaty (NPT), Chairman of the 48th UN General Assembly Committee for Disarmament and International Security (First Committee), and Chairman of the Ad Hoc Committee on Chemical Weapons of the Conference on Disarmament in 1992–1993, where he led the final stage of negotiations on the Chemical Weapons Convention. He currently consults with and advises various governmental and non-governmental organizations.

Mark Wheelis is a senior lecturer in the Section of Microbiology at the University of California Davis. For the last twenty years his research has been focused on the history and control of chemical and biological weapons. He has consulted or served with a number of U.S. and international organizations, including the International Committee of the Red Cross, the World Health Organization, Pugwash and the Program on Monitoring Emerging Diseases (ProMED). Dr. Wheelis is coeditor of *Deadly Cultures: Biological Weapons Since 1945* (Harvard, 2006).